THE KATANGESE GENDARMES
AND WAR IN CENTRAL AFRICA

THE KATANGESE GENDARMES AND WAR IN CENTRAL AFRICA

Fighting Their Way Home

Erik Kennes and Miles Larmer

Indiana University Press

Bloomington and Indianapolis

This book is a publication of

Indiana University Press
Office of Scholarly Publishing
Herman B Wells Library 350
1320 East 10th Street
Bloomington, Indiana 47405 USA

iupress.indiana.edu

© 2016 by Erik Kennes and Miles Larmer

All rights reserved

No part of this book may be reproduced or utilized in any form or by any means, electronic or mechanical, including photocopying and recording, or by any information storage and retrieval system, without permission in writing from the publisher. The Association of American University Presses' Resolution on Permissions constitutes the only exception to this prohibition.

♾ The paper used in this publication meets the minimum requirements of the American National Standard for Information Sciences—Permanence of Paper for Printed Library Materials, ANSI Z39.48-1992.

Manufactured in the United States of America

Library of Congress Cataloging-in-Publication Data

Names: Kennes, Erik, author. | Larmer, Miles, author.
Title: The Katangese gendarmes and war in Central Africa : fighting their way home / Erik Kennes and Miles Larmer.
Description: Bloomington : Indiana University Press, 2016. | Includes bibliographical references and index.
Identifiers: LCCN 2015047636| ISBN 9780253021304 (cloth : alk. paper) | ISBN 9780253021397 (pbk.)
Subjects: LCSH: Katanga (Congo)—Militia—History. | Front de libération nationale du Congo—History. | Congo (Democratic Republic)—History—Autonomy and independence movements. | Angola—History—Autonomy and independence movements. | Africa, Central—History—20th century.
Classification: LCC DT665.K3 K46 2015 | DDC 967.51803—dc23
LC record available at http://lccn.loc.gov/2015047636

1 2 3 4 5   21 20 19 18 17 16

*Dedicated to the memory of Grégoire Kabobo,
son of Antoine Munongo, son and scholar of Katanga*

Contents

	Acknowledgments	*ix*
	List of Abbreviations	*xi*
	Introduction	*1*
1	Becoming Katanga	*18*
2	The Katangese Secession, 1960–1963	*41*
3	Into Exile and Back, 1963–1967	*61*
4	With the Portuguese, 1967–1974	*80*
5	The Katangese Gendarmes in the Angolan Civil War, 1974–1976	*99*
6	The Shaba Wars	*119*
7	Disarmament and Division, 1979–1996	*145*
8	The Overthrow of Mobutu and After, 1996–2015	*166*
	Conclusion	*190*
	Notes	*205*
	Bibliography	*251*
	Index	*279*

Photo gallery follows page 98.

Acknowledgments

OVER THE TWENTY years or so in which this book has been in development, the authors have been assisted by many more people than it is possible to name here.

First and foremost, we are particularly grateful to the former Tigres themselves, without whom this book would not have been possible. Among the dozens who provided invaluable assistance, the most important are: Justin Mushitu, an active member of the Tigres in Angola in 1974–1977 and in Sweden until the 1990s, who patiently explained their history during many visits to his refugee home in Stockholm and who generously shared his archives; Déogratias Symba, influential during key periods from 1977 until the toppling of Mobutu in 1997; Daniel Mayele, who shared his meticulously kept archives, which document the history of anti-Mobutu resistance during the 1970s and 1990s; Henri Mukachung Mwambu and Irung a Wan, key political actors for the movement in Angola, who shared many useful insights; and Jean Pierre Sonck, who shared his invaluable documentation on Katanga and who is one of the foremost experts on its history. Among the military ex-Tigres, we express our deepest thanks to Generals Pascal Kapend, François Kapend, and Sylvain Mbumba "Kadhafi." Colonel Vincent de Paul Nguz was a tremendous help and assisted in research, and Colonel Robert Yav, Elie Kapend, Colonel Yav Nasser, and, last but not least, General Nathanaël Mbumba were valuable sources of information. In Belgium, Colonel René Pire often shared his insights and experience of the Katangese Gendarmerie. From the political wing of the Tigres, we are very grateful to Jacques Cartier Mutombo, Jérôme Nawej, Joseph Kabwit, Yves Nawej and Nickel Rumb.

The initial impetus for this study can be traced back to Filip Reyntjens at the University of Antwerp (IDPM), who greatly facilitated the first research visits undertaken by Erik Kennes between 1997 and 1999. Generous support was also given by the director of the Section for Contemporary History of the African Museum in Tervuren, Dr. Gauthier de Villers, during the years 1999–2009. A first outline of the history of the Katangese gendarmes was as a result included in Erik Kennes's doctoral study, which in turn would never have been possible without the outstanding assistance and creative insights of Bogumil Jewsiewicki.

Miles Larmer's research was generously supported by the UK Arts and Humanities Research Council, which funded a Research Fellowship in 2011–2012; and the British Academy, which provided a Small Grant at the start of his research in 2007–2008. His research was also enabled by many colleagues at the universities of Sheffield Hallam, Sheffield, and Oxford.

Researchers on the subject who assisted with interviews, documents, and contacts include most of all the very knowledgeable Crispin Kalumba Nsanki, Justin Mulangu, Liévain Mwangal, Peter Ngoy Kaodi, Raymond Nshimba, Grégoire Kabobo, Hon. Mwando Nsimba, René Pelissier, John Cann, and the expert journalist Jean-François Bastin. In Portugal, Pezarat Correia, Admiral Rosa Coutinho, Major General Renato Marques Pinto, and Colonel Oliveira Marques were particularly helpful. Nathaniel Kinsey-Powell kindly provided access to documents from the French Foreign Ministry and the Jimmy Carter Library.

We are deeply grateful to the many archivists who assisted our research: José de Quintanilha Mantas of the Torre do Tombo state archives in Lisbon; the UNHCR archives in Geneva; the Portuguese Military History archive; the 25 April Documentation Centre at the University of Coimbra; the US State Department archives in College Park, Maryland; the UK National Archives at Kew; the Contemporary History Library of the Royal Museum of Central Africa in Tervuren; Neels Muller at the Foreign Affairs archives in Pretoria; and the colonial archives housed at the Belgian Foreign Ministry.

The research was developed through presentations at conferences and seminars at the following institutions: the universities of and universities in Botswana, Cambridge, Edinburgh, Exeter, Florida, Kalemie, Kinshasa, Leiden, Leuven, London (SOAS), Oxford, Paris, Pretoria, Sheffield, Sheffield Hallam, Stockholm, Swaziland, and Zambia. Draft research findings were presented at various conferences including the African Studies Association (United States) conference, the European Conference on African Studies, and the African Studies Association of the United Kingdom. Numerous contributors and organizers of these events provided invaluable advice. The authors would particularly like to thank Jocelyn Alexander, David Anderson, Nir Arielli, Filip de Boeck, Daniel Branch, James Brennan, Andrew Cohen, Bruce Collins, Stephen Ellis, Alastair Fraser, Jan-Bart Gewald, Patricia Hayes, Marja Hinfelaar, Lars Huening, Emma Hunter, Bogumil Jewsiewicki, Nathaniel Kinsey-Powell, Prince Kaumba Lufunda, René Lemarchand, Reuben Loffman, Giacomo Macola, Henning Melber, Bob Moore, Justin Pearce, Catherine Lee Porter, Filip Reyntjens, Daniel Spence, Henning Tamm, Thomas Turner, Theodore Tréfon, Harry Verhoeven, Luise White, Benjamin Ziemann, and the anonymous readers of the draft manuscript for their support, insights, and criticism. All remaining omissions, oversights and errors are our own.

The book draws on material previously published by the authors in *Cold War History* and the *Journal of Imperial and Commonwealth History*. We are grateful for permission to reuse a limited amount of that material from those articles, which can be accessed at www.tandfonline.com.

Finally, the authors would like to thank Many Madika and Laura Cole, for their relentless support, encouragement, and patience during the repeated absence of their research-obsessed husbands/partners.

List of Abbreviations

A25A	Centro de documentação 25 de Abril (25 April Documentation Centre, University of Coimbra, Portugal)
ABAKO	Alliance des Bakongo (Alliance of Bakongo)
AFDL	Alliance des Forces Démocratiques pour la Libération du Congo (Alliance of Democratic Forces for the Liberation of Congo)
AHM	Arquivo Historico Militar (Historical Military Archives Lisbon, Portugal)
ANC	Armée Nationale Congolaise (Congolese National Army)
ANTT	Arquivo Nacional da Torre do Tombo (National Archives Torre do Tombo, Lisbon, Portugal)
APARECO	Alliance des Patriotes pour la Refondation du Congo (Patriots' Alliance for re-founding the Congo)
ASLN	Armée Secrète de Libération Nationale (Secret Army for National Liberation)
ATCAR	Association des Tshokwe du Congo de l'Angola et de la Rhodésie du Nord (Assocation of Chokwe from Congo, Angola and North Rhodesia)
BAA	Belgian Army Archives
BCK	Compagnie du Chemin de fer du Bas-Congo au Katanga (Bas Congo and Katanga Railway Company)
BSAC	British South Africa Company
BTK	Bourse du Travail du Katanga (Katanga Labor Exchange)
BTM/Mistebel	Belgian Technical Mission to Katanga/Mission Technique Belge au Katanga
CAD	Centre des Archives Diplomatiques de Nantes (Nantes Diplomatic Archives Centre)
CAF	Central African Federation
CCCI	Compagnie du Congo pour le Commerce et l'Industrie (Congo Company for Trade and Industry)

CCPA	Conselho Coordenador do Programa en Angola (Coordinating Council for the MFA program in Angola)
CEC	centre extra-coutumier
CEDAF	Centre d'Études et de Documentation Africaines (Center for African Studies and Documentation, Belgium)
CEDOPO	Centre de Documentation Politique (Center for Political Documentation)
CIA	Central Intelligence Agency
CNL	Conseil National de Libération (National Liberation Council)
CNR	Conseil National de la Révolution (National Council for the Revolution)
CNS	Conférence Nationale Souveraine (Sovereign National Conference)
Conaco	Convention Nationale Congolaise (Congolese National Convention)
Conakat	Confédération des Associations Tribales du Katanga (Confederation of Tribal Associations of Katanga)
CORAK	Coordination d'Organisation du referendum d'autodétermination pour le Katanga (Coordination for the Organization of a Referendum on Self-Determination of Katanga)
CPK	Congrès des Peuples du Katanga (Congress of Peoples of Katanga)
CRAOCA	Cercle Royal des Anciens Officiers des Campagnes d'Afrique (Royal Society of the Veteran Officers of the African Campaignes)
CSK	Comité Spécial du Katanga (Special Committee of Katanga)
CSL	Conseil Suprême de Libération (Supreme Council of Liberation)
CVR	Corps des Volontaires de la République (Volunteer Corps of the Republic)
DAM	Direction des Affaires Africaines et Malgaches (Directorate for African and Malagasy Affairs)
DEMIAP	Détection Militaire des Activités Anti-Patrie (DEMIAP) (Military Directorate of Anti-Patriotic Activities

DGS	Direcção Geral de Segurança (General Security Directorate)
DRC	Democratic Republic of Congo
DSP	Division Spéciale Présidentielle (Special Presidential Division)
ECP	Étudiants Congolais Progressistes (Progressive Congolese Students)
FAA	Forças Armadas Angolanas (Angolan Armed Forces)
FAC	Forces Armées Congolaises (Congolese Armed Forces)
FAP	Forces Armées Populaires (People's Armed Forces)
FAPAC	Forces Armées Patriotiques du Congo (Patriotic Armed Forces of Congo)
FAPAK	Forces Armées Patriotiques Katangaises (Katangese Patriotic Forces)
FAPC	Forces Armées Populaires du Congo (Popular Armed Forces of Congo)
FAPLA	Forças Armadas Populares de Libertação de Angola (Popular Armed Forces for the Liberation of Angola)
FAR	Forces Armées Rwandaises (Rwandan Armed Forces)
FARDC	Forces Armées de la République Démocratique du Congo (Armed Forces of the DR Congo)
FAZ	Forces Armées Zaïroises (Zairian Armed Forces)
FCD	Front Congolais pour la Restauration de la Démocratie (Congolese Front for the Restoration of Democracy)
FCL	Front Congolais de Libération (Congolese Liberation Front)
FEDEKA	Fédération Kasaïenne (Kasaian Federation)
Fénaco	Fédération Nationale Congolaise (Congolese National Federation)
FLEC	Frente para a Libertação do Enclave de Cabinda (Liberation Front for the Cabinda Enclave)
FLNC	Front de Libération Nationale Congolaise (Front for Congolese National Liberation)
FLNZ	Front de Libération Nationale du Zaïre (Front for Zairian National Liberation)
FNLA	Frente Nacional de Libertação de Angola (National Liberation Front for Angola)

Fodelico	Forces démocratiques pour la Libération du Congo (Democratic Forces for the Liberation of the Congo)
FP	Force Publique (Public Army)
Frelimo	Frente de Libertação de Moçambique (Mozambique National Liberation Front)
Gassomel	Groupement des associations de l'empire Lunda (Grouping of Assocations of the Lunda Empire)
GRAE	Governo Revolucionário de Angola no Exílo (Angolan Government in Exile)
HCR	Haut Conseil de la République (Higher Council of the Republic)
JMPR	Jeunesse du Mouvement Populaire de la Révolution (People's Revolution Youth Movement)
MAE	Ministère des Affaires Etrangères (Ministry of Foreign Affairs)
MARC	Mouvement d'Action pour la Résurrection du Congo (Action Movement for the Resurrection of Congo)
MCS	Mouvement des Combattants Socialistes (Movement of Socialist Combattants)
MFA	Movimento das Forças Armadas (Armed Forces Movement)
MLC	Mouvement de Libération du Congo (Congolese Liberation Movement)
MNC-L	Mouvement National Congolais—Lumumba (National Congolese Movement—Lumumba)
MONUC	Mission de l'Organisation des Nations Unies au Congo (United Nations Mission in the DRC)
MONUSCO	Mission de de l'Organisation des Nations Unies pour la Stabilisation en RDCongo (United Nations Stabilization Mission in the DRC)
MPLA	Movimento Popular de Libertação de Angola (Angolan People's Liberation Movement)
MPR	Mouvement Populaire de la Révolution (People's Revolution Movement)
MRLK	Mouvement Révolutionnaire pour la Libération du Katanga (Revolutionary Movement for the Liberation of Katanga)

NSA	National Security Agency
NSSM	National Security Study Memorandum
OAU	Organization of African Unity
PAF	Pan-African Force
PAIGC	Partido Africano da Independência da Guiné e Cabo Verde (African Party for the Independence of Guinea and Cabo Verde)
PaLu	Parti Lumumbiste Unifié (Unified Lumumbist Party)
PIDE	Polícia Internacional e de Defesa do Estado (International Police and Police for the Defence of the State)
PLC	Parti de Libération Congolais (Congolese Liberation Party)
PNC	Police Nationale Congolaise (Congolese National Police)
PRP	Parti de la Révolution Populaire (People's Revolution Party)
PSA	Parti Solidaire Africain (African Solidarity Party)
RCD	Rassemblement Congolais pour la Démocratie (Congolese Rally for Democracy)
RPA	Rwanda Patriotic Army
RPF	Rwanda Patriotic Front
SACP	South African Communist Party
SARM	Service d'Action et de Renseignement Militaire (Action Service and Military Intelligence)
SGB	Société Générale de Belgique (Belgian General Company)
SGR	Service Général de Renseignements et de Sécurité (General Service for Intelligence and Security)
SNCZ	Société Nationale des Chemins de Fer Zaïrois (National Zairian Railway Company)
SNIP	Service National d'Intelligence et Protection (National Intelligence and Protection Service)
SPLA	Sudan People's Liberation Army
SPLM	Sudan People's Liberation Movement
SWAPO	South West Africa People's Organization
Tigres	Tropas de Infanteria e Guerrilla Revolucionaria (Revolutionary Infantry and Revolutionary Troops)

UDPS	Union pour la Démocratie et le Progrès Social (Union for Democracy and Social Progress)
UFERI	Union des Fédéralistes et Républicains Indépendants (Union of Independent Federalists and Republicans)
UMHK	Union Minière du Haut Katanga (Haut Katanga Mining Union)
UNDP	United Nations Development Programme
UNHCR	United Nations High Commission/Commissioner for Refugees
UNIP	United National Independence Party
UNITA	União Nacional para a Independência Total de Angola (National Union for the Total Independence of Angola)
UNSC	United Nations Security Council
UPA	Union of Peoples of Angola
ZANU	Zimbabwe African National Union

THE KATANGESE GENDARMES AND WAR IN CENTRAL AFRICA

Introduction

THE KATANGESE GENDARMES have over the past half-century fought in many of southern-central Africa's most important wars. Yet their presence, and the significant role they played, often went unnoticed, or was little understood, by most international observers. They were the rank-and-file troops of the secessionist army of the Katangese state, which resisted the United Nations' attempts to reintegrate Katanga into Congo in the early 1960s. They defended Portuguese colonialism in Angola in the late 1960s and early 1970s and then helped bring the Marxist Movimento Popular de Libertação de Angola (MPLA) to power in that country. They fought against the Mobutu dictatorship of Congo/Zaire from exile and helped bring Mobutu's successor, Laurent Kabila, to power in 1997. In all these times and places, they were problematically integrated into other people's armies, mobilized to fight other people's wars, and then demobilized in decidedly imperfect ways that ensured they remained available for armed redeployment. In recent years, armed men fighting in the name or spirit of the secession have mounted rebel attacks in southern Katanga, deploying the symbols and the name by which the gendarmes have become known, the Katangese Tigers. Successive attempts to discipline or demobilize this force have foundered on the refusal of African nation-state leaders, the United Nations, and the so-called international community to recognize what they were ultimately fighting for: not money or ideology, but rather a home, a nation-state in which their Katangese identity would find expression.

The gendarmes have been missed and misunderstood because they acted and defined themselves against conventional frameworks: across the ideological boundaries of the Cold War; the fragile borders of postcolonial states; and conventional definitions of war as constituting conflict between recognized nation-states and involving either national armies or nonstate guerrilla forces. Their illegitimacy, even impossibility, in Mobutu's Zaire and their invisibility in the Angolan wars created additional political and practical difficulties in carrying out our research. The actions and intentions of the gendarmes challenge commonly accepted notions of the meaning of the postcolonial Congolese state, the basis of nationalism and state formation in Africa, and the potential for alternative bases for such formations. They raise important questions regarding relations between "autochthons" and "strangers" in Katanga and the relationship between ethnicities such as the Lunda and the postcolonial borders of Angola, Zambia, and the

Democratic Republic of Congo, which, officially at least, divide them. The gendarmes' identification with "Katanga" as a nation-state remained central to their self-identification and activities, notwithstanding the nonexistence of that state since 1963. Indeed, the attempt to extinguish that identity by external agencies and the Congolese-Zairian state strengthened aspiration to a statehood that was more powerful because it was denied. For these reasons, "Katanga" has provided a malleable but potent sense of identification, a fertile basis for military and political mobilization both for the gendarmes themselves and for sections of the wider Katangese population.

Grasping the meaning and significance of the Katangese gendarmes proved beyond the purview of peacekeepers, politicians, and policy analysts, whose perspective generally stretched to the nearest border and who were equally constricted by their ideological worldview from appreciating the gendarmes' potential for reimagining their identity and rearming themselves. Understanding their significance necessitates a dynamic, mobile historical analysis, following the gendarmes across borders and tracking their changes in ideology and nomenclature, to reveal their enduring affiliations and motivations. As well as utilizing numerous national and international archives, this history also depends on dozens of interviews with former gendarmes, carried out over more than two decades.

Understanding the Katangese Gendarmes

In order to explain the significance of the Katangese gendarmes, an initial truncated narrative of their history is necessary. Following Katanga's secession from newly independent Congo in June 1960, a national Katangese army was hastily assembled; notoriously led by Belgian military officers and later by white mercenaries, its rank-and-file soldiers were raw recruits drawn mainly from the "autochthon" Katangese communities that supported the secession. This new "gendarmerie" saw action against pro-unitary northern Katangese Lubakat societies, the army of the new Congolese nation-state, and UN forces. Following the extinguishing of the secession in January 1963, hundreds of former gendarmes were moved across the border into Portuguese-ruled Angola, while thousands more, hastily demobilized and unpaid, roamed the border areas of Congo/Katanga, Northern Rhodesia, and Angola. After the appointment of former Katangese leader Moïse Tshombe as Congolese prime minister in mid-1964, the ex-gendarmes were recalled from Angola, problematically integrated into the Congolese National Army (ANC), and mobilized against the Mulelist eastern rebellion, which culminated in the fall of Stanleyville in November. They never saw themselves as part of the Congolese nation-state, however, and, after President Mobutu's authoritarian tendencies manifested themselves in his centraliza-

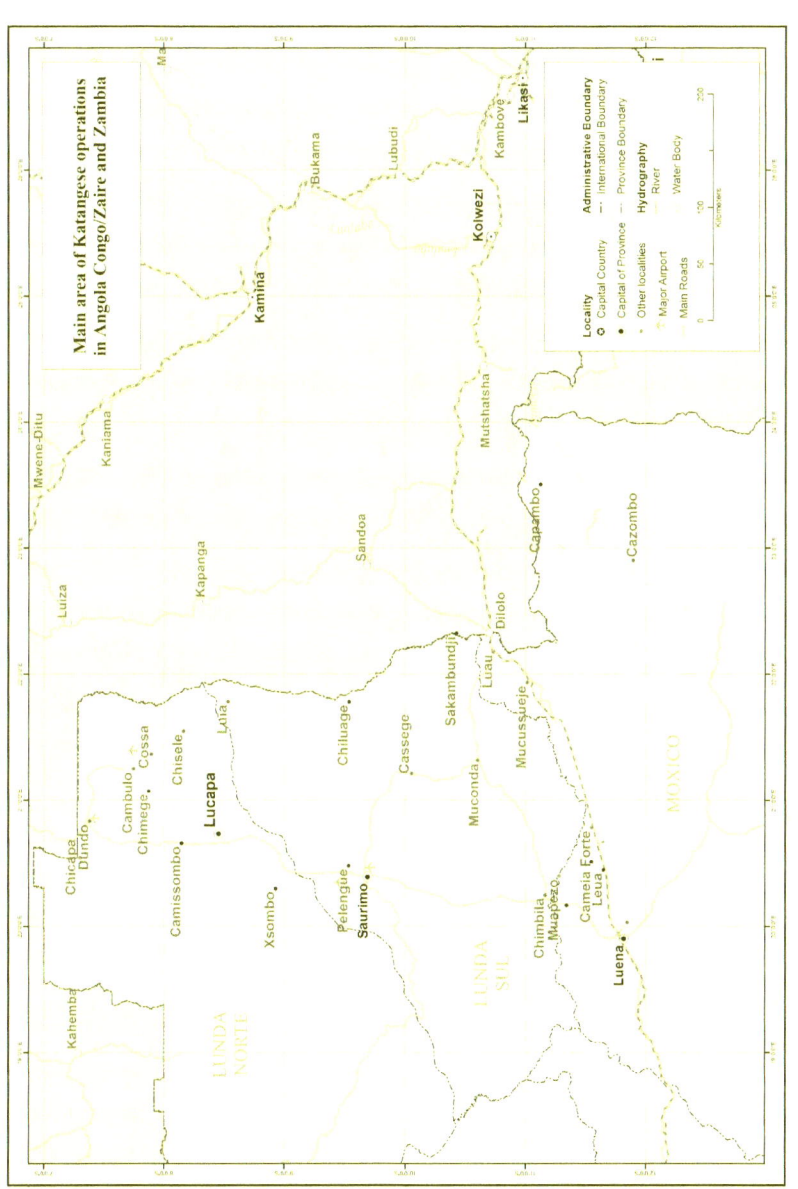

Main areas of activity and bases of Katangese gendarmes and successor organizations in Angola, Congo/Zaire, and Zambia, 1960–1999.

tion of political power in 1966–1967, a mutiny by ex-gendarmes and their mercenary commanders led to a second and more enduring exile in Angola.

There, the ex-gendarmes were mobilized by Portugal against the nationalist forces seeking to achieve Angolan independence, operating mainly from exile in Zambia and Congo/Zaire. Although in many respects reduced to the level of mercenaries and christened by the Portuguese the "*fiéis*," or faithful ones, by the late 1960s the ex-gendarmes were asserting a new identity as an exiled political force seeking self-determination for their homeland: this was symbolized by their adoption of a new organizational identity, the National Front for the Liberation of Congo (FLNC). The situation of the ex-gendarmes was once again transformed by the Portuguese revolution of 1974, which was followed by the rapid decolonization of Angola and civil war, ostensibly among the three Angolan national liberation movements but also involving regional powers and the superpowers. The ex-gendarmes and their FLNC political leadership agreed with the Marxist-oriented MPLA to mobilize their experienced and well-trained troops in support of its cause. FLNC forces saw action in some of the key battles of the civil war, in which the MPLA came to power in 1975. The quid pro quo for this agreement was that the FLNC would use its base on Angolan soil to launch attacks on Mobutu's Zaire. This it did in 1977 and 1978, with the second of these so-called Shaba wars dramatically destabilizing Zaire's strategic mining industry and leading to Western military intervention in a conflict misleadingly framed in exclusively Cold War terms. Angola subsequently brought independent action by the FLNC to an end, expelling its leaders and partly integrating FLNC troops into its own "national" army. Two decades later, however, some thousands of their number were mobilized in the successful overthrow of Mobutu in 1997 by the Alliance des Forces Démocratiques pour la Libération du Congo (AFDL), nominally led by Laurent Kabila. By this route, most ex-gendarmes finally returned to the country that was once again known as Congo and to a very different but still economically strategic and politically important "Katanga." The specific membership of this fighting force had, as will be shown, changed substantially over its decades in exile, but its leadership remained in the hands of those who went into exile in the late 1960s.

Evidently, this brief and simplified narrative raises immediate and important questions regarding the underlying nature of this politico-military group, which was characterized above all by periodic changes to its outlook, ideological positioning, membership, the names it adopted, and the types of activities it undertook.[1] The gendarmes at times sought the outright independence of Katanga, at others meaningful autonomy for Katanga within a decentralized Congolese state, and sometimes even the "liberation" of Congo itself. They evolved from the "neocolonial" armed force of the unrecognized Katangese state in the early 1960s to the ostensibly Marxist Tigres of the mid-1970s. The composition of the exiled force, periodically replenished from within Congo/Zaire to compensate for the many ex-gendarmes who were killed in action or retired from conflict, steadily evolved in the manner of more conventional national armies. Unlike such armies, however, the names by which this force was known also changed periodically in relation to its alliances: the Katangese gendarmes became the *fiéis*, the allies of Portuguese colonial forces faithful to the memory of their homeland; as the FLNC, they were organized along national liberation lines; they adopted an insurgent identity as the Tigres "guerrillas"; and some of their number subsequently became the 24th Regiment of the Angolan armed forces, the FAA. Reflecting these nominative changes, the "ex-gendarmes" also played a range of military roles—a state-based army, an agent of colonial repression, a national liberation movement, a security guard for valuable mining installations, an insurgent force, and a division of someone else's national army—before their problematic (re)integration into the armed forces of the post-Mobutu Democratic Republic of Congo (DRC).

Following from the above, it may reasonably be asked whether this history is best understood as a succession of movements only tangentially related to each other rather than as a singular movement with a consistent form of identity. Addressing the questions adequately will require—and is indeed the justification for—the full extent of the material and arguments presented in this book. Historical research of this kind should, however, not seek to identify a misleadingly singular explanation for an entity as complex as the gendarmes but rather explore its myriad and ostensibly contradictory manifestations as a way to increase our understanding of the nature of political and social change in central Africa. It can certainly be argued that the subsequent memorialization of the gendarmes' various manifestations continued to inform and inspire each successive iteration in important ways, as did the reactions to the movement(s) of their enemies. Indeed, the final chapters will demonstrate that, notwithstanding the extinguishing of the "Katangese gendarmes" as a meaningful politico-military force, the persistent memory of this powerful grouping continues to influence the contemporary and still problematic integration of Katanga into today's Democratic Republic of Congo.

Our aim is, then, to adopt the perspective of the gendarmes as they crossed borders, adopted new identities, and engaged in diverse military conflicts, in order to reveal both the underlying realities of political and military change in central Africa and the effect of those changes on the gendarmes themselves.

Katanga: Acting Like a Nation-State

The African nation-state has long been recognized as a problematic formation.[2] The Katangese secession, with its contemporaneous illegitimacy and enduring political incorrectness, partly prompted the Organization of African Unity's (OAU) reification of colonial borders as the sole legitimate basis of postcolonial states in 1963. This decision was not inevitable, but it led to an intellectual tendency to see the retention of colonial borders—which Kwame Nkrumah and other radical African nationalists had initially railed against—as unavoidable. Thus, the majority of historical writing on African nation-states, while acknowledging their inherent artificiality, nevertheless tended to assume that these states had some legitimacy in a form of proto-national identity or would acquire it by denying the legitimacy of precolonial political identification and by functioning as a Weberian state: by guaranteeing law and order, imposing taxation, and providing welfare and other services, the new state would create a nation from above and make it meaningful in the eyes of its subjects, displacing or undermining alternative forms of identity or belonging, including what we understand as "ethnicity."[3] A vast amount of subsequent work on African political development has demonstrated the fallacious nature of these assumptions, the main conclusions of which are presented here only briefly.[4] First, the capacity of the postcolonial African nation-state to fulfill these functions proved extremely limited. Although this varied within and between particular countries, it is generally true that the optimism surrounding state-led African political and economic development during the 1950s and 1960s had been dashed by the late 1970s or 1980s. It can certainly be argued that in many regions of independent African nation-states, the state was experienced either as an ineffective or distant presence, unable to effectively project its authority far beyond the capital city, or as an authoritarian external imposition, as foreign in its specific manifestations as the colonial state that had bequeathed and considerably shaped it.[5]

In either case, the imposition of nation-statehood within colonial borders did not prevent the continued assertion of alternative bases for "national" belonging. This was particularly true in those countries which contained many diverse ethnicities with a distinct though reconstructed memory of precolonial identity, where colonial-era socioeconomic development had increased regional diversity, and where late-colonial authorities had done little to nurture a genuine sense of proto-national identification in the run-up to independence. All of this was true in the Belgian Congo, where, most pertinently, the outright ban on territory-wide political parties, which remained in place until three years before Congolese independence in 1960, fueled the expression of political grievance and aspiration via ethnoregional associations that then became the basis for most Congolese political parties in the rushed period of decolonization.[6] The southern province of Katanga, marked out as distinct by the precolonial history of its "kingdoms of the savannah" and globally significant mineral wealth, and governed differently as a result, saw the most significant expression of an alternative imagining of national identity. Reconstructed as a colonial province, it enabled the late-colonial articulation by the Conakat leadership of an "authentic" Katangese identity that could accept white settlers as potential Katangese loyalists while simultaneously rejecting Kasaian migrants.

The historical experience of Congo was not, however, qualitatively different from developments in much of the rest of sub-Saharan Africa. Although Katanga and Biafra represented the most overt (although very different) secessionist opposition to colonially constructed nation-statehood, many other such manifestations were visible to observers willing to look beyond the assumptions of the nation-state model. These were commonly dismissed as the result of backward-looking "tribalism" and contrasted to the supposedly pan-ethnic basis of African nationalism, overlooking the extent to which both ethnicity and ethnically based patronage networks commonly pervaded the supposedly modern institutions of the nation-state. At a later stage, African nation-states which had become the arena for ethnoregional conflicts utilized their capacity to bestow citizenship to deny it to those it regarded as disloyal.[7] More recent work has demonstrated both the fertility and the endurance of alternative or "competing" nationalisms, which either sought to reconstruct the ethnoregional basis of the central nation-state or to entirely recast it in, for example, a decentralized or federal form.[8] Historical research does not demonstrate the desirability of following either a centralized or federal path but rather seeks to understand the continued importance of such forms of political expression within and in opposition to externally recognized nation-statehoods. In the light of such studies, and indeed of events such as the independence of South Sudan in 2011, it is possible to reassess the emblematic case of ethnoregional secessionism, that of Katanga, as an initiative driven at least as much by internal alternative imaginaries as by external manipulation by colonial and business interests.[9] It should be noted that, while instructive parallels can be drawn between various expressions of alternative nationalisms in postcolonial Africa, the particularities of each example must equally be understood. Katangese nationalism was multilayered, drawing on reconfigured ethnic identities, self-conscious identification with mythico-historical precolonial states and societies, specific components derived from its particular experience of colonial rule, and—in southern Katanga—a political culture and moral economy shaped by the production of mineral wealth.

One of the important ways in which nation-statehood has been usefully analyzed is by a focus on its specific thoughts and actions, and how these reveal the ways in which state actors understood their territories and sought to act upon them.[10] Understanding the ways in which an African nation-state was expected to act, both in Weberian and more performative terms, helps overcome the ultimately ahistorical impositions placed on researchers by the issue of international recognition and enables a focus on the actual relationship between the governor and the governed.[11] For example, the South African "homelands," rightly regarded as politically illegitimate attempts to construct apartheid, nevertheless demonstrate that the day-to-day relationship of their populations to those states resembled in many respects that of Africans residing in "legitimate" nation-states to the north of the Limpopo.[12] Similarly, the Katangese state, in its brief period of illegal existence, imagined and acted in ways that were characteristic of nation-states elsewhere on the continent, notably in its intolerance for ethnic dissent within its borders and its assertion of national identity via public events and the trappings of nationhood.

In addition to the more performative aspects of "nationhood" in Katanga, central to its self-assertion were, first, its monopoly access to the mining industry that financed the secessionist project; and, second, the monopoly of armed force, the Katangese national army paid for by mining revenue. In the latter case, the construction of a national armed force—which, notwithstanding the focus hitherto on Belgian and mercenary military leadership, was primarily composed of the Katangese gendarmerie—was central to Katanga's assertion of national legitimacy. In many respects, the initial assertion of national military symbolism from without was one of the aspects of the state that was gradually internalized, or "reappropriated," by the Katangese themselves, especially after the departure of Belgian officers in 1961–1962.[13] The capacity for the region's mining wealth to underwrite a range of projects of nation-statehood, development, and more private forms of securitization, to fund the activities of armed groups, but also to become targets for military actions, are all recurring themes in the history of the gendarmes.

Failed Demobilization and Human Land Mines

The negotiated end to conflicts in Africa and elsewhere is commonly marked by self-congratulatory assemblies of the military and political leaders of the parties to the conflict, often alongside Western politicians, UN officials, and civil society experts. Agreements are signed promising free elections; commissions for truth, justice, and reconciliation are organized; and processes supposed to deliver the demobilization and reintegration of opposed armed forces are launched. All of this was true in 1963, when the United Nations' successful termination of the Katangese secession was followed by efforts to ensure the effective unification of Congo's various armed forces. However, this was fatally undermined by the capacity of the gendarmes to escape UN supervision; the continued tendency of the leadership of the ANC to treat the ex-gendarmes as an "enemy within";[14] and the ability of the former Katangese leadership, particularly Tshombe, to reassert the secessionist project. All these factors contributed to the continued existence of a national army without a nation. Even more hazardous in a "postconflict" environment than the quintessential image of a land mine field, whose lethal threat may continue for decades after the ostensible end of conflict, the ex-gendarmes, mobile across national borders and in need of shelter, food, and wages, remained highly vulnerable to subsequent remobilization for different wars in different territories fought for causes other than their own.

In this sense, the ex-gendarmes provide an early example of a widespread problem in postconflict demobilization and reintegration faced across sub-Saharan Africa, and indeed globally, since the early 1990s. The ex-gendarmes were problematically "reintegrated" into Congo's armies on at least two further occasions: between 1965 and 1967, a period that ended with their mutiny against Mobutu's increasingly dictatorial rule of the country; and after 1997, when the ex-Tigres who participated in the AFDL were brought into the post-Mobutu Congolese army. On both occasions, the failure to achieve this process was partly technical but essentially political—for both Mobutu and Laurent Kabila, the threat posed by the ex-gendarmes within the army's midst outweighed the potential benefit of the successful integration of this experienced and effective military force. Comparison may also be drawn with the problems faced in postconflict processes of demobilization and integration in Mozambique and, more recently, in Côte d'Ivoire, as well as in the DRC more generally after the second Congo war.[15]

This enduring threat potential, always linked to the continued prospect of Katangese autonomy, remained, for Congolese centralists, tangible until at least the mid-1990s. Some individual ex-gendarmes were, for example, involved in training the "*jeunesses* UFERI," who sowed fear of a resurgent Katangese autonomy and who played a significant role in widespread ethnic violence against people of Kasaian origin in general and supporters of the opposition Union pour la Démocratie et le Progrès Social (UDPS) in particular, which led to the displacement of at least 150,000 people from their southern Katangese homes. There is, however, a less tangible, almost ethereal element to the perpetual threat of Katangese remobilization, in that it has since the integration of the Tigres into the army of the Laurent Kabila regime in the early twenty-first century become almost entirely divorced from reality. Notwithstanding the practical demobilization of the ex-gendarmes in the twenty-first century, rumors of their potential revival periodically manifest themselves, in support of the perennially potent cause of liberating Katanga from exploitation by the predations of an unaccountable Kinshasa-based central state on both its peoples and its (once again profitable) mineral resources. It is in this context that widespread discontent with the evident disparity between the province's contribution of nearly 50 percent of the DRC's national revenue and the lack of development in Katanga itself finds expression in various forms: demands for federalism, autonomy, or outright secession.

Congolese Political Change from Within and Without

Congo has often been represented as a place apart, the "heart of darkness" which, lacking its own history or agency, has as a result fallen victim to external exploitation and manipulation, from Arab slave trading to King Leopold's brutal regime, from the Cold War (the assassination of Prime Minister Patrice Lumumba and the imposition of the Mobutu dictatorship) to the murderous Congo wars of 1997–2003 in which regional powers imposed puppet presidents and divided up the mineral spoils between them. Many historians have sought to rectify this impression by analysis of the complex, often labyrinthine history of political parties, alliances, and change in Congo.[16] There is nevertheless still a tendency to treat Congo as a place where the normal rules of political power do not apply, where the state is particularly abject, local elites are especially venal, and neighboring powers and Western actors are able to act with impunity. This tends to undermine understanding of the extent to which the problems of Congo are an extreme version of the challenges faced by other postcolonial states in central-southern Africa. Congo's problems may therefore be better understood by placing the country within a regional comparison and in particular by grasping the extent to which the interaction between autonomous movements in border regions and neighboring states has shaped its historical development.

Flowing logically from the above identification of Katanga as in principle a meaningful nation-state is the problematization, or decentering, of the Congolese state as a historically authentic space in which popular identification and political legitimacy should naturally occur. Congo's distinctive political history has generally militated against the creation of conditions conducive to coherent nationwide popular political expression. Belgian colonial rule, particularly the ban on territory-wide political organization that remained in place until 1957, encouraged mobilization via ethnoregional association and severely restricted African nationalists' participation in government until the few months before the sudden arrival of independence. The belated flourishing of political expression during the 1957–1960 period was chaotic, not simply because of the undoubtedly significant attempts at political manipulation by Belgian settlers, politicians, and companies, but primarily because the extraordinary expression of dissatisfaction, anger, and grievance quickly overflowed the shallow foundations hastily dug for new national political institutions and spread like a flood, unevenly and unpredictably, across the diverse Congolese landscape. Taking a single important example, the inability of the Lumumba government to satisfy the entirely understandable grievances of Congolese Force Publique (FP) troops in the first days of self-rule led inexorably to a national crisis and indirectly to the Katangese secession.

Throughout the period of civilian rule (1960–1965), Congolese political life was characterized by an unedifying display of calculated self-interest and a preference for regionally based winner-takes-all political competition that, even when not consciously seeking to delegitimize central authority, had the effect of doing so. Those politicians who found themselves in office but not in power in the capital, Leopoldville, proved unable to construct nationally coherent governments that could be meaningful to the Congolese citizenry and struggled to establish even basic levels of national state legitimacy. Because of this, and because of a legitimate fear of internal regionally oriented opposition movements and their respective external backers, both national and regional leaders commonly sought to secure their position via recourse to external means—the limited but disastrous turn to the Eastern bloc by Patrice Lumumba and the fuller embrace of communist and radical aid by a succession of eastern Congolese Lumumbists, as well as a fuller embrace of Western interests by Lumumba's successors, particularly Cyrille Adoula (1961–1964). Moïse Tshombe's brief period as Congolese prime minister (1964–1965) was equally dependent on Western efforts to shore up Congo from without. Although Joseph Mobutu's 1965 coup was welcomed by many Congolese, it represented above all the judgment of the United States that Congo's strategic position and mineral wealth were too important to be left in the hands of its politicians or its peoples. Mobutu's rule was certainly facilitated by his capacity to deny the legitimacy of grassroots political expression and to truncate it at higher levels. In buying off, suppressing, and/or incorporating (and sometimes all three) ethnoregional political elites rather than addressing the grievances of those who saw such elites as their representatives, Mobutu sought to monopolize the addressing of such grievances in his presidency and person, creating a logical tendency toward totalitarian rule in the early 1970s. This was, however, made possible above all by his relationship with the CIA and other elements of the US politico-military establishment and by his skillful articulation of anticommunism and the characterization of any and all opponents of his rule as, intentionally or not, opening the door to Soviet influence in central Africa. Even at its height in the late 1960s, the capacity of the Mobutu-dominated state to project authority across Congolese territory was uneven and, in some areas, such as Katanga, rested on an effective occupation of enemy territory and the periodic terrorization of the population via the ever unreliable agency of the Congolese National Army.[17]

By the time US support was belatedly withdrawn in the early 1990s, the Congolese state had arguably been in decay for two decades—like some other African states, but with perhaps more dramatic effect, the hollowness of Congolese national sovereignty was cruelly exposed by the disastrous Zairianization experiment, the mid-1970s collapse of the global price of its strategic minerals, and the consequent acquisition of a vast national debt.[18] This exposed the essential externality of political authority in what was now Zaire, fueling opposition among internal actors and Zairian political exiles who took advantage of the political opening that resulted from the Shaba I attack by the FLNC in 1977. The potential for an opposition alliance was skillfully resisted by Mobutu by divide-and-rule tactics, but these tactics were effective because no coherent alliance or alternative vision of the country could be agreed upon by his opponents among the country's political elite, which had no more interest in representing the interests of their clients than Mobutu. By the 1980s, the projection of central state power in much of the country depended on a vast patrimonial machinery that had partly accommodated a new generation of political and military elites but which could ultimately not be paid for. This was temporarily addressed by Mobutu's distinctive form of privatization, the explicit encouragement to officials to help themselves ("*debrouillez-vous*") to state assets, and unsustainable reforms which created chaotic intra-elite competition and simultaneously created surprising spaces for a degree of political expression in the central committee of the ruling MPR party (Mouvement Populaire de la Révolution) and in the country's regional assemblies.

The political opening of the early 1990s had genuine potential for the expression of popular political will. Civil society, churches, human rights organizations, and some political parties coalesced into a huge and highly popular democratization movement focused around the Sovereign National Conference (CNS) of 1991–1992. The Marche des chrétiens of February 16, 1992, a vast demonstration demanding the reopening of the CNS, was the high point of a movement that briefly overcame national division and created the circumstances for a politics without Mobutu. The brutal repression of the march and of the expression of popular will in general, and the subsequent institutionalization and progressive recapturing of these processes both by the presidential movement and by opposition parties with no interest in political accountability, resulted by the mid-1990s in a return to elite-dominated politics, culminating in 1997 with the complete disconnection of the national assembly from the wider population.

Following the withdrawal of US backing, and in the absence of a coherent or effective internal opposition with the potential to remove Mobutu and unite the country around a coherent vision, political change could come only from without. The overthrow of Mobutu by AFDL forces in April 1997 was of course widely celebrated; Laurent Kabila's "Lumumbist" nationalism, more celebrated today than evident during his time in office, nevertheless did briefly re-create a sense of national cohesion and vision, even if it was constructed against external enemies and entirely detached from the CNS's attempts to establish a basis for internal political accountability. Congo's political future was, however, once again decided by external powers that, like their predecessors, masked their manipulation of the country via leaders whose patriotic rhetoric only thinly disguised their dependence on foreign states. The consequence, one of Africa's worst-ever wars and a subsequent absence of peace lasting until today, is matched by a continuing invisibility of the central state in large parts of the DRC.

Nevertheless, we would not suggest, like Herbst and Mills, that the dismantling of the Congolese nation-state would be likely to reduce political or social conflict—indeed, the opposite is highly likely.[19] Congo, despite its size and diversity, is not qualitatively less functional or potentially less governable than a host of other African states. It is also clear that many—probably most—Congolese people believe that their aspirations and grievances can best be addressed by a strengthening of the capacity and legitimacy of Congo as a nation-state.[20] It is noteworthy that, in combating the imposition of political settlements on them by foreign states during the second Congo war, the country experienced a greater sense of national unity than ever before—even if a considerable price was paid by some of its peoples who during this period had their right to Congolese citizenship challenged.[21] The end of all-out war has, however, reduced the impulse toward national mobilization and integration, while the ineffectiveness of the government of Joseph Kabila has led to a resurgence of support for regional autonomy and in some areas—most notably in Ituri but to some extent in Katanga—outright independence. Legitimate discussion about the potential for provincial autonomy, promised by the postwar constitution but as yet not effectively delivered, has, however, been dampened by its manipulation, for example by Rwanda in the Kivus during the second Congo war, as a way of extending its influence over what it considers its hinterland.[22] In this sense, the Rwandan threat to Congolese territory serves the central government's ends, in restricting federalist impulses by rendering them illegitimate—reflecting the historical interaction between neighboring powers, border regions inhabited by transnational ethnicities, and the "national" state in Kinshasa which has created a vicious circle of threat and counterthreat, in which an ahistorical division between autochthons and ethnic strangers is deployed by all sides to depict a reality in which identities and aspirations cannot be neatly contained within national borders.

In this context, the view from the Katangese periphery and from exile in Angola sheds new light on the experience of the Congolese nation-state, the political dynamics of which were themselves modified by Kabila's own (albeit distinct) Katangese identity. It also benefits from documenting the experience of politicomilitary exiles whose problematic vision of national liberation was crushed by armed force and enabled by external agents interested solely in regional security and the profitable exploitation of Congo's mineral wealth.

Armées sans Frontières?

Despite the preeminence of the military as a leading agent in postcolonial African history, it remains a comparatively understudied aspect of political life. Colonial armed forces were established primarily for the internal security of colonial states rather than for their external defense; this certainly shaped postcolonial armed forces, for whom internal repression has been their primary activity and, in countries such as the DRC, their essential role. Early suggestions that African armies might provide one of the building blocks of nation-states have given way to a more considered approach to the complex relationship between state, quasi-state, and nonstate military actors.[23] In order to effectively assess the role and identity of military groupings, we may first consider a typology of armed types. At one end of a spectrum is the army as the embodiment of a rational sovereign nation-state with a Weberian monopoly on the expression of armed force, and at the other, bands of bandits and looters who may use military nomenclature, titles, and uniforms but who seek to control territory solely for personal gain. Between these two extremes we can situate militias such as the Congolese Mayi Mayi, initially established to defend their village or community of origin but coming (in some cases) to engage in state-like initiatives; mercenary forces detached from such origins but displaying elements of operational discipline; ostensibly national armed forces composed primarily of one or more dominant ethnicities which may as a result be regarded as a foreign occupying force in regions where other ethnicities are dominant; and presidential guards whose loyalty is primarily personal rather than national.

All these forms have played a significant role in Congolese military history, but what is often lost in analyses of military formations is their historical agency and specifically their capacity to evolve from one type to another. This tendency has its origins in the FP itself, which originated as a colonial state army but whose role was problematically divided between external defense and internal repression. The Katangese gendarmes, like the Congolese national army itself, evolved out of and in some respects replicated the FP, mirroring its structures and operating procedures but cohering around an idealized Katangese state, acquiring greater legitimacy in the process. This cohering ideal was maintained under a succession of military commanders and advisers: Belgian instructors, white mercenaries, Portuguese colonial officials, Cuban officers, and MPLA and Angolan generals thereafter. During this period, the gendarmes evolved steadily from the colonial-type army of the secession period to a mercenary-led militia force and were then restructured after the model of Portuguese commandos. Alongside their identity as the Katangese army-in-exile, the ex-gendarmes were simultaneously an early example of a transborder army. Following the victory of the AFDL in 1997 and during the two Congo wars, myriad armed groups, some of whom had been roaming central Africa for decades, were "discovered": remnants of the Mulelist rebellion of 1964–1965, subsequently resident in Sudan and Uganda; Lumumbist forces who had been hiding in Tanzania, Kenya, and Uganda; trained Congolese soldiers who fought in every significant war in sub-Saharan Africa; and even Eritreans mobilized to fight a long way from "home."

The ex-gendarmes were, however, different from all of the above in that they aspired to an identity as a state army and had a project to reinstitute that state in some form. In this sense they partly resemble the Rwanda Patriotic Front/Army (RPF/RPA). The latter, arising from the Tutsi population driven into exile from Rwanda in 1959 by the Hutu uprising, resided in Uganda for some decades. Many Rwandan Tutsi born in Uganda went on to serve as a part of the rebel forces of Yoweri Museveni and, having assisted his accession to power, served as a distinct element of the Ugandan armed forces. The RPF utilized this base to launch an armed rebellion against the Hutu-controlled Rwandan state and was in 1994 able to return to Rwanda and gain control of the country, becoming its new government and providing its new armed force. It may, however, be noted that, unlike in the gendarmes' case, the RPF did not exist and did not embody a statist form before Ugandan exile. Instructive parallels may also be drawn with the Sudan People's Liberation Army/Movement (SPLA/SPLM); although it never entered into exile, it fought a decades-long war against what it regarded as the unjust integration of what had during the colonial era been an autonomously ruled southern Sudan, at the moment of independence, into an authoritarian and "foreign" Sudanese state that repressed its people and their culture and that extracted its mineral wealth with no benefit flowing to the areas in which those minerals were produced. Although the SPLA/SPLM was beset by divisions and entered into decidedly problematic alliances with Sudan's regional enemies, it ultimately succeeded in achieving the breakup of postcolonial Sudan, and today the former SPLA is the official army of the world's newest nation-state, South Sudan; it of course remains to be seen whether this will provide a better life for its populace or if it will prove a practical precedent for aspirant secessionists elsewhere in Africa (as we write, the initial indications are, to say the least, not promising).

The SPLA and the RPA certainly resembled one important aspect of the Congolese element of the AFDL, that is, its basis in a mobilized refugee diaspora. In Congo, this was the product of successive phases of political exclusion by the Congolese/Zairian regime. The lack of effective integration of Congolese intellectuals, militants, and combatants into the Mobutu regime, and their subsequent exile across Africa and in western Europe, created the basis for future mobilization against that regime and indeed its successors. In this sense, the ex-gendarmes, one element of the AFDL, were pioneers of what is generally regarded as characteristic of more contemporary politico-military forms commonly associated with the post–Cold War period.

Although the ex-gendarmes' military cohesion largely disappeared with their problematic integration into the reconstituted army of the post-Mobutu DRC, their identity has persisted, fueled by material grievances in the form of low salaries and poor and discriminatory treatment by political leaders. For these veterans, this is explained by the alleged domination of Congolese political and military spheres by northern Katangese Luba, whom the older generation fought against during the secession. The younger generation, the ex-Tigres who went to Angola in the mid-1970s, also remain attracted to the idea of Katangese autonomy, promoted first by Governor Gabriel Kyungu wa Kumwanza in the early 1990s, developed by the province's current governor, Moïse Katumbi, and now more generalized among all of Katanga's population, including Katangese Luba who historically opposed the secession of the early 1960s. While it is clear that no military force now exists capable of fighting for a Katangese nation-state project, this does not prevent new secessionist projects associating themselves with the identity, symbols, and memory of the ex-gendarmes.

Cold War, National Liberation, Local Conflict

Most of the activities described here took place in the context of the global Cold War. To most Western observers of the period, particularly state officials and journalists, Cold War political affiliations and ideas offered the sole or primary explanation for organizations and leaders who portrayed their activities in apparently ideological terms, whether using the language of communism, Maoism, or anticommunism. It is not original to point out the distorting effect of such a singular framework of analysis, in both academic work and among policy makers: most notoriously, the United States' infamous National Security Study Memorandum (NSSM) 39 of 1969 on liberation movements in southern Africa ("the whites are here to stay and the only way that constructive change can come about is through them."[24]), in prioritizing Cold War concerns over self-determination, contributed to the incoherence of US policy during the Angolan civil war, with the decidedly unintended consequence of helping the communist bloc gain a foothold on the continent. Westad's seminal *The Global Cold War* encouraged a new understanding of non-Western agents which drew often reluctant superpowers into Cold War conflicts that turned unintentionally "hot."[25] Today, it is widely recognized that the Angolan civil war, for example, was shaped by parallel and equally important divisions—ideological, but also ethnoregional, reflecting both the support provided to each protagonist by regional powers and the internal dynamics of the respective Angolan nationalist movements. Gleijeses's unparalleled access to the Cuban archives has shed considerable light on that country's decisive role in the war as well as its longer-term role in Africa's Cold War.[26]

This volume not only explains the specific actions of the ex-gendarmes in both the Angolan and later Shaba (the renamed Katanga) wars of 1977–1978 but also deconstructs these events' contemporaneous presentation as Cold War conflicts. Most obviously, the ex-gendarmes themselves, nominally allied to the Western bloc as the ground troops of the Katangese secession and subsequently the auxiliaries of Portuguese colonialism, provided from 1975 vital ground forces for the Marxist MPLA in the Angolan civil war and went on to fight for MPLA-ruled Angola for the remainder of the Cold War. The ex-gendarmes' propensity for ideological shape-shifting is easily dismissed as mercenary opportunism, and certainly there was a decidedly performative aspect to the FLNC's presentation of itself as a Marxist-influenced organization. From the perspective of a less overtly ideological era, it is possible to see how the ideological constructions of Western liberal democracy and Soviet state socialism could prove both complementary and less important to the ex-gendarmes than broader notions of self-determination and nationalism, rooted in their notion of warfare as a pathway home. Such an interpretation was, however, well beyond the understanding of most Western intelligence analysts seeking to make sense of the ex-gendarmes' successive invasions of Katanga (then Shaba Province) in 1977 and 1978, which is here explained from the perspective of its primary protagonists for the first time. While more sophisticated analysts questioned President Mobutu's hysterical presentation of Shaba I and II as crucial battles in the fight against global communism, most US and French observers were happy to see this complex conflict not in its historical context but through a highly circumscribed Cold War prism. This led to the suppression of the most important challenge faced by President Mobutu during his long and mostly venal rule, a missed opportunity for political change that contributed to Congo's contemporary crisis and that today, as we shall see, continues to haunt relations between the central state and its wealthiest and most troublesome province.

1   Becoming Katanga

THIS CHAPTER, IN establishing the history of the area of central Africa that became Katanga, simultaneously and intentionally echoes and challenges the proto-national narratives underlying the creation of nation-states in Africa in the mid-twentieth century.[1] Historians and African leaders sought at that time to retrospectively construct the history of their disparate new territories in order to project a coherent self-conscious national narrative, to encourage national integration, and to discourage alternative and/or competing forms of affiliation.[2] There is a well-established literature stressing the "imaginary" or "invented" nature of nation-states generally.[3] The particular artificiality of African nation-states, constructed largely along the lines drawn by colonists in the wake of the scramble for Africa of the 1880s and 1890s, is equally well known: the process of nationalist imagining in late-colonial Africa was particularly brief; involved a relatively narrow elite, many of whom were Europeans; and allowed little substantive debate over the composition, character, and culture of the new nation-state.

If this general framework applies to (post)colonial Africa as a whole, then it can be witnessed in its most extreme form in the Belgian Congo and its independent successor. Various factors contributed to the extremely late and partial affiliation of most Congolese people to anything approximating a unified nation-state: the nature of colonial administration, which made no substantive effort to project any form of proto-national identity; the related lack of political reform and establishment of "modern" forms of representative institutions until the rushed decolonization of the late 1950s; the very basic level of mass education provided by the colonial state; and infrastructural development that enabled the export of raw materials but did little to integrate the territory within Congo's borders. As will be illustrated below, these and other factors contributed to the emergence in the 1950s of African political expression that was, with few exceptions, primarily ethnoregional in nature. The outright ban on territory-wide political parties maintained until the elections of December 1957 meant that ethnoregional cultural associations provided the main basis for anticolonial political expression and the majority of Congo's political parties in the rapid decolonization process of the late 1950s. This contributed significantly to the forms of political conflict that developed in the run-up to, as well as during and after, independence in June 1960.

In the territory that would become Katanga, there was an equally limited sense of proto-national consciousness, but it was at least as coherent a basis for an imaginable nation-state as the far larger and more disparate Congolese state of which it was a part. This is, then, the precolonial and colonial history of the nation-state of Katanga, a counterfactual history that describes the foundations of the ultimately aborted project of Katangese statehood which, in many ways, closely resembles the parallel projects of nation-making that unfolded simultaneously across postcolonial Africa at this time. This is not to deny that the Katangese nation-state initiative necessitated the artificial projection of unity and belonging onto a highly uneven—geographically, economically, and culturally—territory, the reification of some characteristics of some of its peoples as the dominant features of national identity, and the marginalization or silencing of others. "Katanga" was an elite-dominated project, articulated and instituted by conservative political leaders, chiefly authorities and their European economic and military partners. While the anticommunist orientation of the Katangese political project was distinctive in African terms, it was far from being the only Western-oriented, elite-dominated, or ethnically partial nationalist project in Africa.

The importance of this history is twofold. First, both the precolonial and colonial history of Katanga and Congo shaped these societies in ways that created a strong propensity toward autonomy and even secession among Katangese elites. Second, the reconstructed historical memory of precolonial Katanga, opportunistically asserted with the sudden and largely unanticipated arrival of urban political association and the prospect of self-rule in the late 1950s, was, together with elements directly borrowed from colonial statehood, central to the articulation of a "national" Katanga in the run-up to and during the secession itself. One of the challenges of such an analysis is to distinguish between these two forms of history, that is, the "actual" effect of historical factors on economic, political, or societal change, and the asserted use of history in its memorial and mythical forms. It is suggested that, while the political culture of self-styled "indigenous" Katangese leaders required a highly imaginative interpretation of Katangese history (for example, in its assertion of the so-called Lunda Empire), the political economy of Katanga (particularly the relationship between the territory and its mineral wealth—mining companies almost literally *made* the state structures in Katanga—made it possible to practically envisage an independent Katanga, created the conditions for hostility toward Kasaian labor migration, and yet placed identifiable limits on the ultimate success of the secessionist project. While Katanga's alliance with Belgian advisers and capital had the effect of preserving Katanga's comparatively developed infrastructure development—and, ironically, making possible subsequent Zairianization measures—the practical impact of colonialism on Katanga made it impossible to effectively integrate the territory's diverse population into a cohesive national project.

"Katanga" before the Congo Free State

The social and political formations present in the area of central Africa that ultimately formed Katanga had for centuries been significantly shaped by their trade-based interactions with the wider world. Metalworking, in iron but also in copper, was central to the growing economies of the region. The area around Lake Kisale was an important center for metalworking, and its prosperous inhabitants produced a food surplus, including dried fish, which they traded for, among other goods, copper mined to the south in the modern Copperbelt. In the fourteenth century a centralized kingdom, under the Kongolo dynasty, developed among a people known as the Luba. The origins of the Luba political aristocracy can be traced back to three clans: one Songye, one Kanyoka, and one Lunda. The oral tradition clearly refers to a link between the Lunda and the Luba: around 1400, the female ruler of the Lunda, the Lueji/Ruej, married Tshibinda Ilunga/Cibind Irung, a member of the Luba aristocracy. Luba political principles were incorporated into the Lunda political system, thereby creating an element of unity between what was later southern and northern Katanga.[4]

Several waves of westerly out-migration from the core Luba area (located, according to oral tradition, in a place called Nsanga a Lubangu) took place during the early stages of Luba consolidation, commonly associated with intra-aristocratic conflict and the need to address population concentration at a time of famine, probably around the fifteenth century. This led to the distinction between the Luba Katanga (or Lubakat, also known as Luba Shankadi, probably meaning "faithful") and the Luba Lubilanji in Kasai, a distinction which became increasingly rigid in the subsequent period and which has direct relevance for this history.[5]

The Lunda kingdom meanwhile developed in the vicinity of the upper Kasai River. A Lunda dynasty developed, the king of which became known as the Mwaant Yav, with his capital at Musuumb/Musumba, near to Kapanga territory. The Lunda political system allowed for integration of non-Lunda communities, while granting them significant autonomy. Local communities retained authority over the land and the people living on it. Integration of autonomous territories was, however, assured through the *ciool* (*kilolo*), or tax collector, and the *yikeezy*, or inspector, who preserved political and economic ties with the central Lunda polity. The Mwaant Yav was lord of all land (*ngaand*) as well as the supreme tax collector. A second integrative element was the assertion of nonbiological kinship between the Lunda and non-Lunda groups, creating a meaningful fiction that the successor to any title of authority, whether related to them or not, was identified with the original titleholder.[6] Affiliation to this system was attractive not only for economic reasons but also for the authority gained via association with the prestigious kingdom: this partly explains the willingness of non-Luba peoples to recognize the authority of and pledge allegiance to Tshombe during the secession.

The Lunda system's capacity to absorb neighboring polities under its federal umbrella without requiring their political reconstitution was, Vansina argued, central to its success.[7] In particular, the adoption by the Lunda of Luba political principles not only enabled successful incorporation: it was later suggested that this made for a degree of precolonial unity in what later became "Katangese" territory.[8] Bustin, however, concludes that, although its federal nature aided its successful growth and expansion, the resultant factionalism that arose over succession to the Mwaant Yav title also prevented the Lunda kingdom becoming a more stable state-like system.[9]

Nevertheless, during the seventeenth century the Lunda kingdom grew to become one of the dominant political forces in central Africa. The Lunda developed trading links with the Portuguese in Angola and trade routes to the Atlantic coast which connected them with global trade and, among other benefits, enabled the import of American crops such as cassava and maize.[10] Cassava in particular enabled food surpluses to be produced, leading to population growth and an expansion in the land under harvest. Tribute payments, often in the form of ivory, were redirected to the western trade routes, with guns and other manufactured goods being imported; slaves also became a major export. The possession of firearms strengthened the Mwaant Yav's authority and the kingdom's capacity for slave raiding. Backed by this increasingly powerful central authority, Lunda tribute collectors established new states in the seventeenth century, subordinating and taxing the existing inhabitants, particularly in areas producing attractive goods, such as in the Copperbelt area to the south and east. The most important of these was the Lunda Kazembe in the Luapula valley, which by the end of the eighteenth century had become a major trading center in its own right, linking the Lunda to Indian Ocean trade routes. The Kasanje kingdom, established on the upper Kwango River in modern Angola by Lunda leaders, enjoyed successful trading relations with both the Lunda and the Portuguese.[11] Through these links, the Lunda traded and established relations with coastal societies such as the Bakongo, with whom they would subsequently be integrated into the colonial state of Congo. While this familiarity should not be conflated as constituting a meaningful building block for the emergence of a proto-national identity, Lunda and Bakongo shared a federalist tendency that in the late colonial period reasserted itself in the parallel approaches of the Alliance des Bakongo (ABAKO) and the Confédération des Associations Tribales du Katanga (Conakat) to the future Congolese state.

Long-distance trade expanded throughout the nineteenth century, but as the West African route declined in importance in relation to its East African equivalent (where slave exports had not been effectively outlawed), established central

African powers were destabilized by the activities of societies of armed raiders with their origins in or linked to creole Swahili coastal societies, such as the Nyamwezi. Msiri, one such Nyamwezi trader, was able in the 1880s to extend his control over a large part of Luba and Lunda territories between the Lualaba and Luapula Rivers and to establish a fully fledged state in this area.[12] A small BaYeke core population established a wider polity via the appointment of local chiefs and, crucially, intermarriage with societies indigenous to the territory that would become Katanga.[13] The newly established BaYeke conquest state of Garenganze flourished until the 1890s, trading in copper and ivory and defending its position by force of arms. In comparison, the Lunda kingdom drastically declined, primarily because of the success of its former subject peoples, the Tshokwe, in disrupting and taking over its Atlantic trading routes through military means in the third quarter of the nineteenth century.[14] Lunda chiefs in what would soon become the colonies of Angola and Northern Rhodesia nevertheless retained their fealty to the Mwaant Yav. Memory of this powerful kingdom would, as we shall see, cast a long shadow over the subsequent political history of the region. Similarly, historical conflict between the Bayeke and the Baluba, and the animosity between the Lunda and Tshokwe, would be reconstructed in late-colonial and postcolonial political conflict: as Lemarchand observed in 1964, "memories of past onslaughts tend to fuse with recent experience, thereby intensifying contemporary political cleavages."[15]

The Colonial Takeover

The diverse responses to the colonial invasion of what would become Katanga were shaped by African societies' preexisting relationships to the region's peoples, resources, and trading links. Lunda royalty, having been defeated and driven out of their capital by the Tshokwe in 1888, had effectively collapsed and consequently did not offer a meaningful response to colonization.[16] The smaller but militarily more powerful BaYeke state was somewhat better placed to respond, but it too had been weakened by the 1891 rebellion by the Sanga, one of the indigenous subject peoples under the yoke of Msiri's autocratic rule. It was precisely the mineral resources controlled by the BaYeke (together with persistent rumors about vast gold deposits) that attracted Belgian and British agents to this area in the late nineteenth century.[17] The British South Africa Company (BSAC), established by royal charter in 1889, was frustrated in its efforts to claim Katanga for Britain via a treaty with the Msiri by some skillful reinterpretation by King Leopold of the concession he had been granted by the Berlin Conference of 1884–1885. The founding of the BSAC had provided a stimulus to Belgian surveying of mineral wealth, and the 1889–1891 period witnessed intense competition between British and Belgian agents before the Free State was able to claim Msiri's capital. Copper mining had been carried out in this region since the fifth century AD, and in the nineteenth century production was concentrated in open pits such as Kalululuku and Bwana Mkubwa (the latter in what would become Northern Rhodesia's Copperbelt). However, as Perrings notes, the profits generated by mining did not accrue primarily to those who worked them but to the Lunda Kazembe and later BaYeke overseers who controlled regional trade.[18]

The colonial conquest in the 1890s did not necessitate a uniform or particularly high level of military action against its peoples. The one notable exception was Msiri's direct rejection of entreaties by representatives of the Compagnie du Katanga to fly the Congo Free State flag over his capital of Bunkeya; Msiri was accordingly shot dead by a company representative in December 1891. The memory of Msiri's opposition to Belgian rule later formed an important element in the discourse of "resistance" to colonization.[19] Less well remembered are the actions of his successor as BaYeke leader, the Mwami Mukanda Bantu. He now allied with Belgium, and the BaYeke's well-trained forces were mobilized to ruthlessly suppress other peoples of southern Congo (including the Sanga and other indigenous peoples who hoped to use Belgian colonization to end Yeke oppression) and bring them under effective colonial control—not for the last time in our story, a central African state used a trained military force assembled for one purpose for a very different one. The Lunda themselves were able to use the colonial invasion to seize back much of their territory, which they did in 1898. Negative Belgian experience of Tshokwe raiding and the general instability of the 1890s led the colonists to side with the Lunda, recognizing the chiefly authority of the Mwaant Yav Muteb in 1907 over that part of Lunda territory that remained under Free State control after its 1891 border agreement with Portugal.[20] Localized resistance by Tshokwe seeking to retain their trading routes continued until the Belgians temporarily sealed the Angolan border in 1908.[21] The later anticolonial rebellion (1907–1917) by the Katangese Baluba chief, the Kasongo Nyembo, was later celebrated as one of the most significant military actions against Belgian rule: as we shall see, the later holder of this post would rally to the secessionist cause in the early 1960s.

Katanga under Leopold II

From the outset, Katanga was considered and governed distinctly from the rest of the Congo Free State, reflecting the wealth of its mineral deposits, the commercial interests that sought to exploit them, and the structural weakness of a Belgian colonial system that had little option but to outsource the exploration and exploitation of Katanga to the mining companies.[22] King Leopold directed the Compagnie du Congo pour le Commerce et l'Industrie (CCCI), created in 1887, to establish effective rule of the area and to prospect for minerals.[23] This led to the founding of the Compagnie du Katanga in 1891: this company, in which the

Belgian state held a 10 percent stake, was granted a one-third concession of all Katanga's territory and a charter for the exploitation of 15 million hectares of land for the next ninety-nine years. In 1900 the Comité Spécial du Katanga (CSK) was in turn created to administer this territory; Katanga was henceforth governed by a six-member committee, two of whose members were appointed by the Compagnie du Katanga and four by the King's Congo Free State; profits were divided on the same ratio.[24]

While the rest of the Congo was subsequently overseen by the Belgian parliament and government under the Charte Coloniale, Article 22 of that charter, placing Katangese administration in the hands of the CSK, limited Belgian domestic scrutiny of its operations.[25] The CSK ruled its territory with quasi-state powers; in a precursor of the Katangese gendarmerie, it even had its own police force, with locally recruited platoons amounting to about 650 men, but without military or police training.[26] It should be noted here that, although Belgian armed forces in Congo (known as the Force Publique, or FP) were theoretically divided into "camped troops" (whose role was external defense) and "troops in territorial service" (civilian-administered troops used for policing and public order), their primary role was always the latter.[27]

King Leopold's rule of Congo became notorious for its demands for compulsory labor and for atrocities, particularly in the area of rubber extraction, which generated significant wealth for the king and funded his pet projects but which did nothing for the vast majority of Congo's people. However, this traumatic experience does not form part of the historical memory of Katanga—indeed, the genuine autonomy of Katanga during this period meant that many later prosecessionists sincerely believed that Katanga was politically independent from Congo until 1933.[28] When the Belgian state took over Congo in 1908, it also inherited the challenge of ensuring that this vast territory paid its way; however, the vast mineral wealth of Katanga was by this time providing some kind of answer. Union Minière du Haut Katanga (UMHK), jointly owned by the British company Tanganyika Concessions and the Société Générale de Belgique (SGB), was established in 1906 to bring together the king's mining interests with those of British mining companies active throughout southern Africa.[29] The Compagnie du Chemin de Fer du Bas-Congo au Katanga (BCK) was founded to build the railway that would make UMHK mining activities a practical concern; by 1910 it had connected the Katangese capital, Elisabethville, to the Rhodesian border, enabling copper exports via southern African trading routes.[30]

In September that year, the administration of CSK territory was transferred to the central Congolese government; at this time, the 650 men of the former CSK police were integrated into the FP. Even at this moment of integration, Minister of Colonies Jules Renkin pledged to give Katanga "the greatest possible autonomy."[31] Between 1910 and 1933, a vice governor-general oversaw Katanga's administration; it was the only province in Congo granted such a status, which provided for substantial autonomy and enabled the mining companies to operate with little or no reference to the Congolese capital located at Boma and then Leopoldville. UMHK continued to dominate Katangese administration: Vellut demonstrates that personnel were regularly interchanged between the state and the mining company and that state officials were co-opted by UMHK at the end of their government service.[32] The centralization of administrative power in 1933 in Leopoldville did not substantially reduce the practical independence of mining interests from the colonial state but was nevertheless strongly opposed by Katanga's small community of white settlers, who would subsequently influence the thinking of Katangese secessionists (see below).

The Rise of Katanga's Mining Economy

As already indicated, Katanga's mining industry involved close cooperation among international mining companies, the Belgian state, and their respective local representatives. Following the production of the first smelted copper in Lubumbashi in 1911, the problem of labor supply required Belgian officials to provide ever-greater assistance to recruiters acting for the Bourse du Travail du Katanga (BTK), established in 1910.[33] Despite continual problems of labor supply, arising in part from the comparatively low population density of southern Katanga, production more than doubled during World War I, when copper demand and prices soared and the gross profits of UMHK (managed from London during the German occupation of Belgium) rose from £102,085 in 1914 to £1,603,514 in 1917.[34] Although the postwar downturn affected both production and profits, by 1923 Congo was the world's third-largest producer of copper, producing 65,221 metric tonnes.[35] Although Belgian capital, particularly the SGB, came to control UMHK, it was these private interests rather than the Belgian authorities that dominated the political economy of Katanga.[36]

As already suggested, Katanga's mineral economy meant that it was integrated more into southern Africa than with the rest of Congo: its railroads and supply routes ran southward (and east and west) to Durban, Lobito, and Lourenço Marques. There was no tarred road connecting Katanga to the capital in Leopoldville, which could for decades be reached quicker by rail and ferry via Cape Town than overland. The Benguela railway, which connected the Angolan port of Lobito to Katanga in 1929, diversified Katanga's external linkages but reinforced its separateness from the rest of the Belgian Congo. This was a reality not simply for colonial authorities and skilled white mine workers (many recruited from southern Africa) but also for African societies. A large part of the early Katangese mining labor force was recruited from Lunda- and Bemba-speaking areas of Northern Rhodesia's Luapula and Northern provinces until the mid-1920s (although by the 1930s the process of replacing these by recruits from Rwanda and, most importantly, Kasai had begun).[37] Although many of these mine workers later shifted to work on the Northern Rhodesian Copperbelt, there remained strong ties—economic, social, cultural, and linguistic—between Lunda- and Bemba-speaking peoples on both sides of the Copperbelt border. Thus, mining, as well as the new urban society produced by it, was salient to the identity of much of the population, not only mine workers themselves but also those who indirectly benefited from labor migration and the spending of mine workers' wages.

Importantly, however, Katanga was itself a highly uneven territory, economically and socially. The Compagnie du Katanga concession did not initially include the Lunda heartland, which was integrated into Katanga only in 1912. This suggests the marginality of the once powerful Lunda kingdom at the moment of colonial annexation—once the central power in this land, it was now literally on the margins of Congo and Katanga, and with substantially reduced access to Western trade opportunities across the new colonial border, it continued to stagnate in the first decades of colonial rule.[38] UMHK's administrative purview now covered the area of its operations across an increasingly industrialized southern territory running east-west from Lubumbashi via Kolwezi and toward Angola. The northern part of the province, whose population was dominated by Katanga's largest single ethnic group, the Katanga Luba, was essentially rural, with little mining activity except for that done by Géomines, which would later prove an important economic resource for the North Katanga government of Prosper Mwamba Ilunga.[39] It was also marked by a Catholic mission presence, while the American Methodist mission dominated in Lunda areas of southern Katanga (see below). These divisions—religious, ethnic, and economic—helped provide the basis for subsequent military conflict in the early 1960s, in which the Katangese gendarmes were first mobilized. Thus, while Katanga provided at least as strong a basis for a nation-state as Congo, it is equally evident that the assertion of Katangese national identity involved the privileging of one section of a highly uneven territory over another (as it arguably did in much of nationalist Africa). In Katanga's case, the mining economy, combined with the colonial reconstruction of "tribal" identities, created a powerful imagined community in southern Katanga in a way that appears not to have been similarly possible among the Katanga Luba.

Uneven Economic and Political Development in Katanga

As suggested above, the construction of social and economic relations in Katanga/Congo was shaped both by the mining industry and the infrastructure built to support it and by African reactions to the possibilities this created. Instructive in this respect is the BCK's extension of the northern railway to the territory populated by the Kasai Baluba, which reached what later became Port Francqui in 1928. Kasai thereafter supplied food to Katanga's mines, but this rail route also brought increasing numbers of Kasaian migrant workers to Katanga, and with them profound political consequences for the later period. Although the Baluba Shankaadi in Katanga and the Baluba Lubilanji in Kasai had distant common origins, centuries of living in different environments had by the early twentieth century created two distinct societies. Their respective languages (Tshiluba in Kasai, Kiluba in Katanga) evolved differently. Sociologically, two main divergences are salient: (1) the relative centralization of political authority among the Balubakat vested in the Chief Kasongo Nyembo, considered by some to be the Luba paramount chief, in contrast to the lack of such authority among the Kasai;[40] and (2) the far bigger role played by the mining economy in Katanga—even in relatively remote Lubakat areas—against the central role of agriculture in poorer Kasai Baluba areas. Because of the conflicts between the two groups since independence, many Katangese politicians and academics claim the total cultural and even linguistic independence of the two Luba areas: such claims made regarding Luba history are, as so often, the subject of contemporary political contestation.

Continual problems with labor supply to the mines, and the rising costs associated with it, led UMHK in the late 1920s to break from the short-term migrant labor model pioneered in South Africa. Although religious and humanitarian organizations, as elsewhere in Africa, expressed concern regarding the negative demographic impact of growing labor demands, such concerns were overridden by economic imperatives.[41] In 1927 UMHK extended its twelve-month contract to a three-year scheme, and the following year adopted a wage structure tied to skill levels and length of service, creating powerful incentives for long-term employment. A series of state labor commissions, slavishly supportive of UMHK objectives and comparatively insulated from settler politics of the sort that opposed labor stabilization in southern Africa, endorsed the creation of what amounted to a new multiethnic African working class in the southern mining towns. Workers were encouraged to bring their wives and immediate families to reside with them; primary schooling and basic medical services were provided free of charge. The policy's success was demonstrated by improved productivity; stabilization enabled and stimulated investment in training, specialization, and mechanization.[42] Whereas in the 1920s, UMHK had to recruit 10,000 new men per annum, this had fallen to an average of 1,800 by the 1935–1942 period, by which time 77 percent of workers reengaged.[43] These changes also aided soaring levels of copper production, from 56,221 metric tons in 1923 to 138,949 metric tons in 1930.[44]

The worldwide depression of the early 1930s raised Belgian concerns regarding dependence on unpredictable global markets and led to an emphasis on economic diversification via peasant agricultural production. However, in the absence of significant investment, this policy generally took a repressive and ultimately unproductive form. Labor migration, not just in Katanga but in Congo more generally, was stimulated by imposed cultivation in rural areas, following the compulsory labor decree of 1933 that obliged male Africans in "customary" society to spend sixty days a year on "community" work.[45]

Thus, the identities of each African society in Katanga and its surrounding areas were reshaped partly by their relationships with the mining economy and partly by the demands of colonial rule. Lunda generally remained in rural areas, selling agricultural produce and other goods to mining centers while avoiding what they regarded as dangerous and low-paid employment. In contrast, Luba Kasai were increasingly perceived (in Belgian ethnic stereotyping) as positively attuned to individual advancement via education and employment, and were accordingly recruited and subsequently promoted to increasingly senior positions in the mines and other workplaces. The modern identity of Luba Kasai was, as Jewsiewicki explains, constructed in relation to these urban spaces and opportunities.[46] Catholic missions played an important role in the stabilization of a skilled work force in the UMHK's authoritarian "model camps."[47]

The long-term success of labor stabilization was not, however, matched by official consideration of the social and political consequences. In 1931 a new, specifically urban institution, the centre extra-coutumier (CEC), was established to manage colonial relations with the new urban African population: despite its supposedly "noncustomary" form, the CEC was headed by a "chief," supported by an advisory council, and closely supervised by Belgian administrators with a veto over its decisions. Although CECs were primarily oriented around law and order, they did provide some welfare services, and by the end of the 1930s Belgian policy was comparatively advanced in supporting the development (rather than repressing the existence) of urban African society. This was, however, coupled with an absence of political reform: across the border in Northern Rhodesia, labor stabilization in the late 1940s associated African urbanization with the advancement of "modern" political rights.[48] The failure of Belgian colonialism to seriously envisage similar advances meant that there was initially little correlation between new forms of economic association and new political ones.

This does not mean, however, that there was no "political" resistance to colonial exploitation. The Kitawala messianic religious movement provided radical spiritual explanations for European domination and the devastating effects of the 1930s depression. Separately, the December 1941 mine workers' strike in Katanga followed work stoppages by white mine workers and expressed discontent with the attrition of real wages by wartime inflation; its brutal suppression by armed forces led to about a hundred deaths.[49] Although episodic labor unrest continued to 1943, the militancy of urban workers was not addressed by the formalization of labor representation, in contrast to British and French colonies, which experienced similar labor unrest during this period.[50] Until 1954 workers had to work in the same industry for three years to qualify for union membership; unions were supervised by European advisers, and no national union federations were permitted.[51] There is little evidence to support Nzongola-Ntajala's assertion that these strikes reflected Congolese nationalist awakening.[52] The 1944 soldiers' insurrection in Kasai and Katanga advanced demands that more closely resembled anticolonial manifestos elsewhere in Africa, including the abolition of forced cultivation by peasants; the reduction of the head tax; better treatment of troops by officers; the abolition of corporal punishment in prisons; and the abolition of racial economic privilege.[53] In Luluabourg in 1944, *évolués* (members of the African middle-class recognized by the colonial state) petitioned the governor-general to consider their interests as a "kind of native bourgeoisie . . . [deserving] . . . a particular protection from the government, sheltering them from certain masses or treatment which may apply to an ignorant or backward mass."[54] Each of these expressions of anticolonial discontent, articulating the concerns and aspirations of a particular section of an economically and culturally diverse population, had the potential (as elsewhere in Africa) to coalesce into a more or less representative nationalist movement. Their general failure to do so (compared to most other African colonies) certainly reflected the structural difficulties of establishing a coherent Congolese national identity across the vast spaces and uneven socioeconomic conditions and between the diverse communities of the Belgian Congo, but above all Belgium's unwillingness to seriously contemplate meaningful political change. Most importantly, the ban on all political parties that remained in place until 1957 prevented the organized expression of protonationalist political discontent, which instead found expression primarily through ethnically based "cultural" associations.

Belgian Rule in Congo and Katanga

The ubiquity of force as the basis for colonial rule in Congo did not immediately come to an end with state takeover in 1908: indeed, a decade later, many officials at the *agent territorial* level (often from a military background) were still happier using force than instituting administrative reform. Taxation was forced rather than collected by local African chiefs, who were granted few powers.[55] Significant administrative reform was, however, introduced in the 1920s by Minister for the Colonies M. Louis Franck, who tended toward a Lugardian conservation of native authority.[56] Franck radically reduced the hitherto vast number of recognized local *chefferies* (chiefdoms), which fell from 6,095 in 1917 to 1,212 in 1938.[57] This involved greater recognition of the large-scale chieftaincies that had existed before the advent of colonial rule, effectively reestablishing major powers such as the Luba and the Lunda as the local administrators of public order, tax collection, labor conscription, and the provision of census data. Franck also supported the protection of "national" identities, including the peoples over which the Lunda still claimed sovereignty.[58] An ongoing debate pitted colonial officials who were impressed by Lunda tradition and recognized its potential for effective administration over a wide area against reformers in the influential Commission for the Protection of Natives, notably the Katanga-based Monsignor Jean Félix de Hemptinne, who regarded unchecked chiefly authority as a deterrent to the spread of Christianity.

In the case of the Lunda, not only political power but also the territory of the Mwaant Yav was heavily circumscribed by colonial rule; the tributary payments that had once underwritten the Lunda kingdom were now extracted by Belgian colonial authorities. Indirect colonial rule had simultaneously strengthened what had been the declining authority of both Lunda and Yeke chieftaincies while denying those authorities access to the economic resources that had underwritten their precolonial authority. Among the Lunda, Mwaant Yav Kaumb (1920–1951) was the primary figure in approving or rejecting the appointment of subordinate chiefs and lower-level officials.[59] It is important, however, to recognize that the role and identity of chiefs were substantially reconstituted so that they operated as indigenous civil servants and not in any meaningful sense as the leaders of their people.

This dependency certainly contributed to a general loyalty of chiefly elites to the Belgian authorities, although this was not incompatible with criticism of specific colonial policies. In the medium term, the survival and reconstitution of these societies would later enable their leaders to claim a legitimacy rooted in historical continuity in the run-up to independence (see below). This brief period of colonial loyalty did not prevent recollection and celebration of resistance during earlier periods of colonial rule, for example by the BaYeke Mwami, Munongo Mutampuka, or the Lunda Mwaant Yav Kaumb. During this period, a minority of Lunda had little choice but to engage in migrant labor in construction and mining. The marginalization of this region was reinforced by the relative lack of activity among Catholic missions; in their absence, American members of the Methodist Episcopal Church, founders of the first Christian church in the Lunda heartland in 1913, became highly influential in the future development of Lunda political identity.[60]

Late Colonial Katanga

During World War II, Congo's material and human resources were mobilized by the Belgian government-in-exile in the Allied cause. Congolese rubber and tin production was vital to the war effort following the fall of Malaya, and copper production rose by a third.[61] By 1944 obligatory labor demands had been doubled to 120 days per year. Colonial administrators, their effectiveness measured by their ability to meet production targets, pressured chiefs to extract increased produce and labor from their subjects. This placed the fragile reconstruction of chiefly authority under great pressure and led, among other things, to increased urban migration: the African population living under "customary" authority fell 4.5 percent between 1939 and 1944.[62] Although the postwar Belgian government implemented welfare and development reforms that ostensibly resembled those envisaged in French and British Africa, it clung to the principle that the spending proposed in its Ten-Year Plan for the Economic and Social Development of the Belgian Congo would be funded from Congo's own resources.[63] Urban food price controls disadvantaged rural producers, creating further incentives to migrate.

The global postwar boom had a profound effect on the Katangese mining economy. By 1959, 36 percent of Katanga's population were earning their living as waged employees. The region accounted for 75 percent of Congolese mineral production and earned 50 percent of Congo's income.[64] Even more than in Congo as a whole, where the urban population doubled between 1940 and 1950, the African population of Elisabethville nearly quadrupled during the same period, from 27,000 to 99,000.[65] In these rapidly growing urban societies, social and political aspirations found their most concrete expression in the form of voluntary self-help associations, formed (as in many African towns elsewhere) on ethnic lines. These were not inherently antagonistic to more overtly nationalist tendencies, but the ban on political parties meant that they provided the sole legal basis for the assertion of cultural and political identity. There was, then, little basis for the development of a coherent "Congolese" consciousness: the process of democratically selecting "modern" African political representatives in fact served to heighten ethnic self-awareness.[66]

In Lunda areas, some prosperity was generated by the promotion of commercial cotton production. With the new economic possibilities generated by the boom of the late 1940s and early 1950s, an emergent economic elite of Lunda society, partly aristocratic in origin but often seeking to escape from the confines of tribal authority, began to assert itself. Foremost among this group was Joseph Kapenda Tshombe, the wealthiest and most prominent Lunda businessman, who, however, was not himself part of the Lunda aristocracy.[67] At the same time, Mwaant Yav Kaumb resisted the more proactive Belgian developmental approach of this period; in response, Belgian officials instead engaged with lower level *évolués*, men of aristocratic origin but with a level of mission education and modernist outlook. Kaumb's successor, supported by the Belgian authorities in a succession dispute, was precisely such a modernizing figure: Mbako Ditend, Mwaant Yav from 1951 to 1963, had been, like Joseph Tshombe, one of the first pupils of the American Methodist mission, which provided an important training ground in the ideology of individual advancement and modernization. As such, he was considered a valuable interlocutor by the colonial authorities. As a symbol of his perceived modernist perspective and integration into the material economy of Katanga, Ditend was given a Ford car by the UMHK, the BCK railway, and the CSK.[68] Ditend was regarded as a model chief, presiding over a period of strong cooperation with the colonial authorities. In so doing, he was able to strengthen his authority over subordinate Lunda chiefs and even to appoint some of his sons to these chieftaincies, against the wishes of the Tshombe family, whose favored candidate for the Mwaant Yav title was Moïse Tshombe's maternal uncle, Gaston Mushid.[69]

The subsequent cooperation between Tshombe and Mwaant Yav Ditend during the secession did not overcome the considerable rivalries within the Lunda polity between those whose strong claim to aristocratic authority enabled them to access the benefits of modernization and those who sought to advance in the modern economy and thereby gain a higher position in Lunda society. Indeed, the social dislocation of the late colonial period prompted a growing interest in the history of ethnic identities, not only among the chiefly authorities but also among the younger generation of Western-educated men. Modernizing Lunda elites, those who would go on to support Conakat, had little interest in a simple revival of chiefly authority and recognized that western Katanga was an ethnically heterogeneous area in which Tshokwe and Lunda lived alongside each other. The Mwaant Yav, they imagined, could provide a unifying figure for both populations, but this also opened the door to consciousness of their historical relations rather than a simple notion of ethnic belonging.[70] The Mwaant Yav Ditend, himself partly of Tshokwe ancestry, was likewise wary of narrow ethnic self-assertion. For their part, the Tshokwe had the opportunity to assert their own distinct identity and, in doing so, throw off their historical domination by the Lunda.[71]

Nationalism and Its Discontents

The Belgian authorities, which had previously sought to curtail the Lunda king's authority, were by the early 1950s recognizing the valuable role that could be played by African chiefs as a counterweight to the increasing self-assertion of the Westernized *évolués*.[72] This ran against the tendency in British colonies, where the late-colonial period saw a shift from the defense of chiefly authority to its abandonment in favor of new alliances with ostensibly transethnic nationalist politicians. In Belgian Congo, something of a reverse took place; whereas many urban-based officials had previously treated chiefs with a contempt bordering on overt racism, in the context of rising urban discontent they belatedly discovered the extent to which the chiefs provided a useful conservative bulwark against radical nationalism. The growth of Katanga's mining towns and the urban politics that came with them were regarded cautiously by the Mwaant Yav and his closest advisers. The arrival of large numbers of Kasai Baluba migrants to work in the mines threatened the authority of indigenous chiefs, especially if the former were able to turn their numbers into political power via the ballot box. Lunda self-assertion in the late 1950s is best understood as an expression of anxiety at the rising articulation of political expression among incoming ethnic groups. The Lunda, despite being one of the largest ethnic groups in Katanga, made up only 6.3 percent of the population of Elisabethville in 1957, compared to 22 percent Kasai Baluba.[73] By 1956, 53 percent of the work force of UMHK's Lubumbashi mine in the city was of Kasaian origin.[74] This composition suddenly became of urgent concern in December 1957 with the election of non-Lunda *bourgmestres* (mayors) in Katanga's four urban centers—three of them from Kasai—in the first such election of its kind.[75] This event revealed with shocking clarity the potential marginalization of Lunda authority in a new political environment dominated by modern political practices, including electoral democracy and Western-style self-government. As a result, southern Katanga's chiefs adopted a skeptical, even hostile, approach to the sudden prospect of independence.

Their defense of chiefly autonomy partly resembled that which took place in peripheral kingdoms in many parts of late-colonial Africa at the moment of independence. It had this in common with, for example, Barotseland in neighboring Northern Rhodesia, where the defense of an existing autonomy, here written into legally questionable treaties signed by white and chiefly authorities at the advent of colonialism, provided the basis for claims for continued autonomy or even independent statehood at the moment of decolonization.[76] Similar tensions existed elsewhere, between increasingly dominant African nationalist movements with a vision of a centralized developmental state and previously autonomous chiefly authority or societies that feared a potentially interventionist state authority controlled by African nationalists.[77]

What distinguished Katanga from Barotseland and most other such instances was of course its extraordinary mineral wealth. In the post–World War II period in particular, the long global boom led to a vast increase in the province's mineral output and value, which rose by 80 percent between 1950 and 1957 and amounted to 80 percent of the value of all Congo's minerals in 1957.[78] The exploitation of mineral wealth by colonially linked mining companies such as UMHK was understably viewed by many observers simply as a form of exploitative extraction; many anticolonial activists saw the route to greater "local" control of such wealth via independent nation-statehood. However, with the benefit of hindsight, Katanga's dependency on the technical and economic support supplied by foreign mining companies was, as elsewhere in Africa, more of a structural problem than—as it seemed to contemporary critics of Conakat's close relationship with UMHK—one of political will: political independence and later mine nationalization did not of themselves significantly alleviate the dependent relationship of mineral-exporting countries on international markets over which they exercised no control.[79]

It was certainly the international value of Katanga's minerals that would underwrite the secession. Yet this wealth should not be understood simply as an external factor. Viewed from a local perspective, Katanga's extraordinary mineral wealth was in danger of being exploited by another group of outsiders, namely, the poorer peoples and provinces of Congo.[80] This was compounded by the minerals boom, the visible expression of which was Kasaian migration to urban Katanga and the growing political mobilization of this "foreign" population.[81] The perceived danger of Kasaian domination of "indigenous" southern Katangese ethnic groups, coupled with the likelihood that their political representatives would tie Katanga into a centralized Congolese state, led in 1958 to the formation of the Groupement des Associations Mutuelles de l'Empire Lunda (Gassomel), an explicitly autochthon cultural association which, as its name suggests, looked back nostalgically to what was now proclaimed to have been the "Lunda Empire."[82] Gassomel's most prominent leader, Moïse Tshombe, a Lunda aristocrat and the mission-educated son of Kapend Tshombe, embodied the tacit (but also conflictual) alliance between educated elites and chiefly authorities, symbolized by his marriage to the daughter of Mwaant Yav Ditend.

But Gassomel's Lunda ethnic base was insufficient for an effective political vehicle—alliances were formed with similar elites in other "indigenous" ethnic groups, including some Katangese Baluba, to form Conakat in October 1958. Godefroid Munongo, a pensions clerk, Conakat leader, and brother of the BaYeke chief the Mwami, wrote to Governor André Schöller in February 1959 to express the party's concerns: "The native Katangans have good reason to wonder if the authorities did not accord permanent residence permits to the people from Kasai in our towns so that the natives [of Kasai] can, because of their ever-increasing numbers, crush those from Katanga."[83] Conakat's distrust had some strong foundations: notoriously, Congo's Governor Jean Paelinck had during his investiture spoken in Tshiluba of "you Kasaians, who live in the Katanga . . . I, for my part, will not forsake you. . . . Ask me for what you need and you will get it."[84] Given Conakat's supposed pro-European stance during the secession, it is important to recall its bitter criticism of the perceived bias of colonial officials for the supposedly enterprising and hard-working Baluba Kasai, who were in turn viewed as being in some respects un-African and "close to the whites."[85] Former provincial secretary Henry Rosy later recalled that the 1957 elections were considered "an affair of the white people," and European support was probably a vital element in the election of Kasaians.[86] Alexis Kishiba expressed the danger of an imminent transfer of power from the Belgian colonizer directly to Katangese of Kasaian origin in his seminal article "Katangais, ou es tu?": "Katangan, you are certainly aware of the fact that the issue of use of languages in the Congo will come to the fore in the immediate future. If you don't say anything, a language will be imposed on you and it will not necessarily be a language from the Katanga Province."[87] As Gérard-Libois rightly argued, Conakat was not driven by a simple tribalist reflex but by social competition arising in significant part from the differential effects of colonialism on the respective societies of Congo.[88] The position of Belgian officialdom changed, however, in September 1958 when the pro-Kasai Governor Paelinck was replaced by Governor Schöller, who would go on to support Conakat.

In May 1959, Conakat declared itself in favor of a federal system "in which the reins of command will have to be in the hands of authentic Katangese."[89] It was transformed into a political party two months later, at which point Tshombe took over as its leader.[90] At first, Conakat asserted its authority to represent all Katangese peoples; Balubakat, founded by Jason Sendwe in 1957 to represent the Katangese Luba, initially affiliated with it.[91]

Meanwhile, the Lunda chief reasserted his authority, articulating his own interpretation of history to do so. In January 1959, the Mwaant Yav wrote to the Belgian authorities criticizing the marginalization of chiefs in the emergent political dispensation, attacking the "unforgivable aberration" of "considering the opinions which emanate from the urban centers as representing the general feeling of this province" in the name of the "Lunda Empire, one of the most important demographic groups in Katanga whose sphere of customary authority extends beyond the boundaries of Congo [into] Angola and [Northern] Rhodesia."[92] Anthropological studies were cited to assert the historical continuity of Lunda authority. In particular, the activity of the anthropologist Bruno Crine-Mavar supplied, in Bustin's words, "the Mwaant Yaav and his entourage with a good deal of the theoretical and scientific ammunition they needed to enhance the credibility of the imperial concept."[93] Belgian officials were certainly surprised to discover the scale of the Mwaant Yav's claimed authority and his recent visits to both Angola and Northern Rhodesia to play his traditional role in Lunda ceremonies.[94] Although Lunda political leaders did not overtly seek to redraw colonial boundaries, Conakat's activity certainly encouraged the Mwaant Yav to more strongly articulate his authority and to challenge the potential threat to this from a centralizing Congolese nation-state headquartered in a distant capital that threatened to more permanently separate him from his Angolan and North Rhodesian subjects in a way that the Belgian colonial state had not. Such imaginings were not restricted to the Lunda. It may be instructively noted that the Tshokwe cultural association adopted the name Association des Tshokwe du Congo de l'Angola et de la Rhodésie du Nord (ATCAR), indicating that it, like Gassomel, aspired to represent all Tshokwe across colonial borders.

These chiefly assertions were partly supported by men who in other colonies might have been expected to oppose chiefly authority in favor of antitribal nationalism: mission-trained sons of the elite, now themselves employed in mission schools, hospitals, and offices or enriching themselves via trading opportunities, were among the strongest advocates of a reasserted Lunda imperial identity and were frustrated that the Mwaant Yav did not assert such an identity more strongly.[95] Among such men, "Lunda Empire" had become a ubiquitous term by 1959. While the Mwaant Yav used this notion to revitalize his own authority, Tshombe's instrumental utilization of the same concept to advance his political position was not easily endorsed by the Lunda king, who understood the hazards of ceding to Tshombe the right to speak for the Lunda people.[96]

These growing tensions were further heightened by the economic stagnation that took place during the recession of 1957–1958. Bustin reports that some unemployed urban migrants returned to rural areas such as Sandoa and Dilolo, bringing nationalist political ideas into Lunda areas and challenging the Mwaant Yav's declared opposition to the extension of universal suffrage proposed by Belgium in January 1959. Nationalist ideas were more influential among the Tshokwe: ATCAR affiliated to the pro-unity Balubakat-led Cartel, reflecting the historical and continued distrust between the Lunda and the Tshokwe, tensions that would influence the subsequent history of the Katangese gendarmes in exile.[97] Following its foundation in 1958, Lumumba's Mouvement National Congolais (MNC-L) sought to establish itself across the whole of the Congo; in Katanga it allied with the more radical wing of Balubakat, giving Lumumba's party a distinctly ethnic partiality in the conflict between autochthons and incomers in Katanga's towns. The dominant presence of the MNC-L, itself led primarily by Baluba figures, at the congress of Congolese political parties held in April 1959 at Luluabourg, confirmed for Conakat the danger of Katanga's subordination by an MNC-led, Baluba-dominated Leopoldville government. This contributed, Lemarchand suggests, to the alliance with the settler organization Union Katangaise into which Conakat entered the following month.[98] This temporarily placed Conakat on the same side as some white supremacists, poisoning the party's relations with nationalist parties throughout Congo.

Notwithstanding this alliance, the educated elite that led Conakat did not passively accept the ideas of white settler organizations. Instead, they asserted a vision of the Katangese past that both defended the principle of an autonomous Katangese political unit rooted in indigeneity and rejected settler claims to dominate the same space. The Conakat leader Evariste Kimba sought "to demonstrate to the settlers that Katanga was not a desert before the arrival of the Europeans and that this province could not be made to serve . . . as a region for massive European settlement."[99] Godefroid Munongo offered a similar critique: "To serve certain political designs, people have pretended that Katanga did not exist, that it was a construction of the colonizers. This is to deny that when the first white explorers discovered the part of Africa called Katanga they found three monarchies which were not only bound by family, economic and social links but—and this is by far the most important—their historic destiny had been linked for centuries."[100] These monarchies, with their history as powerful trading and raiding states, provided the necessary mythico-historical basis for a Katangese nation-state that could establish postcolonial trading relationships with corporations such as UMHK without undermining sovereignty—that would indeed ensure that the benefits of such relationships flowed not to foreigners of whatever origin but rather to Katanga's indigenous communities. This, it should be stressed, necessitated a very partial reading of Katanga's past, but not one that was qualitatively different from those articulated by nationalist parties elsewhere in Africa, seeking to present regionally based political projects, often rooted in ambiguous readings of African history, as unproblematic representations of coherent national identities.

As a Luba, Kimba imagined a "Katanga" that stretched out to encompass the former Luba kingdom. Such constructions proved, despite the support of the Luba chief Kasongo Nyembo, to be politically incompatible with the views of Sendwe and his political vehicle, Balubakat. Antagonism between Sendwe and Conakat leaders, and the latter's alliance with Union Katangaise, led Balubakat, representing the Katanga Baluba, to disaffiliate from Conakat and to form a so-called Cartel with the Fedération Kasaienne (FEDEKA), established to represent Kasaian interests within Katanga and the Tshokwe organization ATCAR in November 1959.[101] As independence approached, political competition spilled out into ethnic clashes between autochthonous groups and Kasai Baluba in Katanga's towns. Conakat, like nationalist parties elsewhere in Africa, asserted control over public space by insisting on the carrying of its membership card by Africans engaged in economic activity, but in Katanga such demands took on an unmistakably ethnic autochthon-outsider form. Rioting occurred in January and March 1960 as each party prepared for the May 1960 elections that paved the way for independence.

In those elections, which Young characterizes as amounting to an ethnic census, Conakat won eight of the sixteen national assembly seats in Katanga and twenty-five of sixty provincial seats, securing 32 percent of the vote, a lower percentage than the Balubakat Cartel.[102] Conakat, however, skillfully constructed a broader coalition of support, establishing a bloc of thirty-eight of the sixty provincial seats.[103] Although efforts were made to establish a broader-based government, at independence the provincial government was composed with no Cartel members; Balubakat protested at electoral fraud and refused to take its seats, leaving its northern Katangese supporters unrepresented. The ethnic and economic divide between southern and northern Katanga had now taken on political form and would soon become the basis of a military conflict.

A Contested Independence, 1959–1960

Although Congolese *évolués* and other sections of society had of course long considered political and particularly social solutions and actions to address their grievances and aspirations, these only belatedly took the form of overt nationalism. Young points to the travel restrictions preventing most Congolese from direct experience of Belgian or African political life outside the Congo: passports were prohibitively expensive to obtain and, in contrast to the long-established British or French African students' movements, only fifteen Congolese students were studying in Belgium in 1959.[104] The primary stimulus to Congolese nationalism was the 1955 Van Bilsen Plan, a modest proposal for decolonization over a thirty-year period.[105] The plan prompted the seminal publication of the manifesto of Conscience Africaine, in which Congolese political intellectuals demanded "total political emancipation" for the first time, while not directly challenging Van Bilsen's overall time frame.[106] The following year, ABAKO's manifesto demanded full political rights and that "emancipation should be granted us this very day."[107] The conversion of some ethnocultural associations into overt political organizations was sparked by the visit of the Belgian Group de Travail in 1958, designed to formulate plans for decolonization of the Congo. Belgium's initial proposal for a four-year transitional process was rejected by ABAKO and the MNC-L, which insisted on the immediate transfer of power. A central issue in this process was the distribution of power between the capital and the regions.[108]

With the sudden approach of a largely unplanned independence, Conakat found itself out of kilter with nationalist thinking in Leopoldville, which was increasingly in favor of noncooperation with Belgian reforms and immediate self-determination. Elections for communal and territorial councils, boycotted by parties based in Leopoldville, saw an 81 percent turnout in Katanga.[109] Of the eight Katangese delegates to the watershed Round Table conference held in Brussels in January 1960 to decide Congo's future, two were from Conakat (advised by Europeans) and two others were chiefs sympathetic to the party. Despite the fact that many other organizations present in Brussels ostensibly shared its federalist stance, Conakat, having initially been part of the federalist Front Commun, failed to establish effective alliances with other federalist parties such as ABAKO. Demonstrating the influence of European advisers linked to UMHK (see below), Tshombe asserted that "the resources of each province be properly its own," demanding that control over mining activities and revenue should be at a provincial level.[110] Authority over mineral resources was instead vested in the central government, which was charged with ensuring that each province received a fair share of mining revenue. Conakat's unmistakably conservative position on other issues—limiting universal suffrage; a prominent role for chiefs in the Senate; giving the vote to Belgian residents; and retaining an oversight role for the Belgian king until a full national constitution had been put in place—was comprehensively rejected by parties wishing to achieve full and immediate independence.[111] Conakat's evident inability to establish an influential position, in the context of the rapidly approaching decolonization of Congo, led it to strengthen its already close ties with Europeans.

Conakat's European Relationships

At independence, there were 32,000 Europeans in Katanga, 2 percent of the total provincial population of 1,654,000. Only about 3,000 of these were, however, "settlers," making the European population very different from that of settler-dominated states such as (Southern) Rhodesia and Algeria.[112] Most Europeans were salaried employees, relatively recent arrivals, and had no long-term commitment to a settler-based political project. In 1958 the settler body Ucol had established the Union Katangaise to provide political representation. Conakat's relations with Union Katangaise grew closer in the rapid run-up to independence, but this was never an easy relationship given the racialized views of most settlers.

By 1960 close relations had developed between Conakat and leaders of the Central African Federation (CAF), bordering Katanga to the south. Roy Welensky, CAF prime minister, proposed the incorporation of Katanga into the federation on the basis of the mineral wealth it shared with the Northern Rhodesian Copperbelt. Conakat also, however, met the leaders of Northern Rhodesia's nationalist organization, the United National Independence Party (UNIP), indicating a wish to keep its options open and an unwillingness to be viewed simply as a representative of settler interests.[113] A distinction should also be drawn between the urbane and wealthy Tshombe, at ease in European company and open to its influence on him, and men such as Jean-Baptiste Kibwe and Munongo, ideologically committed to the Katangese project and suspicious both of settlers and of the mining interests that had brought tens of thousands of outsiders into Katanga over previous decades. These tensions, reflecting ideological, personal, and ethnic divisions within Conakat's leadership, would persist throughout the secession.

It is nevertheless true that in the months before Congolese independence, Conakat was probably more than ever under the influence of European advisers from the now disbanded Ucol; its leaders, such as George Thyssens, continued to advise Conakat. Conakat also received funding directly from UMHK, the owners of which had for a number of years been considering how to secure their interests and continued profits in a very different political environment.[114] Lemarchand, however, points out that the executives of SGB, themselves divided over their preferred political relationship between Katanga and Congo, provided financial aid to both Conakat and (albeit to a lesser extent) Balubakat in 1960.[115]

Conclusion

The Congo, first as royal possession and then as colonial state, was, like most African colonies, an artificial territory that brought together a disparate group of kingdoms and polities with only limited prior relations. This disparity was reinforced by the weakness and incoherence of colonial policy and the sheer scale of the land that Belgians had conquered but did not fully control. The lack of territory-wide infrastructure, the abject neglect of economic and social development before World War II, and the failure to associate development with self-government after it, as well as the selective reinforcement of tribal identity and the lack of meaningful political reform of the sort carried out elsewhere in colonial Africa, all militated against the development of a proto-national identity among many of its peoples, even in the run-up to independence. The fact that most political parties established in the brief run-up to independence sought support from an ethnically identifiable electorate was a sign of this.

The minerals boom of the postwar period had drawn large numbers of Kasai migrant workers to live and work in the mining area, and the political expression of Kasaian migrant identity in the 1957 elections prompted the foundation of new ethnically based cultural and political organizations, among both incomers (for example, Kasai Baluba) and autochthons (for example, Gassomel and ATCAR). The external value of Katanga's mineral resources, which underwrote the secession, was well understood by local African elites, who had historically controlled this trade; it had the potential to enrich Katangese Africans but was in danger of being exploited by another group of outsiders, namely, the poorer provinces of newly independent Congo, particularly under a more centralized and interventionist government in Leopoldville and, of the greatest importance, by the Kasai immigrant community and its political leadership.[116]

In seeking to turn their imagined community into a real nation-state, following the contours of political authority molded by colonialism, Katangese political leaders constructed a usable version of the past, emphasizing certain aspects of the territory's history and silencing others, a process central to nation-state building across the continent.[117] Notwithstanding its lack of recognition by the international community, the Katangese political project closely resembled the assertion of national independence in the rest of Africa at this time. There were evidently major contradictions inherent in the Katangese state-building project, but these were not qualitatively different from similar contradictions and tensions inherent in many nationalist projects in Africa, most obviously that of the Congo itself, that sought to carve nation-states out of ambiguous historical claims and territories of highly uneven socioeconomic development and "differential modernisation."[118]

2 The Katangese Secession, 1960–1963

CONGO DECLARED INDEPENDENCE from Belgium on June 30, 1960. On July 11, the southern province of Katanga declared itself independent from Congo.[1] The Katangese secession is normally understood, primarily or exclusively, as the result of external machinations by forces hostile to the independence of the Congolese nation-state. Belgian colonial and military officials, as well as multinational mining capital, are portrayed as the main protagonists, seeking to maintain their economic and political interests against the potentially radical nationalism of the Congolese central government led by Prime Minister Patrice Lumumba. The indigenous leaders of the Katangese state, to the extent they are analyzed at all, are commonly viewed as the puppets of these forces, denied political agency or legitimacy. The apparent role of the Katangese political leadership in the murder of Lumumba certainly reinforced the illegitimacy of their state among contemporary observers and the leaders of newly independent African states. Patrice Lumumba himself, meeting US secretary of state Christian Herter weeks after the declaration of the secession, exemplified this position in claiming: "There is no problem in Katanga. There could be a referendum, and you would see that the people did not want secession. Tshombe is simply an instrument of the Belgians."[2]

This stance has been maintained in most subsequent analyses of the Congo crisis of the early 1960s, the UN intervention, and the coming to power of Mobutu Sese Seko as Congolese leader. For example, in Ludo De Witte's generally exemplary analysis of the assassination of Lumumba, the idea that there could be any indigenous basis for the secession is constantly, if indirectly, dismissed: "Officially, power was held by Africans in secessionist Katanga. In fact, Belgians were pulling all the strings."[3] While the secession was undeniably shaped by the interests and actions of colonial settlers, mining capital, and sections of the Belgian political and military authorities, this unwillingness to recognize an alternative indigenous basis of political authority to that of the Congolese central state means that no attempt has been made to explore the motivations of the southern Katangese political elites, who initiated the secession in a context in which the restricted space available for political practice under colonialism enabled these nonstate and reconstructed ethnic leaders to politically express their hostility to that state and the Kasaian peoples they viewed as dominant within it.[4] This was certainly enabled by the emphasis on federal authority in the 1960 "Loi Fondamental" that provided the basis for the transfer of power. While their alliance with Belgian advisers and capital had the effect of preserving Katanga's considerable (in comparison to other regions) infrastructural development—and, ironically, making possible later Zairianization measures—the colonial inspiration for Katanga made it impossible to effectively integrate the territory's diverse population into a cohesive national project.

There is no intention herein to romanticize the Katangese project or to revive older conservative portrayals of Lumumba, who was clearly an articulate spokesperson for a meaningful African independence in which the resources of the continent would be utilized for the benefit of its people.[5] However, the tendency of his retrospective supporters to assume the existence of popular support for the new central state and its government in all parts of the country, with no recognition of the evidently uneven and contradictory nature of the Congolese territory and the variable extent to which the people of Congo related to it, is ultimately ahistorical, denying agency to those Africans who adopted a sincerely held opposition to the central state. This chapter does not seek to justify or to offer retrospective legitimacy to the Katangese secession but merely to suggest that it rested in significant part on local factors, one of which was the distinct identity of peoples who saw themselves as indigenous and who were hostile to linked processes of demographic, economic, and political change that, they believed, threatened their position of relative dominance in Katanga.

A full understanding of the secession requires a thorough investigation of its local indigenous leaders and advocates and the political dynamics within which they operated. Their alternative conceptualization of the boundaries of the region's postcolonial states was, at the time of the secession, only one of a large number of such reconstructive projects—notwithstanding the 1963 decision by the Organization of African Unity to recognize colonial borders as the basis of independent state borders, there was no historical inevitability that the existing borders of the colonial state would be replicated in the postcolonial period.[6] The fact that the Katangese national project was primarily imagined and pursued by only part of the province's political leadership, representing only one element of its diverse population's social and cultural outloook, arguably makes it more, not less, similar to nation-building projects elsewhere in Africa during this period.

Despite its lack of international recognition, the Katangese political project closely resembled the assertion of national independence in the rest of Africa, including Congo itself. This chapter explores the ways in which Katangese leaders and officials (along with their foreign sympathizers) sought to project and perform an authentic nation-state, rooted (like its Western models) in a mythico-historical sense of ancient belonging, and the use made by Katangese leaders of both public and media space to perform and assert the nation-state in which they sincerely believed. This is not, however, to assert that autochthonist claims made by some nationalist politicians were a more "authentic" reflection of indigenous culture than their more cosmopolitan counterparts: while Katangese politicians sought, as will be shown, to associate themselves with the authority of indigenous chiefs, they were no more willing than their political opponents to concede meaningful power to them.[7]

During the secession, an image of Katanga was constructed that united the province's southern ethnicities (Lunda, Bayeke, Tshokwe, Batabwa, and so on) behind a political project designed to maintain and advance its relative prosperity in alliance with settler interests and mining capital, while simultaneously resisting and reducing the influence of "outsider" migrant labor the mining industry had hitherto encouraged. Conakat sought to assert a Katanga-wide indigenous inclusivity, initially based on an alliance with Jason Sendwe's Balubakat, and then (when this was rejected) on the support of the Luba paramount chief Kasongo Nyembo, whose relative, Evariste Kimba, was a prominent Conakat leader. The subsequent "sub-secession" of northern Katanga and the formation of the northern Lualaba Province in October 1960 demonstrated the failure to integrate this area as a whole into the secessionist state.

Conakat is nevertheless best understood as an essentially "nationalist" movement: like some other nationalist movements seeking power in Africa at this time, it sought to ensure that a greater proportion of the revenues resulting from local mineral wealth stayed within the territory producing them, and it tried to ensure that more of the jobs created within that industry went to local people. René Lemarchand rightly concluded that one of the three important factors explaining the claim to self-determination, alongside settler and Belgian metropolitan interests, was

> the sense of economic grievance which permeates the attitude of the so-called "genuine" Katangese towards the inhabitants of the other provinces. As already noted, regional differences in the distribution of economic resources operated to aggravate latent tensions among ethnic groups, so that economic stratification tended to coincide with tribal divisions. In a sense, therefore, tribal antagonisms must be viewed as symptoms of economic grievances. The fact that the Conakat succeeded in rallying the support of otherwise unrelated tribal entities (Bayeke, Lunda, Batabwa, etc.) suggests indeed that these grievances were an important source of solidarity among its members.[8]

The gendarmerie was vital to the defense of the secessionist state against the Congolese armed forces and to its (ultimately unsuccessful) attempts to forcibly incorporate northern Katanga into its nationalist project. As will be seen, negotiations to bring an end to the secession focused and often foundered on how the gendarmerie, quickly established as a potent military force, would be incorporated into the Congolese National Army (ANC). While the secession was brought to a sudden end at the start of 1963, the failure to reach agreement on this thorny issue ultimately led the Katangese gendarmes to slip the reins of their now defunct nation-state and keep its flame burning outside its decidedly porous borders.

Declaring the Independent State of Katanga

Conakat leaders effectively trialed the declaration of independence in the weeks before Congolese independence on June 30, 1960. Indeed, it was thought necessary to do so because secession was believed to be far more difficult once a unitary Congo had been granted independence. In practice, it was the mutiny of the FP, angered at the disjuncture between the rise to power of civilian politicians and the lack of equivalent advancement by the military, that provided the excuse for the relatively opportunistic declaration of an independent Katanga on July 11. In the brief reformist period before Congolese independence, a legal distinction was finally introduced in March 1958 between "internal" and externally oriented forces: FP commander in chief Emile Janssens had in April 1959 designated the latter as "gendarmerie units," a term introduced in law in May 1960, though never implemented in Congo.[9]

The nationwide mutiny of FP soldiers from July 5 onward created an atmosphere of instability and led to attacks on Europeans, which prompted thousands of European residents to seek refuge in Northern Rhodesia and elsewhere. The mutiny spread to Elisabethville's Camp Massart on July 9–10. Given the tiny number of skilled Congolese and the dependence of both government and the economy on Europeans (particularly in the strategic mining industry), Belgium, settler representatives, and Conakat leaders were able to present the potential collapse of the economy and society as the result of Lumumba's malign leadership and communistic agitation and as a justification for action. Following Lumumba's appointment of the Kasaian Victor Lundula on July 8 as the commander of the now renamed Congolese National Army and his refusal to accept Belgium's "offer" of military intervention to bring about order, elements of the divided Belgian government threw their weight behind an accelerated effort to secure the region's mineral and strategic interests via secession. Accordingly, on July 11, Conakat, the largest party in the Katangese provincial assembly, declared independence in the following terms:

> The independence of the Congo is an established fact since June 30, 1960. What do we behold at present? Throughout the Congo and particularly in Katanga and in Leopoldville province, we see a tactic of disorganization and terror at work, a tactic which we have seen in . . . many countries now under Communist dictatorship. . . . Katanga cannot bow to such proceedings. The Katangan government was elected by a provincial assembly, itself elected on the basis of a program for order and peace. Under these circumstances, and before the dangers we would bring down upon us by prolonging our submis-

sion to the arbitrary will and Communistic intentions of the central government, the Katangan government has decided to proclaim the independence of Katanga.

THIS INDEPENDENCE IS TOTAL. However, aware of the imperative necessity for economic cooperation with Belgium, the Katangan government, to which Belgium has just granted the assistance of its own troops to protect human life, calls upon Belgium to join with Katanga in close economic community. Katanga calls upon Belgium to continue its technical, financial, and military support. It calls upon her to assist in re-establishing order and public safety.[10]

In the subsequent Katangese constitution promulgated in August 1960, it may be noted that a "Grand Council" of twenty chiefs was established; ten chiefs, including the Mwaant Yav, were appointed as ministers of state. None of this, however, translated into practical political authority over the new state itself; while the chiefs were granted substantial autonomy in their own areas, control over the levers of state power and relations with the mining industry remained with Conakat's leaders.

The Congo Crisis and UN Intervention, 1960

Breaking diplomatic relations with Belgium, Congolese prime minister Lumumba gave a green light to efforts by the ANC's new chief of staff, Joseph Mobutu, appointed on July 10, to forcibly end the secession. He, however, recognized that greater force would be needed against the well-armed and well-trained Belgian forces that were rallying behind the Katangese state. As is well known, Lumumba called upon the United Nations to bring a rapid and forcible end to the secession.[11]

Despite the relative unanimity of anti-Lumumba feeling in Western capitals in late 1960, on the basis that he was the source of communist influence in the country, the United States did not see this as a reason to support the strongly pro-Western Katangese government. In the run-up to independence, State Department officials believed that fragmentation of the country would provide the greatest opportunity for communist infiltration and that "a united Congo would enable the West to compete more advantageously with the [Communist] Bloc than a fragmented Congo which would be born in disorder and anarchy and offer the Bloc an especially fertile ground for penetration."[12] Although US policy did vary between the Eisenhower and Kennedy administrations, its consistent aim was the establishment of a central Congolese government that was sufficiently broad to claim some level of national representation and sufficiently stable to protect Western interests and guard against communist infiltration. Throughout 1961 and 1962, therefore, it supported the rapid resolution of the Katangese secession, but if possible through peaceful means.[13]

The United Nations accordingly passed resolutions recognizing the unity of the Congo and calling for the withdrawal of Belgian forces from Katanga. At Lumumba's request, it dispatched its only second-ever "blue helmets" peacekeeping force; by the end of July, 8,400 UN troops (many from recently independent Asian and African nations) were in Congo.[14] However, the UN Security Council, while resolving on August 9 that "the entry of the United Nations Force into the province of Katanga is necessary for the full implementation of this resolution," simultaneously affirmed that "the United Nations Force in the Congo will not be a party to or in any way intervene in or be used to influence the outcome of any internal conflict."[15] Much then depended on whether the secession could be ended by negotiations or would require the use of force. When the UN secretary-general Dag Hammarskjöld's special representative, Ralph Bunche, visited Elisabethville, he (and Hammarskjöld) became convinced that UN entry into Katanga would involve confrontation with the recently mobilized armed forces of Katanga (see below) and would therefore breach the Security Council resolution.[16] The failure of the United Nations to forcibly end the secession prompted a frustrated Lumumba to seek logistical and military support from the Eastern bloc. This led to Lumumba's conflict with President Joseph Kasavubu and the former's removal from office in September 1960, and ultimately to his murder in January 1961 at the hands of Belgian soldiers and Katangese leaders. Lumumba's supporters, led by Antoine Gizenga, would go on to establish an alternative Congolese government in the eastern city of Stanleyville.[17]

Arming the Secession, 1960–1961

The United Nations' fateful decision involved, according to Hoskyns, a successful bluff on the part of the Katangese authorities, given the barely trained Katangese army that it was still bringing into existence.[18] Although dozens of Belgian officers rallied to support the state, bringing some materiel with them, Katanga urgently needed an indigenous armed force to mobilize against its many enemies.[19] Ironically, given the role of the FP mutiny in prompting secession, it was FP forces that formed the kernel of what, following Janssens's terminology (see above), became known as the gendarmerie. After the intervention of other Congolese and some Belgian troops, notably the so-called Liberation Battalion from Kamina under Major Guy Weber, the former FP troops based at Camp Massart were disarmed, and only those of Katangese origin and residency, numbering around 350, were retained for the new force.[20] They were initially supplemented with volunteers, primarily but not exclusively from Lunda communities, mobilized in cooperation with the Lunda king the Mwaant Yav. Added to these were a number of local units: Baluba warriors, recruited by Kasongo Nyembo, but under the effective command of the Belgian officer Robert Lamouline; a group of 2,000

Bazela in the region of Pweto, under the territorial administrator Walter Engels; Bayeke recruited around Bunkeya; and a small group of white volunteers from Kaniama.[21]

By July 13, Major Jean-Marie Crèvecoeur had been appointed commander of what was becoming the Katangese "army," established with the support of former FP officers and the Belgian Technical Mission (BTM/Mistebel), which was vital to the day-to-day administration of Katanga.[22] Although Belgian officers played a vital part in the organization of the Katangese army, it was equally recognized that the substantive part of the army must be indigenous. Gérard-Libois writes: "During the entire month of August, a veritable race against the clock took place with the objective, for Tshombe and his advisers, of building a more or less efficient Katangan gendarmery before the eventual withdrawal of the Belgian troops."[23] Although these forces were officially designated as the "Katangese armed forces" in November 1960, the term "Katangese gendarmerie," despite not being an accurate depiction of their role, has passed into memory and history.[24] A first contingent of 1,500 men was planned, composed solely of men born in Katanga or who had resided in Katanga for more than ten years.[25] By November 26, the gendarmerie's manpower had reached around 7,000. In the final quarter of 1960, the gendarmerie, although still in the process of being trained, was already on the front line.

The initial conception and organization of the gendarmeries was, for the period during which they were under Belgian supervision (July 1960–August 1961), strongly dependent on colonial precedent.[26] According to René Pire, a former Belgian officer, the gendarmes' organizational charts and tactics were adopted wholesale from the regulations of the FP.[27] The urgency of the period, particularly the need to defend the Katangese borders against the ANC, made it imperative and certainly easier to resort to a well-established formula of colonial military organization. In this context, some of the FP's white and African officers provided supervision and command. These former officers had, according to Frédéric Vandewalle, a "colonial predisposition/prejudice" that placed whites above blacks.[28] The inevitable consequence was that the Katangese gendarmes initially operated according to the colonial model of repressive discipline.

Although the gendarmerie had been established in opposition to the renamed FP/ANC, this did not mean that the issues that led to the mutiny were not relevant to it. Its soldiers, just like their FP counterparts, aspired to rapid grade advancement. Although not all soldiers were advanced (as Lumumba had done with the ANC), some rapid promotions were made. Colonel Crèvecoeur, commander of the gendarmerie, wrote in June 1961: "We have 142 Katangese officers: some have been appointed for their conduct and their courage, the others for their loyalty, 10% for the normal valour of an officer.... We do not have any illusions about the real value of our troops. But it is certain that they are however better than the ANC troops, principally because of their superior discipline."[29] The very real problem of supervision and the training of these officers was partly resolved by a recall of some repatriated Belgian officers and the organization of several stages of training in Belgium. Following the departure of the Belgian officers in August 1961, these training programs came to an end and were followed by the transfer of several units to the supervision and tutelage of mercenaries (see below). Some Belgian officers, however, remained, most notably Lamouline, who commanded the battalion of the Kasongo Nyembo.

Despite this training, the discipline and organization of most units often left much to be desired. Commandant Weber complained in September 1961 that "the gendarmerie was not being commanded and as a result lacked discipline and morale."[30] In addition, there were personal rivalries among the various Katangese and Belgian political and military commanders, for example Crèvecoeur, Guy Weber, military counselor to Tshombe, and André Grandjean, *chef du cabinet* to the secretary of national defense. Many senior Belgian officers preferred to remain in Elisabethville instead of physically leading their front-line troops into combat in the north.

The War against the Balubakat

The northern Katanga state, controlled by Balubakat and supported by the Lumumbist government in Stanleyville, threatened to cut Katanga's lines of communication.[31] Katanga's need to suppress the Balubakat rebellion meant that partly trained soldiers, organized in mobile groups of around sixty troops apiece, together with some policemen, were mobilized and dispatched to the front line.[32] Vandewalle later recalled the resort to brutal tactics by the as yet semitrained gendarmes, still small in number: "On their side, the forces of order met with many losses, especially [those] amongst their number exposed to the greatest risks made by the insufficient hardening of their troops. For our part, ... warriors in the trained supplementary units inevitably ... resorted to certain methods of customary warfare, with burning of huts and pillage."[33] Young, however, suggests that these terror tactics did not reflect inexperience but were in fact entirely intentional: "The 'pacification' efforts periodically conducted by the ... Katanga gendarmes in Balubakat areas of North Katanga were often little more than terrorization carried out by indiscriminate reprisals against whole regions."[34] This behavior did not, however, distinguish the gendarmerie from other Congolese military forces of this and earlier periods, including the ANC and the FP, nor from the Balubakat forces who opposed them.

These brutal tactics did not initially enable the gendarmes to reverse the impressive gains of the Balubakat forces. An interim agreement with the United Nations of October 17, 1960, created neutral zones and bought time for the gendarmes to reorganize, while doing precisely the same for the Balubakat forces. At the start of 1961 the Katangese forces initiated three military operations (named Banquise, Mambo, and Lotus) which reduced the territory held by Balubakat almost as rapidly as it had been obtained. Balubakat retained control only of the town of Kabalo, and only because of protection provided by UN troops in the area. By this time, February–March 1961, the Katangese army was composed of 600 Europeans and 8,000 Katangese troops.

These three operations brought a degree of order to this area of northern Katanga now under the control of Katangese army forces, but only as a result of a highly repressive military occupation. Vandewalle provides the following account: "The gendarmerie sought to protect the people by pre-emptive actions, but these, because of the same tribal war character and the use of drugs that they imposed, led to inevitable killings which made the operation appear as a savage repression. To be effective, it had to give to the Baluba the distinct feeling of defeat."[35]

Despite Vandewalle's attempts to place responsibility for the violence that occurred in the hands of "customary warriors" and (later) the mercenaries, force was undeniably the principal strategy of the gendarmerie as developed by Belgian officers. A note by Chief of Staff Perrad of December 1960 reads: "Attempts to hold talks may be a feint designed to get a break or lull the vigilance of our forces. It is therefore important not to relax efforts to establish our supremacy in the rebellious regions; redoubled efforts can sometimes have a salutary effect on the opponent, and accelerate the acceptance of our terms."[36]

The International Politics of the Secession, 1961

Following the brutal killing of Lumumba in January 1961, a significant reorientation took place in Belgian policy toward Katanga, which was also hastened by the fall of the Eyskens government in April 1961 and its replacement with that of Théo Lefèvre, which was more hostile to Katanga. Belgian opinion was strongly divided between Mistebel supporters who strongly supported an independent Katanga, and others (linked to Justin Bomboko and Mobutu) who advocated a strong unitary Congolese state. Official Belgian support for the secession had always been limited, did not involve recognition of Katanga as an independent state, and was motivated primarily not by active enthusiasm for the secessionist project but rather by concern that a communist-oriented central Congolese government would not protect Belgian interests. For example, the threatened takeover of the Catholic school network proposed by Minister of Education Pierre Mulele and the mooted nationalization of the mining industry had turned both the Belgian Catholic Church and the mining industry against the Leopoldville government. Once such threats were removed, Belgian policy was driven primarily by a desire to reconcile the Katangese leadership with the central authorities in Leopoldville, leading to a political settlement involving some form of federal structure. The underlying aim of many Belgian politicians was to secure effective control or influence over Katanga's mining wealth, not to preserve Katanga as an independent state. Following Lumumba's death, there was an increasing emphasis that control could best be secured via the government in Leopoldville, and Belgium gradually withdrew support from the secessionist state.[37]

The official Belgian position should not of course be conflated with the powerful pro-Katanga lobby in Brussels or with the enduring sympathies of many senior political and military figures, some of whom continued to provide considerable backing to the secession. Tshombe remained dependent on Belgian advisers such as George Thyssens (who drafted the declaration of Katangese independence) and Professor René Clemens (who wrote the Katangese constitution).[38] Clemens was an important figure in Mistebel, established by Harold d'Aspremont Lynden to channel Belgian support to the secessionist state. In addition, the local directors of UMHK assiduously developed relationships with Katangese political leaders and, crucially, continued to direct the company's royalty payments to the Katangese exchequer.[39]

While on the international stage Belgium resisted efforts to forcibly reincorporate Katanga, the Brussels authorities privately sought to pressure the Tshombe government to accept reintegration. Belgium also channeled financial support to the Leopoldville government and provided military support and advisers to the Congolese national army, the ANC. Indeed, Katangese political leaders believed the Belgian government had betrayed their cause and regarded its diplomatic efforts with suspicion. In February 1961, for example, Belgian efforts to encourage talks with Leopoldville were angrily rejected by Tshombe, who declared that "Belgium was responsible for the negative evolution of the situation by refusing . . . to recognise the state of Katanga. The menace of the ONU [UN], in which Belgium has assisted the triumph of unitarist views, doesn't impress Katanga which will never renounce its independence. . . . [W]hilst Katanga has tried to cooperate with the weak regime of Kasavubu in Leopoldville, the bad advice given to Leopoldville by the Belgian government has prevented any agreement."[40] As Belgium was forced in August–September 1961 by the United Nations and the United States to withdraw many of its advisers and officials from Katanga, including many officers of the Katangese armed forces (see below), a considerable number simply remained in or returned to their positions in unofficial guise, while others were replaced by a new, more wholly mercenary officer class (see below). In the first few months of 1961, Belgian government officials organized the transfer of hundreds of Belgian volunteers (and those of other nationalities) to fight in Katanga.[41]

In the wake of the international outcry following Lumumba's death, a new and far stronger UNSC Resolution 161 was passed in February 1961, authorizing "all appropriate measures" to "prevent the occurrence of civil war in the Congo, including . . . the use of force, if necessary, in the last resort." Because the presence of Belgian officers and advisers was believed by the United Nations to be central to the functioning of the Katangese state in general and its army in particular, the resolution, reinforced by a Congolese government decision in April, empowered the forced removal and repatriation of such officials. UN forces advanced to take key positions in northern Katanga, and by August, 338 "mercenaries" and 443 Belgian "political advisers" had been detained and expelled.[42] It was widely believed that such measures would result in the effective collapse of both the Katangese economy and its military.

Meanwhile, in the first four months of 1961, the Western powers and the United Nations, viewing the Gizenga-led Lumumbist state in eastern Congo, with its capital in Stanleyville, as the major threat to national stability, actively sought to reconcile the Leopoldville and Elisabethville governments; an anticommunist axis, based on contacts between Mobutu and Tshombe, would potentially provide the basis for a pro-Western bloc in Congo. The United States was meanwhile open to the arguments of its Western European allies, particularly Belgium and Britain, that the secession should not be ended forcibly; this reflected its desire to protect Katanga's strategic mineral assets and to ensure peaceful reintegration into a Western-oriented Congo.[43] Moïse Tshombe remained the pivotal figure who, in the first half of 1961, engaged in drawn-out negotiations to resolve the conflict; it was widely envisaged that this would lead to Conakat leaders becoming part of a Leopoldville unity government that could more effectively combat the anti-Western Lumumbists in Stanleyville. Numerous roundtable summits were arranged and interim agreements reached, but these commonly foundered on two issues central to the secession: the flow and distribution of UMHK-derived taxation revenue; and control over the Katangese military forces (see below).

Katanga: Acting Like a Nation-State

Had Katanga been solely or overwhelmingly an externally imagined project, the state and its manifestations would surely have collapsed in early 1961. In fact, the secession was maintained for a further two years. During this period, Katanga's leaders, with the help of their Belgian advisers, projected the secession through a visible performance of a state, directed at both the international community and its subjects: the issuing of national stamps and banknotes, the flying of the national flag (which incorporated precolonial copper ingots or *croisettes* in its imagery), and the singing of the national anthem (which refers in its lyrics to the same symbolism).[44] International propaganda was issued against UN military actions, for example during Operation Rumpunch.[45] If Katanga's performative claims to statehood only partially masked its material and structural weaknesses and its dependence on foreign personnel, then this was equally true of many new African states engaged in the process of making nations from above. Alongside the imagery, Finance Minister Jean-Baptiste Kibwe sought to ensure that UMHK paid its taxes, and indeed implemented additional ones, incurring displeasure and occasional resistance by the company's directors, in ways closely resembling relationships between postcolonial states and multinational mining corporations elsewhere in Africa.[46] The economic policies of Katanga, including the commitment to support agricultural development via state intervention and support, strongly resembled those in newly independent Africa as a whole.[47]

Elisabethville was host to celebratory and commemorative events, including the arrival of foreign visitors; negotiations with Congolese state officials were presented as diplomatic meetings of equals.[48] Katangese leaders themselves went abroad on fact-finding missions. Important events took place at the Université d'État d'Elisabethville, "a high-level institution of world renown."[49] Local newspapers provided a powerful outlet for state propaganda; published by self-appointed spokespersons for European interests in Katanga, they portrayed the heroic actions of Katangese gendarmes against their foreign enemies, often through iconographic photographs.[50] Commemorations of the glorious fallen dead were held at Elisabethville's Cathedral of St. Peter and St. Paul.[51] In August 1961 honors were granted to Katangese war veterans at a reunion organized by the Association des Anciens Combattants du Katanga.[52] Senior chiefs such as the Mwaant Yav and the Kasongo Nyembo were likewise pictured in earnest discussion with military and political leaders. Government proclamations were solemnly issued and reproduced in full in the newspapers, which denounced "invasions" of Katangese territory by Lumumbist and UN forces and the threat of international communism. In July 1961, Katanga's apotheosis as a state of supposedly international significance was demonstrated at the international fair (here, as elsewhere in Africa, the replication of a colonial-era event), where Tshombe's position as Katangese president was acted out on a "national" stage.

As in the late-colonial period, claims to a legitimacy rooted in the precolonial authority of its composite societies were central to Katanga's identity and representation. Newspapers stressed the special status of Katanga within the Belgian Congo, giving it its "independent character."[53] Such historically rooted ideas were equally promulgated in its international propaganda. Alongside the trumpeting of Katanga's anticommunist stance was a powerful autochthonous rhetoric that, although appealing to (and often advanced by) Western sympathizers, was rooted in the notion of a precolonial supremacy disconnected from European settlement. In a section entitled Proto-histoire, the 1961 publication *4000 ans d'histoire* placed Katanga alongside other great precolonial African kingdoms such as Great Zimbabwe. Its wealth, generated by copper mining, had enabled the development of a sophisticated hierarchical society: in the sixteenth century, central

Africa had witnessed "the formation of great empires, which were long preserved in Katanga, making this country a true nation whose history, without its continuity being dissolved, continues up to the 20th century."[54]

The state also sought to claim the allegiance of all the province's peoples. Katangese leaders, particularly Evariste Kimba, continued to lay claim (via the allegiance of Kasongo Nyembo) to the Baluba as an essential component of the Katangese nation—mirroring, in so doing, the insistence of Congolese national politicians that Katanga was integral to its territory.[55] Radio Katanga, which like its colonial predecessor broadcast daily in Lunda, Kihemba, Kiyeke, Kisanga, and Tshokwe, also broadcast programs targeted at Katangese women in Kiluba and about the folklore of the Baluba in Manono, one of the areas of northern Katanga occupied by the gendarmerie.[56] Tshombe himself addressed a group of Balubakat women on January 5, 1961, in autochthonous terms: "We are all part of the same family: I am the President of all and all, you are in Katanga, because you are born, because you live there. Our food comes from the same soil, fertilizes our work in the same fields . . . in Katanga, we are all in the same family."[57] While Tshombe's attempts to incorporate Katangese Baluba within Conakat's "national" project were certainly tendentious, the strenuous and continual efforts of his party and administration in this regard are not what would be expected of a "puppet" administration that existed only to meet the needs of its foreign masters.

Pressure and Negotiations, 1961

From mid-1961 onward, and particularly following the appointment of Cyrille Adoula as Congolese prime minister in August (strongly supported by the Kennedy administration), the Leopoldville government became increasingly determined to end the Katangese secession. Antoine Gizenga's agreement to recognize the authority of the Adoula government made it the first undisputed Congolese government for nearly a year and created a united anti-Katangese front in the rest of Congo.[58] The United States took a noticeably firmer line than the main Western European powers, which still sought to prevent the forcible reintegration of Katanga into Congo and a negotiated settlement to the crisis. Ultimately, the defenders of the central state were the US government and its Western allies. Indeed, while De Witte portrays the United Nations as effectively complicit in the Katangese secession—and Hammarskjöld had himself been arguably supportive of Lumumba's elimination—in practice it was precisely the United Nations, rather than the perennially ineffective forces of the ANC, which was to bring Katanga forcibly under the control of the increasingly Western-aligned Leopoldville government in 1962–1963.[59] Tshombe, albeit from an opportunistic position, frequently attacked the United States for using the Congo crisis as a way for American financiers and capitalists to gain control of Katangese copper.[60] The Belgian government, while protesting against any forcible action against Katanga, applied increased pressure on the Tshombe government to reach a negotiated settlement.

From this point onward, Katanga fought a mainly diplomatic and partly military rearguard action against what was in retrospect the inevitable end to the secession. During the long, drawn-out negotiation process, Tshombe demonstrated his preparedness to make substantial concessions; however, following his return to Elisabethville, Tshombe commonly repudiated the essence of such agreements, reverting to a position wherein full Katangese independence would be surrendered only in exchange for the realization of a fully federal Congolese constitution. Western observers believed that Tshombe's preparedness to make substantive concessions was not shared by "extremists" such as Munongo, Jean-Baptiste Kibwe, and Evariste Kimba, who were also critical of Tshombe's overdependence on Belgian advisers.[61] Certainly, the Katangese president's ability to deliver his government's accession to any agreement reached in negotiations was limited; however, the perception that he was more amenable to the reintegration of Katanga into a Western-oriented federal Congo is not generally supported by the evidence. In practice, it was under Tshombe's leadership that the secession was maintained, and it was Tshombe, rather than Kibwe or Munongo, who would subsequently remobilize Katangese political identity in the mid-1960s.

Central government frustration over these never-ending negotiations led to the detention of Tshombe and Kimba in Coquilhatville in April 1961. The Katangese leaders were released in June, having signed an eleven-point agreement apparently resolving the major issues of conflict: a path was proposed toward the unification of Congo and Katanga's political structures, finances, and diplomatic representation. Katanga was forced to concede, alongside the sovereignty of a unified Congo, the integration of the gendarmerie into the national army, the ANC. Gérard-Libois explains that "under the terms of this accord, the reorganization and staffing of the Katangan gendarmery would be accomplished under the authority of General Mobutu; the execution of this plan would begin with the dispatch to Katanga of 102 Congolese officers newly trained in Belgium and placed under the orders of Colonel Eugene Ndjoku."[62] However, as previously, Tshombe insisted on his return to Elisabethville that the accord was merely a starting point for further negotiations.

The failure of the Tshombe government to fully comply with the demand to expel foreign military advisers led the United Nations in August 1961 to launch Operation Rumpunch, the most offensive operation so far in its efforts to implement UNSC Resolution 161.[63] However, the United Nations' targeting of Belgian personnel, coinciding as it did with the effective advance of the ANC into northern Katanga, raised tension between Katanga and the United Nations, which also facilitated the entry of Balubakat into Albertville. The following month, the

United Nations' Operation Morthor sought to capture the remaining foreign mercenaries and political advisers and to implement arrest warrants for Tshombe and other Katangese leaders issued by the Adoula government.[64] However, Operation Morthor was a political and military fiasco; it quickly escalated into open warfare as blood was shed on both sides. Once again, this operation was undermined by a successful bluff by Munongo that convinced Western observers that the gendarmerie was stronger than it in fact was. The Katangese gendarmerie resisted UN attempts to gain control, a level of resistance for which it was unprepared.[65] During this period, thousands of Baluba civilians resident in southern Katangese towns were forced by violence into UN-organized refugee camps.[66]

The United Nations prematurely announced the end of the secession after seizing key installations in Elisabethville. Jean-Baptiste Kibwe, arrested by the United Nations, was coerced into stating that the secession was at an end, something for which he was never forgiven by Munongo and Tshombe.[67] The latter was, however, able to escape to Northern Rhodesia, while Irish UN forces suffered a humiliating defeat in Jadotville. At the end of the first day of the operation, the United Nations announced over Katangan radio that the secession was at an end. This statement was premature and caused controversy because the United Nations was not specifically mandated to end the secession, only to prevent civil war and expel foreign mercenaries. On September 13, Tshombe fled to Ndola in Northern Rhodesia, from where he urged the gendarmerie to continue resistance. A propaganda campaign against the alleged brutality of the UN operation was mounted by Katanga's international supporters, particularly via the publication of *46 Angry Men*.[68] Reports of UN attacks on civilian installations came from Elisabethville and caused anger among Western European powers that sought a peaceful end to the secession. UN secretary-general Hammarskjöld's attempt to negotiate personally with Tshombe led to the former's death in a plane crash.[69]

After these reversals, the United Nations was forced to agree to a cease-fire on disadvantageous terms, handing back public buildings and military posts to Katangese authorities. Tshombe returned to Elisabethville. In November, Security Council Resolution 169 resolved that the United Nations should "take vigorous action, including the use of the requisite measure of force, if necessary," to remove foreign military and other personnel not under UN command. A new military operation in December 1961 led to significant casualties on both sides but finally gave the United Nations control of strategic positions in Elisabethville and removed the threat potential of the Katangese air force. At the end of the year, Adoula and Tshombe signed the Kitona agreement, accepting in principle the unity of Congo and (among other things) the need to place Katangan forces under central government control.[70] Conakat also agreed in principle that its representatives elected to the Congolese parliament in 1960 would finally take their seats.

Tshombe nevertheless succeeded in delaying the end of the secession for another year through drawn-out negotiations with the central government.

The Katangese Gendarmes at War, 1961–1962

Throughout 1961 the Katangese gendarmerie was engaged in military action against Balubakat forces, primarily the "Jeunesses" Balubakat (in which Laurent Kabila was a local deputy commander). The latter were supported by the military forces of the Gizenga-led Stanleyville-based Congo government, which provided stiff opposition to the Katangese gendarmes. Following the expulsion of Belgian supervisors in August–September 1961 under UN pressure, information and accounts about the gendarmerie's activities became rarer. The Katangese officers were now commanded by Lieutenant General Norbert Muke, formerly of the military police of Elisabethville.[71] The United Nations estimated that in September 1961 Katangese forces totaled 13,000, with the vast majority based in northern Katanga: 1,400 in Manono, 535 in each of Albertville and Kongolo, with just 270 men in Kolwezi and 135 in Jadotville.[72] The gendarmerie had succeeded in militarily defeating the Balubakat revolt. Balubakat, however, continued to receive political support, not least from Leopoldville and among UN officers such as Cruise O'Brien, who took on aspects of the colonial notion of the Luba as a more "advanced" people than, for example, the Lunda.[73]

Despite the withdrawal of most Belgian officers, the Forces Armées Katangaises did not collapse, as certain observers, including many of those officers, had anticipated. With the assistance of foreign mercenaries, discipline was maintained, as well as a military efficacy in its operations countering UN attacks. Its actions were supported by the Katangese government's propaganda operations, which gave the gendarmerie a unity of objectives while stressing, somewhat inaccurately, their entirely indigenous nature.[74] It is true that the withdrawal of Belgian military advisers coincided with a substantial increase in the presence of mercenaries: some were themselves former Belgian soldiers, while others were recruited from Rhodesia and South Africa; most notorious among their number were Bob Denard and Jean Schramme, the latter not a mercenary per se but a former Belgian settler. From 1962 to 1967, these mercenaries would play an important role in the subsequent history of the so-called Katangese Armed Forces. However, it is important not to overestimate their authority during the secession itself: the mythology that has developed around these mercenaries, perpetuated until today through their niche publications and sensational novels, has a tendency to attribute to them qualities of military leadership and organization out of all proportion to their actual role, particularly during this period.[75] In practice, day-to-day command of the gendarmerie rested in the hands of Katangese, while the mercenary groups operated with relatively significant autonomy. The fighting between UN and Katangese forces outlined above demonstrated that the departure of most Belgian officers had not substantially undermined the operational capacity of the gendarmerie.

In the final twelve months of the secession, the drawn-out negotiations between the Leopoldville and Elisabethville governments were periodically undermined by continued fighting between the gendarmerie and Congolese government forces, which, with the effective protection of UN forces, were now able to advance into northern Katanga. In March 1962, Adoula wrote to Tshombe refuting the latter's criticism of an attack by ANC forces in Kongolo and indeed denying that the ANC was waging war in Katanga: it was, he argued, merely seeking "the restoration of peace and legality to the province." The Congolese army would, Adoula claimed, fire only to defend itself from attack. He continued: "The attack on Kongolo by Katangan gendarmes headed by mercenaries, at a time when you speak of a peaceful solution, can only be considered a sign of your bad faith. . . . According to troops there, Katangese gendarmes who claim to be instruments for peace and security were implicated in the massacre of a hundred civilians killed only because they opposed secession."[76] The ANC made steady advances into northern Katanga during 1962.[77] The US consul in Elisabethville and, he claimed, Tshombe himself were concerned about "the steady deterioration of discipline and efficiency in the present gendarmerie and even para-commandoes and the fear that the ANC pattern may be repeated in Katanga."[78] In May, US State Department Congo desk officer Charles S. Whitehouse supported the consul's recommendation that the United States prioritize efforts to retrain and reorganize the gendarmerie: "Certainly every reasonable step should be taken to prevent the gendarmerie from becoming a lawless and undisciplined military organization."[79] The CIA warned that, in the unwelcome event of a nonnegotiated military end to the secession, "Katanga forces are likely to resort to guerrilla type operations and could severely harass UN forces for some time."[80] Such concerns help explain the United States' focus on Tshombe as central to its efforts to enable a peaceful end to the secession and bring Katangese forces under the auspices of the Congolese state.

Ending the Secession: The Limits of Negotiations, 1962–1963

By May 1962, Belgium and the United States were working in close concert to bring a rapid end to the secession. While Britain still took the view that all-out war in Katanga would be politically and economically disastrous, adversely affecting substantial British investments in Katanga and upsetting the delicate negotiations over the future of both Northern and Southern Rhodesia, the other two relevant Western powers now shared the view that regional stability depended on a rapid resolution of the crisis.[81] For its part, the United States understood that active Western support for the Adoula government's efforts to end the secession was vital; anything less could encourage radical elements in the coalition government to seek military support elsewhere, undermining Adoula's fragile leadership. By this time, Katanga had lost all support from Belgium; its only meaningful foreign support came from the soon-to-be-abolished Central African Federation and Portuguese-controlled Angola. The latter had supplied arms and logistical support to the Katangese armed forces and would come to play an important role in the future of the gendarmerie.[82]

In the second half of 1962, negotiations revolved around the peace plan proposed by U Thant, Hammarskjöld's successor as UN secretary-general. The U Thant Plan sought to secure Katangese reintegration into the central Congolese state, in exchange for an agreed division of powers between central and provincial administrations on overtly federal lines.[83] Mineral revenue would be divided fifty-fifty between the central government and the province that produced it. A key issue in these negotiations was the incorporation of the gendarmerie into the ANC. As part of his efforts to defend Katangese autonomy in an envisaged federal Congo, Tshombe strenuously resisted the full integration of the gendarmes into the ANC until a new federal constitution was in place. In mid-1962, the United States believed it was still possible to find a place for Tshombe in the administration of a unified Congo, but not for those they regarded as "extremist," such as Munongo and Kibwe.[84] It remains unclear whether Tshombe was not in a position to deliver Katangese agreement to the U Thant Plan even if he had wanted to, or if he simply convinced Western leaders and sympathizers of his moderation while continuing to pursue his own secessionist agenda. It is, however, clear that, far from being a puppet of Western interests, Tshombe played a skillful role in an increasingly difficult situation.

In late 1962, Tshombe periodically made positive public and private statements regarding the reintegration of Katanga into Congo, including the unification of the gendarmerie with the ANC, to be symbolized by these troops taking an oath of allegiance to Congo. However, he continually delayed formal agreement until he was satisfied with the new federal constitution being negotiated under the U Thant Plan. His obfuscation was aided by periodic advances by ANC forces, for example into Kamina in late August, which enabled Katanga to protest to the United Nations at its failure to prevent the violation of neutral bases.

By the end of 1962, matters were finally brought to a head for a number of reasons. The United Nations' lengthy, troubled, and expensive operation in Congo, largely underwritten by the United States, was increasingly regarded as unsustainable. By November 1962, the US ambassador to Congo, Edmund Gullion, was maintaining that the United States must insist on free movement for UN forces throughout all of Congo, including Katanga: "The key to the termination of Katangan secession peacefully is prevention of reinforcements to the illegal gendarmerie.... [T]he heart of the problem remains military and political."[85] The United Nations and the United States, recognizing that the U Thant Plan had failed, and facing the imminent withdrawal of forces by some UN member states, sought to bring the crisis to a conclusion. The United States and Belgium issued a joint statement on November 27, 1962, declaring the plan's failure and publicly conceding the need for increased economic pressure on Katanga. This was swiftly followed by an increase in US military provision for UN operations; in Katanga, anti-US demonstrations were organized in Elisabethville. Amid rising tension, a UN helicopter was shot down on December 24, 1962. Five days later, Tshombe's refusal to sign a document ordering the withdrawal of roadblocks in Elisabethville manned by the gendarmerie left no alternative but to end the secession by force, as US diplomatic sources later noted with a tone of regret: "Compliance with UN demands would have still left Tshombe in a good negotiating position with his forces intact, but he seemed unsure of his ability to control his gendarmerie and perhaps feared discrediting himself in the eyes of his supporters.... [I]t is certain that he did not foresee that the UN victory over the Katangan forces would be so rapid and complete."[86]

Certainly, the end to the secession was surprisingly swift; gendarmes dispersed into the bush when faced by direct UN military action, sometimes taking the local population along with them.[87] Kipushi, a key mining and transportation center, was occupied without a fight on December 30. Britain and Belgium protested the violent UN action, and Tshombe, meeting Roy Welensky, prime minister of the Central African Federation, in his capital, Salisbury, vowed to fight on. UN forces entered Jadotville (today's Likasi), supposedly a strong redoubt of secessionist forces, on January 3, 1963. Kolwezi was the final base of the Katangese government, where ministers, mercenaries, and the gendarmerie under Muke's command remained in place. Before it could be taken by force, the Katangese government declared a formal end to the secession on January 14.[88]

Conclusion

In order to grasp the underlying reality of the Katangese secession of 1960–1963, it is necessary to understand the motivations and actions of its internal political leadership. While the secession was certainly driven by the interests and actions of some Belgian politicians, military officers, and mining interests, it could not have taken place, and would certainly have not taken the form it did, without the actions of Katangese political leaders whose outlook was fundamentally shaped by their vision of a Katanga rooted in both its precolonial history and its distinctive colonial-era trajectory. Far from acting as puppets of Belgian interests, self-defined indigenous Katangese leaders expressed hostility to specific socioeconomic results of colonialism, especially the influx of Kasian labor into Katanga and the potential loss of political control to this group of "strangers." The leaders of Conakat sought to express their ethnoregional identity in a modern territorial form—and when it became evident that this could not be achieved via a unified Congolese state, they sought to establish a Katangese nation-state. In order to defend this state from its external enemies, Conakat leaders and their Belgian military allies mobilized that central manifestation of the sovereign state, the national army. This took the form of the Katangese gendarmerie, which—in parallel with Conakat's political actions to defend the state—acted militarily against the state's enemies in northern Katanga: the forces of Balubakat and those of Stanleyville, the Congolese national army, and the troops of the United Nations.

While the United Nations was delighted to have defeated these forces and thereby secured the ending of the secession, it remained preoccupied with dismantling the Katangese state's relationship with its twin pillars of support: the UMHK and the gendarmerie. The former was secured by UMHK's agreement, the day after the Katangese government formally declared an end to the secession, to pay foreign mineral earnings to the central Congolese government.[89] As will be shown, effective control over the gendarmerie would not prove so easy to achieve.

3 Into Exile and Back, 1963–1967

ONE OF THE major problems in ending conflicts in Africa has been the effective demobilization of armed forces and the creation of unified national armies. For example, the recent inability of the Democratic Republic of Congo to disarm and integrate myriad armed groups, or to find alternative economic opportunities for young men who have previously survived by force of arms, has arguably perpetuated predatory conflict by such militia, often in new or hybrid forms, over the past decade.[1] The defeat of the Katangese secession presented, on the face of it, precisely this problem to the Congolese state, the United Nations, and the international community that had supported UN intervention. A major concern of these actors was the former Katangese gendarmerie, well trained but now detached from the state that had created it and, as a consequence, unpaid. It is clear, however, that insufficient foresight was given to the issue of demobilization and that this process was at best poorly implemented. More specifically, the Egge Plan of June 1961, which set out how the integration of Congo's various armed forces would take place, was incompatible with the desire of the Congolese National Army (ANC) to crush its Katangese enemies. As with later conflicts, the various Congolese armed forces, including, most significantly, the undisciplined and predatory Congolese army itself, represented "human minefields" whose potential for violent disruption of the supposed peace remained long after the end of overt warfare.

Unlike a minefield, of course, the Katangese gendarmerie was mobile, and while part of it was integrated, decidedly imperfectly, into the ANC, a large number of the gendarmes were, at the very extinguishing of the secession in January 1963, transported to Portuguese-controlled Angola for a first and relatively brief period in exile. Others spent 1963 roaming the border areas of Congo, Northern Rhodesia, and Angola; while some returned to the communities from which they had been recruited, others came to be seen as a predatory force on the local population. The Congolese army's efforts to defeat this force equally constituted a threatening force to the local civilian population. This reinforced the collective view of some Katangese that the state was still worth fighting for, if not now, then in the future. Not for the last time, however, the Leopoldville government, unremittingly hostile to the political project of which the gendarmes were now an important residual symbol, overstated the danger they posed to its Western supporters: US reports of gendarmes' activity and the threat they represented consequently contrast sharply with those of the Portuguese authorities in Angola, who saw the gendarmes in their midst as more of a refugee burden than a military threat.

Despite the loathing of the Congolese state for what the gendarmes represented, however, the state's weakness meant that the gendarmes would be called upon to play a role in its defense. A year and a half after the ousting of the Katangese government, Moïse Tshombe was appointed prime minister of all of Congo; under his leadership, the gendarmes and their mercenary commanders were returned from Angolan exile and put to work defending the Congolese state against which they had previously fought, this time against the radical Mulelist movement seeking to build an independent Lumumbist nation-state in eastern Congo.[2] The successful suppression of this rebellion with the entry of Belgian paratroopers into Stanleyville in November 1964 was followed by a further, more-sustained attempt to reintegrate the gendarmes into the ANC, now dominated by the singular figure of Joseph Mobutu. In 1965 Mobutu's second coup was carried out with the support of the United States, which ultimately concluded that protecting Western interests and preventing communism from gaining a foothold in central Africa necessitated the denial of self-determination for the Congolese people.[3] Just as the ex-gendarmes were problematically semi-integrated into the ANC, so were many of their former political leaders drawn into the Congolese political establishment, with the notable exception of Tshombe himself (see below). As a result, when Mobutu centralized all decision making in 1967, granting himself the power to rule by decree, there was little or no resistance by the former political leaders of the Katangese state. It was instead the former Katangese army and its mercenary officer class that mutinied against Mobutu's emergent dictatorship, presaging a far longer period in Angolan exile.

The Demobilization of Katanga, 1963–1964

With the formal end of the secession in January 1963, UN and ANC forces took control of Elisabethville and, both jointly and separately, began patrolling the reincorporated province of Katanga. Following an agreement on January 17, Moïse Tshombe facilitated the entry of UN forces into Kolwezi, the last redoubt of the secessionist army. As part of this agreement, the gendarmerie was supposed to surrender its arms and ammunition in a process overseen by the United Nations, under the provisions of the National Reconciliation Plan (also known as the U Thant Plan).[4] The Adoula government granted a general amnesty to Katanga's political leaders.[5] Economic integration was achieved relatively swiftly; UMHK concluded an agreement with the Leopoldville government in early January that transferred the payment of taxes and royalties from Elisabethville to the Congolese government.[6] Despite Katangese finance minister Kibwe's efforts to delay the process, the Congolese state took over the Katangan National Bank in the second half of January.

Katanga was, with the rest of Congo, divided as of July 1962 into separate provinces, a process that weakened Katanga and (more generally) decreased the potential for the mobilization of provincial opposition to the central state.[7] North Katanga was created in July 1962, with the other provinces established the following year. This division was bitterly attacked by Tshombe as the "Balkanization" of Katanga; he nevertheless established a South Katanga provincial government in April 1963.[8] Tshombe's authority, notwithstanding his leadership of the secession, was regarded as vital for maintaining public order.[9] However, his rivalry with Balubakat's Jason Sendwe, who also sought to rule a Katanga integrated into Congo, led to ethnic clashes in Jadotville in April in which an estimated seventy-four people were killed.[10] In May 1963, ANC forces raided Tshombe's residence, and he was accused of maintaining a private militia. Tshombe himself, after initially promising Conakat's support to efforts to unify the country, fled Congo for Paris in June 1963 (he later relocated to Madrid), claiming persecution and fearing arrest after the Congolese government had seized documents demonstrating his continued contacts with mercenaries. He remained in close contact with the commanders of his former forces, seeking to utilize them to return to Congo and to power. Tshombe's departure further undermined efforts to bring his former soldiers in from the cold.[11]

In mid-1963 the remainder of the former province of Katanga was split into the new Lualaba (also known as South Katanga) and Katanga Oriental provinces. Notwithstanding their opposition to such measures, many former Katangese leaders took up positions in the new provincial governments. The nonimplementation of the U Thant Plan, ostensibly accepted by the Adoula government as the basis for the postwar settlement, created resentment among the former Katangese leadership. A new constitutional commission was appointed in January 1964 and two months later recommended a presidential system of government to replace the parliamentary one established at independence.[12]

Military reintegration was to prove a much tougher problem and proceeded slowly. The commander of the gendarmerie, General Norbert Muke, and twenty-five of his officers took an oath of allegiance to the Leopoldville government in early February.[13] However, the Congolese government's new resident minister in Elisabethville, Joseph Ileo, expressed skepticism that "Gen. Muke and [the] Katangans [were] really giving wholehearted support to [the] effort to collect them [i.e., the gendarmes from the 'bush']. Many gendarmes seemed to be taking seriously word spread by Katanga authorities . . . that surrender [was] merely temporary and [that] Katanga would carry on [the] fight after 2–3 months when [the] UN leaves. . . . [This meant that the] . . . collection of gendarmerie weapons was made difficult, and [it was] possible that [the] only resolution would be patrols to comb every village in Katanga."[14] Tshombe meanwhile complained that without assurances regarding the treatment of former gendarmes, he could not persuade them to "come in with their weapons."[15] The United States recorded that only 3,500 of an estimated 14,000–17,000 gendarmes registered for integration into the Congolese army. It should, however, be noted that at least 7,000 of these had not been given military training and had quickly returned to civilian life after the end of the secession. Young reports that only 2,000–3,000 gendarmes became part of the ANC at this time, and the figure is probably nearer the lower number.[16] The remainder, approximately 8,000 well-trained soldiers, disappeared from political control.

While US officials, influenced by the Leopoldville politicians with whom they closely cooperated, focused on the technical aspects of integration and stressed the "chaotic" nature of the ex-gendarmes, the underlying difficulty was political. Congolese politicians, particularly Adoula, Justin Bomboko, and (to a lesser extent) Ileo, saw Katanga not as part of Congo that needed careful reintegration but rather as an enemy to be conquered militarily: their attitude thus resembled that of the victorious Allied forces who imposed reparations on Germany in 1919 rather than that of those who sought to rebuild it in 1945.[17] This particularly applied to the "integration" of ex-gendarmes into the ANC: in August 1963, Mobutu secretly ordered the award of lower ranks—that is, the effective demotion—of those gendarmes. Those who did join the ANC, such as Colonel Charles Babah, report physical violence and the fear of being killed by their new fellow soldiers.[18]

The immediate concern for nonintegrated ex-gendarmes was financial: while some were quickly employed as security officers for mining companies, others were now penniless. In mid-February, ex-gendarmes in the town of Kapanga went on a rampage, complaining that they had not been paid; the United Nations sent General Muke to calm them down.[19] In March, it was reported that "in the bush in South Katanga roam large bands of gendarmes, in uniform and carrying arms, but receiving no pay, who have failed to respond to the call to enrol in the central army. . . . [T]hey are to be counted in thousands, not hundreds."[20] Returning to their villages was not always an option: an American Methodist missionary reported that "large numbers of gendarmes are being treated as outcasts in their own villages. Even fathers are allegedly disowning sons."[21] Tshombe acknowledged that the "gendarmerie in [the] bush represented [a] serious threat to public order."[22] Indeed, the combined effect of insecurity and harassment by ANC soldiers threatened a new exodus of the skilled European expatriates on whom the Katangese mining economy depended.[23]

The United Nations sought, initially via reconciliatory messages but increasingly through the display of overt force, to bring in the gendarmes from the bush. Their efforts were, however, undermined by the ANC.[24] Despite operating officially under UN leadership, ANC soldiers lacked "discipline and self confidence" and, in the words of US consul Jonathan Dean, "tended to see lurking Gendarmerie behind every bush."[25] In August 1963, under pressure from Ileo and Mobutu, the United Nations ended its efforts to reconcile and integrate former gendarmes. US secretary of state Robert McNamara expressed concern that Mobutu's attempt to end the problem by armed means reflected his own "dreams of glory. Worse than inaction would be [the] failure of [the] operation, or . . . [a] bloodbath. [The] Gendarmes are reportedly well armed, know the country and have [the] African population with them."[26] UN officials, focused on withdrawing their forces by December 1963, publicly played down "any suggestion that all was not calm and peaceful in Katanga."[27] However, in late September, UN helicopters dropped pamphlets in French and Kiswahili in which the Katanga Oriental provincial government urged the ex-gendarmes to return to civilian life.[28] As the United Nations gave up on reconciliation, and as the ANC operated with increased autonomy, reprisal raids were carried out in supposedly pro-secessionist communities: "[The] ANC descent on [the] village [of] Bayeke chief Antoine Munongo has left permanent resentment and unpaid ANC troops engaging in widespread, continual theft in Baudouinville-Pweto area. South of Pweto . . . they have pressed [the] search for ex-gendarmes with [a] very heavy hand, burning several villages and leaving male inhabitants of others bound in [the] sun with shrinking rawhide cords. Some villages [are] still wholly deserted as [a] result [of] this treatment."[29]

An ANC operation in September to capture the former gendarmerie base at Kasenga was frustrated when 300 ex-gendarmes crossed the Luapula River into Northern Rhodesia, where border populations ethnically resembled their Congolese counterparts. British officials, who believed the negotiated surrender of the ex-gendarmes was both possible and desirable, criticized the ANC's approach: "The Congolese National Army now consider that they have won a splendid victory. They have entered Kasenga, which was previously occupied by ex-gendarmes. They have, however, like a sick man scratching a boil, disseminated the poison throughout the body, whereas a text-book encircling operation might have removed it definitively."[30]

Indeed, bands of ex-gendarmes roamed the border areas of Congo, Northern Rhodesia (then still part of the Central African Federation [CAF]), and Angola during the second half of 1963. Some sought to trade with civilian populations on both sides of the border, while others engaged in armed banditry. British officials reported in September: "Small numbers [of] unarmed ex-Katanga gendarmes in mufti [are] periodically crossing into Northern Rhodesia to barter for food. Their food position is reported acute."[31] Reports were received of up to 300 ex-gendarmes in Northern Rhodesia's Solwezi District, at the Kafue headwaters and at Kansanshi mine. Smaller groups of ex-gendarmes assembled in Kakoma in Mwinilunga District, the heartland of the Lunda polity in Northern Rhodesia.[32]

Congolese government and UN officials appealed to CAF authorities to arrest these gendarmes.[33] While the latter were concerned about the ex-gendarmes' lawless activities, they simultaneously opposed any UN or ANC incursion into federal territory.[34] Northern Rhodesian officials argued: "While we deplore the practice of these gendarmes crossing into Northern Rhodesia we must[,] up to a point, regard them as refugees and accord them humanitarian treatment."[35] The governor of Northern Rhodesia, Evelyn Hone, stressed the difficulties in policing Mwinilunga, where "many of the tribesmen are in sympathy with Tshombe due to strong tribal affiliations. We certainly do not want them to become directly involved in the Congo/Tshombe dispute, nor do we want Armée Nationale Congolaise to undertake further incursions into this Territory, as they have already done on two occasions." He noted, in any case, that "the large majority of them are unarmed." Hone continued: "We have certainly not gained the impression that the Armée Nationale Congolaise are particularly energetic in trying to deal with the ex-gendarmes who are at large in the bush. From time to time half-hearted operations are mounted but they come to very little, and their security is so bad that the ex-gendarmes seem to ... vanish into thin air."[36] This capacity of the gendarmes to melt away into the ethnically identical civilian populations of these border areas would enable them, on a number of occasions, to evade both their enemies and the effective control of their ostensible patrons.

Into Angola, 1963–1964

It was only in October 1963 that US and British diplomats belatedly discovered the extent of mercenary and ex-gendarme presence in Angola itself, following a visit there by a Special Branch officer based in Mwinilunga.[37] In November it was subsequently reported that "approximately 2,500 unarmed Katangese ex-gendarmes crossed over [the] border into Solwezi District ... [from Katanga]. They were friendly and well behaved though [they] showed some reluctance to return across [the] border. They stated they were proceeding en bloc to Angola on instructions of Tshombe and it is believed they will collect others en route."[38] This was the first but not the last time that ex-gendarmes would travel to and from Angola via Lunda areas of Northern Rhodesia / Zambia. This process was aided by the significant ethnic homogeneity of the populations straddling the borders of the three neighboring territories.

It should be recalled that relations between the Katangese secessionist government and colonial Portugal had been excellent, as shown in the letters exchanged between their respective security services and the fact that two of Tshombe's younger brothers, Jérôme Nawej and Benjamin, had studied in Portugal.[39] Pascal Kapend, a Katangese intelligence officer in Dilolo, recalls the systematic cross-border exchange of information between Katanga and the Portuguese intelligence services.[40] The Portuguese colonial regime and the Katangese government shared the same obsession with anticommunism, and the former had begun to face cross-border attacks from Congo by Angolan nationalists organized in the Frente Nacional de Libertação de Angola (FNLA). While there are suggestions that Tshombe had planned to transfer some of the gendarmes to Angola in the event of the secession's defeat, Portuguese officials had clearly not anticipated the arrival of such a large group at this point.

A variety of sources indicate that a first group of 500 Katangese troops entered Angola in January–February 1963, via Teixeira de Souza.[41] The majority, led by the mercenary Jean Schramme and numbering about 400, moved on to Vila Luso. The Portuguese authorities were unprepared for their arrival, but given the Leopoldville government's support for the Angolan Government in Exile (GRAE) of FNLA leader Holden Roberto, Portuguese intelligence (Polícia Internacional e de Defesa do Estado, or PIDE) officials were quick to see their potential as a counter to the growing Angolan nationalist presence in Congo.[42] In late 1963, Ileo, concerned about potential Portuguese aggression, sought to deter Roberto from establishing a military training camp in Dilolo.[43] Portuguese officials were, however, also concerned that the ex-gendarmes might be a potential source of destabilization within Angola, and that harboring them would further increase international criticism of Portugal's colonial policy. This was partly disguised by presenting the camps as a humanitarian operation; Portuguese colonial intelligence constantly referred to Katangese "refugees" in correspondence about the gendarmes and mercenaries.[44]

A steady stream of ex-gendarmes arrived in Angola in late 1963; these were transferred to a number of additional camps, at Cazombo (where 1,798 were based by January 1964), Cazage, Lutuai, and Lunguebungo.[45] Notwithstanding their depiction as refugees, military organization remained strong. Parallel command structures appear to have existed in Angola, separate from those under Muke: Major Ferdinand Tshipola was formally the ex-gendarmes' commander, with Antoine Mwambu his chief of staff. In addition, however, four groups operated under their respective mercenary commanders (some of whom were to remain with the ex-gendarmes until 1967—see below). Schramme certainly refused to recognize Tshipola's authority.

The gendarmes lived in Angola in very difficult circumstances and lacked virtually everything, in contrast to their officers, who were housed in hotels paid for by Moïse Tshombe.[46] By the start of 1964, two of the above-named camps appear to have become so-called training camps.[47] White mercenaries were reported to be traveling from Katanga to Angola via Ndola in Northern Rhodesia, relaying messages among Tshombe, the mercenaries, and the ex-gendarmes, with

Southern Rhodesian assistance.[48] Tshombe, in exile in Paris and then Madrid, remained in contact with the ex-gendarmes seeking his underlying objective, namely, to regain his lost power. He was entirely pragmatic in his efforts to build alliances with forces in Congo; notwithstanding the ideological gulf between them, he initially made overtures toward the radical leadership of the Conseil National de Libération (CNL),[49] leading to an anti-Leopoldville agreement known as the Madrid Accords.[50] In Leopoldville, the Madrid Accords raised fears of a military alliance between the ex-gendarmes and the Mulelists (of whom, see below).[51] Accordingly, around April 1964, Tshombe appears to have directed the remobilization of the ex-gendarmes.[52] According to J.-P. Sonck, Tshombe and the Portuguese sought to transfer command of the gendarmes to Schramme, but this was firmly opposed by Tshipola and Mwambu.[53] During this period, some 3,000–4,000 new recruits seem to have been brought to Angola from Katanga as part of the preparations for Tshombe's (subsequently aborted) rebellion.[54]

The southern Katangese character of the gendarmes enabled the mobilization of the Lunda and Tshokwe population on both sides of the frontier in support of their operations, if only for their protection and as a network of information. The Mwaant Yav, the Lunda king, now played a crucial role in the ex-gendarmes' informal structures of authority. This was aided by the demise of Mwaant Yav Gaston Mushid (1963–1965), who had been reluctant to involve himself directly in political life. From the appointment of his successor, Daniel Tshombe, the Mwaant Yav Muteb II Mushid (1965–1973), until today (and in a break with the previous alternation of succession between royal lineages), every Mwaant Yav has been a brother of Moïse Tshombe. Previous Mwaant Yavs had been discontented with and sometimes challenged their relative marginalization by Tshombe. Now, the monopolization by the Tshombe family of the dignity and authority of the Mwaant Yav made him a vital instrument of influence in South Katanga and over the cultural and political life of the ex-gendarmes, to which he was intimately linked. During this period Daniel Tshombe, the man who would soon be Mwaant Yav,and his brother, Jérôme Nawej, were actively involved in mobilizing support for the ex-gendarmes.[55]

Many inside Congo—government and US embassy officials and the Angolan GRAE, as well as journalists—expressed considerable alarm about the ex-gendarmes in Angola and in the border areas, whether as a chaotic threat to law and order, as the basis for a new Tshombe-initiated secessionist rebellion, or as an anti-GRAE force initiated by the Portuguese. In February 1964, ANC general Louis Bobozo, highlighting Portuguese support for the "ex-gendarmes" in Angola and support provided by Daniel Tshombe, demanded that ANC troops then being mobilized against the Mulelist rebellion in Kwilu (see below) be used against the ex-gendarmes.[56] The same month, one State Department official expressed his concern about what might happen after the withdrawal of UN forces:

Katanga will be very vulnerable after the departure of the UN troops; the Portuguese are vitally concerned about incursions of [Holden] Roberto's guerrillas from the Congo; Portugal's and Tshombe's aims coincide nicely. All this would seem [to] add up to the possibility that Portugal may be building up a Katanga pro-Tshombe force that could be used as a threat to Adoula with a view to inducing Adoula to restrict Roberto's activities. If this failed, it would not appear beyond the realm of possibility for the Portuguese to unleash gendarme elements into Katanga in support of Tshombe's cause.[57]

It appears, however, that the latter possibility was not seriously entertained at this stage. US observers, desperate to shore up the weak Leopoldville government, tended to see such threats where they lacked much basis in reality. US officials were acutely aware that the ANC, supposedly the "chief instrument" to deliver security in the Congo, was in fact a major cause of instability and that the Adoula government had no way of addressing this.[58]

The UN operation in the Congo was finally brought to an end in June 1964, amid (not coincidentally) new radical challenges to the authority of the Leopoldville government. It was not, however, southern Katanga, but other regions of Congo that provided the greatest threat. The Kwilu rebellion led by Pierre Mulele promised a "second independence" in western Congo, while Mulele's allies in the east were similarly fueled by Lumumbist radicalism and supported by communist states.[59] The fall of the northern Katangan capital Albertville to the leftist "Simba" rebels of Gaston Soumialot in June was a warning of what was to come, but it was the fall of Stanleyville (today's Kisangani) and the declaration of Soumialot and Christophe Gbenye's "people's republic" under their CNL, that exposed the weakness of the Leopoldville government. This presented a new communistic threat to Western political and economic interests in central Africa and prompted the return of Moïse Tshombe, in the unlikely guise of Congolese prime minister.

The Road to Stanleyville, 1964

General Mobutu, recalling his previous efforts to construct a Leopoldville-Elisabethville alliance against the Stanleyville-based Lumumbist government of Antoine Gizenga in 1962, now used his influence with President Kasavubu to persuade him to name Tshombe as Congolese prime minister. As the United Nations finalized the withdrawal of its forces and Stanleyville fell to the CNL rebels, Tshombe arrived in Leopoldville on June 26, 1964, and was named prime minister on July 9. Tshombe's unity government, whose members included former secessionists such as Godefroid Munongo and South Kasai's Albert Kalonji, was reviled by most African states, and Tshombe was banned from representing Congo in meetings of the OAU.[60]

Tshombe quickly arranged the return of the gendarmes and the mercenaries from Angola, as well as the mobilization of some who had remained in Congo.

Two units were commanded by Ferdinand Tshipola and Jean Schramme, respectively, until they were integrated into the force organized by Vandewalle to capture Stanleyville; thus, one of the most important Belgian officers in the former Katangese army now led operations designed to reestablish Leopoldville's control over eastern Congo.[61] As early as July 11, a group of 150 ex-gendarmes was recruited in Jadotville to form the second commando, which subsequently participated in fighting at Kabongo, Kabalo, and Albertville against the Simba rebels. Others were recruited in Elisabethville; many of these ex-gendarmes were among those who had been living in the bush and who reenlisted primarily to claim their salaries. This commando operated in conjunction with the 12th Battalion of the ANC, under the command of Lieutenant Colonel Eustache Kakudji. Commandos from the ANC's 3rd Battalion under Colonel Tshatshi who were still in Katanga were sent to Kamina, with the 2nd Katangese Company (approximately 150 ex-gendarmes) under Captain Niembo. These forces were integrated into a column led by Kakudji that pushed Simba forces back toward Kabalo and Albertville, where they arrived at the end of August. From there they progressed toward Lulimba.

The troops who returned from Angola expected to resume the fight for Katangese autonomy or independence, only to be told by Tshombe that their immediate task was to defeat the eastern rebellion on behalf of the Congolese state. They refused to obey any person other than Moïse Tshombe—their political leader but also the man previously responsible for the payment of their wages, which many had not received since 1963. This last demand was not resolved until Tshombe personally intervened. ANC troops were, unsurprisingly, hostile to the new alliance with their former enemies, but this only partly explains why their reception in Congo was badly executed.[62] The Schramme-led "Batabwa" group arrived separately to avoid a conflict with the units commanded by Tshipola; Sonck reports clashes between the separate Batabwa and Lunda troops, but this probably reflected rivalries between mercenary and Katangese leaders rather than ethnic hostility.[63] Contrasting views exist in sources regarding the "great discipline" of the ex-gendarmes about which Schramme boasted. Vandewalle certainly reports that, among the Tshipola-led ex-gendarmes, "discipline was satisfactory and the troops were content."[64] The uneasily unified forces of the ANC, the ex-gendarmes, and mercenary commanders were now mobilized in operations against the Mulelists. Given their unimpressive record, US officials were skeptical about the capacity of both the Congolese government and its armed forces:

> There is in this part of the country and the adjacent areas a strong sentiment of dissatisfaction against the Congolese government, a practically general sentiment. All the layers of the population in this area are profoundly outraged with the first four years of independence, of which corruption, inefficiency, the violence of the state and the economic decline contrast bitterly with the prom-

ise of independence.... These sentiments of dissatisfaction are equally shared by the troops of the ANC. The principal reasons for their failures in combat are not so much a lack of military capacity and the superstitious fear of the rebels (which are nevertheless important factors) but that they do not want to fight.[65]

Gleijeses cites diverse US diplomatic sources:

It is not only the case that the troops refuse to fight. They also contribute to reinforcing the rebel case by their "acts of brutality and pillage." The US ambassador notes that the killings committed by chance, the pillage and the rapes were "normal activities" of the ANC and it is a complaint of the general population that is welcomed by the rebels "who, in most cases, treat them better than the ANC."[66]

The US authorities were, however, equally hostile to autonomous operations by the ex-gendarmes and their officers. Tshombe called for Western powers to supply military equipment and logistical support and was personally in favor of mercenary-led operations; fearing being tarred with the brush of foreign intervention, he publicly insisted on the use of African soldiers.[67] Given their subordinate role in the operation, the Katangese themselves did not have the opportunity to develop an autonomous command, and their position depended entirely on Tshombe's precarious position in the Congolese political system.

Without giving an exhaustive account of the Stanleyville operation, the role and importance of both the Katangese and the mercenary elements within the wider Leopoldville-backed forces need to be explained. These included the 5th Battalion of mercenary South Africans under Mike Hoare; a newly recruited 7th Battalion of Hemba; Katangese gendarmerie formerly based in the garrison of Kongolo, commanded by Belgian officers; a battalion of the Luba of Kasongo Nyembo, but now without either Belgian or mercenary leadership; the 9th Battalion, consisting of the Luba of Manono under Major Protin; and the 10th Battalion of Batabwa led by Schramme (around 250 troops). From August 1964, these combined forces steadily advanced against the Simba rebel forces. Both sides were supplemented by foreign troops and supplied by international backers—anti-Castro Cuban pilots flew American support planes, while the rebels were supported by many radical African states, including Uganda and Egypt.[68] However, when hundreds of white hostages were taken by the Simba forces and held in Stanleyville, the Tshombe government received direct assistance from the Belgian armed forces, supported by the US Air Force. Belgian paratroopers were dropped into Stanleyville on November 24, rescuing most of the hostages and paving the way for the entry of ANC and mercenary forces into the city.[69]

The ex-gendarmes now provided immediate reinforcements to secure and control Stanleyville, and also participated in mopping-up operations against the

Simba rebels in early 1965. The 9th and 7th Battalion commandos played an important role in the subsequent struggle against the eastern front during 1965–1966, still led by Soumialot, as well as the young Laurent Kabila. The 14th Commando of Mboyo saw action in the zones of Watsa-Kilo and Moto-Faradje. Having been integrated into the ANC, some sources suggest that this unit attempted to return to Stanleyville in July 1966 to join the revolt by the Baka Regiment, part of the ANC's 5th Brigade, led by Ferdinand Tshipola (see below). Some sources note the ruthless attitude of "gendarmes" (who were among those recruited in Katanga, and not the Angola returnees) during the repression of the Mulelists, for example in this eyewitness report from Albertville: "We saw in a hospital all the patients suspected of sympathy for the rebels killed without pity in their beds. Since we sensed equal menace for us by the Katangese, we decided to escape no matter what."[70]

A further five battalions (numbered 11 through 15) composed of the ex-gendarmes and led by Ferdinand Tshipola were repatriated from Angola to Congo only in September 1964, in an operation documented by the Portuguese intelligence services.[71] In total, 2,935 ex-gendarmes and 15 officers returned to Congo, leaving a similar number behind in Angola.[72] These latter five battalions arrived too late to participate in the operation to reconquer Stanleyville in the second half of 1964 and were instead allowed to visit their families after their absence in Angola. They were, however, deployed in the subsequent occupation of Stanleyville, having been dispatched to Albertville on November 21.[73] It is noteworthy that these well-trained troops, independent of mercenary command, closely linked and loyal to Tshombe, were not deployed in the most important battles against the Mulelists. It appears that their deployment was ultimately more political than military, and that the perceived political nature of their presence was why they were immediately attacked by Mobutu's ANC forces when Tshombe was ousted from power the following year (see below).

Congo and Katanga under Tshombe and Mobutu, 1965–1967

During much of 1965, Tshombe sought to establish himself as a legitimate Congolese national politician, with his new political vehicle, Conaco (Congolese National Convention). Under his premiership, a new federal constitution was promulgated in August 1964, granting substantially increased provincial autonomy. Notwithstanding his past record, and despite still being ostracized by other African states, Tshombe achieved considerable internal popularity, partly as a result of overseeing the defeat of the eastern rebels. He now sought to position himself in the mainstream of African nationalism, going so far as to antagonize his former Belgian allies by reappropriating some mining concessions.[74] Elections were held in government-controlled areas in March–April 1965. In these

Tshombe and Conaco and its supporters won a majority (80 of 167 seats) in parliament, which met in September for the first time since its dismissal by Kasavubu two years earlier.[75] Tshombe's confrontation with President Kasavubu (who declared himself opposed to political parties and called for a "Government of National Union") led to the former's removal from his position as prime minister in October. In an event that marked the disintegration of the former Katangese political elite, he was briefly replaced by his former Katangese ally Evariste Kimba (now leading Balubakat), whose position as prime minister was twice rejected by the pro-Tshombe parliamentary majority.[76] When Mobutu seized power in November 1965, Tshombe undeniably enjoyed significant popularity across Congo. Mobutu subsequently oversaw the show trial and execution of Kimba and three other former ministers in the brutal May 1966 event known as the *pendus de la pentecôte*.[77] Tshombe fled Congo for Spain, from where he continued to organize secretly for his return to power.

Mobutu initially adopted relatively conciliatory and pragmatic policies, appointing a balanced cabinet including eight members of Conaco in a government endorsed by the newly elected parliament.[78] Tshombe, however, was a useful lightning rod for discontent and was accordingly scapegoated for all Congo's ills: an international warrant was issued for his arrest, and he was charged with treason and sentenced in absentia to death in 1967 for attempting to recruit mercenaries.[79] Over the next two years, Mobutu proceeded methodically and with great skill to first incorporate and then neutralize various provincial power bases. This was to culminate in 1967 with a confrontation with the Katangese, politically and militarily.

As part of his wider centralization initiatives, Mobutu twice undertook to reunify the divided provinces of Katanga. In April 1966, he announced that Lualaba and Katanga Oriental would merge to become South Katanga, to be led by Godefroid Munongo, a decision characterized at the time by Benoit Verhaegen as a "last minute concession seeking to promote the unity of Katanga in exchange for the loyalty of the Elisabethville leadership to the central authorities."[80] This was essentially a tactical move to further divide the Katangese political leadership. Katanga was nevertheless reunified at the end of December 1966; for less than a week, Paul Muhona, a Tshokwe and a former member of the Katangese secessionist government, served as its governor. Such measures briefly raised hopes that Katanga could regain some of its old autonomy, and most of the former political leaders of the secession were ready to engage (or arguably compromise) with the new central authorities. Mobutu, however, had no intention of reestablishing any substantial provincial autonomy. Rather, he adopted an opportunistic but highly effective approach to the granting and withdrawal of regional powers to particular individuals, which served to steadily reinforce his effective control over an increasingly centralized political system.

At the start of January 1967, Muhona was replaced by a new governor, Jean-Foster Manzikala. Manzikala had been president of the Orientale Province government under the Lumumbist government of Antoine Gizenga in 1960–1961. He was, unsurprisingly, strongly opposed to Katangese autonomy and, acting no doubt on orders from Leopoldville, organized and encouraged the harsh repression of all Congolese suspected of "Tshombist" sentiments and whites suspected of supporting them. Manzikala was replaced in turn by Denis Paluku (in August 1967) and then by Leon Engulu (in August 1968), the latter a key figure from the increasingly dominant Equateur Province in Mobutu's new governing vehicle, the Mouvement Populaire de la Révolution (MPR), established in May that year. Under these leaders, a "de-Katangization" of the provincial administration was carried out.

Utilizing the Africanist revolutionary rhetoric of this period, the Mobutu regime radically centralized state administration, one element of which was the appointment of provincial governors from other areas. In the late 1960s, Mobutu managed to integrate many important secession-era leaders into his administration, skillfully manipulating the short-termist ambitions of, and divisions among, Katanga's political elite. Political representation was reduced to the (temporary) appointment of prominent individuals from particular regions and provinces to high office, raising expectations that those individuals would in turn direct the resources they controlled and the jobs they oversaw to their area of origin, in classic patrimonial style. All such appointees thereby placed themselves in a "tribalist" trap, in which any independent political assertion was seen as essentially parochial and self-serving. Even the most limited hopes that a degree of Katangan autonomy could be recovered were now dashed.

Mobutu's political centralization went hand in hand with a nationalist economic policy; the Congolese government's lengthy negotiations over its future relationship with Katanga's mining industry, which had appeared close to agreement, were suddenly thrown into turmoil by the unexpected nationalization of UMHK in December 1966, presented by Mobutu as a radical blow to foreign control of Congo's mineral resources. UMHK operations were suspended and a new company that came to be known as Gécamines established in its place.[81] Jean-Baptiste Kibwe, a key figure in the Katanga secession but one who had not joined Tshombe's national government in 1964, was appointed president of the Gécamines council. Kibwe's appointment created an (entirely unjustified) sense that this nationalization reflected Katangese interests, further dividing the (ex-) Katangese political leadership. Gécamines' capacity to initiate a truly "national" policy was, however, dependent on the retention of skilled expatriate employees, on which UMHK operations depended; the new company was similarly incapable of replicating the international marketing operations of Belgian companies. Although Union Minière's name disappeared, it continued to effectively oversee the production, processing, and selling of copper via the Belgian company Société Générale des Minerais.[82]

The special position of Katanga, however, could not be entirely suppressed: some Katangese continued to articulate autonomous aspirations and, for reasons already established, possessed some of the tools to realize them. In the absence of a unified political leadership, such aspirations came to rest primarily on the military force that the secession had brought into existence and which focused on the hope of a second return by Tshombe, who continued to plot his return from exile in Madrid.

The Katangese Gendarmes: Integration and Mutiny, 1965–1967

Following the fall of Stanleyville in 1964, a far larger number of ex-gendarmes (at least 4,350) became part of the 30,000-strong ANC. In addition, at least 6,000 ex-gendarmes were integrated into the "police" force of South Katanga—this force appears to have received military-style training, suggestive of a role involving the authoritarian internal policing of a civilian population regarded as disloyal to Leopoldville.[83] The perpetual reform of the eternally dysfunctional ANC meanwhile entered a new phase, with the Belgian army providing training for 1,800 troops, supported by US funding for equipment.[84] Notwithstanding the ousting of Tshombe, the units of former gendarmes who had returned from Angola in 1964, known as the Baka Regiment of the ANC's 5th Brigade, remained at the uneasy service of the central Congolese state in its ongoing efforts to end the leftist rebellions that continued to challenge its hegemony.

In mid-1966 the ex-gendarmes remained in stand-alone units, with their own commanders. Around 1,000 mercenaries and 3,000 ex-gendarmes were based in the east of Congo, fighting leftist rebels in South Kivu and the outskirts of Stanleyville/Kisangani (the names of some Congolese cities were "Africanized" in July 1966).[85] In this form, they were militarily effective but, for that precise reason, relatively autonomous from central political control. It proved ultimately necessary, therefore, for Mobutu to curtail their capacity on a permanent basis.

Tensions between the ANC and the ex-gendarmes in its midst first came to a head in July 1966, when the units of Colonel Tshipola (roughly 3,000 gendarmes and 240 mercenaries) took control of Kisangani in a military rebellion against the ANC that led to the deaths of Colonel Joseph-Damien Tshatshi (notorious as a leader of the postsecession repression of Katanga in 1963) and other senior ANC officers.[86] It was reported that the gendarmes, who were "technically part of the national Army but [which] have retained their own officers and identity," had not been paid as regular ANC troops had been.[87] In a memo following the uprising, Tshipola not only accused the ANC commander of discrimination in the treatment of the ex-gendarmes, particularly regarding promotions; he also questioned the legitimacy of Mobutu's coup of the preceding November.[88] Although the mercenaries under Bob Denard remained neutral, others took control of Watsa and Isiro, looted banks, and descended on Kisangani. Strengthened by these reinforcements, Tshipola defied the central authorities. Mobutu appealed to Godefroid Munongo to resolve the mutiny in Stanleyville; Munongo was simultaneously approached by the rebels to give them political leadership. Although he refused to provide such leadership, Munongo was nevertheless imprisoned by Mobutu. Attempts at reconciliation failed, and the ANC took military action to defeat the mutiny. On September 23, Kisangani was retaken from the ex-gendarmes, this time with the aid of Denard's mercenaries and to a lesser extent the units commanded by Jean Schramme, which helped disarm retreating gendarmes.

The extent of Tshombe's involvement in this operation—which was evidently poorly prepared—remains uncertain. The recruitment of mercenaries for a new operation to return Tshombe to power had taken place, and the support of the Portuguese government seemed to have been agreed; Congo broke off diplomatic relations with Portugal in October 1966.[89] One reading of these events suggests that Tshombe certainly planned an operation to retake power, with the help of his Katangese army, in Angola and in Congo itself. Documents in the Portuguese archives refer to an Operation Tshombe, in which Tshombe would be transferred to Elisabethville/Lubumbashi in September 1966 with the assistance of Portugal and South Africa; there he would proclaim himself Congolese president.[90] It remains unclear, however, whether the mutiny was the signal to put this plan into effect or an unplanned operation arising from the local grievances of the ex-gendarmes. Tshombe tended not to rely directly on the ex-gendarmes in this period and appears to have preferred European mercenaries—at this time, there was an attempt to recruit and train mercenaries in France in apparent support of his attempt to retake power.[91]

In the wake of these events, a certain number of ex-gendarmes and/or the Katangan police fled to Angola: one of the first groups was led by Pascal Kapend, a police officer during the secession and by this time a security officer in Dilolo; and Antoine Luembe, future chief of staff of the "ex-gendarmes," both of whom entered Angola on May 24, 1967.[92]

Even before these events, the central authorities had hardened their attitude toward Katanga and its political leaders. As noted, Munongo had been placed under house arrest in Kinshasa during the mutiny; he was suspended from his functions on November 4, and these were taken over by the region's military commander, General Massiala. On December 24, Munongo was dismissed as governor of South Katanga. A subsequent parliamentary commission of inquiry found that he had not been involved in any plot but did identify the existence of a network of friends of Tshombe within Katanga. It raised the potential menace emanating from the *police nationale* of Katanga: "For the moment, the ANC authorities fear that the high number of the police (plus or minus 6,000) is positioned as an army, and is composed of many elements which previously served in the gendarmerie of the Katangese secession."[93] In March 1967, the trial in absentia by military tribunal of Moïse Tshombe took place alongside that of Lieutenant Colonel Tshipola. Tshipola, like Tshombe, was condemned to death for his supposed role in the mutiny, as was Captain Kalonda Moanda, accused of killing Colonel Tshatshi; other ex-gendarme officers were given lengthy prison sentences.[94] Thomas Tshombe, brother of Moïse Tshombe (and the future Mwaant Yav), was condemned in his absence to fifteen years in prison for having arranged and secured contacts between the mutineers and the ex-gendarmes in Angola. In addition, the verdict against Tshombe condemned his earlier establishment of an "irregular army," called the "Katangese gendarmerie," constituted of uncontrollable louts and mercenaries recruited principally from South Africa.[95] With this army, the prosecution statement declared, "he proceeded to systematically exterminate the population of North Katanga who were hostile to his authority and [who] opposed the Katangese secession. . . . [T]he bombardment of more than 80,000 refugees in a UN camp was executed on the orders of M. Tshombe after considered thought."[96]

Thus, despite the general amnesty agreed following the Katangese secession, and notwithstanding Tshombe's subsequent position as Congolese prime minister, his actions and those of the ex-gendarmes during the secession were retrospectively criminalized. This remained the official position of the Mobutu regime until its fall in 1997. The Congolese press now spoke of the ex-gendarmes as "mercenaries," making no distinction between them and their mercenary commanders; this misleading conflation would continue in subsequent representations of the gendarmes by the Congolese/Zairian authorities and media for decades to come. Tshombe himself was never to return to Congo; his plane was hijacked and flown to Algiers on June 29, 1967, where he was held in detention and from where he did not return alive.

There is strong evidence that Tshombe was, before his capture, preparing a further operation to retake power, once again supported by the Portuguese authorities in Angola.[97] This operation was to depend on an alliance of Denard and Schramme's mercenary forces, the ex-gendarmes, and on reinforcements to be brought from South Africa by the mercenary Jerry Puren.[98] The conflict that did in fact break out in July 1967 (see below) was, however, sparked by the ANC's plan to dismantle its mercenary units rather than by the capture and jailing of Tshombe. Indeed, the detention of Tshombe should have dissuaded the mercenaries from going ahead, but Schramme decided to proceed with a decidedly adventurous operation to capture the provincial capitals of eastern Congo. This second mutiny accordingly broke out at Bukavu and Kisangani on July 5, 1967, on the anniversary of the death of Colonel Tshatshi. In a broadcast on July 5 declaring a nationwide state of emergency, Mobutu denounced "foreign commandos" who had occupied Kisangani airport, depicting his former mercenary allies as a gang of "Belgians, Spaniards, Frenchmen and Englishmen" who attacked the Congo "in order to make money."[99] The Congolese government used diplomatic channels and the media to characterize the fighting as a foreign intervention, not a mutiny: Mobutu declared that South African former mercenaries "had involved several Katangan gendarmes 'in their adventure, which was as fruitless for them as for their masters.'"[100] At the United Nations, Congo claimed that Belgium, Spain, and Portugal had foreknowledge of the attacks.[101] Three months later Mobutu sought to further boost his Africanist credentials when he unveiled in Kinshasa a monument to the memory of "national hero" Patrice Lumumba, the man who in 1961 he had sent on a plane to his death in Katanga.[102]

The military operation was badly executed by Schramme, who clearly underestimated the capacity of freshly trained units of the ANC, supported in its anti-mutiny operations by US C-130 aircraft.[103] The reinforcements promised by Puren and Denard did not arrive and, despite the presence of 600 "Katangese," Schramme had to evacuate from Kisangani. In retreat, his small army of 300 mercenaries and a few thousand former gendarmes reached Bukavu on August 7–8. There, on August 10, Colonel Leonard Monga was proclaimed as president of an anti-Mobutu "government of public salvation," but this had no practical basis of authority. These forces held Bukavu until November 3, from where they retreated into Rwanda. It was initially proposed that 900 Katangese gendarmes (together with their wives and children) would be evacuated to the now independent state of Zambia under Red Cross auspices.[104] However, Mobutu's insistence that all mercenaries and ex-gendarmes be returned to Congo scuppered this arrangement.[105] Many of this group would eventually find themselves in Angola, either for the first or second time.

Bob Denard's failure to deliver reinforcements was without doubt a result of a change in the position of the French government, which initially expressed private support for the overthrow of Mobutu.[106] He did, however, organize a small diversionary insurgency from Angola at the start of November, named Operation Lucifer. Despite the lukewarm support of Portuguese intelligence for this operation, Denard and his men crossed into Congo by bicycle and reached their target, the Kisenge Manganese company operations, on November 1; there they seized sixteen trucks belonging to the company as transportation. They briefly occupied Kisenge and Mutshatsha (where they tried to recruit additional ex-gendarmes to their cause) before being attacked by the ANC, whose military capacity was on this occasion underestimated by the mercenaries.[107] According to a Katangese member of the expedition, the Portuguese authorities withdrew their support after the mercenaries stole 8 million Belgian francs from the Kisenge Manganese company safe.[108] By November 5, Denard's forces were beating an ignominious retreat into Angola.

Conclusion

Throughout this period, it was possible for Katangese political and military leaders to believe that the fragile Leopoldville-based Congolese state, with its all-too-limited hold on the country's vast territory, could be defeated and that the Katangese nation-state, terminated in 1963, could be revived. Many demobilized Katangese gendarmes, both those taking refuge in Angola and those living in the bush along Congo's borders with Northern Rhodesia / Zambia and Angola, looked to Katangese leaders, particularly Moïse Tshombe, to revive the secessionist project. Certainly, their experience of the Congolese state, and its physical manifestation in the form of the ANC, reinforced the belief that Katanga's integration into Congo represented in effect an occupation by hostile foreign forces.

When Katangese forces were reassembled in mid-1964 under the Congolese premiership of Tshombe, this was understood as a first step toward what they saw as a more just representation of Katanga. Their integration into Congolese national armed forces, always problematic and never complete, anticipated a subsequent rebellion in collaboration with Katangese political leaders, mercenary soldiers, and foreign allies, particularly Portugal. Yet while the ex-gendarmes were consistently ready to rebel against Mobutu-led Congo, the divisions among the Katangese political leadership and (with the exception of Tshombe) their general unwillingness to pursue Katangese independence and/or autonomy via military means rendered any such movement vulnerable to decapitation. When Tshombe was detained by Algeria in 1967, where he died in custody two years later, the ex-gendarmes, now without their political leadership, found themselves marooned in Angolan exile.

It might then have been expected that any further pursuit of a Katangese political project would expire with Tshombe's detention. However, this simply marked the beginning of a much longer-term project of exiled political organization; this would take many forms, both political and military, over the following decades, but would consistently pursue the underlying aim of Katangese liberation.

4 With the Portuguese, 1967–1974

When the former Katangese gendarmes went into Angola for a second time from mid-1967 onward, they had no notion that this exile would last for decades rather than years and that for many of their number it would be a final destination—they would either die there in combat or live out their lives as exiles.[1] Certainly, the retreat into Angola, and the wave of political repression of Katanga and its Lunda population that followed, left the ex-gendarmes and the political movement they problematically represented at a new low. Their inability to define their own future led them to become the most important of the African forces that fought for the Portuguese colonial state against Angolan nationalists, struggling for independence from their own exile in Zaire and Zambia.

The relationship between the Portuguese military and intelligence services, on the one hand, and the ex-gendarmes and their Katangese political allies and leaders, on the other, was a delicate and evolving one. It belies the simplistic characterization of the ex-gendarmes as "guns for hire": their opportunistic relationship with Portuguese colonialism rather enabled them to maintain a limited and decidedly problematic war against the increasingly Mobutu-dominated Zairian state. While this relationship was never one of equals, the ex-gendarmes retained (unlike the better-known Flechas—see below) meaningful if limited autonomy regarding their position in Angola; indeed, conflict periodically arose among their senior officers over the best way to further their aims. Like all the state and nonstate forces that sought to utilize the well-trained and relatively disciplined Katangese forces for their own ends over their lengthy career, the Portuguese found they could not be treated as a blank slate—they had enduring political aims and motivations that shaped their participation in the Angolan nationalist war and their relationship with the colonial state, even if their externally oriented ideological perspective shifted significantly and opportunistically during this period. As the Portuguese military authorities recognized in 1975: "Nobody who pays attention to the politico-military panorama of this area in Africa, more particularly Angola, can deny the importance of [such] a military force: approximately 2500 disciplined men who benefitted from Portuguese commando training, competently accompanied and with several years of war experience. This is reinforced by the fact that, until today, they are sufficiently motivated for maintaining their internal cohesion, for reasons of survival as well as for political reasons."[2]

This relationship, and indeed the composition of the Katangese army-in-exile itself, constantly evolved up until the Portuguese revolution of 1974. The vulnerable "refugees" who arrived in 1967 had high hopes of a rapid return to the Congolese fray and retained strong relationships with the Lunda royal family that, it was hoped, would enable this. However, this was prevented by the capture in 1967 of Moïse Tshombe and his detention in Algeria (where he died in custody two years later) and the loss of mercenary leadership. The arrival in 1968 of Nathanaël Mbumba, one of a group of former Katangese policemen, led ultimately to the severing of the ex-gendarmes' previously vital ties to the linked authorities of the Tshombe family and the Lunda king, the Mwaant Yav. The creation in June 1969 of a new political organization, the National Front for the Liberation of Congo (FLNC), led, on the one hand, to the upgrading of the ex-gendarmes' military capability by greater integration into the Portuguese army and, on the other hand, placed significant control in the hands of Mbumba, its new leader. Mbumba took advantage of his good relations with the Portuguese authorities, who were happy to use his organizational abilities to neutralize the influence of the Tshombe family. Mbumba's vise-like grip on military organization was, however, matched by his inability to establish an effective political body and his consistent refusal to have one foisted on him by any external agency. Having made himself indispensable as the sole authority controlling the ex-gendarmes, Mbumba was then unable to craft and pursue any political program other than the simple takeover of power, whether in Katanga or over Congo as a whole (see below).

Our knowledge of this period rests on a number of sources, most particularly the documents of the Portuguese armed forces and colonial intelligence services. These are supplemented by histories of the Portuguese colonial wars and the memoirs of some protagonists, both Portuguese and Angolan. These are of course sources that tend to reflect one side of this relationship far better than the other, but they provide indirect access to the ideas and aspirations of some Katangese leaders. The authors have also carried out interviews with both FLNC leaders and ex-gendarmes (including Mbumba himself) and Congolese officials from this period. These, together with documents produced by the FLNC itself, provide unprecedented insight into how and why they pursued their problematic alliance with the Portuguese army and intelligence services.

Background: The Portuguese Colonial War

Portugal had since World War II engaged in a rearguard action against both international and local forces for decolonization and self-rule; this authoritarian and relatively poor European power continued (unlike France, Britain, and Belgium) to regard its African colonies as an asset, not a burden. Frustrated nationalists in Angola and Portugal's other African colonies took up arms against their colonial masters. Following separate uprisings in urban and rural areas, Holden Roberto's Union of Peoples of Angola (UPA), operating from a Congolese base, launched a significant incursion into Angola in March 1961, sparking a primarily armed struggle for independence that lasted until the Portuguese revolution of 1974. This was fought both from exile and within Angola: the successor to the UPA, Roberto's Frente Nacional de Libertação de Angola (FNLA), operated across the Congolese border in northern Angola, while the Movimento Popular de Libertação de Angola (MPLA) operated from western Zambia and in neighboring eastern Angola. Jonas Savimbi's União Nacional para a Independência Total de Angola (UNITA), which split from the FNLA-led Govêrno Revolucionário de Angola no Exílo (GRAE) in 1964, operated largely within Angola, though it concluded a nonaggression pact with the Portuguese that lasted until shortly before the Portuguese revolution.[3]

By 1967 the Portuguese anticolonial wars had stretched the financial and demographic limits of this comparatively undeveloped European nation (Portugal was second lowest among European nations in per capita income). The task Portugal faced was enormous: its forces were fighting in three territories that were geographically distant (Lisbon to Luanda is a distance of 7,300 kilometers) and with extensive rural areas advantageous to guerrilla activities. In 1961, at the time of the first major FNLA offensive, the Portuguese army had 79,000 soldiers and an annual budget of US$93 million.[4] Portugal's difficulties were further aggravated by the increasing international illegitimacy of its colonial enterprise. Although Portugal's attachment to its colonies was driven by the genuine contribution they had made to the country's development, the reality was that, when military costs were taken into account, they were a huge drain on its resources.

As the colonial war progressed, military recruitment became increasingly difficult. The Portuguese population was stagnant at around 9 million people, and the nation's lack of development and its authoritarian government led to high emigration. Meanwhile, the wars demanded the acceleration of recruitment by 11 percent per year.[5] The Portuguese Military Academy could not train enough officers, forcing the army to use noncommissioned officers in their place and to abandon seniority as the basis of promotion. These pressures necessitated the recruitment of increasing numbers of various supplementary African forces. Before 1961, 14.9 percent of the Portuguese troops in Angola were African, but this proportion had increased to 42.4 percent by 1973.[6] In Angola, these African forces were of a very diverse nature, as is revealed by identifying them in turn:[7]

1. The Special Troops (Tropas Espeçiais) were composed of former soldiers of Holden Roberto's UPA/FNLA/GRAE who had operated in the Cabinda enclave in the early 1960s. Having defected to the Portuguese, they operated in Cabinda and the northwestern provinces of Uíge and Zaire before being

deployed to the eastern front (see below) in 1966. Their original complement was supplemented by some former members of the MPLA and came to number about 640 men. After Angolan independence in 1975, part of this force was successfully demobilized and the soldiers returned home; another section joined the Cabindan independence movement, the Frente para a Libertação do Enclave de Cabinda (FLEC).

2. The Special Groups (Grupos Espeçiais) were recruited from civilians in eastern Angola, from 1968 onward. They operated in small groups of approximately thirty soldiers, whose overall contingent numbered 3,069 by 1974. They were integrated in the commando forces of the Portuguese for certain operations.[8] Three-quarters were demobilized after 1974; a quarter went to Zaire.

3. The Commandos, also known as the Companhias de Cacadores Espeçiais, were a unit formed primarily for countersubversion or counterguerrilla operations. In Angola they were deliberately drawn from a range of ethnic groups in order to form mixed units.

4. The Flechas, or *fleches noires*, are the most well known of these auxiliary forces: they were "bushmen" who provided tracking skills and used bows and arrows (hence the origin of the name *flechas*, or arrows/black arrows) in their skirmishes with African nationalist forces. They operated in local units under the authority of the Polícia Internacional e de Defesa do Estado (PIDE) secret police, initially tasked with collecting information. However, following the capture and torture of Portuguese agents at Luso in 1967, the Flechas were trained and armed so as to provide a force that could operate behind enemy lines without being easily detected. The Portuguese, profiting from the antagonism between the bushmen and "Bantu" black Africans, organized the former in combat groups and trained them as military commandos. Their number reached 2,270 men.[9] The term *fleches noires* is sometimes incorrectly applied to all "loyalist" African forces, including the gendarmes. After independence, the majority joined UNITA, with around a quarter joining the MPLA.[10]

5. The Loyal (Leais) were political refugees from Zambia, organized militarily by the Portuguese. Their number is estimated at 450 men.[11]

6. The ex-gendarmes were known as the *fideles* or *fiéis* (that is, those who were faithful to their "homeland" of Katanga) and also as the Catangueses. The term *fiéis* was a code name conferred by the Portuguese following their 1970 Operaçao Fidelidade. They were the numerically largest of the "Special Groups" and constituted roughly 28 percent of all auxiliary African troops and 19.7 percent of those in the Eastern Military Zone.[12]

These various African forces were integrated into the overall operational structure in a military strategy adapted to the situation. In the early 1960s, the Portuguese developed a flexible doctrine of counterguerrilla struggle, drawing on the experiences of the British (for example in Malaya and Kenya) and French (in Algeria) colonial systems and their own experience.[13] The doctrine was standardized in the manual *O exército na guerra subversiva*.[14] This placed an emphasis on a decentralized approach, deploying small combat groups and using psychological warfare tactics in ways designed to deter popular support for the guerrilla movements.[15]

However, this doctrine and the structures based on it no longer proved sufficient after 1966, as the operations of Angolan nationalist forces increased in both scale and effectiveness. The MPLA opened its eastern front in April 1966, relocating most of its troops to western Zambia in order to infiltrate Angola across its eastern border. The existing Portuguese military structures, oriented toward the war in the north against the Zaire-based FNLA, struggled to adapt to this new and more substantial threat. The Portuguese also initially underestimated the political work carried out and the military infiltration achieved by the MPLA in eastern Angola.[16] The late 1960s saw the Portuguese military struggle to adjust to this profound challenge; in this context, the presence of the ex-gendarmes from 1967 provided a partial answer to their problems.

The Gendarmes under Portuguese Control, 1967–1969

Immediately after the evacuation of Schramme's troops from Bukavu, a new wave of repression was inflicted by Congolese army forces on both military and civilian Katangese. According to many sources, important leaders of the ex-gendarmes were executed in Kinshasa, Mbandaka, and elsewhere.[17] A small number who managed to flee later became important commanders of the FLNC, among them Vindicien Kasuku Kiyana (a.k.a. Mufu) and Simon Kasongo. This brutal subjugation acquired a central place in the memory of the Tigres in Angola and became a motive for their refusal to accept Mobutu's control of Congo over the next three decades.[18]

From June 1967—as some of their number had done in 1963—ex-Katangese soldiers entered Angola in small groups, principally at Jimbe, at the three-way frontier with Congo and Zambia. They were brought to Caianda and Cazombo. According to PIDE reports, the number of arrivals steadily grew, and the points of entry multiplied over time, as the level of repression in Congo increased. One report in November 1967 mentions the plan of one Colonel Elente, military commander of Kolwezi, to assassinate the Lunda without discrimination, including the family of Tshombe and the Mwaant Yav.[19] On December 11, 1967, the Portuguese Ministry for Overseas Territories officially designated the new arrivals as refugees.[20] They were regrouped in the Gafaria camp (in Cazombo), known as "the first group," with the "second group" in the Camissombo camp (Verissimo Sarmento). In February 1969, the Katangese negotiated the establishment of a headquarters at Chimbila, between Camissombo and Cazombo, where their leadership was henceforth based.

According to archival documents, the Portuguese quickly perceived the dual advantage they were able to gain from the presence of the ex-gendarmes. First, they provided a legitimate (for the Portuguese at least) basis for hostility toward and actions against Mobutu; until the death of Tshombe, the Portuguese hoped to assist in overthrowing Mobutu, whose support for the FNLA was a threat to their continued rule of Angola. Second, it enabled their deployment directly against the MPLA and FNLA. The first of these objectives was paramount in this initial period, while the second was uppermost in the early 1970s.

These two aspects were reflected in the dual management of the Katangese camps. The PIDE managed political and administrative relationships with the *fiéis* (of which more below), while the armed forces handled military operations. These relationships built on the collaboration between the Portuguese and Tshombe's secessionist regime in the early 1960s, when the Portuguese, the Katangese, and their Belgian advisers saw themselves as part of the worldwide struggle against "communist subversion."[21] Pascal Kapend had for example met regularly with PIDE officers in Angola during his time as a Katangese intelligence officer based in Dilolo in 1962–1963.[22]

In the late 1960s, collaboration between the Portuguese and the Katangese forces was focused not on opposition to the Angolan nationalist threat but primarily on the continuing Katangese struggle against the Mobutu regime. Accordingly, the promotion of "liberty" and independence for Katanga was favorably welcomed and supported by the Portuguese.[23] During this period, Mobutu was still consolidating his hold on power, and the Portuguese were keen to assist Katangese efforts to destabilize what they understood as a radical Africanist regime. However, in June 1967, plans to return Moïse Tshombe to power were scuppered by Tshombe's abduction by and detention in Algeria. The Portuguese thereafter sought to establish some form of legitimizing political organization for the Katangese.

Accordingly, in March 1968, the first (and little-known) political organization of the Katangese in exile was created.[24] It was named Fédération Nationale Congolaise (Fénaco). Fénaco's program, which was without doubt written by the Portuguese, presented a program for all of Congo, not only Katanga. It is therefore doubtful whether this program, prepared for propaganda purposes, reflected in a meaningful way the aspirations of the Katangese military forces themselves, but its appeal to Congolese rather than Katangese interests was indicative of the subsequent development and tactics of the FLNC (see below). Fénaco was presided over by Raphaël Lumuna and based in Cazombo. An armed wing, the Armée Secrète de Libération Nationale (ASLN), was also to be established.[25]

At the same time, the Portuguese army cooperated with the ex-gendarmes in carrying out sabotage attacks inside Congo; initially, just one hundred of their number were mobilized in actions in Katanga and Kasai, which had as a secondary aim to disrupt FNLA activities. These initial operations were conducted in small combat groups of around thirty troops each. They had the linked aims of gathering military intelligence, subverting the Mobutu regime, and targeting FNLA guerrillas based in areas bordering Angola.

For the Katangese, combating the FNLA was an extension of their war against the Congolese state. Holden Roberto had undermined efforts to broaden the UPA/FNLA base in Congo among Angolan exiles based in Katanga; instead, the movement remained highly dependent on its close relationship with the Leopoldville authorities.[26] This relationship had been briefly interrupted during Tshombe's Congolese premiership (1964–1965), which was of course unsupportive of the Angolan nationalist cause; but Roberto's position was decisively strengthened by the coming to power of Mobutu and the free hand he granted the FNLA leader to suppress dissent within its diverse ranks.[27] The FNLA did not, however, mount a significant military intervention across the Angolan-Zaire border in the late 1960s or early 1970s, and instead became embroiled in internal Zairian politics. FNLA soldiers who challenged Roberto's leadership were violently suppressed by Zairian troops, and militants of the rival MPLA were detained at the FNLA's Kinkuzu base.[28] In 1971 the Organization of African Unity withdrew its recognition of the FNLA's government-in-exile (GRAE) because of its failure to practically advance the Angolan struggle. Gleijeses suggests that Mobutu's restraint on FNLA activities resulted in part from the potential reprisal threat of the Katangese gendarmes in exile.[29]

The *fiéis* were also mobilized against MPLA forces in eastern Angola (see also below). Most of the MPLA's troops, led by Daniel Chipenda, were from northeast Angola, and a majority were Tshokwe in origin: the historical animosity between Lunda and Tshokwe found expression in local hostility to the *fiéis* and Chipenda's recruitment from this population.[30] The number of ex-gendarmes deployed in these actions was relatively small in relation to their strength (1,130 men at Gafaria, 1,555 at Camissombo), suggesting that they were not designed as an all-out military operation.

Their actions, however, had a destabilizing effect in Congo, especially after Fénaco claimed that some Congolese National Army (ANC) officers were members of this movement. Amid an atmosphere of suspicion, General Massiala, ANC commander in Katanga, was arrested.[31] Customary chiefs in the Sandoa region were likewise arrested because they had in their possession lists of ex-gendarmes.[32]

The primary Portuguese directive setting out the organization and functioning of the Katangese camps was issued in April 1968. It established a formal basis for the presence of the ex-gendarmes within Angola and defined the framework for the management of the camps, based on the aforementioned division of responsibility between PIDE and the armed forces. It was at this time that it was christened Operation Lucifer.[33] However, this formalization of their presence in Angola, despite heralding a much-desired improvement in their abject living conditions, led nevertheless to many desertions and contributed to at least one revolt. Most Katangese remained focused on returning to Congo, both to combat the Mobutu regime and (in a more personal sense) to be reunited with their families. This reflected the substantive differences in perception and approach between the Portuguese and Katangese. The former sought to disrupt Congolese support for Angolan liberation movements, with the military support of the *fiéis*; although they were initially willing to provide limited support to the Katangese "independence" project, the physical overthrow of Mobutu was beyond their capacity or intention, bearing in mind the international opprobrium that would have resulted. The Katangese sought a rapid return to take the fight to the Congolese state; as with other exiled liberation movements of very different political hue, such as the Zimbabwean or South African movements then based in Zambia and Tanzania, tensions between host state and the exiled movement were common. The Katangese were never simply the puppets of the Portuguese, nor indeed of the many other forces that sought to utilize their military capacity in their own interests, during their long history.

The *Fiéis* and the Mwaant Yav

The notion of direct military operations against the Mobutu regime was strongly supported during this period by Lunda royalty. The authority of the Mwaant Yav, the Lunda king, stretches across vast areas of Congo, Angola, and Zambia. His authority is, however, challenged by the Tshokwe, who, as noted in chapter 1, overthrew Lunda supremacy at the end of the nineteenth century. However, Tshokwe history includes instances of both self-assertion against the Lunda and submission to Lunda prestige, with the Tshokwe at times even identifying themselves as Lunda. The authority of the Mwaant Yav is consequently considerable among Angolan Lunda and Tshokwe. Because, as noted, every Mwaant Yav since 1965 has been a brother of Moïse Tshombe, the family was able to retain considerable political influence, albeit in rural rather than urban areas. David Tshombe (Mwaant Yav from 1965), the most militant and well-organized Lunda ruler, apparently remained opposed to President Mobutu until his death in 1973. He and his brother Thomas requested arms from the Portuguese, as well as replenishing the ranks of the *fiéis* with new recruits sent across the border.[34]

Thomas Tshombe unsuccessfully demanded that the Portuguese rehire the mercenary Jean Schramme to improve the training of the Angola-based Katangese forces.³⁵ However, the Mwaant Yav himself, under close surveillance by the Mobutu regime, seemed to think that the moment was not right. The Portuguese, while lacking confidence in Thomas Tshombe's leadership abilities, nevertheless used the Tshombe family members for political propaganda purposes, including distribution of the FLNC pamphlet *Réveil Congolais* in 1971.³⁶ Acting on the authority of the Mwaant Yav and utilizing his networks, Jérôme Nawej and Joseph Kabwit (a former commando and member of the Force Publique who was close to both the Tshombe family and the *fiéis*) traversed Lunda territory to recruit young men to send to Angola to reinforce the ranks of the Katangese.³⁷ The proximity of the Lunda and Tshokwe populations to the Angolan border, as well as the cross-border ties of prominent Lunda families, helps explain their disproportionate representation in the *fiéis*, the composition of which was steadily evolving from that of the more diverse Katangese state army of the early 1960s.

Congo-Zaire under Mobutu, 1967–1974

It is necessary to explain the basis of Mobutu's authority in Congo during this period in order to appreciate the repressive context that drove some southern Katangese into Angola, thereby providing new recruits for the Katangese forces in exile. It must first be recalled that Mobutu's coup of November 1965 was widely welcomed as a solution to the venality and selfishness of civilian politicians during the First Republic.³⁸ Mobutu, supported by the United States, carefully and assiduously incorporated important political forces into his administration. These included prominent Katangese politicians, most of whom proved susceptible to the skillful manipulation of their own rivalries, which allowed Mobutu to incorporate them into the neopatrimonial power structure he constructed in the late 1960s.

The Mobutu regime consolidated its power by first using and then eliminating most of the leading actors of the Katangese secession. Evariste Kimba, briefly Tshombe's replacement as prime minister in 1965, was summarily sentenced on treason charges along with three other ministers in June 1966; all four were executed in front of a vast crowd. The former Katangese finance minister Jean-Baptiste Kibwe was appointed president of the board of directors of the new nationalized mining corporation, Gécomin (later renamed Gécamines), when it was established in January 1967. He was nevertheless arrested in February 1968 and, together with all other Katangese on the Gécomin council, condemned to penal servitude. Godefroid Munongo, who had served in Tshombe's short-lived Congolese government and was subsequently appointed governor of Katanga Orientale Province, was initially left untouched by the Mobutu regime. He was, however, arrested in September 1966 amid rising tension within the Congolese military and, having been deposed from his position as governor, was imprisoned, first on the island of Bula Bemba and then in Kisangani, before being freed in August 1968.[39] According to the testimonies of many former *fiéis*, Munongo had, after Tshombe's detention in Algeria, been approached about taking political charge of the Tigres, but he had refused. He was subsequently reintegrated into public life as the chief of the Bayeke and, in the early 1980s, served as a state commissioner and a member of the ruling party's Central Committee. Men like Kibwe and Munongo were among the first to discover the perpetual insecurity and consequent surrender of autonomy that was intrinsic to membership of the fragile ruling elite of the Second Republic.[40] The one figure who represented a continuing threat to the survival of the Mobutu regime and who therefore could not be successfully incorporated was Moïse Tshombe himself. Tshombe had been tried and sentenced for treason in 1967 in absentia but remained in contact with the gendarmes until he was kidnapped and transported to Algeria. In his absence, it was left to Katanga's military forces, and to the Tshombe family's leadership of the Lunda community, to carry the flame for its legitimacy and (later) for its memory.

As Young and Turner argue, Mobutu's demonization of Tshombe enabled him to build hitherto unlikely (and characteristically cynical) alliances with Lumumbist forces to which he had hitherto been strongly opposed.[41] In the late 1960s, Mobutu showed political aptitude in consolidating his New Regime via administrative reforms that concentrated power first in Leopoldville/Kinshasa and ultimately in the hands of the presidency of which he was the embodiment. As has been well documented, Mobutu successfully incorporated the memory of "national hero" Patrice Lumumba and thereby gained the support of a student movement whose position he considerably advanced; this was dramatically and permanently reversed in 1969 and 1971, when student protests were ruthlessly suppressed. The dominance of Belgian capital was successfully diluted with the entry of new international investors into the Congolese economy. At the end of 1966, apparently successful negotiations with Union Minière regarding reforms to its ownership of mineral resources were suddenly reversed, replaced with the apparent unilateral nationalization of the mines, with the establishment of Gécamines.[42] This decision was substantially revised when it became clear that Congo lacked the means to extract and market its minerals without outside assistance; although this undermined the confidence of some of Mobutu's Western backers, it nevertheless enabled him to present himself as a radical nationalist. This image was reinforced by his sponsorship and support of Holden Roberto's FNLA in its fight against Portuguese colonialism.

Mobutu's authority was consolidated in 1970 with the establishment of his "party," the Mouvement Populaire de la Révolution (MPR), as the central institution of the Congolese state. Party and state bodies became the sole channel of economic development; appointment to such bodies enabled personal enrichment by elites and supported patronage networks that tied many more individuals into a web of loyalties dominated by Mobutu. In the early 1970s, Mobutu sought increased regional influence and a greater international profile. While his new ideology stressed Africanist cultural "authenticity," grandiose development plans were advanced that could be achieved only by mortgaging the country's mineral wealth to external investors. The contradictions between radical rhetoric and reality reached their apex with the Zairianization program of 1973. This, and 1974's "radicalization" program, supposedly sought to place the country's economy in the hands of Zairian citizens, but actually violently disrupted economic activity and investor confidence. By the time these measures had been reversed, the global recession of the mid-1970s had driven up the international price of oil and led to a massive slump in the value of the minerals on which Zaire was economically dependent; these prices did not recover in real terms until the twenty-first century.

A 1972 directive gave the MPR political direction over the armed forces, while a legal change the following year sought to abolish the customary authority of local chieftaincies. A major clash with the established Christian churches over the provision of education and other social services revealed, with Mobutu's retreat, the limits of his ability to turn directives into reality. The new constitution introduced in 1974 made the MPR (of which all Zairians were automatically members) the sole institution vested with political authority. Mobutu was granted unlimited power to change the constitution, and his supposed ideology of "Mobutism" was given constitutional authority.[43] It was at this moment of official supremacy that the practical weakness of the Zairian state was revealed; the humiliation of the country's army in Angola the following year would prove a powerful demonstration of the hollowness of Mobutu's apparent hegemony.

Young and Turner argue that, until this period, Mobutu was largely successful in consolidating the previously fractured governance of Congo/Zaire, and that its weaknesses arose with the overreach of Zairianization, the Angolan invasion, and the global economic crisis from 1974.[44] Mobutu's apparently successful consolidation of his predatory rule in the country's peripheral rural areas in the late 1960s was achieved partly by the use of terror, but also by the integration of most provincial and ethnic identities into the political symbolism of his unitary, Lingala-speaking regime. However, Swahili-speaking Katanga was, as a result of its distinctive history and development and the memory of the secession, qualitatively different from the rest of Congo in this regard.

Regionalism and Ideological Opposition to Zaire

The failed integration of the Katangese gendarmes into the ANC in 1963 and the continued failure to fully integrate those gendarmes who returned to Congo from Angola in 1964 created an atmosphere of mutual distrust and suspicion that led to conflict between these forces and the Congolese army in 1966 and 1967. These military tensions reflected the wider failure to achieve the effective incorporation of postsecession Katanga into the Congolese state, perpetuated by the physical presence of the ex-gendarmes. While, as noted, some prominent secessionist leaders were temporarily incorporated into the New Regime after 1965, the underlying forces—economic, social, and cultural—that had created the circumstances for autonomy remained in place. As has already been indicated, the Lunda royal establishment, now dominated by the Tshombe family, continued to resist political centralization of the state and the negation of chiefly authority. The U Thant Plan's proposed fifty-fifty division of mining revenue between Katanga and the central government was never realized; while the province's mining industry, increasingly focused on Kolwezi rather than Elisabethville/Lubumbashi, boomed in the ten years following the end of the secession, the revenue it generated went directly to and underwrote an extraordinarily centralized Kinshasa-dominated Congolese state, just as Conakat's leaders had once feared. Although southern Katanga's towns expanded rapidly, their growing population—mirroring urbanization elsewhere in postcolonial Congo/Zaire—found few opportunities for formal employment in an increasingly mechanized mining industry. Rural southern Katanga remained, not without good reason, under constant suspicion of harboring opposition to the Mobutu regime. The consequent repression of southern Katanga in general, and the Lunda in particular, which began with the ANC's occupation in 1963, continued under Governor Jean-Foster Manzikala from 1967 and involved periodic violence against the Lunda over the next decade. This repression fueled local sympathy for the exiled gendarmes' resistance to Mobutu's rule, which in turn fed paranoia about Lunda disloyalty in a destructive cycle of repression and nascent revolt.

The Zairian state's concern about the regional threat posed by both internal and external Katangese resistance is suggested by the extent of the politico-military repression of the province, but also by the periodic attempts by the Mobutu government to make contact with and neutralize the *fiéis*. Mobutu took the menace of the Katangese presence in Angola extremely seriously, but he was not consistent in his response to this threat. In 1970 alone this took three, arguably contradictory, forms: attempts by Congolese officials to enter into direct negotiations with the ex-gendarmes; the reinforcement of Congolese troops on the Angolan frontier (at Dilolo, Kisenge, and Luashi) in advance of that year's presidential election campaign; and the offer of an amnesty by Mobutu.[45]

The Katangese under Mbumba, 1969–1973

From 1969, the growing effectiveness of the MPLA's operations necessitated a change in the operational practice of the *fiéis*. From 1971, their military operations were integrated into Portugal's Eastern Military Zone, although their political operations continued to be coordinated with the PIDE, renamed the Direcção Geral de Segurança (DGS) in 1969. In April 1969, it was decided to develop the organization of the *fiéis*, whose command was moved to the new Chimbila camp established in 1970; most of the decisions taken at this time were, however, implemented only in 1971, a delay that led to an internal revolt in January 1970. Finally, as the Lunda royal establishment had urged, a higher level of military instruction was provided; and the *fiéis* were given salaried employment from May 1971, something that distinguished them from most other African forces fighting for Portugal in Angola.[46] Some Katangese troops were permitted to bring family members across the border to reside with them. Support was also provided in establishing a more permanent political body, presented as a government in exile. However, this was to prove a decidedly Faustian pact—the price of increased military effectiveness and conditions was closer integration into Portugal's colonial armed forces and a reduced focus on their war against Mobutu. The ex-gendarmes' relationship with their Portuguese masters is usefully summarized in the following PIDE statement of June 1969: "In addition to the need to improve their living conditions, including the arrival of their families, it is essential to make them understand their status as refugees, and to make it clear to them that we cannot by any means support a political and military adventure in Katanga without it being useful to our own policy. . . . [W]ithout this we will be in difficulty in our own fight against subversion."[47]

Tshombe's death in Algiers in June 1969 was preceded by the appointment as the *fiéis*' chief of staff of the man who would be the most important leader of the Katangese forces over the next decade. Nathanaël Mbumba, one of a number of Katangese policemen who left for Angola in 1967–1968, lacked historical roots in the gendarmerie, though not in the secession (see below). It was partly for this reason that he was able to take the *fiéis* in a new political direction, away from the project of reviving the Katangese secession. Mbumba transformed the *fiéis* into a significant military force and established a basic political platform that achieved limited autonomy from the Portuguese military, notwithstanding Mbumba's ultimate dependence on them for his authority. This was symbolized in the name of the political organization he led and indeed dominated, the FLNC.[48]

Mbumba proved to be a perfect instrument for Portuguese efforts to mobilize the Katangese more effectively against the Angolan liberation movements. He understood that the Portuguese could help him to realize his personal ambitions, but this necessitated a rupture with the Mwaant Yav and the Tshombe family and the revival of the secession. Unsurprisingly, documents in the PIDE archives show that the Tshombe family opposed the closer alignment of the *fiéis* with the Portuguese and their war against Angolan nationalists.[49] This rupture pleased the Portuguese, since they no longer had to manage a problematic alliance with a powerful royal figure based in a foreign nation-state. Mbumba's break with Lunda royal authority would ultimately lead him, during the first Shaba war of 1977, to attack the Lunda queen mother in an attempt to capture the *lukanu*, or symbol of traditional power. Mbumba had by that time enlarged his ambition from being a leader of an armed force capable of toppling Mobutu, or at least reestablishing the secession, to himself becoming the Mwaant Yav.[50]

Mbumba was born in the Mwaant Yav's Lunda capital, Musumba, on January 5, 1940.[51] A Methodist, he started secondary school at Mulungwishi but did not complete his studies. During the secession he was a police subcommissioner in Kolwezi. He also headed the Lunda cultural association, Gassomel, in Kolwezi. In 1964 he was appointed chief police commissioner in Lualaba Province.[52] In 1966 he was transferred to Dilolo.[53] According to his testimony, Mbumba opposed Governor Manzikala's development of the provincial section of the "thuggish" Corps des Volontaires de la République (CVR), the forerunners of the Jeunesse de Mouvement Populaire de la Révolution (JMPR), the youth wing of Mobutu's ruling party, and claims to have liberated people detained by the CVR. Mbumba claims that this put him in conflict with Manzikala and led him to go into exile in Angola.[54]

Mbumba, while at times an advocate of Katangese secession, later came to see himself as a potential future president of Congo. Like many Congolese politicians, Mbumba attributed his political calling—in retrospect, admittedly—to a religious experience, a dream incorporating both Christian and military elements:

> Before I went to Angola, I had a vision. . . . I was asleep. I was in the Catholic Church. Me, I am Protestant but I was in a Catholic Church. The one who was preaching was the Pope, surrounded by many Monsignors. After the Mass, they started to distribute the vestments, the ballots. . . . But when it came to me, I saw a Monsignor who came with many keys. Amongst the keys he had one large key, he said to me, "Take this." Me. I looked at him but [said, "W]hy give me the keys, to [do] what with them?" I saw the others with the vestments. My intention was to also receive the habits. The Monsignor demanded of me, "Nathanaël!" three times. I looked at him, he turned around. The Pope came himself. He called me "Nathanaël!" "Lord!" I went down on my knees. He took the keys. He said to me "Take them. Take them to your breast." Two times! "You have only need of vestments? Look at the habits they have received." I looked at the others: in torn shirts.
>
> > "You know what this is?"
> > I said "Lord."
> > "It is the strength of the country."
> > I woke up.

[That was the f]irst day. [On the s]econd day:
I was in military dress. Me, I was in the police [in reality], but I was in military uniform [in the dream]. There were officers that saluted me and showed me respect.
I woke up. This was the decision to go to Angola.[55]

Nathanaël Mbumba crossed the Angolan border on his own initiative, probably in January 1968, without having the explicit authorization of the Mwaant Yav. He succeeded nevertheless in being named the commander in chief of the new FLNC. According to many interviewees, it was the preponderance of former police officers (like himself) among senior ranks of the movement that explained his selection, in preference to the highest-ranked officer, Lieutenant Colonel Jean-Beauvin Kalenga, a senior ex-gendarme. In fact, seven former gendarmes and four former policemen were present at the meeting where Mbumba was confirmed in this position. It is equally likely that the Portuguese authorities provided decisive support for Mbumba's candidacy. However, claims in this regard are based more on Mbumba's subsequent decisions than on evidence from this period. Kalenga was more or less marginalized from this time, before reappearing later in the 1978 Shaba war as chief of command. For a good understanding of subsequent events, above all the factional struggles for authority that subsequently developed, the military hierarchy of *fiéis* officers already in place at the time of Mbumba's selection as commander in chief needs to be identified:

Lieutenant Colonel: Jean-Beauvin Kalenga
Majors: Jean-Delphin Muland, Stéphane Lubange, Nathanaël Mbumba
Captains: Antoine Luembe, Pierre Kazadi Cobra
Lieutenant: Vénance Yolhamu
Adjutant: Georges Nawezi.[56]

Within this hierarchy, military and political organization remained divided: the military organization was at this time known as the so-called Secret Army of National Liberation, run by Kalenga. Political activity was carried out by the executive committee, run by Mbumba.

Military Training and Deployment, 1971–1974

The Portuguese insisted on preparatory political work being carried out in Congo before the FLNC's new military activities were launched. While this was perhaps necessary, it also reflected a (partly concealed) aim of delaying any new attack on the Mobutu regime. PIDE continued to organize political work, including the printing and distribution of *Le Réveil Congolais*. The military activities of the *fiéis*, however, were increasingly directed against nationalist "subversion" within Angola rather than action inside Congo/Zaire. During the long wait for an opportunity for such action, Mbumba, with commando training provided by the Portuguese, formed the *fiéis* into an efficient and powerful army that was firmly under his dictatorial control.

Once installed in command, facing multiple desertions and low morale, Mbumba installed an iron organizational discipline on the *fiéis*. Simultaneously, however, he made great efforts to improve their living conditions, which were described in the following manner by one Portuguese officer: "They live with their families in a practically primitive fashion, refusing to be integrated (into the colonial army), hoping always to return to their country of origin."[57]

Mbumba successfully negotiated with the Portuguese to improve their supplies and pay. Whereas the Katangese troops had previously been paid only during military operations on a daily rate, from November 1970 they received a monthly salary; this was increased in May 1971. Most importantly, from March 1971 until 1974 they received commando training in the Chimbila and Camissombo camps. In total, commando training was delivered to fourteen companies, each led by an officer, several of whom (like Vindicien Kiyana "Mufu") would play an important role in the subsequent history of the FLNC. It was this training that led to the adoption of the name Tigres—granted by the Portuguese to each company as it completed commando training—the designation by which the Katangese troops would subsequently become known.[58]

From February 1971, the *fiéis* were officially integrated into Portugal's "irregular" or "auxiliary" forces. In charge of training in Camissombo was Captain Elísio de Carvalho Figueiredo, who became the *fiéis*' most trusted Portuguese officer and who would play a key role in arranging their alliance with the MPLA in 1974–1975.[59] They nevertheless retained considerable autonomy within the Portuguese colonial armed forces. Their primary objective, to retake power in Katanga and if possible all of Zaire, remained a permanent source of tension with the Portuguese colonial authorities; as always, the Katangese refused to become simply the passive tool of their political masters. It is possible that this is the reason the *fiéis* are barely mentioned in the wider literature in the eastern war against the MPLA and UNITA.[60] It is nevertheless clear that, according to documents in the PIDE and Ministry of Defense archives, the *fiéis* participated in many raids against the MPLA in the early 1970s. Accounts also confirm their involvement in protecting the operations of the diamond mining company Diamang, in the Dundo region.[61] According to Colonel Almeida Santos, liaison officer with the *fiéis*, they provided security against nationalist attacks on road construction equipment and operations.[62]

Portuguese commanders nevertheless firmly resisted requests by the *fiéis* for heavier armaments than their guns and light mortars, fearing this could lead to direct military action against Zaire, something the Portuguese now clearly opposed. As well as increasing criticism of Portugal in international diplomatic circles, any such armament and operation would have made it more difficult to control the *fiéis* politically and militarily.[63] As we shall see, uncannily similar issues would arise in relations between the *fiéis* and Angolan and Cuban officers after the Angolan war for independence.

Mbumba was certainly not passive in the face of Portuguese authority: he wrote detailed entreaties to senior Portuguese officials, seeking a greater role for his forces in the struggle against Angolan nationalists. He highlighted the threat posed by Chinese assistance to Mobutu and the FNLA, but also the potential weaknesses of the Mobutu regime and its vulnerabilities in Katanga.[64] In hindsight, however, it can clearly be seen that the price paid for Mbumba's successful efforts to ameliorate the condition of his forces was their uncritical deployment in the Portuguese war against the Angolan liberation movements. Certain officers, such as Kalenga and David Mwakasu, were not in agreement with this approach.[65]

The leadership of Mbumba was nevertheless arguably profitable in the medium term. He was able to transform the *fiéis*, turning a disparate group composed of ex-gendarmes, police, and newer recruits, into a real army. In this he was also aided by a visit to Portugal in June 1972, from which he returned having negotiated a more senior position with the Portuguese authorities. He obtained the promise of new recruitment and better-trained military staff. Having severed links with the Lunda royal establishment and the Tshombe family, Mbumba now imprisoned Joseph Kabwit, the envoy of the Mwaant Yav.[66]

In many respects, Mbumba's exercise of authority in the FLNC mirrored that of his enemy and the man he sought to replace, President Mobutu. A speech of welcome after his return from Portugal in July 1972 used the same slogans as the MPR.[67] Mbumba signed letters with his "authentic" African names, exactly in the style of the MPR of the time: "Nathanaël Mbumba Mwizi-Kicha Kalal Pa Mbal Wa Mwanza." All witnesses attest to his authoritarianism and his suspicion of "intellectuals" and, indeed, anyone more educated than him; he was intolerant of anything that threatened his monopoly of power. This explains why, for example, a political official such as Raphaël Lumuna, previously the leader of Fénaco and more highly educated than Mbumba, was imprisoned from 1971 to 1976.[68] This attitude arose partly from Mbumba's failure to give the FLNC a coherent political framework: never, in effect, did the *fiéis* possess a leadership capable of making substantial political dividends out of their undoubted military strength. Although Mbumba was an excellent organizer and militarily courageous, his narrow political vision ultimately prevented the FLNC posing a credible bid for political power in Congo.

The FLNC certainly struggled to turn its feared military capacity into political influence and effectiveness *within* Congolese/Zairian borders. It may be compared instructively in this regard to the People's Revolutionary Party (PRP) of Laurent Kabila, constructed out of the remnants of the CNL.[69] The PRP was created in 1967 as a Marxist-inspired guerrilla movement; it utilized a cross-border hinterland in Tanzania that was vital to its survival. Despite its radical identity, the PRP offered no substantial military threat to the Congolese authorities, but this did not prevent it ultimately providing the basis for Laurent Kabila's "leadership" of the AFDL in the mid-1990s. The PRP's microstate, in an economically marginal border region, represented little threat to the Kinshasa authorities and could therefore be tolerated. In contrast, the strategic importance of the southern Katangese mining industry meant that antiregime threats had to be repressed insofar as was possible and restricted to the ex-gendarmes' presence in Angola.

The Angolan War in the Early 1970s

By the late 1960s, the actions of the MPLA and UNITA had achieved an impressive expansion of the territory under their control or influence. By December 1970, this had been expanded to the whole of the province of Moxico, a large part of Cuando Cubango, part of Lunda Sul, and the eastern part of Bié Province. In response, the Portuguese armed forces developed a new concept of war against "subversion" in 1968. It combined a more flexible territorial division, a more integrated command, and significant psychological activity. It was not, however, fully implemented until the arrival, in May 1970, of Costa Gomes, the new commander in chief of Portuguese forces in Angola. Costa Gomes fundamentally modified the Portuguese military structure and withdrew some elements of the military doctrine formulated in 1963. A decentralized structure was also put in place for the Eastern Military Zone under the command of General Bettencourt Rodrigues. Thanks to a series of integrated operations, involving all the Portuguese and auxiliary units, the area of nationalist operations in the east was reduced. The Portuguese offensive utilized all the military actions at its disposal, including the use of defoliants and the forcible relocation of at least one million people into *aldeamentos* or "protected villages."[70]

Three years later, the nationalist presence had been reduced to a small frontier zone between Zaire, Zambia, and Angola held by the MPLA, as well as an area controlled by UNITA southwest of Luso. The Portuguese army's limited resources were used in an appropriately parsimonious way, flexible and adapted to the situation at the time. This was arguably the sole reason for the prolongation of the war. According to Daniel Chipenda, the MPLA's eastern front commander, in August 1974: "For us, the crisis of the Eastern Front began toward the end of 1968, when the Portuguese colonists began a new strategy against our forces. The offensive started in September 1968 with an action combining aerial forces (reconnaissance planes, bomber planes, transport planes, helicopters and parachutists), marine territorial forces, special groups (Angolan military special forces), special troops (Angolan troops of the second line) and the militias of the PIDE. When they started the scorched earth strategy, they formed the barrage on [the] Eastern plateau and practiced a psychosocial politics of recovery at all levels."[71]

Frustration at these military setbacks, coupled with the fissiparous tendencies inherent in the Angolan exile movements (and indeed in exile movements in general), led to splits in the MPLA. It is important to recall the military weakness of the MPLA at this time in order to understand the conflicts within the movement: Chipenda himself, following this split, ultimately took most MPLA troops into the FNLA. This, coupled with UNITA's nonaggression pact with the Portuguese, left the MPLA at a substantial military disadvantage in the subsequent conflict to decide who would rule independent Angola.

Conclusion

In highly unpromising circumstances, the exiled Katangese forces carved out for themselves a significant military role in Portugal's war against Angolan nationalist forces. While this certainly involved a degree of mercenary activity, it also enabled a continuation of the secessionist project from exile—with support from the Mwaant Yav and the Tshombe family inside Congo—until Moïse Tshombe's death in Algeria. The leadership of Mbumba and the conversion of the secessionist ex-gendarmes into an effective army-in-exile significantly altered the dynamic of the FLNC's opposition to the Zairian state. This reorientation improved the conditions of the *fiéis* and made them a more effective fighting machine but reduced their direct links to Katanga. The ex-gendarmes remained alive as a politico-military force but were arguably less directly oriented on their political aims, preoccupied as they were with the anticolonial war in Angola, in which they served with some distinction.

Although the prolonged war was a military victory of sorts for the Portuguese, they were simultaneously losing the political conflict. The colonial ideal, linked closely to the "New State" of António de Oliveira Salazar, was increasingly unpopular among young officers. They found themselves confronted on one side by older officers who blocked their promotion, and on the other by a necessary softening of recruitment standards that reduced their status. Prompted by the growing social and economic crisis, to which the Marcelo Caetano regime responded with an authoritarian attitude, left-wing officers formed the Armed Forces Movement (MFA). The crisis reflected discontent regarding the commitment of ever more Portuguese resources in the prolonged colonial war, which had successfully reversed nationalist gains in Angola but failed to do so in Guinea-Bissau and Mozambique. The end came in April 1974, when the MFA put an end to the Caetano regime and (as a result) the alliance between the dying Portuguese colonial system and the FLNC. The Portuguese revolution, which threatened the very existence of the Katangese exile movement, led instead to a new politico-military alliance that helped bring the MPLA to power and that laid the groundwork for the FLNC's most effective military action against Zaire.

Colonel Guy Weber and Katangese gendarmes, June 1961. Courtesy of JP Sonck.

Moïse Tshombe and Lieutenant General Norbert Muke, September 1961. Courtesy of JP Sonck.

Katangese gendarmes in Kongolo, November 1961. Courtesy of JP Sonck.

Nathanaël Mbumba (slightly off to the right, in light-colored shirt) and, to his left, Albert Onawelho and Justin Mushitu, with others, Angola, October 1975. Courtesy of JP Sonck.

Mbumba inspects his *fiéis* troops, undated but circa 1976. Courtesy of Justin Mushitu.

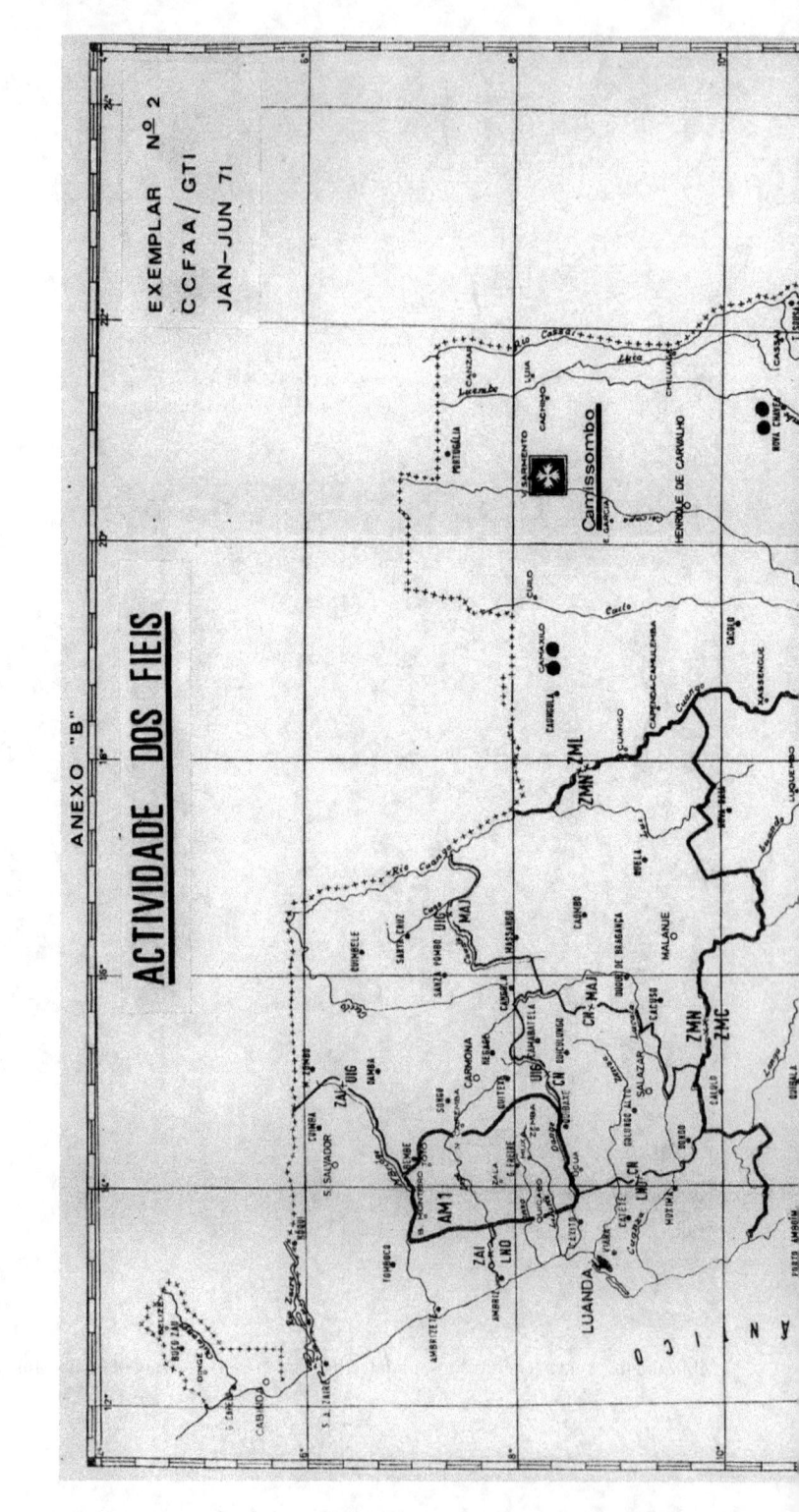

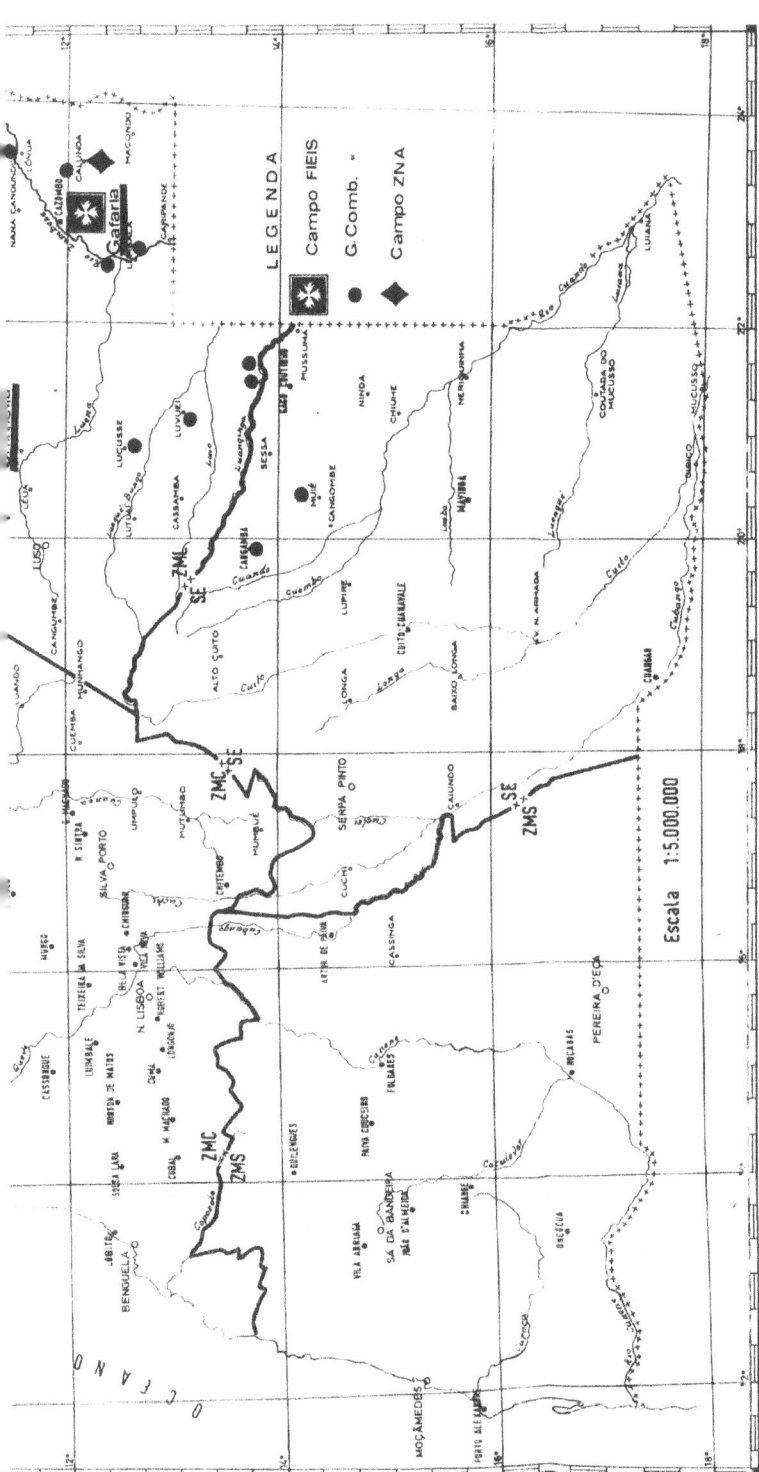

Portuguese military map showing activities of *fiéis*, January–June 1971. Courtesy of Arquivo Historico Militar.

Nguz Karl I Bond (second from left) with Justin Mushitu (left, semivisible), Maurice Bendera, and Vindicien Kiyana "Mufu" (right). Courtesy of Justin Mushitu.

Nathanaël Mbumba (right) and Mwaant Yav Kawel, Sovereign National Conference, Kinshasa, 1992. Courtesy of Henri Mukachung.

Ex-Tigres in Viana, Angola, 1991. Courtesy of JP Sonck.

Generals Simon Kasongo (left) and Stany Kalala, 1992. Copyright SONUMA, from documentary "Ailleurs au Congo. Les orphelins du Katanga"; RTBF, Brussels, 1992.

Deogratias Symba (in civilian clothes, left) and Irung a Wan (right), with Katangese ex-Tigres, 1997. Courtesy of Deogratias Symba.

5 The Katangese Gendarmes in the Angolan Civil War, 1974–1976

The position in Angola of the ex-Katangese gendarmes, politically organized as the FLNC and now known as the Tigres, was inevitably transformed by the Portuguese coup of April 1974. Their effectiveness in the cause of Portuguese colonialism counted for nothing—was, indeed, a potential liability—in a political environment that threatened to leave them without sponsorship or support. However, the FLNC, under the last vestiges of departing Portuguese tutelage, now entered into a new and surprising alliance with the MPLA, one of the Angolan nationalist groups against which it had previously fought on behalf of the Portuguese. The FLNC's demonstrative ability to change sides in a conflict commonly constructed as an ideologically based battle within the wider Cold War not only demonstrates the limited relevance of such a framework for the Tigres themselves but also casts doubt on the ways in which the Angolan "civil war" is commonly imagined, suggesting that such political affiliations were of far less importance than the ability of each side to establish military superiority by whatever means.

The Tigres played a significant but underreported role in aiding the MPLA's ultimate victory in the Angolan conflict. Building on Gleijeses's work showing the belated (though ultimately vital) intervention of Cuban forces in this conflict, this chapter demonstrates that one of the more important ways in which the MPLA's military weakness was initially addressed was via the mobilization of FLNC forces in the military confrontations that took place in 1975.[1] Although the still patchy evidence available limits the claims that can be made in this regard, it is increasingly clear that this war in Angola was fought to a large extent by foreign forces, with "Zairians" active on both sides.

The undeniable military utility of the FLNC's forces, demonstrated once again in this phase of their existence, can lead to their characterization as an empty mercenary vessel, vulnerable to political manipulation and willing to sign up to whatever cause would pay their wages and provide them with weaponry. While the alliance with the MPLA was certainly one of convenience, the FLNC demanded and received explicit support from the MPLA for their primary goal, the toppling of the Mobutu regime in Zaire, in the form of the Cossa Accords (see below). The military and political victory of the MPLA, achieved with the support of the FLNC, not only represented a military defeat and political humiliation for Mobutu; it also placed the Tigres in a far more powerful position to weaken and potentially destroy their Zairian enemies.

Background: The Portuguese Revolution and Its Consequences for Angola

The so-called Carnation Revolution of April 25, 1974, fundamentally and irrevocably changed the future of Angola and that of the ex-gendarmes and other Katangese exiles, now organized into the FLNC and led by Nathanaël Mbumba. When a grouping of young Portuguese officers called the Armed Forces Movement (MFA) overthrew the Caetano regime, General António de Spínola (whose book *Portugal and the Future*, published in February of that year, had provided a powerful critique of the country's colonial policy) became president of a provisional government, the "junta of national salvation."[2] On May 16, a provisional government was installed as a parallel structure to the junta. The MFA was fully committed to the withdrawal of Portuguese forces from the country's overseas territories and to a negotiated but rapid end to colonialism. Although not initially persuaded of the need for immediate decolonization, Spínola declared in a televised broadcast on July 27 that Portugal's colonies would be given total independence.[3]

The MFA was a movement explicitly of the Left, nonpartisan but influenced by Portugal's hitherto repressed socialist and communist parties, and found itself in unavoidable confrontation with the Salazarist military old guard. During the remainder of 1974, revolutionary forces pushed Portuguese politics to the left, although not without considerable resistance and occasional reverses by the MFA's liberal-reformist opponents. Ironically, given the desire of most Portuguese actors to rapidly end colonialism, the domestic Portuguese political context continued to shape the competition for power in Angola, influencing the outcome of the civil war that culminated in the MPLA's victory in November 1975, an outcome that had critical consequences for the FLNC. Portugal's new rulers, if they wished to be consistent, had little choice but to establish interim structures to govern the country's colonies until the handover of power.

Elsewhere in Portugal's African empire, the Partido Africano da Independência da Guiné e Cabo Verde (PAIGC) in Guinea-Bissau and the Frente de Libertação de Moçambique (Frelimo) in Mozambique had established themselves as dominant revolutionary guerrilla movements and thereby achieved a relatively unproblematic accession to power. In Angola, however, three movements were in fairly open competition, and no neutral interlocutor existed to oversee the handover of power. Notwithstanding their frequently expressed commitment to cooperation in the national interest, each movement (but particularly the FNLA) had previously attacked its nationalist rivals, and in the case of UNITA cooperated with the pre-1974 Portuguese military.[4] While Spínola and other moderate Portuguese figures sought to exclude the communistic MPLA from power, leftists within the MFA sought to strengthen its hand in negotiations. In the event that these negotiations failed, this leftist group sought to ensure that the MPLA was well positioned in any ensuing military conflict .

By the end of April 1974, the MFA had created a "committee of representation," or cabinet, in Luanda, led by Brigadier Pedro Pezarat Correia; this radical officer helped create the conditions in which negotiations with the three liberation movements would take place.[5] In July 1974, the Junta Governativa para o Estado de Angola was established under the presidency of Vice Admiral António Alva Rosa Coutinho, a member of the Portuguese junta. Rosa Coutinho sought to transfer what he saw as the positive achievements of the Portuguese revolution to Angola itself, drawing on his extensive experience in Africa.[6] Rosa Coutinho had in 1960 participated in the evacuation of Portuguese and Belgian refugees from Matadi during Congo's postindependence crisis. In 1961, as part of a Portuguese contact mission that obtained a navigation agreement with Congo, he was briefly imprisoned by the Congolese authorities and accused of espionage.[7] He had then made his career in Mozambique before his appointment in Angola in 1974.

Although never a Communist Party member, Rosa Coutinho clearly had left-wing sympathies (he was known as the "red admiral"), the extent of which were perhaps not fully appreciated by Spínola.[8] Rosa Coutinho, along with many colleagues, believed that the MPLA had the greatest number of trained and competent cadres and was best placed to govern an independent Angola.[9] He later publicly explained his aim to prevent Angola being dominated by a coalition of a Spínola-dominated Portugal, former agents of PIDE, and the Salazar state, in conjunction with President Mobutu.[10] Most of all, he feared that any MPLA disadvantage would allow President Mobutu, together with the FNLA, to take power and ultimately "Mobutize" Angola.[11] Rosa Coutinho was supported in his efforts by Pezarat Correia and by José Emilio da Silva, the MFA representative in the Junta Governativa.[12]

As should already be clear, the period from July 1974 until Angolan independence in November 1975 saw the creation of many supposed governing institutions.[13] A provisional Angolan government was created in September 1974, hierarchically subordinate to the junta headed by Rosa Coutinho. This structure was somewhat simplified in November 1974 with the creation of a new provisional government under interim high commissioner Rosa Coutinho.[14] With the resignation of General Spínola on September 30 (amid the general radicalization of Portuguese political life), the MFA was better placed to execute rapid decolonization.[15] Spínola was succeeded by General Francisco da Costa Gomes, who had himself been military commander of Angola from May 1970 to

August 1972.[16] The MFA, supported by Rosa Coutinho, now accelerated the decolonization of Angola and established structures in the Portuguese army to bring this about.[17]

UNITA and the MPLA had agreed to de facto cease-fires with the Portuguese in June and July 1974, respectively. The FNLA moved its forces from Zaire into Angola in August and September; by the time it signed its cease-fire on October 12, it had established a considerable military presence in the northwest of the country.[18] Subsequent negotiations led to the Alvor summit in January 1975, where accords were signed creating a transitional government designed to be in charge of the country until independence, the date for which was fixed as November 11, 1975.[19] It was also agreed at Alvor that a national Angolan army would be created out of 8,000 men from each of the three nationalist organizations; it was an agreement that inevitably highlighted the issue of non-Angolan military forces such as the Tigres (see below).[20]

In line with the Alvor agreement's de facto exclusion of all irregular forces, a process began to disarm the Tigres, starting at a rate of 200 men per day and ending in mid-March 1975.[21] However, because it was feared that their dispersal would place them at the disposal of competing liberation movements, a "survival allowance" was to be paid to them for the following six months.[22] As a consequence of the Portuguese revolution, the Tigres were disoriented about their own uncertain future. Although the Portuguese initially retained their military capacity, once the three liberation agreements officially suspended armed activity by November 1974, this capacity served no ostensible purpose. They were reclassified against their wishes as "political refugees."[23] They nevertheless hid many of their weapons and, as we shall see, were probably rearmed by other Portuguese officers. Even before the Alvor agreement was signed, Rosa Coutinho and Captain Elísio de Carvalho Figueiredo—the man who had given commando training to the Katangans and whom they trusted more than anyone else—had maneuvered to create an alliance between the Tigres and the MPLA.

The Angolan Nationalist Movements in 1974–1975

November–December 1974 was a crucial period of positioning, as the three liberation movements sought to reinforce themselves politically and militarily. The issues and stakes involved in Angolan decolonization were far wider than simply Angolan and Portuguese "national" interests; its outcome was of relevance to bordering countries (such as Zaire, Zambia, Rhodesia, and Congo-Brazzaville), much of central and southern Africa (South Africa and its colony Namibia, and Tanzania, for example), and the superpowers and their Cold War allies. This problematic context, together with divisions among Portuguese authorities amid the collapse of colonial authority, had the effect of undermining any potential cooperation between the Angolan movements and instead fixed them in their confrontational militarized positions. Partly as a result, no party—Portuguese, Angolan, or other—could gain effective control over the course of events. The three liberation movements, suddenly faced with establishing a meaningful legal presence inside Angola, were generally unprepared for an unexpected and sudden transition to self-government. Each was in general less concerned with strengthening its support among the Angolan population than with mobilizing external assistance and military force as the means to take power. Each, however, relied on a strong internal ethnoregional base whose support it could claim or at least assert. The FNLA remained under the direction of an authoritarian leader, Holden Roberto, whose unwillingness to break from his Bakongo base (only 15 percent of the indigenous Angolan population) and Zairian patronage made him a deeply problematic prospect as a national leader.[24] This did not prevent the FNLA making substantial military advances in late 1974, supported by the Zairian armed forces. UNITA, which drew its support largely from the Ovimbundu, had the advantage of a consistent internal presence but was militarily weak and compromised by its collaboration with the Portuguese.[25] Nevertheless, not having mounted effective military action for more than five years, UNITA found itself over the next twelve months the subject of patronage and support from Zaire, Zambia, the United States, and South Africa.

The MPLA, with support among the Mbundu and the mestizo population, was ideologically aligned with the leftist parties coming to power elsewhere in Lusophone Africa and had some support from more radical African regimes. It also had considerable intellectual and organizational capacity, and was probably the most widely recognized nationalist organization across the country. Led by Agostinho Neto, the MPLA enjoyed the sympathies of the MFA and officials such as Rosa Coutinho, but Neto's relations with the Soviet Union were, Shubin suggests, in a poor state at the time of the Portuguese revolution.[26] It was also both politically divided and militarily weak. A Brazzaville-based leftist faction of the MPLA, Revolta Activa, criticized Neto's "undemocratic" leadership, but the main threat came from its military leadership.[27] Daniel Chipenda, who had been the eastern front commander since 1966, had been in open conflict with Neto since 1972, and the prospect of political victory now brought this conflict to a head.[28] An MPLA congress in August 1974 concluded with the apparent victory of Chipenda, who was strongly backed by Zambia, whose president, Kenneth Kaunda, opposed the more radical Neto.[29]

However, Neto had always benefited from greater external recognition, and he continued to negotiate as the MPLA's "true" president.[30] Neto strengthened his hand when, in August 1974, he formally proclaimed the MPLA's armed wing, the Forças Armadas Popular para Libertacao de Angola (FAPLA), present inside Angola.[31] This was followed by a MPLA "conference" in Mexico in September, at which a new and unified internally based leadership was established under Neto.[32] Portuguese authorities signed a cease-fire agreement with Neto's MPLA on October 21, effectively recognizing him as the organization's president. In February 1975, Chipenda, conceding defeat in this struggle, took with him to the FNLA the majority (2,000–3,000) of the MPLA's battle-hardened troops.[33] Zairian president Mobutu encouraged this split and facilitated the integration of Chipenda's forces with those of the FNLA.[34] Although Neto had won control of the MPLA, the loss of its most experienced combatants threatened to render this victory a pyrrhic one, given the increasingly militarized struggle for control of Angola.[35] Neto could count on the MPLA combatants led by Nito Alves in the first military region in the northwest, but his only other immediate option was the African forces formerly in the service of the Portuguese, but then being demobilized. In this context, the Tigres came to constitute an essential element of Portugal's support for the MPLA.

The Tigres as an Object of Desire

In the context of intra-Angolan military competition, in which trained soldiers and armaments of whatever provenance became the primary basis of power, the Tigres were the object of solicitations from all the Angolan parties. Attitudes toward such foreign forces mirrored the wider unreality of Angolan political negotiations: each actor argued publicly for an outright ban on foreign troops, while each sought to gain control of such forces and to mobilize them in their own interests. The Tigres were equally courted by the movement of white settlers that sought to carry out a coup d'état against the new Portuguese authorities in Angola. Rosa Coutinho sought at all costs to avoid a Rhodesian scenario, in which the whites might proclaim a unilateral declaration of independence.[36] Certainly, one group of settlers tried to claim the support of the Tigres; Pezarat Correia claims to have dissuaded them from collaborating with these white colonists.[37]

It should be recalled that the problem facing the Tigres was far from unique. As decolonization advanced, the Portuguese authorities had to consider the future of their various African auxiliaries. The fact that these groups had been central to the Portuguese colonial war did not deter nationalist movements from seeking to utilize them. For example, a meeting between the MPLA and the Flechas was held on October 29, 1974. Despite both significant animosity between the two forces and opposition among some MPLA leaders to this strategy, the MPLA promised to protect them after independence.[38] However, in comparison to the Flechas, with whom no agreement was ultimately reached, the FLNC, with its genuinely (if problematic) autonomous political leadership and organization, was considerably better equipped to articulate and pursue its interests and avoid the danger of simply being treated as a tool of one or another of the various nationalist or regional state forces. As former allies of Portuguese colonialism, they were in a position of great political weakness, but this was counterbalanced by their considerable military capacity at a time when what was at stake was a *military* and not a political victory.

As early as November 18–19, 1974, during a meeting held in Algeria between Portugal's National Commission for Decolonization and an MPLA delegation, it was agreed that the Tigres should be accorded special treatment by the transitional government.[39] For Mbumba and the wider FLNC leadership, their future in exile or otherwise had of course been a burning issue since the Portuguese revolution. During an extraordinary meeting held at the Chicapa base on November 21, 1974, the FLNC resolved not to leave Angola. The minutes of this meeting reveal that they refused a number of other options for their future advanced in August by senior Portuguese officers, including the following possibilities:

- their integration into Angola, with the award of Portuguese nationality
- their return to Zaire in exchange for an amnesty from President Mobutu
- their transfer to a third African country, most likely South Africa, where they would "continue the defence of the white race."[40]

The latter option was ultimately taken up by some former Flechas, who were forced to become part of South African "third forces" based in Namibia after a quarter of their total were killed by Angolan liberation movements following the Portuguese revolution.[41]

In the weeks before a summit of the three liberation movements called by the Portuguese authorities for December 18, 1974, negotiations focused on the integration of their troops into the proposed national army and the related role of "foreign" forces such as the FLNC.[42] The issue was of particular importance to Neto's MPLA, whose negotiating position was weakened by its lack of troops. Rosa Coutinho, who expressed his fears about the "Mobutu-ization" of Angola in the event of a FNLA victory, sought to address this weakness by bringing about an alliance between the MPLA and the FLNC.[43] The MPLA was happy to agree to such an arrangement; having requested the creation of a transitional government as part of their efforts to resist an FNLA takeover, they similarly envisaged the Tigres as a way of resisting the FNLA's military advances despite the MPLA's lack of a substantial army of its own.[44]

The prospect of such an alliance was of major concern among the opponents of the MPLA and the FLNC alike. A telegram sent by Zaire's consul in Luanda on December 6 to Rosa Coutinho alludes to evidence that the ex-Katangese gendarmes were being enrolled in the ranks of the MPLA.[45] In mid-December, the FNLA similarly accused Rosa Coutinho of seeking to integrate the "4,000 ex-Katangese gendarmes" into the MPLA army.[46] As Marcum suggests, President Mobutu, who had long taken a direct interest in the outcome of the Angolan anticolonial struggle, was deeply troubled by this emergent alliance. Mobutu's decade-long patronage of Holden Roberto had played an important role in the liberation struggle, but Congo/Zaire's active military support of the FNLA had been tempered by the retaliatory potential of the ex-Katangese forces.[47] Zaire's dependency on Angolan rail routes for its exports was a further disincentive to a more militant stance. In 1974, however, the sudden end of Portuguese colonialism prompted Mobutu to substantially increase military aid to the FNLA, a policy reflecting his ostensibly radical Africanist position in the early 1970s. The People's Republic of China, which Zaire had recognized in 1972, provided (in competition with Soviet backing for the MPLA) military aid and training to the FNLA.[48] In June 1974, around 120 Chinese military instructors arrived at the FNLA's Kinkuzu base and, along with 100 Zairian paratroopers, provided training for an FNLA force of around 15,000 men.[49] A further group of Chinese trainers, along with 450 metric tons of military equipment, arrived in August.[50]

As well as seeking to place his ally Roberto in power in Luanda, Mobutu wished at all costs to prevent the Soviet-aligned MPLA from gaining power on his doorstep. On September 15, 1974, Mobutu met with General Spínola on Ilha do Sal, where they privately agreed to facilitate the formation of an Angolan coalition government that would be headed by Holden Roberto, Chipenda, and UNITA's Jonas Savimbi, but which would exclude Neto.[51] Mobutu sought assurances from Spínola that Zaire would not face hostile action from the Tigres.[52] The ousting of Spínola by the radical MFA officers (discussed above) scuppered this plan and made an alternative approach necessary. The Zairian government, fully aware of the threat posed by an FLNC-MPLA alliance to its allies and itself, accordingly sought to defuse this long-ticking time bomb by bringing the exiled Katangese forces home. One suggestion of Mobutu, according to António Silva Cardoso, was that the Tigres then be allied with the FNLA forces.[53] Mobutu's diplomatic offensive was launched with the declaration of an amnesty for the Tigres on November 24, 1974. The Zairian government officially demanded that the Portuguese authorities enable direct talks, something that was accepted by the FLNC and by Rosa Coutinho. Such an offer was ostensibly attractive to many ex-gendarmes, whose hostility to Mobutu was offset by their desire to return home. However, mindful of the brutal execution of some ex-gendarmes after the operations in Kisangani and Bukavu in 1967, the FLNC expressed its lack of confidence in any promise from Kinshasa.[54]

Mobutu's plans were ultimately frustrated by Rosa Coutinho's successful efforts to bring together the MPLA and the FLNC. Indeed, initial contact between the two organizations had taken place in mid-November 1974, outside the authority but not the knowledge of the Portuguese. Mbumba dispatched a mission to Dar es Salaam, probably in mid-November 1974, to contact Neto, where the latter was based until January 1975.[55] The envoys were Captain Paul Kalenga (the

FLNC's security chief) and Deogratias Symba.⁵⁶ Although Symba claims he proposed an alliance with the MPLA, he was in reality acting on behalf of Jean-Baptiste Kibwe: this former minister of the Katangese secessionist government had fallen from favor with President Mobutu and hoped to position himself as the political leader of the FLNC.⁵⁷ Nathanaël Mbumba subsequently presented Symba to Rosa Coutinho as an FLNC official.⁵⁸ According to Portuguese military intelligence reports, a group of MPLA eastern front officers met Mbumba at its Camissombo camp, promising a "frank and true collaboration."⁵⁹ For his part, Mbumba was initially unwilling to accept the MPLA's offer unless it was supported by the Portuguese.⁶⁰

At a secret meeting at Cossa on December 17 (the day before the planned summit of liberation movements called by the Portuguese) held in Lunda Norte Province close to both the Zairian border and the FLNC bases, this alliance was formalized.⁶¹ Rosa Coutinho promised to prevent any forced return of FLNC troops to Zaire and continued financial assistance, in exchange for which the FLNC would ally with the MPLA and defend the Angolan border from FNLA incursions.⁶² The agreement implied that the FLNC would be rearmed and reequipped should conflict between the liberation movements occur.⁶³

According to Mbumba, in attendance were, on the Portuguese side, Rosa Coutinho, Captain Elíso de Figueiredo, Silvino Almeida, and the director general of the Dundo-based Diamang company, whose Cossa offices provided the venue for the meeting; from the MPLA, Lucio Llara, Lopo de Nascimento, Lopes Ludy, and (perhaps) Jose Eduardo dos Santos; and for the FLNC, Nathanaël Mbumba, Jacques-Antoine Luembe, Pierre-Damien Tshiniama, Jean-Delphin Muland, Justin Mushitu, and Deogratias Symba.⁶⁴ That day, Mbumba accordingly announced the FLNC's refusal to accept the Zairian amnesty at a press conference.⁶⁵ This was confirmed at a meeting with Zairian representatives in Luanda three days later. Following this setback, the Zairian authorities sought to blame, not without reason, the Portuguese authorities in general and Rosa Coutinho in particular for the MPLA-FLNC alliance. In a communiqué dated December 23, Kinshasa officially protested against the pro-MPLA position of the Portuguese authorities and (incorrectly) claimed that Neto secretly visited an FLNC camp.⁶⁶ Rosa Coutinho protested the offensive tone of the Zairian communiqué.

Zaire now sought to undermine the FLNC by various means. Deogratias Symba, recognized as the FLNC's political representative by High Commissioner Rosa Coutinho in December 1974, was kidnapped on January 31, 1975, by FNLA members based in Luanda.⁶⁷ He was taken to Kinshasa, where he was imprisoned. Symba successfully escaped from his detention and returned to Angola.⁶⁸ The Zairian authorities in Lisbon, Luanda, and Shaba nevertheless continued their diplomatic efforts to persuade the Tigres to return to Zaire.⁶⁹ In April 1975, Thomas Tshombe was dispatched by Mobutu, in a further attempt to persuade them to return.⁷⁰ The FLNC-MPLA alliance was nevertheless formally approved by Neto after his arrival in Luanda in February 1975 at a meeting with FLNC leaders. Once it became clear that his efforts had no chance of success, and amid rising military conflict in Angola, Mobutu focused his efforts solely on military support to the FNLA.

The Significance and Legacy of the Cossa Accords

The Cossa Accords and the apparent disappearance of the physical document in which they are set out are a vital part of this story, since they subsequently acquired a mythic status for the FLNC. The authors' lengthy efforts to obtain a copy of the agreement proved unsuccessful, and it is therefore necessary to rely on secondhand accounts. According to Mbumba's written "history" of the FLNC, this meeting formalized the assistance of the FLNC to the MPLA in the latter's struggle for independence, in explicit exchange for Angolan help for FLNC operations that ultimately sought to take power in Kinshasa.⁷¹ Every subsequent demand that Mbumba and the FLNC presented to the Angolan authorities was framed in implicit and often explicit reference to these accords. According to one rumor, there were no more than two copies of the document, one for the MPLA and the other held by Mbumba.⁷² It is suggested that the Angolans subsequently stole the latter, so that there was no proof of the promises made by the MPLA. No mention of the Cossa Accords appears in the PIDE archives or those of the Portuguese Angolan army in Lisbon. The signing of the agreement is, however, confirmed by Américo Cardoso Botelho, then employed by Diamang, in his memoir, and by a Portuguese officer serving in the area.⁷³ The strongest evidence for a written agreement is provided by Captain Figueiredo himself.⁷⁴ In an April 1975 report he recalled: "In December 1974, the contacts with the MPLA resulted in an agreement which stipulated that the *fiéis* would join the MPLA in their struggle if a generalized conflict would break out in Angola. As a counterpart, they would receive arms, protection and future MPLA support to further their own objectives."⁷⁵

The continuing significance of the agreement was clearly understood by Figueiredo:

> The *undersigned* agreements remain valid. The mutual contacts were intense and there is on both sides an interest in the rearmament (of the Katangans). This could be done as soon as the MPLA has arms at its disposal. The influence of the MPLA and their political position is obvious in the political program of the Katangans, in the political training given to its military, in the propaganda they sent to their country Zaire, and in the use of "comrade" in the way they address each other. From the point of view of the refugees, the agreement with the MPLA may only be disrespected if there is a strong reason to do so. They call it the "survival agreement."⁷⁶

The Cossa agreement would afford the FLNC much more than mere survival. It provided the basis for Angola's subsequent provision of military and logistical aid to the Tigres, which ultimately enabled the latter to participate in the successful overthrow of Mobutu some decades later.

It is certainly significant that the FLNC was, in circumstances of decidedly limited maneuver, able to reach an agreement designed to further their political aims. If they had been "guns for hire," then the material conditions available under South Africa's proposed patronage would have been significantly more favorable. Why was Mbumba, an ideologically conservative figure who had previously cooperated with the Portuguese colonial armed forces, willing to establish an alliance with the MPLA? As well as white settler groups (as noted earlier), Mbumba was in contact with Jonas Savimbi and appears to have seriously considered an alliance with UNITA; UNITA was, however, initially weak militarily and was moving toward an alliance with the FNLA during this period. In any event, UNITA was at the end of 1974 a movement with little military capacity or significant external support.[77] The FNLA, despite its apparent military strength, was not considered an attractive alternative, given that its "patron," President Mobutu, might attempt to eliminate the FLNC once the FNLA came to power. Ultimately, the alliance with the MPLA appears to have offered the FLNC the best opportunity to pursue its activities against the Mobutu-dominated Zairian state.[78]

It may nevertheless appear surprising that the Tigres were prepared to ally with the MPLA, the organization they had fought in the Eastern Military Zone in the early 1970s. The main body of these MPLA forces, led by Chipenda, had, however, defected to the FNLA.[79] In contrast, the MPLA leadership with which the FLNC concluded the Cossa Accords had resided in exile and had no experience of combating those previously known as the *fiéis* on Angolan soil. The Portuguese authorities, in the person of Rosa Coutinho, strongly supported and influenced Mbumba's decision, whose position at the head of the FLNC had always rested on his willingness to follow Portuguese guidance.[80] In addition, the military weakness of the MPLA, which could have made cooperation less attractive, was in fact a great advantage, in that it gave the FLNC, with its ready-made army, considerable negotiating strength. For Mbumba, ideological considerations had little or no importance. He was instead focused on the short-term survival of his movement, and on the long-term possibility of achieving political change in Zaire. Finally, the Tigres' loyalty toward the Portuguese in the person of Captain Figueiredo seems to have been a decisive factor.[81] Silva Cardoso believes that the loyalty of the former *fiéis* toward the Portuguese authorities helped convince them to sign.[82]

What was the benefit to the MPLA of these additional forces? Written estimates for January 1975 suggest that the MPLA had a total of between 5,000 and 8,000 guerrillas. The Portuguese army estimated it had 10,300 troops at its disposal in May 1975.⁸³ It is not always clear in such estimates what proportion of these troops were combat-ready or in training, and some estimates may include the FLNC fighters themselves. Marcum suggests that the MPLA/Neto–aligned forces consisted of 2,300 soldiers "in field" and 5,700 "in training," as well as 4,000 ex-Katangese gendarmes.⁸⁴ This indicates that, at the start of 1975 at least, the FLNC constituted the majority of MPLA-aligned combat-ready forces. Marcum elaborates: "By this time [April 1975] the MPLA had recruited the 3,500 to 6,000 man anti-Zairian, Katangese gendarmerie who had previously served the Portuguese in fighting Angolan nationalists. Kept intact after the coup as a security against Zairian designs, this well-trained, ex-Tshombe force added significantly to the MPLA's military capacity. But it also incensed President Mobutu, and as of mid-May, twelve hundred Zairian soldiers were reported to have moved across the Angolan border to operate alongside the FNLA's then in-place army of ten thousand."⁸⁵

Conflict between the Nationalist Movements

Following the outbreak of skirmishes in Luanda between newly arrived MPLA and FNLA forces in November 1974, the three nationalist movements engaged in an increasingly bloody war for control of Angolan territory.⁸⁶ Conflict steadily escalated with the arrival of armaments supplied by the external supporters of each side and was barely affected by periodic treaties in which they supposedly agreed to end the fighting.⁸⁷ As noted, the January 1975 Alvor Accord, signed by the three movements and endorsed by regional states including Zaire, established a transitional government led by a presidential council composed of representatives of all three parties and overseen by Portuguese high commissioner Rosa Coutinho.⁸⁸ However, following criticism expressed by the FNLA and UNITA, on January 28 (days before the Transitional Government took office) Rosa Coutinho was replaced by the more conservative General António Silva Cardoso.⁸⁹ Silva Cardoso had, his predecessor believes, pro-FNLA sympathies.⁹⁰ However, the preoccupation of all Portuguese leaders was by then control of the violence that was increasingly being used by the liberation movements; Silva Cardoso certainly wished to prevent the MPLA coming to power by military means. The Tigres were already concealing their existing stocks of weapons, and when Soviet arms shipments for the MPLA began to arrive in May 1975, some were, according to one former Tigre, dispatched in secret to their camps.⁹¹ Figueiredo was suspected of involvement in these transfers but was cleared after an inquiry.⁹²

Documents suggest that High Commissioner Silva Cardoso wished to see the Katangese returned to Zaire, and the Tigres remained afraid of this possibility. Mbumba alluded to this scenario as late as July 1975 during talks held in Chicapa.⁹³ However, Portuguese official capacity in Angola had waned considerably by mid-1975; wracked by its own revolutionary "Hot Summer" of clashes between moderates and radicals, Lisbon could no longer enforce its authority throughout Angolan territory.[94]

This situation made it easier for radical officers to secure the alliance with the MPLA and rearm the Tigres. High Commissioner Silva Cardoso, seeking to control and potentially demobilize the Tigres, appointed Figueiredo as his personal representative to the FLNC, unaware of Figueiredo's pro-MPLA position. Carefully disguising his own sympathies, Figueiredo assured Silva Cardoso that the Tigres could be effectively controlled and indeed recommended strengthening them:

> Although it is impossible . . . to try to stop the initiated contacts (notably with the MPLA . . .), we could still, with the trust they have in the MFA and the help we could give them in the future, control the development of the situation and avoid exposing us without us being informed or having agreed. We could thus guarantee
> - That they do not act against the Republic of Zaire, at least not this year and if this is not advisable;
> - That they do not engage themselves irreparably with the MPLA, while maintaining an agreement that would not end up in the integration of the *Fiéis* with the MPLA and provide them with arms from this movement;
> - That all their political activities (contacts with other countries or parties) would be oriented by us;
> - That they would remain in our hands for the most convenient orientation.
>
> To realize these objectives, they should get tangible support and also be convinced that we are not against their objectives, but that the latter cannot be achieved as long as there is no possibility of success. The ex-*Fiéis* must feel that we are acting in good faith. It is difficult to cheat them because they are hardened by the lies of the previous regime over the last seven years.[95]

Figueiredo's recommendations were reinforced by those of the MFA's Conselho Coordenador do Programa en Angola (CCPA), which pushed for a military strengthening of the MPLA and even an alliance with UNITA against the Mobutu-backed FNLA. In its report, the CCPA secretly advised:

(a) To guarantee them [i.e., the Tigres] social assistance, more specifically support for their agricultural activities and the improvement of their equipment . . . ;
(b) Guarantee their physical security by the installation with them of Portuguese forces as well as rapid and direct communications with Luanda;
(c) Guarantee the possibility of, if necessary, a rapid rearmament, for an offensive or a defensive use or as an element of dissuasion;
(d) Guarantee the maintenance of a level of training so that they do not lose their operational capacities.[96]

Even while the Tigres were mobilized by the MPLA over the next six months, they continued to be supported financially by the MFA authorities. As late as October 1975 the CCPA, well aware of their alliance with the MPLA, was nevertheless prepared to transfer 15 million escudos to the Tigres.[97]

In response to the rising tide of violence, African governments cajoled the three movements into the Nakuru Accord of June 21, 1975, which called for immediate disarmament of all sides.[98] In this increasingly unreal environment, in which earnest and universal calls for adherence to peaceful cooperative negotiations were constantly belied by armed conflict and preparation for it, the Tigres could not avoid becoming involved. To deal with rising insecurity in northeast Angola, the Diamang company demanded government authorization to use the Tigres (with whom its relationship dated back to the colonial period) for the protection of their installations in Dundo.[99] The Tigres would continue to protect and benefit from their diamond concessions for two decades.

Cuba, the MPLA, and the Tigres

Cuban military intervention was of course a decisive element in the MPLA's ultimate victory in Angola. Since the revolution of 1959, Fidel Castro and Che Guevara (until his death in 1967) had sought to export Cuban socialism to the "Third World": Cuban forces had previously supported the Lumumbist revolutionary forces in eastern Congo in the mid-1960s, while anti-Castro Cuban exiles had flown CIA-backed flights in support of the Tshombe government in 1964.[100] In the late 1960s and early 1970s, however, Cuba's active role in Africa was mainly limited to support for the PAIGC's campaign against Portuguese colonialism in Guinea-Bissau.[101] The Soviet Union, which provided only limited military aid to radical movements in Africa during that period, was, according to Shubin, unimpressed by the MPLA's internal divisions and Neto's independently minded leadership in particular.[102] Following the Portuguese revolution, they initially insisted that the MPLA establish internal unity before Soviet aid (which had been suspended in 1972) could be resumed; by the end of 1974, however, the quickening pace of events led the Soviets to prepare the provision of large quantities of arms for Neto's movement.[103] In January 1975 a specific request for political and military aid was made in a letter to the Cuban authorities written by Neto while in Dar es Salaam.[104] Initially, however, it was envisaged that preparations were being made for a military clash that might follow the elections then planned for October 1975; the arrival of Soviet weaponry would take at least five months. A Cuban delegation that visited Angola in January 1975 welcomed the agreement between the FLNC and the MPLA and did not, to our knowledge, raise concerns about their ideological background. According to Gleijeses, they reported to Havana in March 1975 on their December 1974 meeting with Neto as follows:

"The MPLA are eager to respond to their [the ex-gendarmes'] overtures, so that, if necessary, they could count on their assistance."[105]

Cuban aid was not, however, quickly approved and had not arrived by the time fighting broke out in Luanda between the MPLA and the more numerous FNLA forces in March 1975. With Portuguese troops unwilling to intervene, the MPLA relied on hastily mobilized popular forces from Luanda's shantytowns (the so-called *poder popular*) to repel FNLA attacks.[106] Although a truce was agreed, FNLA attacks resumed at the end of April; but the MPLA's military wing, FAPLA, was able to effectively counterattack the following month using newly arrived Soviet weaponry before another short-lived cease-fire was arranged by the increasingly impotent Portuguese forces.[107] Large quantities of Soviet weaponry arrived between March and November 1975.[108]

Although earlier studies suggested that Cuban forces were on the ground and participating in fighting in Angola by May or June, Gleijeses (whose access to Cuban sources is unrivaled) has convincingly demonstrated that, apart from a handful of advisers, they arrived considerably later. In May and again in June 1975, the MPLA issued increasingly urgent requests for Cuban assistance.[109] Cash was provided, but not the military instructors that Neto most wanted. Although Cuba ultimately provided substantially more such trainers and equipment than Neto requested, Gleijeses stresses the surprisingly slow pace of Cuban intervention—the vast majority of Cuban military trainers arrived in Luanda only in October 1975, bringing their number to about 1,000.[110] Cuban support was further limited by the Soviet emphasis on global détente at this period and by treaty restrictions on the use by third parties of weaponry supplied by the Soviet Union to Cuba.[111] Only in the days before the date set for Angolan independence, November 11, 1975, were the 650 elite Cuban troops flown into Luanda in Operation Carlota, which made a crucial difference in the run-up to independence.[112] In the interim, FLNC forces played a significant role in bolstering the MPLA's military position in Angola.

The Angolan War for Independence and the FLNC, 1975

This section provides an account of the FLNC's involvement in military confrontations of the Angolan war in the run-up to independence day. The battles for control of Luanda from late 1974 onward indicated that control of the capital city was considered decisive by both the MPLA, which controlled it from mid-1975 onward, and the FNLA, which sought to conquer it, with the support of heavy artillery operated mainly by the Zairian army.[113] FNLA forces had begun arriving in Luanda as early as October 1974; it was the first nationalist movement to establish a strong military presence in the capital.[114] Neto himself returned to Luanda in February 1975 to a hero's reception, securing his own leadership position in the eyes of his Soviet and Cuban allies and inspiring some thousands of young Angolans to fight for the MPLA (Shubin cites a figure of 6,000 fighters[115]); these were, however, untrained and probably of limited use in the conventional military conflict that followed.[116] In July a new wave of violence broke out that spread across the country, during which the MPLA successfully forced the FNLA out of the capital.[117] One report suggests that Figueiredo organized the transfer of Tigres under the command of Captain Grégoire Mulombo from Camissombo to Luanda, where they were commanded by FAPLA's Colonel Antonio França Ndalu.[118] They participated in the battle to evict the FNLA from the city. They were subsequently deployed in the defense of Luanda during August.[119]

Meanwhile, additional Zaire-based FNLA forces advanced on Luanda from the north, while UNITA troops engaged MPLA forces in battles to the south in August. As the war intensified, Portuguese efforts at reconciliation were undermined, not only by the Angolan movements themselves, but also by the pressure applied by their foreign allies. The transitional government collapsed, and as its impotence in the face of rising conflict became clear, Portugal advanced its scheduled date for full withdrawal from February 1976 to November 11, 1975, meaning they would depart on or before the date set for Angolan independence.[120]

Substantial numbers of the Zairian Armed Forces (FAZ) started moving into Angola in May 1975.[121] Two additional companies of paracommandos entered Angola in August, and Zaire later invaded the oil-rich Cabinda enclave in the days before independence in November.[122] They were skilled in the operation of their military equipment, but their chronic lack of discipline hampered their effectiveness. Although Zaire's growing economic problems limited Mobutu's support to the FNLA, President Gerald's Ford's approval of covert aid to both UNITA and the FNLA brought US arms supplies to Kinshasa by the end of July.[123] Zaire's international position in the mid-1970s was, to say the least, confused. Mobutu had in July 1975 expelled the US ambassador and arrested a number of CIA agents, accusing them of plotting his overthrow. This was linked to his desire to expel US-trained officers from the FAZ.[124] Mobutu publicly condemned the United States for its failure to support African liberation struggles, while simultaneously pressing for additional US military aid for the FNLA.[125] However, as MPLA victory in Angola became a likely prospect, contradictions in US policy toward Zaire also revealed themselves—pressure on Mobutu for economic reform was trumped in June 1975 by an emphasis on military cooperation against the communist threat in Angola and the provision of aid to address this.[126] The United States was, however, entirely aware of the weakness not only of UNITA and the FNLA but also of the FAZ itself: many of the latter's senior officers had been detained and tortured following coup accusations.[127]

Many witnesses speak of the substantial assistance that the Tigres provided to the MPLA, particularly before the arrival of Cuban forces. However, the scale and specificity of this is hard to evaluate, because many observers were not in a position to, or were not concerned with, differentiating clearly between FAPLA and the Tigres. Both forces wore the same uniforms and could not be separately identified by most observers.[128] Thus it is possible that some of the well-organized MPLA forces (compared to the FNLA) observed during this period were in fact those of the FLNC. We have no choice but to admit that the relative poverty of the sources at our disposal allows us to offer no more than a provisional analysis of the extent and value of the help given by the Tigres to the MPLA during the period from 1975 to 1976.

According to one subsequent history of the FLNC, the movement was engaged in the recruitment and instruction of MPLA combatants in the provinces of Lunda Norte and Lunda Sul.[129] According to Mbumba, the Tigres were deployed against advancing FNLA forces, with two battalions dispatched to Moxico (Luso, now Luena), two battalions to Luanda, two companies to Benguela, and two companies to Dundo (Lunda Norte).[130] The MPLA and FLNC forces took control of the town of Moxico and continued fighting with UNITA in the vicinity of the Benguela railway. As noted above, they took part in the expulsion of the FNLA from Luanda between the end of May and June 7, 1975; they then successfully participated in the defense of the capital before taking Caxito (a coastal town to the north of Luanda) from the FNLA on July 24.[131] Samuel Chiwale, the UNITA commander at the time, recalls in his memoir that in mid-August 1975, a column of twenty-eight armored cars brought Katangese soldiers from Sao Rimo, "armed to the teeth," to attack the UNITA base at Luso. UNITA's lack of ammunition forced it to withdraw to Chicala; Chiwale notes that many UNITA soldiers were unarmed, compared especially to the Katangese forces.[132] When the town was retaken by UNITA, the Katangese withdrew north to Biula and then to Luau (Teixeira de Sousa) as they awaited the arrival of Cuban forces.

On October 23, about 200 Katangese formed part of an approximately 1,000-man Cuban-led offensive which halted the FNLA's advance at Morro do Cal.[133] When South Africa's considerable forces crossed into Angola and joined with UNITA forces in its Operation Savannah from October 1975 onward, Mbumba shifted his general headquarters south from Chicapa to Saurimo (in Lunda Sul) to defend the area.[134] Four battalions participated alongside Cuban forces in the attack on UNITA-held Luso in late October; they also fought against South African forces at Luena, Cacala, Cangumbe, and Cangongue.[135] UNITA leader Jonas Savimbi asserted that FLNC forces were more redoubtable than the regular FAPLA troops: he told Stockwell, "The MPLA is no problem to us.... They run away ... [but the Katangese] ... are very strong and they don't run away."[136]

There is evidence that 200 FLNC forces took part in the war's decisive battle for Quifangondo, to the northwest of Luanda, on November 10, 1975, against FNLA and Zairian army forces.[137] According to Shubin, the recently arrived

Soviet-trained so-called Ninth Brigade of the MPLA was significant in repelling the FNLA's advance on Luanda. Cuban troops, including the 650-man elite force flown from Havana to Luanda on November 4, also fought in these operations. Young and Turner state that "Katanga gendarmerie units, which had been brought into alliance with the MPLA in January 1975 . . . helped blunt the Zairian offensive."[138] More specifically, Gleijeses reports that Quifangondo was successfully defended on November 10 by "850 FAPLA, 200 Katangans, 88 Cubans, and Yuri, the Soviet adviser."[139] The then Belgian chargé d'affaires in Luanda, who witnessed the battle from a distance, confirms the deployment of four battalions of Katangese troops.[140] Meanwhile, MPLA forces elsewhere, including the Tigres, had gained ground on UNITA forces and controlled much of the country, including diamond mining areas in the Lunda provinces.[141] The price that the FLNC troops paid in these battles was high: their complement was effectively reduced from 2,100 to around 1,600 soldiers.[142] These losses explain why the Shaba I war in 1977 was planned partly as a war of recruitment.

For its part, the FAZ, despite its heavy artillery, failed to play an effective role in the attack on Quifangondo and was soundly defeated by Cuban and FAPLA forces as it was repelled from Cabinda.[143] By January 1976 the FNLA offensive in Angola had crumbled in the face of Cuban/FAPLA action. FNLA and Zairian forces did not so much retreat as flee; in the words of the *New York Times*, they "pillaged the towns to which they withdrew. . . . Refugees report that these towns . . . have been completely sacked and that their populations have fled. . . . The Zaire army units were said to have been the most active element in the looting."[144] Even Holden was critical of the FAZ's performance, damaging relations between him and Mobutu.[145] The embarrassing passage of anti-MPLA mercenaries through Kinshasa was stopped in mid-February, and all Zairian forces had left Angola by the end of that month.[146] This humiliating defeat was not simply a military blow for Mobutu; the exposure of his tacit alliance with US and South African forces was a devastating and permanent blow to any pretensions he had to pan-African leadership. It revealed the weakness of his armed forces and strengthened the hopes of his opponents, inside and outside Zaire, that he could be defeated.

The New Politics of the FLNC

Parallel to their military engagement on the side of the MPLA, the FLNC simultaneously adjusted to the postindependence political realities of Angola with new political initiatives that would enable them to attack Zaire. The military strength of the forces now known as the Tigres was consistently mirrored by the weakness of their political organization. The success of the FLNC forces in the Angolan conflict now made them an attractive ally to leftist opponents of Mobutu who had previously regarded them with anti-Tshombist suspicion. Mbumba was, however, habitually hostile to such alliances, especially because potential partners often lacked forces of their own; he was suspicious (not without cause) that his own ambition for political power was unlikely to be advanced as a result of such cooperation. The retrospective adoption of the more overtly leftist nomenclature of the Tropas de Infanteria e Guerrilla Revolucionária as the basis for the name Tigres suggests the political reorientation of the FLNC during this period.[147] Unsurprisingly, the MPLA in general and Neto in particular, whose own communistic orientation was reinforced by Eastern bloc aid during the war for power in Angola, sought to place the Tigres' activities in a radical framework and to link them to leftist Congolese forces.

The first political contact of the FLNC during this period was probably with Laurent Kabila's People's Revolutionary Party (PRP). Agostinho Neto had become acquainted with Kabila in 1974 in the course of his enforced stay in Tanzania, where Julius Nyerere gave some limited support to Kabila until 1975.[148] According to many Congolese testimonies, Neto sought to entrust Kabila with providing political direction to the FLNC. After a covert meeting with Kabila in November 1974 at his lakeside base at Wimbi, Deogratias Symba was decidedly unimpressed by the offensive capacity of the PRP.[149] A letter from Mbumba to Kabila, dated May 10, 1975, suggests Mbumba's state of mind and perhaps his knowledge (gained from Symba's 1974 report) of the poor state of the PRP's forces:

> Comrade,
>
> If I contact you, it is not to say that we lack the force to liberate our country, [because] we have an extraordinary force capable of liberating our country. It is necessary to collaborate with us because we know that you . . . do not have the means to . . . liberate our country. . . . Dear Liberator, I conclude that you must understand that you have a thousand chances to take advantage of this opportunity which now presents itself.[150]

Given the personality of Laurent Kabila, it is unlikely that he would have responded positively to such an invitation. Nevertheless, this potential alliance of these two anti-Mobutu movements, with their respective internal bases of support in northern and southern Katanga, made that province (now officially known as Shaba) a genuine threat to the Zairian authorities. This problematic relationship persisted into the late 1970s, consistently demonstrating the resistance by the FLNC in general, and by Mbumba in particular, to the group's potential domination by radical political movements without meaningful military capacity of their own.

Conclusion

The threat to the FLNC's very existence posed by the Portuguese revolution of April 1974 provided in practice the circumstances for the movement to negotiate a new military alliance with the MPLA, a marriage of convenience that led to the deployment of the *fiéis*, now renamed the Tigres, in the Angolan war for independence in 1975. As previously, the ex-Katangese fighters and those who had joined them in exile found themselves deployed and dying in someone else's war, although their deployment against the FAZ and its FNLA allies clearly constituted taking the fight to the Mobutu regime, albeit on Angolan soil.

The test of whether this sacrifice was worthwhile would come in the aftermath of the war, when the FLNC leadership sought to hold the MPLA to its side of the Cossa agreement. The two Shaba wars of 1977 and 1978, launched from Angolan territory by a well-resourced and highly trained FLNC armed force, dealt the most serious blow the Mobutu regime experienced until the 1990s. In so doing, these conflicts brought the Cold War to central Africa in a decisive way.

6 The Shaba Wars

THE MPLA'S POLITICAL and military victory in Angola in November 1975 radically changed the political outlook throughout central Africa.[1] The establishment of this overtly Marxist state, supportive (like Frelimo-ruled Mozambique) of revolutionary nationalist movements in southern Africa, placed the region's racist settler regimes on the defensive and destroyed the assumptions on which Western policy toward the region had been built. It also led to decades of civil war with UNITA, backed by South Africa and (during the 1980s) the United States. No less significantly, it created new tensions with Zaire, which had suffered a military humiliation in Angola and which, facing economic crisis and reduced Western support, appeared particularly vulnerable.

This weakness represented an unprecedented opportunity to Mobutu's many enemies inside and outside Zaire, not least the FLNC. Rearmed by the MPLA's Cuban and Soviet allies, and strengthened by the Cossa Accords, they seized this opportunity, first to strengthen their numbers and then to invade the former territory of Katanga (renamed Shaba in 1971), but now with significantly altered aims and political direction. The first Shaba war of 1977 led President Mobutu to make significant political reforms, with effects that last until today. The second Shaba war of 1978, in which the Tigres seized the town of Kolwezi and severely destabilized the country's strategic mining industry, posed the greatest threat the Mobutu regime faced until the 1990s. This was the first time that the FLNC had, as an independent political and military actor, pursued its aims on an international stage in ways that would attract the attention and response of a wide range of international actors, including both superpowers.

It was, however, Mobutu's very political and economic weakness, coupled with his successful presentation of the Shaba attacks as local skirmishes in the wider Cold War, that mobilized Western support and enabled him to retain power. The FLNC, with its historical origins in the supposedly "neocolonial" Katangese state, was, at this moment of its greatest military success, portrayed as a Marxist guerrilla movement allied to the Soviet bloc. Although many external observers believed that the FLNC was doing the bidding of Angola and Cuba, the evidence presented here demonstrates once again the agency of the FLNC and its pursuit of its own aims. Indeed, it was precisely the unwillingness of the FLNC's leaders to accept the direction of the state under whose authority they officially operated that ultimately led to the loss of their political autonomy over the next two decades.

This chapter first explores the position of the FLNC in the aftermath of the war for Angolan independence, the allies they now attracted, and the plans they made to pursue their cause. It then focuses on the two Shaba wars, exploring their key events but also explaining the FLNC leadership's strategy and the divisions this provoked with their supposed Angolan and Cuban allies. Using a range of official and unofficial archives, it also analyzes Mobutu's response to these attacks and his complex relationships with his Western allies. It concludes with an explanation of Angola's break with the FLNC and its destruction as a coherent force.

The FLNC in Angola, 1975–1976

In the aftermath of the Angolan war for independence, heavy fighting continued into 1976, with 36,000 Cuban troops leading a rout of the remaining FNLA and mercenary forces in the north and pursuing South African forces southward until their departure in March 1976.[2] Cuba was, however, divided between desiring a rapid end to its expensive commitment and the need to secure full control by the MPLA of all Angolan territory. The deployment of inexperienced FAPLA troops against UNITA, while most Cuban troops remained in garrison towns, was unsuccessful, since UNITA provided a more significant military threat than expected.[3] In this context, the well-trained and experienced Tigres remained a significant military asset. Limited evidence exists of direct Cuban and Soviet training of Katangese forces, and the Tigres certainly benefited from new Soviet equipment, supplied to them by the MPLA.[4]

However, Cuba's prioritization of Angolan stabilization led it to discourage support for the Tigres. Gleijeses provides evidence of Cuban skepticism and even hostility toward the FLNC.[5] Jorge Risquet, head of the Cuban mission in Angola, met FLNC leader Nathanaël Mbumba in February 1976; Mbumba requested (according to Risquet) "heavy weapons, political instructors, and money"; these would enable the FLNC to recruit additional troops in Zaire and then mount a major attack, seizing a city and toppling the Mobutu regime.[6] Risquet was unconvinced by Mbumba's claims that "his ideology is Marxist and that he intends to lead his country towards socialism": he reported to Castro and Neto that the FLNC had "tainted pasts: they were Katangan gendarmes, secessionists, and supporters of Moïse Tshombe."[7] Cuba refused to provide the large-scale military aid (including tanks and antiaircraft artillery) Mbumba had requested.[8] The picture that emerges is of a relatively conservative Cuba that prioritized protecting its gains in Angola and was wary about the potential of the FLNC to advance them in Zaire; the Soviet Union was significantly more reluctant to be drawn into Cold War conflict in Africa following the Helsinki Accords of 1975.[9] The MPLA, however, initially shared the FLNC's aim of removing President Mobutu, who had supported their Angolan rivals during the anticolonial and independence wars and who might continue to do so, given the continued presence of FNLA/UNITA forces on Zairian territory and periodic incursions by Zairian forces into Angola.[10]

The FLNC's Chicapa headquarters, near Dundo, was in a diamond-mining region, which Mbumba used to develop economic activities that enabled the movement to achieve significant self-sufficiency. If we believe figures provided by Mbumba, the Tigres' assets grew to the extent that they constituted something of a state within the state.[11] Mbumba certainly improved the military effectiveness of the FLNC forces—now numbering less than 2,000—that had survived the war for independence. However, Mbumba's authoritarianism and suspicion were coupled with a lack of realism in his military evaluations. While he did not hesitate to execute officers who were unable meet the (probably) unrealistic tasks he set them, his iron discipline was probably necessary to impose order on this military force, even if his primary purpose for doing so was to advance his own position politically and economically. Mbumba thus developed the political autonomy of the FLNC while simultaneously ensuring that he did not lose control of it. Following the abduction of Deogratias Symba by Zairian forces, he named Justin Mushitu and Pierre Tshiniama in March 1975 as the FLNC's representatives to the Angolan government—both were given the rank of major.[12]

The FLNC's role in bringing the MPLA to power raised the movement's international profile; it had demonstrated its effectiveness as a fighting force, while the Angolan war had exposed the weakness of the Zairian army and Mobutu's willingness to collaborate with Apartheid South Africa. The former gendarmes of the Katangese secession, hitherto considered beyond the Tshombist pale, were now, under MPLA auspices, partly rehabilitated in left/nationalist eyes. Their dubious ideological record was less important—to many Zairian and Angolan eyes, if not to Cuban observers—than their military capacity.[13] From 1975, many opponents of Mobutu came to Luanda seeking an alliance with the FLNC. One of the first such initiatives, in October 1975 (that is, before Angolan independence), proposed the FLNC's "total fusion" with four opposition groups: the MNC-L, led by Roger Mokede and Albert Onawelho; the PRP of Laurent Kabila; Raphael Mumba's Conaco; and Robert Maïkissa's ABAKO.[14] This proposed alliance allowed Mbumba to make links with the Lumumbist opposition to Mobutu; in doing so, he overtly renounced the political heritage of the Katangese secession, of which the Tigres were the legacy. In a subsequent letter, he claimed credit for abolishing the symbols of the Katangese struggle from the moment he took charge of the FLNC: "It is because on 19 June 1968, I created the FRONT DE LIBÉRATION NATIONALE CONGOLAIS, whereby after I had presented to you my politico-military programme, our ideology, that continued with the

POLITICAL IDEAS ... of our Valiant National Hero Comrade Patrice Emery LUMUMBA.... I proceeded to boycott all Katangese activities, such as the flag and the anthem of Katanga."[15]

The proposed alliance was not, however, formally established; Mbumba claims this was because the funds he had allocated to it disappeared, a perennial problem that apparently occurred every time the FLNC funded external allies and that contributed to Mbumba's distrust of external links and representatives.[16]

Among the other Congolese leaders who approached the FLNC were the following:

- Mathias Kemishanga and Felix Mukulubundu, former allies of Pierre Mulele now based in Brazzaville (against whom many ex-gendarmes had fought in 1964–1965);
- Cartier Mutombo, a journalist at Radio Katanga during the secession and personal secretary to Moïse Tshombe. He became the FLNC representative in France;[17]
- Congolese painter Pierre-Victor Mpoyo, who arrived in Luanda from Nigeria. He agreed to fund the FLNC on condition that he was named its president;[18]
- Daniel Monguya Mbenge, provincial governor of West Kasai and Katanga in the early 1970s, who visited Luanda in December 1975–January 1976.[19] Monguya was appointed president of the Mouvement d'Action pour le Résurrection du Congo (MARC), which was in the mid-1970s the most prominent Zairian opposition movement in exile;[20]
- Jean-Baptiste Kibwe, former Katangese finance minister, who arrived in Luanda around May 1976. Kibwe's representative Deogratias Symba had been an important figure in the FLNC, and Kibwe now sought to position himself as its political leader. Mbumba, suspecting a plot, sought the arrest of Kibwe, who escaped only with help from the Belgian ambassador.[21]

Several of these visitors were granted FLNC membership and appointed as its external representatives. This did not, however, lead to effective cooperation: while they complained of Mbumba's refusal to listen, he accused them of misappropriating funds that he had placed at their disposal. In general, each such initiative foundered on Mbumba's suspicions and unwillingness to share leadership.

The MPLA, while broadly supportive of the FLNC's aims, consistently sought to ally it with left-leaning Congolese leaders, most notably Antoine Gizenga, the former Parti Solidaire Africain (PSA) leader and head of the Lumumbist government in Stanleyville in 1960–1961, and Laurent Kabila, whose People's Revolutionary Party (PRP) continued to offer limited guerrilla resistance in eastern Zaire.[22] Gizenga was apparently welcomed to Luanda in May 1977 by Neto, whose hopes that he would ally with Mbumba were dashed by the latter's failure to meet him.[23] In the mid-1970s, Gizenga's Parti Lumumbiste Unifié (PaLu) had allied with the PRP, with Gizenga named as the PRP's external representative.[24] Toward the end of 1976, a plan (not enacted) was developed by the Tigres to attack Congolese territory (specifically Mbuji Mayi) from Angola, in coordination with a PRP attack against Kalemie in the East.[25] It has been suggested that this pincer operation to overthrow Mobutu was supported by several African countries.[26]

Kabila may have visited Luanda in March 1977, just before the first Shaba war.[27] Although a joint attack was no longer practical because of the PRP's limited military capability, the idea was not abandoned.[28] Antoine Gizenga was ready to provide political leadership to this movement, but he, Kabila, and Mbumba all struggled to sublimate their individual leadership ambitions within a unified movement.[29] Subsequent French analysis concluded that "the troublesome personality of M'Bumba is the primary obstacle to the extension of the [opposition] Front. Despite the efforts of Luanda, he has refused integration with the other Zairian opposition movements."[30] Mbumba was, however, the only leader able to take the military fight to Zaire itself, as he was about to demonstrate.

Shaba I: The War of Eighty Days

On the night of March 8–9, 1977, the FLNC launched an invasion of the renamed Shaba Province. Under the command of Grégoire Mulombo, a force of approximately 1,500 Tigres entered Zaire on foot or on bicycles. Three or possibly four battalions advanced simultaneously: the 1st Battalion, led by General Mufu, advanced toward Dilolo and then Kasaji, in the direction of Lubumbashi; the 2nd Battalion occupied Kasaji, then advanced to the east, toward Sandoa; the 3rd Battalion was charged with taking Kisenge and Malonga before also targeting Sandoa; and the 4th Battalion's mission was to first take Kapanga to the north before continuing to Kamina.[31] The towns of Kapanga and Kisenge were taken on March 8, then Dilolo (March 9), Mutshatsha (March 10), and Sandoa (March 13).[32] Belgian intelligence and diplomatic reports show that the progress of the Katangese troops was slow thereafter, advancing about 250 kilometers in fifteen days.[33] This mode of operation supports the claim made by all the protagonists that Shaba I was designed as a war of recruitment, to enable a subsequent operation of greater scale.[34] The Tigres also occupied territory where FNLA and UNITA forces were based, including Kisenge, where a camp of Angolan refugees was controlled by these movements. The Tigres probably had orders to destroy FNLA/UNITA bases in the region, something of evident benefit to the Angolan government and its allies.[35]

However, it appears that, at least in principle, a plan existed to attack the whole country. Interviewees confirm contemporary intelligence bulletins reporting widespread rumors of impending attacks in Bas-Congo and Kasai as a prelude to the seizure of Kinshasa.[36] However, the unexpected presence of the Zairian Armed Forces (FAZ) at strategic points prevented such a plan being implemented (as well as raising suspicions that plans for the invasion had been leaked).[37] Mbumba accordingly limited the operation to Katanga. The focus of the Tigres on the Dilolo-Mutshatsha route rather than that to Kapanga suggests that their aim was to take Kolwezi: this town was now the center of Shaba's mining activities, producing 75 percent of Zairian copper and 80–90 percent of its cobalt.[38]

The slow pace of progress toward Kolwezi resulted from the difficulties in providing logistical support inside Zaire, not because of significant resistance by the FAZ, which quickly retreated after the first gunfight. The FLNC, setting off explosions to imitate the heavy artillery they did not possess, succeeded by this method in scaring away Zairian soldiers.[39] This embarrassing defeat of Zaire's army followed and was partly a result of its increasing politicization, reflecting Mobutu's suspicion of his senior officers.[40] The introduction of MPR "political commissars" in the FAZ; the removal of many Western-trained officers, now dubbed counterrevolutionaries; and finally the creation of the enormous Kamanyola division, trained more to goose-step than to fight—all these factors had damaged the FAZ's capacity for combat.[41] The US embassy in Kinshasa warned that the FAZ's unwillingness to fight meant that "the loyalty of the military and the tolerance of the people for Mobutu's government could be drawn into serious question."[42] A coruscating Belgian military intelligence service report suggests that it was only the timidity of the Katangese advance that prevented a greater victory:

> The Katangese attack revealed the level of courage of the FAZ. . . . [Its] soldiers [were] limp, demoralised, drunk, lacking ideals, stating openly that they had only come to the frontline because they were forced to. . . . [G]uns were fired so as to whip up the aggressive mood of the soldiers who had no desire to risk their lives to prevent the return to the country of the Katangese. . . . From a tactical viewpoint, all these combined admirably: the atmosphere, the FAZ's lack of enthusiasm for combat, the total support of the majority of the population for the Katangese. [I]t was only because t]he commanders of the Katangese offensive . . . advanced [so slowly] that, despite their fear, despite their disgust for fighting, the FAZ was finally able to emerge as winners.[43]

For his part, Mobutu framed urgent appeals for Western military aid by claims that Cuba and Angola had initiated and were participating in the invasion.[44] On April 2, Mobutu informed the Organization of African Unity (OAU) of "the aggression to which my country is subjected by a horde of mercenaries in the pay of the Cuban-Russian coalition."[45] Zairian chief of staff Bumba Moaso claimed (without providing evidence) that Russians and Cubans had been fighting with the Tigres.[46] In fact, while the operation was certainly supported by the Angolan authorities, Shaba I came as a surprise to the Cubans.[47] Risquet, out of Angola at the time, subsequently criticized the attack for providing an opportunity for retaliatory Western-backed action.[48]

However, the reaction of Western countries to Mobutu's appeal was decidedly lukewarm: the Carter administration was predisposed against African intervention after the Angolan debacle, while the Belgian government feared that active participation might lead to its civilians being taken hostage by the FLNC forces in Shaba. President Carter stated publicly on March 24, "We have no hard evidence, or any evidence as far as that goes, that the Cuban and Angolan troops have crossed the border into Zaire."[49] This diplomatic confusion certainly reflected poor intelligence, but also the lack of clarity in—or at least the poor communication of—the FLNC's objectives. In press interviews, Mbumba declared his desire to drive out the Mobutu regime; otherwise, communication was carried out by FLNC representatives in Brussels (primarily Célestin Luanghy) and Paris (Cartier Mutombo).[50] Their contrasting ideological positions—Lumumbist and Marxist in Brussels, Tshombist in Paris—indicate both the lack of clarity and the improvised nature of the FLNC's political positioning and external representation.[51]

Diplomatic efforts to resolve the unfolding crisis revolved around Nigeria, Western-aligned but with considerable standing as an independent African power. The OAU and powerful African states (whose defense of territorial integrity generally trumped their enmity toward Mobutu) lobbied Angola to ensure an FLNC withdrawal, while preventing hot pursuit by FAZ forces into Angola that might escalate the conflict. In a meeting with Nigerian foreign minister Joseph Garba on March 21, US secretary of state Cyrus Vance stressed the need to maintain Zairian territorial integrity and "US interest in a solution within an African framework."[52] Zairian foreign minister Nguz Karl I Bond, himself of Katangese Lunda origin, was closely involved in these negotiations. In pressing European ambassadors to take a stronger stance, Nguz emphasized the leftist nature of the FLNC:

> In the occupied area of Shaba Mobutu's photograph had been replaced by Lumumba's. The invaders, who hailed from other regions as well as Shaba, addressed each other as "Comrade," in Spanish or Portuguese. Zairian opposition elements in Europe spoke of establishing a "socialist regime" and there was evidence of close contacts between them and Soviet and/or Algerian embassies. The invaders' aim was clearly not secession but the overthrow of Mobutu.... If Zaire, given its vital position in Africa, were to fall into the hands of Moscow-sympathisers, the rest of Africa would certainly, in time, follow suit.[53]

Belgian and French observers, persuaded by such reports, constructed the Tigres in Cold War terms:

> Not only are their units equipped with conventional weaponry ... but they also use infiltration methods of the "Vietcong" type, with the invaders arriving in their village in plainclothes, where they are greeted as ... the liberators of Katanga. Their success is achieved by the fact that their behaviour contrasts with the brutality and corruption of the forces of order in Zaire. Such a technique bears the hallmarks of those who have been trained and armed as part of a long-term strategy that exploits tribalism for Marxist-Leninist aims.[54]

The left-leaning Antoine Gizenga was attributed a role in this operation that he certainly did not play—his telephone calls, which were monitored by the French authorities, emphasized his pro-Soviet allegiances.[55] Gizenga himself encouraged this erroneous analysis, which was complementary to his outreach to the FLNC, described above; in a message to the French president he claimed that Zairian opposition forces (including the PRP) were strong, organized, had Eastern bloc support, and supported the actions of the "Katangese gendarmes."[56]

Such an analysis was, however, rejected by the Mwaant Yav, Daniel Tshombe: the Lunda king assured the US consul in Lubumbashi that "the current aid of Cuban mercenaries [to the FLNC forces]—if there is any–should not be a fear for the future, since the ex-Katangese had not been indoctrinated and were only seeking to return home." He claimed that the goals of the invading forces included "overturning the present political system, establishing a round table to establish a new government, perhaps led by Gizenga; [and] a [Congolese] federation with an independent Shaba."[57] On a subsequent visit to the French consulate, the Mwaant Yav described the approach of the FLNC forces:

> They arrive in a community, present themselves to the population, bringing flour and cassava; they explain to the population the goals they pursue and depart after two hours. This intoxicating tactic is applied several times; the Zairian soldiers have laid down their arms refusing to fight with them and also asking if they can go with them. They are not Marxists, though there may be some amongst them.... They leave the existing [local] administration in place if they are accepted by them.[58]

Angola meanwhile claimed that the Katangese action was wholly internal and denied responsibility for it. In mid-April, Angolan president Neto, asked by UK foreign secretary David Owen whether Angola was supporting the Katangese, replied that "the Katangese had decided to go to Zaire of their own free will. Angola only gave them food."[59] Britain, keen to build strong relations with Angola to resolve conflicts in southern Africa, was more willing than other Western states to give Neto the benefit of the doubt. Rejecting the French belief that "Soviet influence is the direct cause of most of the current tensions in Africa," one

British official suggested: "There has clearly been some degree of Angolan support and the Cubans trained the ex-Katangese, but the Shaba operation is a good example of the kind of local problems that litter Africa and which can erupt without external prompting."[60]

It was only on April 7, with the FLNC apparently on the verge of seizing Kolwezi, that Morocco sent a contingent of 1,200 soldiers to aid the Zairian cause: this was made possible by an airlift provided by France, whose president, Valéry Giscard d'Estaing, was increasingly worried about US weakness in the face of a rising communist threat in Africa.[61] Morocco's King Hassan II, drawing public attention to the secessionist origins of the FLNC, justified the intervention by the OAU's policy of territorial integrity of African states.[62] Arriving in Kinshasa on April 8, Moroccan forces left almost immediately for Kolwezi and Kamina. They made rapid advances, taking Mutshatsha on April 25. Two captured Katangese troops, questioned on Zairian television, suggested that large numbers of Cuban forces were fighting with the FLNC and that Gizenga was "running operations from Angola."[63] Celebrating his victory in the "liberated" town of Mutshatsha, Mobutu declared: "We will do our best to prevent Soviet influence in Africa. If Europe trembles every time Brezhnev coughs, it is not for me."[64] After the retaking of Dilolo by the FAZ and their Moroccan allies on May 21, the Tigres regrouped around Kapanga in order to mount an organized retreat to Cazombo in Angola.[65] Belgian intelligence officers were, however, worried that the apparent rout of the FLNC disguised a "melting away" of Katangese forces into the civilian population, ready to reemerge after Moroccan forces left.[66]

As this brief account of the "war of eighty days" shows, some analysts and diplomats (strongly encouraged by Mobutu and some of the FLNC's own allies) interpreted these events primarily through Cold War perspectives, obscuring the underlying motivations and methods of the FLNC itself. The lack of reliable information on the latter indicates the deficiencies of Zairian intelligence in predicting the invasion, but also the lack of importance accorded by external actors to the issues underlying the conflict. External intelligence tended to interpret events in solely geopolitical or ethnic terms, ignoring or failing to comprehend the centrality of Katanga in informing the Tigres' actions.

The FLNC between the Wars

Although ultimately a military failure, Shaba I provided a significant number of new "recruits" (both voluntary and involuntary) for the Tigres. This recruitment was aided by subsequent reprisals by the FAZ against Lunda civilians suspected of prior collaboration with the FLNC (see below). Before the first Shaba war, the number of Congolese civilian refugees living among the Tigres was very limited. Due to their recruitment efforts during the two months of the Shaba I operation and a subsequent population flight from Zaire, an estimated 152,000 refugees were present in Angola by June 1977. They were initially housed in camps close to the border in Moxico and Lunda provinces. Following President Neto's October 1977 speech announcing the removal of the refugees from both the borders and diamond mining areas, they were moved to other camps in Moxico and Lunda Sul in early 1978. Many were subsequently resettled in other provinces (Bengo, Malanje, Cuanza Norte, Cuanza Sul), but several of the civilian camps continued functioning in Moxico and even in Lunda Norte, some of which are still in use as of this writing. About a dozen civilian refugee camps were created in Moxico Province and about six in the Lunda provinces.[67]

Many of the new military recruits were initially brought to the Chicapa base, where they received intensive training. According to an internal document, the FLNC's overall strength increased during this period from three battalions of 500 (1,500 in total) to fourteen battalions of 660 soldiers each, totaling 9,240 soldiers.[68] Five new military camps housed the new arrivals, where Mbumba established a characteristically efficient system to ensure that they were properly fed. Discipline was draconian, and according to some sources, the death penalty awaited those who challenged Mbumba's authority.[69] For example, Antoine Luembe, head of the general staff, was executed in 1977 in the wake of Shaba I.[70] The FLNC continued to engage in cross-border infiltrations into Zaire in the second half of 1977 as preparation for a second major offensive.[71] For example, an FLNC patrol infiltrated Zairian territory south of Dilolo on November 14.[72]

The FLNC was now the subject of greater international attention, although the quality of intelligence varied considerably. The major concern of Western observers was the degree and form of support being provided to the FLNC. French reports subsequently alleged that the FLNC was reequipped during this period by Cuba, Algeria, and Libya.[73] It was suggested that some new recruits had been trained under "Cuban leadership" in the use of antiaircraft and other heavy weaponry. French intelligence gathered in Kinshasa claimed that "ideological training would also be pursued [and] the influence of Gizenga would supplant that of Nathaniel Mbumba."[74] Certainly, some Tigres recall military training under Cuban supervision, while Soviet advisers provided training for their military intelligence operations.[75] One interviewee reports that the Cubans provided training in the use of heavy artillery, in an arrangement brokered by Mbumba outside direct Angolan control.[76] However, training should not be conflated with control. Western embassies and intelligence organizations tended both to exaggerate the extent of communist influence and to assume that left-wing actors (both Zairian and Cuban) would by their engagement with the FLNC automatically acquire political influence over it, assuming a lack of agency within the organization itself.

Certainly, the attraction of the FLNC for Mobutu's radical opponents increased in the wake of Shaba I. Among these was the Progressive Congolese

Students movement (ECP).⁷⁷ From July to November 1977, ECP representatives visited Angola, where its members were incorporated into the FLNC central committee. ECP leaders provided external representation for the FLNC but experienced characteristically difficult relations with Mbumba; they were not informed of the launch of the Shaba II attack.⁷⁸ For their part, the FLNC's new radical allies were not blind to the nature of their new partners. One member of a Europe-based Lumumbist delegation that visited Chicapa during this period remarked:

> The FLNC is an organisation that says it is revolutionary. However, when one considers the ... discipline that reigns within the liberation army, a discipline appropriate to a colonial army with all the consequences involved, the use of the whip as an instrument for punishment, the use of imprisonment for a minor fault, the relationship between officers and soldiers which is far from being the relationship between comrades, one can objectively conclude that this army is not an army of liberation.⁷⁹

Although the FLNC's approach during Shaba I indicated that it understood how to fight a "people's war," it made no pretense of being organized along Maoist ideological lines.⁸⁰ Its conventional military hierarchy arguably made the Tigres a more effective fighting force than more ostensibly ideological African "liberation" forces; it was also comparatively independent and efficiently organized. At this time, Mbumba seemed to be at the peak of his power. He claims to have obtained arms from Libya and Algeria and possessed a significant war chest, funded from revenue generated by Chicapa's farms, diamond trading, and payments received first from the Portuguese and subsequently from the MPLA.⁸¹ Mbumba himself had ambitions not only for Katanga but also to obtain for himself the traditional authority of the Mwaant Yav. Despite lacking any royal ancestry, during the first Shaba War he had ordered his forces to capture the symbols of power of the Mwaant Yav in the royal capital of Musumba, in the absence of the king himself. Some items were taken but not, it appears, the main symbol, the *rukan* or royal bracelet. During the attack, the Queen Mother Rukonkish Kamin was tied up and ultimately died of her wounds.⁸² Other evidence for such ambitions comes from a Portuguese officer's report of a visit to Camissombo in 1975. After a copious meal, a drunk Mbumba sketched his dream of restoring the Lunda-Tshokwe kingdom—with himself at its head.⁸³

However, the FLNC's Achilles' heel remained its incoherent political position. The relative success of Shaba I only increased the pressure from Neto to bring the Tigres under what he regarded as a legitimate form of political leadership.⁸⁴ Accordingly, further contacts took place between Laurent Kabila and Mbumba. An alliance with the PRP would make the FLNC, "tainted" by association with the Katangese secession, more acceptable to "progressive" African states such as Tanzania, Botswana, Mozambique, and Zambia. The FLNC political representative Deogratias Symba, in possession of an Angolan passport and apparently also acting as a PRP representative, was dispatched on a mission in 1976 to obtain external support.[85] Kabila meanwhile traveled to Luanda in July–August 1977 to formalize collaboration between the PRP and the FLNC, in negotiations facilitated by Justin Mushitu, FLNC representative to the Angolan government.[86] These concluded with the creation of what was known as the Supreme Council of Liberation (CSL) in an agreement signed in Luanda on August 26, 1977. This made it clear that collaboration, rather than merger, was the aim:

- Article 4: The CSL has as its principal objective to combine efforts for the struggle for national liberation.
- Article 13: Each of the two parties affiliated to the CSL has the right to protect its total autonomy.[87]

Given the PRP's substantially reduced military capacity following an FAZ offensive in Fizi in June–July 1977, the only possibility for collaboration was the transfer of all or some of the Tigres to eastern Zaire, or for Kabila to take political charge in Angola.[88] Understandably, Mbumba saw no reason to accept either alternative; his army was now both sufficiently autonomous and demonstrably effective enough for it not to require an externally imposed strategy or leadership.

Partly because of Mbumba's characteristic approach, the CSL treaty did not lead to practical cooperation. His unhappy experience of appointing external FLNC representatives with diverse political ideas and outside his immediate control increased his mistrust of such alliances. In contrast, Justin Mushitu engaged politically not only with Kabila but also with MARC (see above), becoming its joint secretary-general.[89] Mbumba suspected that Kabila might use a mooted FLNC/PRP/MARC coalition to take control of the FLNC with the blessing of Neto and the aid of Mushitu.[90] In Luanda in October 1977, Mushitu warned Kabila that he faced assassination if he returned to Chicapa. Kabila left Luanda, and Mushitu himself sought asylum at the Swedish embassy.[91] Unsurprisingly, Mbumba rejects this explanation, claiming simply that Kabila left Luanda without implementing the agreement. Mbumba accused Kabila of acting against him in Europe and of having revealed to France and Belgium plans for the imminent second Shaba war. In any case, on April 10, 1978, the FLNC central committee annulled the accord creating the CSL.[92] The following month, the FLNC launched the second Shaba war without the participation of the PRP or Kabila.

Zaire between the Wars

As noted above, Shaba I was launched at a time when international support for the Mobutu regime was at a low ebb. Although it was ostensibly a military victory and was presented as such by the Zairian state, it was a propaganda disaster for the Mobutu regime. The Carter presidency was critical of previous US support for so-called Third World anticommunist dictators; Secretary of State Cyrus Vance and Ambassador to the United Nations Andrew Young sought to replace "neocolonial" Western interventionism with African solutions to African problems, backed by a more interventionist OAU. Indeed, Gleijeses demonstrates that the Carter administration was willing to normalize relations with Cuba in 1977 if Cuba could be persuaded to withdraw its troops from Angola.[93]

France now stepped into the space vacated by the United States' hitherto close relations with Zaire. Giscard d'Estaing saw the MPLA victory as a communist threat to Western interests and sought to draw Zaire, the largest and potentially the wealthiest French-speaking nation in Africa, into its Francophone sphere.[94] Giscard's visit to Zaire in August 1975 had provided a much-needed boost to Mobutu's battered esteem.[95] French diplomats stressed, in characteristically Napoleonic style, the desirability of political centralism and the menace of ethnic diversity; Mobutu had tried "to create national unity, [but] the fire of ethnic particularism has never ceased to burn under the ash."[96] In Shaba I, however, "Zaire [had been] the victim of subversive armed activities from abroad.... Whatever the origin of the attackers, their action cannot be considered as a popular insurrection, nor therefore an internal matter . . . it is an *external aggression*."[97] France, satisfied that its transportation of Moroccan troops had enabled Zairian victory in Shaba I, subsequently strengthened its military engagement.[98] This meant enabling a more effective Zairian military, perhaps via a longer-term presence of Francophone African troops. Belgium, while not opposed to such measures, pressed more strongly for political reform to defuse popular support for the overthrow of Mobutu, possibly sparked by a second Katangese invasion. Belgian foreign minister Renaat Van Elslande expressed concern that Mobutu could not survive without foreign troops in the event of a second FLNC incursion.[99]

The disastrous state of the Zairian economy and the equally disastrous performance of the FAZ in Shaba I placed substantial pressure on Mobutu to make meaningful economic and political reforms. During Shaba I, Zaire had received a guarantee of external support in the form of an IMF loan of US$85 million, a signal to private banks that the regime was still financially viable.[100] The price to be paid was the implementation of political reforms, formally announced during a speech by Mobutu at N'Sele on July 1, 1977.[101] In a subsequent message to Carter, Mobutu claimed that the "underlying meaning . . . [of the reforms was] the liberalization of our national system through profound political decentralization; economic decentralization; and full implementation of the norms governing human rights."[102] Mobutu announced that eighteen of the thirty members of the MPR's supreme Political Bureau would henceforth be directly elected from candidates resident in each of the nine provinces (two from each).[103] Members of the National Legislative Council and urban councils would also be directly elected (rural council members would be appointed). Mobutu also proposed a degree of decentralization—eventually introduced in 1982—via greater autonomy for the regional commissioner. The Zairian presidency remained, however, an uncontested position.

Elections to these bodies were accordingly held in October 1977; despite the fact that all candidates belonged to the single party, the MPR, they proved highly competitive: more than 2,000 candidates stood for 270 parliamentary seats, and 167 contested the 18 elected Political Bureau seats.[104] In December 1977, however, Mobutu was elected unopposed to a third seven-year term as president. When the dust had settled on these reforms, even Mobutu's supporters in the French Foreign Ministry concluded: "It is difficult to see anything other than a parody in the elections of last October and December.... Political reforms... have been implemented in form only and have created a facade of democracy."[105] In the medium term, however, these reforms, instigated as a result of the political fallout from Shaba I, had a significant impact, enabling the creation of an active parliamentary opposition to Mobutu that coalesced in 1982 into the opposition party Union pour la Démocratie et le Progrès Social (UDPS).[106] The new Legislative Council, with powers to question and scrutinize decisions made by the government (now led by a prime minister, known as the first commissioner of state), provided an important focus of political dissent in the late 1970s and early 1980s.

These political reforms were matched, in November 1977, by Mobutu's famous speech condemning the *mal zaïrois* and advancing the "Mobutu Plan" to resurrect the national economy.[107] This apparent opening of the economy to liberalized investment was positively received in international markets, and an additional loan of US$220 million was provided by a consortium of Western banks.[108] Meanwhile, the disastrous economic situation showed no signs of improvement: inflation stood at 250 percent per annum in November 1977, and that year's budget deficit alone was US$340 million.[109]

These reforms coincided with increased repression of the local and regional proponents of more radical reform. Most immediately, the retreat of the Tigres in May 1977 was followed by a new reign of terror in Lunda areas, where the "victorious" FAZ carried out revenge attacks against Lunda civilians assumed to support the FLNC (about which Mobutu's Western allies were silent). As noted, this had the effect of driving hundreds of thousands of additional refugees into Angola, providing potential new recruits for the FLNC.[110] In addition, a decree was put in place preventing the hiring of officials from Katanga and North and South Kasai. In the military, this measure was used by ambitious officers from Equateur Province to remove their rivals from these provinces.[111]

Meanwhile, in June 1977, the Mwaant Yav, Daniel Tshombe, was placed under house arrest, accused of having assisted with recruitment for the FLNC. In December he was formally arrested and accused of possessing documents that proved his collusion with Nathanaël Mbumba.[112] Nguz Karl I Bond, only recently reappointed as minister for foreign affairs, was dismissed from this position in August 1977, allegedly because he had been informed by Jean-Baptiste Kibwe six months earlier that an attack on Zaire was being prepared.[113] Nguz was probably ousted because Western policy makers had identified him as a possible replacement for Mobutu.[114] After an obviously rigged judicial process, Nguz was condemned to death in September (his sentence was subsequently commuted to life in prison).[115] His conviction highlighted the broader exclusion of southern Katanga's political elite in the new political dispensation.

Finally, in February 1978, about 250 soldiers and civilians were arrested, accused of involvement in actions designed to destabilize the state. The following month, a case was opened against sixty-seven soldiers and twenty-four civilians. Nineteen were condemned to death, eighteen of whom were executed. Monguya Mbenge of MARC (see above) was alleged to be the mastermind behind this "terrorist plot.[116] Some FAZ officers trained at overseas military academies, mostly in Belgium, were eliminated or marginalized. On March 17, seventeen FAZ officers (of whom two were Katangese) were shot. At the end of March, officers and noncommissioned officers from Bandundu were suspended as a result of a revolt in Kwilu, which was harshly suppressed.[117] As Belgian intelligence later noted, these actions had grave consequences for the FAZ: they led to a total paralysis of the Department of Defense and the general staff headquarters, an oppressive climate of fear and suspicion, the loss of experienced officers who were not immediately replaced, and a resultant profound discontent among those who were relocated.[118] These destabilizing and demoralizing events occurred less than two months before the FLNC mounted its second attack on Zaire.

Shaba II, May 1978

The Invasion

The second Shaba war, far shorter but more significant than Shaba I, raised the stakes of the conflict: the FLNC, taking a more direct route via Zambian territory, seized Zaire's globally important mineral assets. This led not only to a more urgent response by Mobutu but also to a far more rapid and larger-scale international intervention. It was the high point of the ex-Katangese gendarmes' impact on Zaire since the secession, but its very success ultimately led to the dismantling of the FLNC as an autonomous politico-military force.

The extent of Angolan approval and direction of Shaba II is disputed. FLNC forces were stationed near the Zairian border for defensive purposes. According to Mbumba, Angola's minister of national defense, Henrique "Iko" Carreira, ordered the FLNC to infiltrate groups of twenty-five men each day into Zaire.[119] However, other witnesses insist that Mbumba, fearing an imminent rapprochement between Neto and Mobutu, acted without Angolan authority (see also below).[120] Gleijeses demonstrates that the Cubans, having learned about the possibility of a second Shaba attack, expressed clearly to Neto their opposition to any such operation, which they feared would prompt a more substantial Western intervention on the side of Mobutu—as it indeed did. While Neto apparently expressed his agreement with this analysis, he did not prevent the instigation of Shaba II. Gleijeses concludes that his actions "did not match his words" but apparently did not consider the possibility that the FLNC acted without Neto's permission; he does, however, quote Neto's "evasive" reply to Cuban criticism following the attack, in which he stated: "In the case of the Katangans, there was much sentimentality on the Angolan side. . . . [W]e decided that they should not launch another attack from Angola, but we took no measures to stop them."[121]

On March 21–22, 1978, Katangese forces had begun infiltrating Zaire and advanced toward Mutshatsha, where they clashed with both FAZ and UNITA forces in heavy fighting that led to the death of approximately forty FLNC soldiers.[122] Some days later, on March 27, Mbumba was apparently directed to assemble all the Tigres at the Chicapa base. He then took the decision to limit the FLNC's operation to areas of Shaba Province away from the Zairian-Angolan frontier. This is consistent with the subsequent entry of FLNC's forces into Zaire via northwest Zambia, through the same Lunda-speaking areas they had traversed in 1963 on their way to Angola. Mbumba established his headquarters at Jimbe, close to the Zambian and Zairian borders; he had roughly 5,000–6,000 troops at his disposal, which he transported from Chicapa to Jimbe during April.[123] Because of Luembe's execution (see above), command of Shaba II was entrusted to Vindicien Kiyana, nicknamed Mufu.[124] The operational commanders were Gaston Nawej and Pascal Kapend.

According to Mbumba, the attack was launched in three phases: a first wave of 3,300 advanced toward Kolwezi on May 1, 1978; another 1,650 Tigres entered Zambia on May 5, so as to attack Mutshatsha and the route linking it to Kolwezi; and a third wave of about 1,000 troops was to attack Kasaji.[125] Zambia's alleged failure to prevent the movement of FLNC forces through its territory was characterized by Mobutu as facilitating the rebel attack, damaging relations between the two countries (see also below).[126] The unexpected route of attack caught FAZ forces, concentrated on the Angolan border, by surprise.[127] Kolwezi was "defended" by the 14th Brigade of the Kamanyola Division, considered the FAZ's weakest unit.[128] Between 2,000 and 2,500 of the FLNC forces, their uniforms initially hidden beneath civilian clothes, entered Zaire; their surprise attack on May 13 captured the city in a few hours, destroying twelve Zairian air force planes in the process.[129] A witness's statement described the capture of the town and suggests the use of sacrificial magic by the FLNC:

> We had suffered a lot during the nocturnal infiltration. . . . Kolwezi was less than one hour's march. Strangely enough the town seemed ever further away, time passed by and we did not reach it. But as a chief, I had a rope made of skin of an unknown animal that I wore on my arm as a bracelet. It felt ever tighter, to signal to me the presence of the enemy. Physically we didn't see anything and Kolwezi seemed to move ever further away. This . . . led to an exchange among us because the situation seemed disquieting. We thought we should usefully sacrifice a combatant. After the sacrifice it was as if a veil was lifted from our eyes. We were already in Kolwezi without even noticing it. It is this way we took over Kolwezi while the FAZ fled in all directions like little rabbits.[130]

A further FLNC column subsequently captured Mutshatsha. Also in FLNC hands were approximately 2,500 European employees of Gécamines, SNCZ, and other mining operators in Kolwezi. Six French soldiers, part of France's existing military cooperation with Zaire, were killed at the Hotel Impala. The majority were Belgian (1,750) and French (400) nationals, and for this reason Belgium and France took the lead in the international response.

International Appeals and Response

On May 14, Mobutu appealed for assistance from the United States, France, Belgium, Morocco, and China to repel the invasion.[131] Once again, Zaire portrayed the attack as an action controlled and initiated by Cuba and the Soviet Union. In a briefing of Western ambassadors, Zaire's acting foreign minister, Umba Di Lutete, claimed that "white faces" had been seen among the Katangese troops, implying the physical presence of Cubans.[132] Zaire's representative to the United Nations protested the invasion of "pretend" refugees, "armed and supported by the Luanda government, under the instigation of Soviet-Cuban imperialism."[133] The British Foreign Office was briefed by Zaire's special emissary, Lengema Dulia, on May 18; he claimed (contrary to the evidence) that the Brussels-based Monguya "faction" of Shaba exiles had planned the FLNC attack and that these factions had been brought together by the "Russians."[134] For its part, Angola consistently denied supporting the FLNC: a press statement issued on May 15, emphasizing the supposedly internal nature of the conflict, stated: "Angola is completely alien to any movements of Zairois elements in armed opposition to Kinshasa authorities."[135]

International analysis nevertheless focused on the form and extent of Angolan and Cuban involvement in the FLNC in the run-up to and during the attack. A Diamang employee told the British embassy in Luanda that "many Cubans . . .

were certainly integrated with the Katangese when they set off... but so far there is no way of knowing whether the Cubans crossed the border with the Katangese."[136] CIA intelligence suggested that in early May "the Cubans were already organizing the movement of a large number of FLNC troops from northeastern Angola towards the Zambian border and that Cuban advisors were accompanying this force. They had no confirmation the Cubans planned to stay with the rebels once they left Angola."[137] During the invasion, a CIA report, while skeptical of Cuban presence inside Zaire, argued that "Cubans have been involved in training and advising the ex-Katangan exiles... the Cuban government clearly had foreknowledge of the attack... [and] Cuban advisers doubtless assisted the rebels in their preparations for the incursion."[138] This report continued:

> The FNLC probably has some freedom of action regarding tactics and local objectives, and, to a degree, the timing of specific operations.... The rebels... would be capable of training their own recruits and launching a one-shot operation independently if they were willing to take the risk that such wholly independent operations might put them at cross-purposes with the Cubans, Soviets, and Angolans. Once inside Shaba, the degree of Cuban/Soviet/Angolan control over them would probably be much smaller. The FNLC can also draw on a large number of sympathisers and guerrillas in place throughout the Shaba region to support its operations.[139]

As is suggested above, evidence implies that Cuba was directly opposed to any such attack. Seeking to secure Angola as a base for the struggle against white minority rule in southern Africa, Cuba sought to avoid any pretext for attacks on Angola and, both publicly and diplomatically, denied any role in Shaba II.[140]

The position of Angola toward the invasion remains somewhat unclear: apparent incoherence in the Angolan government may reflect the impact of the Nito Alves affair on the MPLA.[141] Despite the order allegedly given by Defense Minister Carreira (as noted above), Mbumba was ordered by the Angolan government to return to Luanda for a meeting. He was held there under house arrest until the completion of Shaba II.[142] It remains unclear at what level of the MPLA this order was approved, but this and other evidence suggests either divisions within the MPLA leadership or else an abrupt change in its position between the start of April and early May. Carreira was reputedly close to Neto, and it is unlikely that the attack would have been approved without consulting the Angolan president. Gleijeses cites Neto's claim that "I knew nothing of this until the Cubans [Risquet] informed me."[143] Risquet himself thought it possible that Neto's instructions were not being respected, a position that is held by some ex-Tigres.[144] A former Zairian ambassador to Angola believes that a radical faction of the MPLA approved the operation against Neto's orders.[145] Rosa Coutinho held the view that Shaba II was launched at the instigation of a group of Cuban advisers, but this seems unlikely.[146]

Some former Tigres also believe that Mbumba feared an imminent accord between Neto and Mobutu, in which an end to Zairian support for the FNLA and UNITA would be matched by the expulsion of the Tigres to Zaire.[147] Although Mbumba's house arrest certainly suggests disapproval of the operation by the Angolan presidency, Tigres who participated in Shaba II report that Mbumba continued to give instructions by telephone during the operation (see below): Mufu, the operational commander, recalls many telephone messages from Mbumba during the full course of the operation.[148]

Events in Kolwezi and the "P2 Massacre"

Despite the apparent threat to its nationals, Belgium initially played down the prospect of using armed force. Even the French, initially hopeful that the FAZ would be able to recapture Kolwezi, delayed responding to Mobutu's request for military aid.[149] By May 17, 1978, however, by which time the failure of Zairian forces to retake Kolwezi was apparent, a briefing note for the British cabinet spelled out the dangers of the situation: "If President Mobutu cannot deal with the problem quickly, his position could be seriously threatened, leading to chaos and the opportunity for external interference, which the Russians would no doubt exploit. He could face an army revolt. The loss of Kolwezi will damage Zaire's already bankrupt economy."[150]

The FLNC forces occupying Kolwezi were initially relatively disciplined. However, faced with a lack of clear instructions from Mbumba and limited supplies, disorganization took hold, above all among the young recruits from Shaba I. "Popular tribunals" issued summary judgments, and the young troops, some using drugs, were trigger-happy and did not always follow the orders they had been given to protect expatriates. A report based on a Gécamines source claimed that on May 15, eight Belgians and one Italian had been killed.[151] The following day, the French ambassador in Kinshasa reported: "The attitude of the Katangese [gendarmes] in ... [Kolwezi] has suddenly changed[;] indifferent to discipline, its occupiers have lost all restraint, and are looting and killing foreigners regardless of occupation, age or nationality."[152] A general panic took hold among the expatriate population.[153] Reports of such attacks accelerated Western efforts toward establishing an intervention force. Before international forces could be mobilized, however, President Mobutu directed the 311st Battalion into action, parachuting into the area around Kolwezi on May 16.[154] This was despite CIA concern that the attack might be unsuccessful and that "the threat to the European community in Kolwezi could increase if the Zairians attacked the residential sector."[155] This fear proved well founded; this disastrous operation left most of the Zairian paratroopers dead, injured, or captured. FAZ forces were, however, able to recapture Kolwezi airport, located ten kilometers south of the town, which Mobutu briefly visited on May 18. This action reinforced awareness of the vulnerability of the Mobutu regime but simultaneously increased pressure for outside intervention.

On May 18, what came to be called the P2 massacre took place. The FAZ took custody of fifty Europeans in the Baron Levêque company offices in the so-called P2 quarter. As FLNC forces approached, grenades were thrown, and thirty-seven of the fifty Europeans were killed. This massacre shaped the international image of Shaba II, with the estimated 800 Zairian dead largely forgotten. Media reports which assumed FLNC responsibility were supported by Zairian foreign minister Umba Di Lutete, who "said the rebel troops had been ordered to massacre the whites they were holding. . . . [M]essages intercepted by his government showed that Gen. Nathaniel M'Bumba . . . had given the order to kill Europeans after it became apparent his invasion was doomed."[156] It remains difficult to determine who perpetrated these killings, but the weight of evidence suggests that responsibility in fact lay with the FAZ. Belgian intelligence reports state that the expatriates were killed by the Tigres after FAZ troops fled.[157] According to Odom, the Tigres had been unnerved by the FAZ airdrop.[158] However, the detailed testimony of Yambuya accuses the FAZ troops already in the area.[159] Lourtie argues that the P2 massacre could not have been committed by the FLNC because its forces had already retreated by the time it occurred.[160] Lourtie spoke with two expatriates hiding in a false ceiling above where the massacre took place: they were certain that the FAZ paratroops were responsible.[161] In addition, none of the Tigres who participated in Shaba II interviewed for this study recalls this event, suggesting their lack of involvement.

Whatever the evidence, one conspiratorial rumor in later circulation claimed that the FAZ had deliberately killed these Europeans to spark a foreign intervention. Certainly, Zaire desired such an intervention, and a massacre could have been aimed at inciting Belgium and France to intervene. However, this theory is undermined by the fact that the international decision to intervene had already been taken (see below).[162]

Western Intervention

Since Shaba I, US policy toward Africa had altered in ways that would shape its reaction to Shaba II. Cuba's deployment of some of its Angola-based troops in the Cuban-Ethiopian force that successfully reversed the Somali invasion of the Ogaden in late 1977 through early 1978 contributed to a shift in US policy. Vance's moderate "Africanist" policy was increasingly seen as ineffective, and National Security Adviser Zbigniew Brzezinski won support for a stronger military response to Cuban implementation of Soviet "aggression" in Africa. In this context, the United States agreed to provide logistical support to an emerging Franco-Belgian "evacuation" plan (Operation Red Bean). In the early hours of

May 18, the White House agreed to a request for ten C-141 aircraft to airlift Belgian equipment to Zaire, on condition that the planes themselves did not enter the combat zone.[163] The presentation of the military operation as "strictly limited to evacuation of expatriates ... [and] in no way connected with the broader conflict between the Zairians and Katangans" was a diplomatic fiction designed to avoid the accusation that Western states were interfering in African affairs.[164]

When, on the afternoon of May 19, a first group of 420 French legionnaires parachuted into Kolwezi, the Tigres had already retreated.[165] The situation the French troops found on the ground was chaotic, with FAZ paratroopers carrying out revenge attacks against civilians.[166] The chaotic nature of the Zairian military response is confirmed by a senior FAZ officer who recalls that he was assigned to command several companies unknown to him and never received an operational command. One legionnaire confirms the involvement of some French troops in the random killing.[167]

The unexpectedly early French airdrop irritated Belgian politicians, who saw it as an attempt to take sole credit for the liberation of Kolwezi and who questioned the supposedly "humanitarian purpose of the French drop."[168] France's foreign minister, Louis de Guiringaud, claimed that the sudden deterioration of conditions and the threat that expatriates would be killed en masse necessitated prompt action.[169] However, French actions went well beyond securing the expatriate community; French troops worked with FAZ forces to secure control of Kolwezi itself and pursued FLNC forces as they retreated in vehicles they had seized. As a result, Mobutu was able to blur the line between humanitarian and political intervention; he quickly requested that France extend its military assistance beyond the immediate "rescue."[170] Belgian paratroops arrived in Kolwezi on May 20 and played a leading role in evacuating the expatriates—they did not participate in overt military action. Their supposedly late arrival and limited role were criticized by Mobutu, who publicly contrasted their actions to France's more interventionist approach. The final death toll in Kolwezi was around 160 expatriates, 150 Zairian soldiers, 200 Katangese, 3 French soldiers, and at least 800 Zairian civilians.[171]

The Diplomatic Fallout: Finding the Cubans

On the day of the French airdrop, Foreign Minister Louis de Guiringaud was already claiming that France's troops in Kolwezi had "identified the presence of a motorised company of Cubans ... [and] several Cuban vehicles."[172] He declared on June 16: "We now know from several different sources ... that Cuban instructors in Angola helped train the Katangans to launch the attack against Shaba."[173] Cuban president Fidel Castro not only denied his country's involvement but insisted that he had sought to prevent the Katangese action.[174] He publicly outlined his country's prioritization of the southern African theater of operations: "The fundamental problems of Africa are in southern Africa. . . . This is why, for political reasons, we have been absolutely opposed to this kind of action on the part of the Katangans."[175] Castro suggested that Neto's instructions to prevent the FLNC's attack had not been followed. Neto himself publicly insisted that "Angola did not train or arm any army nor did it organise any expedition against Zaire. Our Soviet and Cuban allies did not intervene in any way on Angolan territory to provoke the rebellion." In claiming that Angola's involvement arose solely from the presence of "Zaire refugees on its territory," Neto, like his Portuguese predecessors, sought to conceal the FLNC's military capacity by intentionally blurring the division between refugees and soldiers on the Angola-Zaire border.[176]

US president Jimmy Carter meanwhile castigated the Soviet Union for its continued "interference in the internal affairs of African nations" via its Cuban ally.[177] In response to Castro's denials, the White House released a CIA memorandum suggesting Eastern bloc training for the FLNC, Cuban military support during Shaba I, and advisory support in the run-up to Shaba II.[178] Gleijeses convincingly demonstrates the poor quality of this intelligence, which tended to assume that any competent military action by the Katangese could have occurred only under close Cuban direction.[179] A more dispassionate CIA assessment drew an instructive distinction: "It is impossible for a military expedition, such as that mounted against Kolwezi this year . . . to have occurred without the knowledge and logistic support of the Cuban government and its representatives in Angola . . . [but] we do not have evidence that Cuban personnel physically accompanied the basically ex-Katangan gendarme elements who invaded Shaba in 1977 and 1978."[180]

This did not, however, prevent a continuing search for evidence of a physical Cuban presence in Shaba II: on June 2, an NSA staffer wrote excitedly to Brzezinski: "Recent overhead reconnaissance of the Shaba region has turned up evidence of Cuban participation in the recent invasion of Zaire . . . a photograph of what appears to be—according to the best analysts at CIA—a half-smoked Cuban cigar (Cohiba brand). . . . While it is possible that the cigar was smoked by a Katangan, this is highly unlikely . . . the Cubans do not like either the Katangans or the Angolans. . . . Thus, the Cubans might pass arms to the Katangans, but NOT their best cigars. We have, to paraphrase the expression used during Watergate—found the 'smoking Cuban.'"[181] Curiously, this supposedly definitive piece of evidence did not convince the White House, which never publicly claimed that Cuban troops were inside Zaire. For their part, only a few Katangese participants in Shaba II insist on the participation of a "Cuban" inside Zaire; several interviewees claim that an albino, named Kalau, was mistaken for a Cuban.[182]

Sergio Martinez of the Cuban Interest Section (one of Cuba's few links to the United States) explained that Cuban "involvement in Shaba is contrary to Cuba's interest since Cuba knows that the Katangese are uncontrol[l]able and any support could prove to be embarrassing."[183] Although Cuba had trained and armed the FLNC (though not to the extent of its demands), the *purpose* of this training was essentially defensive. Cuba and, to a lesser extent, Angola were by the time of Shaba II unhappy about their lack of control over the FLNC, which destabilized the fragile balance of the Cold War in Africa.[184] By 1978 Mobutu had reinforced his position internationally, making Angola more reluctant to support a military operation: Mbumba, appreciating both a growing threat to the FLNC's autonomy and a potential détente between Mobutu and Neto, gambled on an adventurous attack on Kolwezi without the direct support of either Cuba or Angola.

Retreat via Zambia

The majority of FLNC troops retreated from Shaba back through northwest Zambia; one column was sighted near Sakeji mission school in Mwinilunga district on May 22.[185] A French report identified a convoy of 300 vehicles, mostly captured in Zaire, passing through Kalene Hill on May 23–24.[186] British sources reported affinity between local Zambians and the rebels: "The Zambian locals, who are from the same tribe (the Lunda) as the Katangese, seemed very friendly towards the retreating rebels. They were lining the road and were giving the rebels food in exchange for their Zairean loot."[187] A *Times of Zambia* journalist was told by fleeing Zairian refugees that Mobutu's repression of the Lunda in general and against the Mwaant Yav and Nguz Karl I Bond in particular had fueled Lunda recruitment to the FLNC. FLNC guerrillas had apparently "pillaged" Zairian villages between Mutshatsha and Kolwezi and had forced Zairian farmers to provide them with supplies as they had prepared their operation over the past few months.[188]

Zaire sought Zambia's cooperation in preventing the free movement of Katangese forces in their retreat to Angola, but this remained difficult, for reasons uncannily similar to those facing the colonial authorities in 1963. British officials reported: "All the indications are that the Zambians are highly embarrassed [by the presence of FLNC forces] and simply do not want to know. Both in public and in private . . . they have admitted [that] only unarmed refugees have arrived from Zaire. Even if they wished to try to prevent the passage of the rebels, they do not have the means to do so."[189] President Kenneth Kaunda, having denounced Mobutu's allegations that Zambia was being used as a base for attacks on Zaire, was embarrassed when his denial that armed Katangese rebels had passed through Zambia was challenged by journalists who had witnessed them. The *Times of Zambia* subsequently criticized the fact that "upwards of a thousand heavily armed rebels can cross ninety kilometres of Zambian soil without our security forces knowing and reporting it."[190]

Following skirmishes between Zambian army forces and retreating Tigres, Britain's Lusaka embassy stressed both the lack of forces available to police the border and the danger that local Zambians "would be sympathetic toward the Katangese if the Zambian Army tried to move against the rebels in strength."[191] Some FLNC soldiers were, however, captured and interrogated by Zambian intelligence officers; the CIA's resultant report claimed that "hundreds of armed guerrillas now in place in Shaba are preparing to attack other towns including Likasi, Lubumbashi, and Kipushi. The guerrillas are supported by secret bases and supply centers throughout the region."[192] In fact, most (but not all) FLNC forces were in full organized retreat into Angola and would not again present a substantive threat to Mobutu's control of Zaire for nearly two decades.[193]

After Shaba II

Following the invasion, FLNC forces withdrew to Angola with their numbers largely intact, having dealt a considerable blow to the Zairian economy; the Kolwezi occupation had driven up the world price of cobalt by 24 percent and forced Western donors to inject an additional US$100 million to prevent the collapse of Zaire's economy. US officials recognized their achievement: "In the space of one week, the ... FLNC ... successfully accomplished their prime mission ... of impairing the mining complex ... [in a] swift, well prepared, well organized attack. ... The extent of that impairment in terms of psychological, economic, political and social consequences has deep significance for the viability of the Mobutu regime."[194]

French officials admitted in early June that the "gendarmes" continued to pose a threat because of their ability to move among the civilian Lunda population "like fish in water."[195] Britain argued that the lesson of Shaba II was the need for greater reform; its Foreign Office insisted, "We do not want to see Mobutu get away with a series of cosmetic reforms as he did in 1977."[196] The reality was, however, that, in contrast to the aftermath of Shaba I, both France and the United States had in practice reinforced Mobutu's position. As in the mid-1960s, the West was unable to imagine an alternative political model for Zaire that would not imperil both vital Western mineral supplies and create an opening to communism in central Africa. Ultimately, both invasions, by demonstrating the weakness of Mobutu's authority, forced the West to provide significant military and financial aid.[197] Mobutu's awareness that Western states had no alternative to his rule made it possible for him to delay or disregard demands for reform. In the aftermath of Shaba II, Brzezinski, reflecting the more hawkish policy of the Carter administration he had successfully advocated, argued: "Zaire is too important and the global stakes too high for the United States to continue its past posture of marginal support for the Zaire economic [reform] effort.... Not participating in this effort would probably lead to a rapid economic collapse in Zaire and political fragmentation of the country.... Any long-term economic recovery could not take place unless there was an improvement in the security situation."[198]

Immediate negotiations therefore focused on the provision of an African military force that could secure control of Shaba's mineral areas and guarantee the security of expatriates based there, against the continued threat posed by the Katangese—without this protection, the mining industry vital to the Zairian economy would grind to a halt. At French instigation, a new Pan-African Force (PAF) or Inter-African Force, under Franco-Moroccan leadership and consisting of 2,400 African troops from Morocco, Senegal, Togo, and Gabon, was established in Kolwezi and Lubumbashi to provide security for mining activities and expatriate employees, thereby guaranteeing government revenue and Western investments. It also "prevented the Zairian Army from committing its usual excesses against the civilian population."[199] This remained in place until mid-1979; by the time it was withdrawn, the military threat posed by the FLNC had been largely extinguished.[200] Nevertheless, Belgium maintained a significant military presence in the area throughout the 1980s to guarantee expatriate safety.

Under international pressure, diplomatic relations were established between Zaire and Angola in July 1978. Neto, with Moscow's endorsement, visited Kinshasa in mid-August, with both leaders seeking to normalize relations and agreeing to terminate support to groups hostile to each other's regimes.[201] This was followed by Mobutu's own visit to Luanda in October. Zaire also improved its strained relations with Zambia, with a visit by Kaunda to Lubumbashi in June 1978 and a meeting of the Zaire-Zambia commission held to address border tensions in August.

Cuba, keen to focus international attention on South African aggression in the wake of the Cassinga raid of May 1978, pressured Neto to end Katangese military autonomy.[202] As the Tigres returned to Angola, they were immediately disarmed. Following the normalization of relations between Angola and Zaire, it was agreed to move the Tigres away from their shared frontier.[203] With the withdrawal of Angolan patronage, the FLNC was finished as a coherent political force, and its leadership was expelled from Angola.[204] One contemporary observer rightly concluded, "It seems that Mbumba did not think about military categories or tactics and did not have a comprehensive plan that included political factors."[205]

Zaire's promulgation of an amnesty in June 1978 and the normalization of relations with Angola led to the return of approximately 52,000 refugees from Angola and Zambia to Zaire (although many more remained). France, actively involved in refugee repatriation, noted in September that "some of the ... [FLNC soldiers] are ready to return to Zaire and benefit from the amnesty. Those most involved, Mbumba and those close to him, are wary. Previous experience has created fear that there will be a sudden catch. But Angola does not want to keep them."[206] Some returnees were indeed accused of sympathies with the FLNC and executed as a result.[207]

As in 1963, the demobilization of ex-Katangese forces raised the prospect that bands of armed men would disperse into the triborder area, potentially to emerge as a threat at a later date. In December 1978, Belgian and French intelligence warned of the danger posed by "rebel bands" of the FLNC commanded by Lieutenant Colonel Mufu, which "seemed to have entirely escaped the control of Luanda and were operating from Angolan and Zambian [border] areas."[208] There was, in fact, no realistic possibility of a "Shaba III" attack: France's accentuation of the Tigres' threat was, however, a taste of the widespread disjuncture between image and reality that would develop in the years to come.

Cuba had clearly provided military training and support to the FLNC forces, as a major part of the military forces at the disposal of the MPLA. There is, however, no evidence that they did so, as was alleged by Zaire and France, in order to facilitate the attacks by the FLNC against Zaire—rather, the overwhelming priority of Cuba was strengthening the defense of Angola against its many enemies and the capacity of its fighting forces (including the FLNC) against UNITA. Cuban officers perhaps underestimated the capacity for autonomous action by the FLNC, but they were certainly unwilling to provide them with the heavy weaponry needed for a more effective attack on Zaire. Cuba was critical of Shaba I and actively sought to prevent Shaba II; it also encouraged the Angolans to break links with the FLNC in its aftermath. The attitude of the French mirrored this Cuban stance in some respects: they were apparently unable to imagine that the FLNC could and would act independently and indeed against the expressed wishes of Cuban forces, and (in Shaba II) be so effective in doing so. Because the FLNC did not fit neatly into the Cold War prism through which both sides—and indeed international observers more generally—viewed these events, its aims remained misunderstood and ultimately unfulfilled. The failure or unwillingness of non-African states, on both sides of the Cold War, to understand this led them to marginalize one of the few Congolese forces with the capacity to effectively challenge Mobutu's predatory regime.

The following chapter will explain the aftermath of the destruction of the FLNC as an autonomous force capable of challenging Mobutu's domination of the Zairian state. It explains the fragmentation of its leaders and soldiers into a series of factions and the problematic incorporation of many of its soldiers into the Angolan armed forces. It nevertheless illustrates how, at the nadir of the fortunes of the Katangese-in-exile, geopolitical change in Africa and globally created new possibilities for political change which, in the late 1990s, led many Katangese exiles to realize their dream of returning home to a post-Mobutu Congo.

7   Disarmament and Division, 1979–1996

With the ending of formal support from Angola to the FLNC, the group rapidly disintegrated into a series of factions, while most of its political and military leadership was deported to Guinea-Bissau. Under the Portuguese, and initially under the MPLA, the Katangese forces in Angola had for more than a decade been deployed in actions against the Zairian state and Angolan forces backed by that state. Now, having lost their political leadership, they were semi-integrated into the Angolan armed forces and, from 1988, deployed militarily by the Angolan state in a form mirroring their use by the Portuguese two decades earlier.

The Katangese nevertheless continued to claim ownership of the identity and history of the FLNC. They faced a profound dilemma in doing so: their political identity and credibility rested on their history of effective resistance against the Mobutu regime, most notably the Shaba operations of 1977 and 1978. Now, the loss of their autonomous military organization and leadership severely limited their capacity to capitalize on this history. Moreover, the removal of their leader, Nathanaël Mbumba, responsible for the Shaba I and II attacks that had destabilized Zaire but that had also led Angola to withdraw the FLNC's Angolan support base, sparked a series of internal conflicts. These divisions were complex and multisided, but at their heart was the issue of whether and how to return in some version to the homeland to which they laid claim and which remained central to their identity. Herein lay their unique challenge to the Zairian state: while President Mobutu had proved his extraordinary ability to incorporate all the regional identities of Zaire in the projection of his authority, he failed to find a way to reconcile his rule to the dream of Katangese autonomy, forcefully symbolized and kept alive by the now ex-Tigres.

Although the ex-Tigres posed no genuine challenge to President Mobutu for much of this period, they remained a potent if undeployed weapon. As is indicated by documents in the archives of the United Nations High Commission for Refugees (UNHCR), the Angolan authorities were reluctant to allow them to return to Zaire. This was not only because they would lose a force that, detached as it was from Angola's own political divisions, could be easily mobilized, but also because they feared that Zaire might use them militarily against Angola, possibly in cooperation with UNITA. Inside Zaire, the memory of the "ex-gendarmes" was kept alive both by the military and security forces, which sought to exaggerate the threat posed by external enemies, and by part of the Katangese population, which cherished the memory of the secession and of the continued potential of the ex-Tigres to achieve Katanga's "emancipation."

These factors created opportunities for the ex-Tigres to enter into political alliances with opposition movements inside and outside Zaire, although their attempts to do so were weakened by their own political and ethnic divisions. Some groups allied with the Katangese politician Nguz Karl I Bond, hoping that he would, on becoming president, facilitate their return. Others made alliances with Lumumbist groups, while a younger generation, recruited during the Shaba wars and with no direct memory of the secession, worked with Marxist groups, encouraged to do so by the Angolan state. Many such attempts to establish an independent political organization strained relationships with their Angolan hosts.

In this context, one faction of the ex-Tigres, together with some civilian refugees, returned in 1989 to their home country, with the assistance of UNHCR. Their return heightened the historical antagonism between the Katangese and the security apparatus, dominated by Mobutu's Equateur region. As a way to control the returnees, some were integrated into the paramilitary Civil Guard. During this period, the pro-democracy movement that swept Africa in the early 1990s, along with the related post–Cold War withdrawal of US support to Mobutu, stimulated internal political change in Zaire and the creation of new opposition movements. This created a new politicization of the ex-Tigres, in both Zaire and Angola. Their presence in Katanga helped the Union des Fédéralistes et Républicains Indépendants (UFERI), a new autochthonous political movement, establish its authority. Several groups of ex-Tigres meanwhile seized the opportunity to return to Zaire and establish political parties; some participated in the landmark Sovereign National Conference (CNS), including Nathanaël Mbumba.

However, the political movements of the early 1990s ultimately failed to effectively challenge Mobutu's hold on power. The withdrawal of US support failed to bring Mobutu down but instead made his state an increasingly cancerous presence harboring opposition groups from a number of Zaire's neighbors. Ultimate responsibility for the removal of Mobutu fell to his regional enemies. In this process, those ex-Tigres who had remained in Angola became one of the forces instrumental in the overthrow of Mobutu.

Managing the "Refugee" Problem

Before we turn to the ex-Tigres themselves, it should first be recalled that a large number of young men were, forcefully or not, recruited during the Shaba I operation. Only some had received military training, and most of them—interviewees refer to a probably exaggerated number of 15,000—did not participate in Shaba II but remained in Angola. A second wave of refugees arrived after Shaba II: UNHCR documents for 1980 refer to a total of 18,000 Zairian refugees to be housed in

Angola.¹ The Angolan military established a network of military camps to manage the ex-Tigres, some of which still exist. Those who had participated in Shaba II were relocated to Sangondo camp (Moxico Province), while the troops who had remained in Angola during the operation were moved to the new Chimbila camp, located between Cazombo (Moxico) and Camissombo (Lunda Norte).

However (and not for the first time in this study), there was some confusion between "civilians" and "soldiers": the UNHCR's figure included former soldiers, as these had technically become refugees since their disarmament in 1979. It is ultimately impossible to definitively assess the numbers of ex-Katangese fighters still resident in Angola: UNHCR did not distinguish between military and civilian refugees, and the Angolan government had no wish to publicize the continued presence of foreign troops in the country.

Following established UNHCR procedure, a first repatriation of 9,300 refugees to Zaire took place in early 1979; these were mainly repatriated from Lunda Norte and Sul provinces—probably, as is suggested in a UNHCR report, to prevent their involvement in the diamond trade. However, reports were received of violence against and even the murder of returned refugees, discouraging any further returnees.² For the next decade, the UNHCR and the International Red Cross sought to provide the remaining refugees with humanitarian assistance. Internally, they were the responsibility of the Angolan Ministry of Social Affairs, but it often deferred to the de facto authority of FAPLA, the Angolan army. While Angola needed international assistance for this large refugee population, it refused to give the UNHCR any decision-making authority.³ This became clear when Angola decided to relocate this population away from the Lunda and Moxico provinces bordering Zaire, independent of a UNHCR evaluation mission.⁴ They were transferred in 1980 to other camps in the provinces of Malanje (a camp called Quitota), Kwanza Norte (Mawa camp), Kwanza Sul (Cacanda), and Bengo (Nambwangongo / Santa Eulalia), the latter located close to the strategic Mabubas dam, a target of UNITA attacks.⁵ The parlous situation in which these men found themselves prompted a steady stream of individual returns to Zaire, while attacks drove some of the now unarmed ex-Tigres away from these camps, with many subsequently resettling in Viana, close to the capital, Luanda.

The main division within the ex-Tigres was between those wanting to return and others who preferred to stay in Angola. UNHCR reports reveal the existence of sometimes violent conflict on the basis of this division. For example, a 1986 report indicated that most of those in the Santa Eulalia camp wished to return to Zaire, while those in Mawa camp refused; in both cases, the majority harassed the minority group. For their part, provincial-level Angolan authorities appear to have favored those wishing to stay, probably because of their potential to combat the growing UNITA threat.⁶ Zaire simultaneously harbored its own Angolan refugee population, many of whom were ostensibly opposed to the

Angolan government. The presence of politicized refugee populations (some of whom had military training and/or experience) created, for both host countries, a rough equivalence of mutual threat that can be compared to the nuclear threat in the wider Cold War: they could be deployed politically and/or militarily, but their value was primarily in their threatened rather than actual use.

The Ex-Tigres in Zambia and the 1980 Coup Attempt

After Shaba II, one group of Tigres stayed in Zambia, having been disarmed by the Zambian authorities. Detailed information about this group is scarce, other than that among its leaders were Musonda Mukandasa Kingandya and Simon Kafunga. Deogratias Symba, resident in the Zambian Copperbelt city of Kitwe during this period, was implicated (alongside other ex-Tigres living inconspicuously among their Lunda kin in the Mwinilunga district of North-Western Province) in an attempted coup d'état against President Kenneth Kaunda. Symba met with Zambian dissidents and agreed to recruit former FLNC fighters to support their coup attempt. Once the dissidents were in power, their government would, it was agreed, allow Zambian territory to be used as a base for a renewed attack against Mobutu.[7]

Symba accordingly brought fifty to sixty men (some Katangese, some Zambian ethnic Lundas) from North-Western Province to a farm south of Lusaka recently purchased by a coup plotter.[8] Valentine Musakanya, one of those involved, tellingly describes the Chilanga recruits as "men from the Zambia-Katangese border at Mwinilunga who were legitimately both Zambian and Katangese rather than Zairoise."[9] Another 140 Katangese were kept in reserve on a farm near Kalulushi on the Zambian Copperbelt. In October 1980, the planned coup was preempted shortly before its implementation by the arrest of the coup plotters and their Katangese allies, following an army raid on the Chilanga farm during which one man was killed and four wounded. In total, thirteen people, including four Zairians (Symba, Albert Chimbalile, Laurent Kanyimbu, and Roger Kabwita), were publicly charged with involvement in the coup attempt. Eight of the accused were found guilty in January 1983, and seven (including Symba) were sentenced to death.[10] Symba remained in prison in Zambia before being pardoned in 1990 and acquiring political asylum in the United States. It was from there that he subsequently became involved with various Zairian opposition movements, established his contacts with Emile Ilunga, and engaged in the mobilization of the ex-Tigres for the AFDL (see below).

Factionalism among the Ex-Tigres in the 1980s

After Nathanaël Mbumba's house arrest in Luanda during and after Shaba II, he was transferred to and imprisoned in Huambo. On December 5, 1979, following the normalization of relations between Zaire and Angola, he and the entire political and military leadership of the FLNC, together with their immediate families, were flown to Guinea-Bissau. Mbumba was to remain there in a new exile for only a few years before leaving for Libya and Tanzania to pursue his political aims (see below).

Following Shaba II, the majority of the ex-Tigres were transferred to Sangondo camp (Moxico Province), where François Kapend was the commander.[11] A former gendarme, Kapend played a leading role in reconciling the ex-Tigres with the Angolan authorities, partly by surrendering their resources (including their weaponry) to the Angolan government.[12] Tensions did, however, arise over what Mbumba later characterized as Angola's "seizure" of the FLNC's considerable wealth. According to Mbumba, this amounted to 17.3 million kwanzas (US$596,551), cars, jeeps, trucks, bulldozers, 2,500 cows, 700 pigs, and 400 hectares of farmland.[13] These goods remain a point of dispute between the FLNC and the Angolan state, but the more substantive result of this transfer was to render the ex-Tigres economically and militarily dependent on the MPLA government.

The removal of Mbumba, their authoritarian but unifying leader, opened a Pandora's box of internal conflicts among the ex-Tigres, fought out along generational, ethnic, military, political, and personal lines. These divisions also soured already fragile relationships with the Angolan authorities. As a further indication of the fragmented composition of the ex-Tigres at this time, while many were resident in military camps, others lived in civilian camps and worked in civilian employment, mainly in industry and in the diamond trade; some were even teachers. The ex-Tigres tried to construct new alliances with the outside world without their former patron. They did not, however, regain their former unity, and great effort was expended in interminable factional and personal struggles. Contrary to the period when Mbumba zealously guarded his control over the movement, those who claimed the ex-Tigres' leadership now sought out any kind of political alliance that would give them leverage, some control over their future, and/or resources for survival.

In this situation, various Zairian intellectuals again tried to position themselves as the leaders of the political movement in exile. The scenario always played out in the same way: the Zairian visitor came in person or sent an emissary to a group of ex-Tigres that was now in a state of material distress, promising to alleviate their parlous position. The latter readily signed alliances or declarations in the hope of returning to Zaire under conditions of their own choosing. These politicians subsequently used these declarations as proof that they had at their disposal a military force capable of pressuring the Mobutu regime to make political reforms or concessions. In certain cases, this political capital was utilized to raise funds which were not always deployed for political purposes; certainly, none of these projects effectively challenged Mobutu's control of Zaire. A central element in this strategy was the articulation of the mythic power of the "ex-Katangese gendarmes," generated via recourse to memories not only of the Katangese secession but also of the two Shaba wars that had shaken the foundations of the Mobutu regime. Such myths, never of course tested in practice, nevertheless retained considerable influence both in Katanga and, for opposite reasons, in Kinshasa.

Meanwhile, the political capital of the ex-Tigres inside Angola remained closely tied to the assistance they had given to the MPLA to capture and retain power in 1974–1976. Therefore, as their own declarations constantly stated, the December 1974 Cossa agreement provided the legitimizing basis for the ex-Tigres' claim for assistance to topple the Mobutu regime—or at least to ensure their personal security in the event of their return to Zaire. The only resource they could deploy in support of this claim was their own existence as an organization that embodied a virtual threat.

The ex-Tigres' self-identification was confused by the evident contradictions in an organization with its roots in the Tshombist secession that now, as a result of its problematic alliance with the Marxist Angolan state, had come to embody elements of radical Lumumbist Congolese political identity. Similarly, a generational fault line divided a still-powerful older generation of ex-gendarmes and pre-1974 exiles which looked to an essentially Katangese identity from the younger post-Shaba generation, most of whom had no memory of the secession and some of whom sought to integrate into Angolan society.[14] We trace below only five main lines of these developments, characterized as they were by an endemic factionalism.

FAPC/FAPAC and Nguz Karl I Bond, 1980–1989

Jean-Beauvin Kalenga, the leader of the *fiéis* before Nathanaël Mbumba, was chosen in August 1978 as general commander of what was now named the Popular Armed Forces of Congo (FAPC).[15] This was militarily and politically the most significant group of ex-Tigres during this period. The fact that Kalenga was a Katangese Luba led to conflict with some Lunda officers, such as Gustave Masela (see below), who felt that their ethnic group was, as the majority of the ex-Tigres, entitled to lead what it asserted was the "real FLNC."[16] This latter group consisted mainly of the older generation of secession-era and pro-Tshombe Katangese.

Probably under pressure from the Mobutu regime and the UNHCR, and with the authorization of the Angolan government, Kalenga engaged in negotiations with Zaire. A first meeting was held in Luanda in June 1980 with a Zairian delegation. However, after three days of talks and a dismissive speech from Kalenga, no agreement was reached.[17] In July a meeting took place in Kinshasa between the FAPC and representatives of President Mobutu. The conditions set by Kalenga for reconciliation were partly political (democratization, federalism, recognition of the FLNC as a political party, freedom of association, and so on) and partly of a military nature. These latter demands were, for the ex-Tigres, the more important and remained constant during their exile in Angola: recognition of their military ranks and organizational structure; rearmament; recognition as a separate division following integration into the Zairian army (the FAZ), and their stationing in Shaba Province. Sources suggest that these military demands were initially accepted by the FAZ.[18] It appears that they were later rejected at a senior political level, probably by Mobutu himself.[19]

With this refusal, FAPC sought to pursue an apparently promising alternative strategy. In April 1981, Nguz Karl I Bond, the former first commissioner of state (prime minister), arrived in Brussels; the most prominent Lunda political leader following the death of Tshombe, Nguz aimed to construct a credible opposition movement in exile. He enjoyed significant support among Zairian exiles in Europe, who saw him as a potential successor to Mobutu. Kalenga, faithful to his Katangese roots, accordingly rallied to Nguz. He sent a delegation of his close colleagues (notably David Kilala, Stephane Lubange, and Denis Kisunka) to Brussels, which in February 1982, along with Justin Mushitu—by then aligned with Nguz—signed an agreement creating the Front Congolais de Libération (FCL), a politico-military alliance designed to succeed the FLNC. Simultaneously, the FAPC was renamed the Patriotic Armed Forces of Congo (FAPAC) and declared to be the military wing of the FCL. This alliance bolstered Nguz's political credentials with a significant degree of potential military strength.[20] Among the Angolan authorities, however, links between these "Tshombist" soldiers and Nguz, a long-term ally of Mobutu, were viewed with suspicion.

Nguz now established a broader alliance with other opposition parties. Signed into existence in September 1982, the new Congolese Front for the Restoration of Democracy (FCD) defined its objective as "restoring democracy and putting in place a transitional government."[21] Notwithstanding his ideological differences with Nguz, Laurent Kabila of the PRP was one of the signatories to the creation of the FCD 's Charter.[22] A "shadow government" was formed on this basis. Emile Ilunga, who would subsequently position himself as a would-be political leader of the ex-Tigres, was at this time introduced into the Katangese political milieu in his capacity as the Belgian representative of the PRP. Ilunga would subsequently attempt to use his influence with Vindicien Kiyana "Mufu," the operational commander of the Shaba II war (who shared Ilunga's Hemba ethnicity), to attain leadership over the ex-Tigres. Mufu traveled to Luanda on behalf of the FCL in 1984. In 1986 a "new FCL" was established, ostensibly bringing together Ilunga, Mufu, Justin Mushitu, Simon Kasongo, and others.[23] Despite these efforts, the FCL and its successors fell apart, and Ilunga remained a marginal figure during this period.

Despite the potential for this Front to unite disparate Congolese opposition forces, tensions immediately arose within the ranks of the ex-Tigres over these links to the FCL and FCD. On its return to Angola, the three-man delegation was accused of having squandered the US$4,000 that they had received from Nguz. David Kilala was relieved of his duties and questioned by an internal military tribunal. When Jean-Beauvin Kalenga died of an illness in March 1983, Kilala was accused of having used witchcraft to kill him and was beaten to death.[24] This internal conflict took on an ethnic hue because Kilala's supporters were primarily Babemba, a minority group within the mainly Lunda ex-Tigres. Kilala was suspected of having allied with Jean-Delphin Muland (see below) to take over the movement.[25]

After a meeting of the ex-Tigres' leadership in Sangondo in April 1983, Nguz designated General Simon Kasongo as FAPAC commander.[26] The headquarters was then moved from Sangondo to Mawa, where Kasongo was based. However, a splinter group led by Stephane Lubange, a prominent commander of the Tigres before 1974, denounced Kasongo to the Angolan authorities. Angola, irritated by the contacts with Nguz, arrested Kasongo and twenty-five FAPAC officers in October 1984.[27] They were transferred to Luanda and placed in a camp at Viana, south of Luanda. The Mawa camp was then placed in the hands of the Mouvement des Combattants Socialistes (MCS) faction, ideologically close to the MPLA (see below); the Angolans thus made it clear that they did not support the links between the ex-Tigres and Nguz.

Nguz, having failed to effectively challenge Mobutu from exile, returned to Zaire in June 1985.[28] Shortly thereafter, in July 1985, a second attempt at a negotiated reconciliation between the FAPAC and the Zairian authorities—undoubtedly a condition set by Mobutu for Nguz's return—was organized in Luanda. Talks took place between the Zairian ambassador and Justin Mushitu, acting as an envoy of Nguz. The FAPAC group evidently wished to return to Zaire, because of their poor living conditions and the increasing threat from UNITA attacks against their unarmed forces.[29] Again, however, the conditions they put forward—exclusively of a military nature—were rejected by the Zairian authorities, probably because they included the maintenance of the ex-Tigres' autonomous military status during a transitional period. The Zairian regime likely feared that the group would thereby become a potential instrument for internal resistance, a de facto private militia, in Nguz's hands.

Following the failure of these negotiations, Nguz disassociated himself from the FCL and was appointed Zairian ambassador to the United States in 1986; Justin Mushitu would, however, continue to be involved in political leadership.[30] FAPAC continued to operate under Simon Kasongo.

Masela's "Real FLNC" and Repatriation to Zaire

As noted earlier, the Lunda-dominated "real FLNC" faction led by Gustave Masela refused to accept the leadership of FAPAC. They saw their group as the real FLNC because they considered themselves as having ousted Mbumba and reestablished a more "authentic" Lunda leadership. This group, originally based in Chimbila, later relocated to Cacanda camp. In the late 1980s it became the focus of efforts at repatriation of the ex-Tigres.

Following a meeting of Presidents Mobutu and Eduardo dos Santos in November 1986 and a subsequent meeting of the bilateral Zaire-Angola commission the same month, a total of 3,297 refugees were identified for repatriation to Zaire, a first step toward an envisaged total of 6,000 over the next two years.[31] This operation finally started in December 1987, focused on "real FLNC" forces based at Cacanda camp. To the surprise of all involved, however, the Zairian immigration and security services suspended the repatriation process and, one week into the operation, on December 21, 1987, returned the refugees to Luanda.[32] This was certainly consistent with the position of these services, which tended to overstate the threat from the ex-Tigres and considered their return to be a security risk for the regime—a fear that, as will be seen, was not wholly unfounded.

When a new repatriation initiative was launched by the UNHCR, the ex-Tigres involved explicitly refused to return without fulfillment of the conditions previously put forward.[33] The repatriation operation nevertheless resumed in September 1989, and by February 1990, 8,249 "refugees" had been returned to Zaire.[34] Due to a rapidly changing political situation in Zaire, these forces would find themselves involved in new forms of political and military mobilization (see below).[35]

The Mouvement des Combattants Socialistes

If FAPAC broadly represented the "pre-1974" elements of the FLNC, the MCS became the focus of the young people recruited during Shaba I, who were now attracted to the radical ideology of their Angolan hosts and more amenable to Lumumbist notions of a unitary Congolese heritage. The MCS was led by Ambroise Mashiku and Martin Mukalayi. Mukalayi was born in Nyunzu to a Luba family. After completing a degree in industrial sociology at the University of Lubumbashi, he entered Angola in December 1977 in the wake of Shaba I, where he became the FLNC's political commissioner. After Shaba II, Mukalayi and Mashiku were moved to the Mawa camp. Mashiku had studied in Prague, and because of his ideological proximity to the MPLA, he clashed with FAPAC. When Kasongo and his officers were removed to Viana (see above), Mashiku was made the commander of Mawa camp with Angolan support. There he created the leftist MCS. This group worked very closely with the authorities and security services, to the point where it policed the operations of the ex-Tigres on behalf of the Angolan state. In January 1988, the MCS established a short-lived alliance with Laurent Kabila's PRP and the Tanzanian-based Parti de la Libération Congolais (PLC) movement of Antoine Marandura, a network of like-minded resistance movements.[36]

During the second half of the 1980s, as a consequence of growing Western aid in general and US policy under the Reagan presidency in particular, a much-strengthened UNITA mounted increasing attacks from bases in eastern Angola, seeking to take control of the important diamond mines in the Lunda area. President Mobutu actively supported UNITA: its front line provided a bulwark against the potential threat of the ex-Tigres.[37] Several thousand UNITA troops moved into Lunda Sul and Lunda Norte provinces in 1983, and they were supplied across the Zairian border.[38] The ex-Tigres appealed for assistance and protection to the Angolan authorities and the UNHCR. To the dismay of the latter, in 1988 Angola began to rearm some sections of the ex-Tigres, beginning with their MCS allies in Mawa camp.[39] When this group failed in their assigned task of dislodging UNITA's communication link between Quibaxe and Caxito, the same mission was given to those based at Nambwangongo.[40] When the latter successfully accomplished this mission, the Angolan authorities started rearming the other groups of ex-Tigres (see below).[41] This rearmament process was a crucial turning point, creating as it did a new set of obligations from the Angolan government toward the ex-Tigres, something the latter would claim explicitly and repeatedly over the next decade.[42]

Jean-Delphin Muland and FLNC II

The division between FAPAC and MCS revolved primarily around an enduring loyalty (on FAPAC's part) to Katanga, versus (for the MCS) affiliation to Angola and the MPLA. Other tensions, however, developed around issues of hierarchy and seniority. Jean-Delphin Muland refused to accept that Simon Kasongo and not himself was chosen as Kalenga's successor; as a result, he turned for nearly a decade to civilian life in Angola before reemerging as one of the main military leaders of the ex-Tigres in the 1990s.

Jean-Delphin Muland is without doubt the most unpredictable personality among the Tigres' leaders. Born in Kaniama in 1939, but of Lunda origin, he was a member of Moïse Tshombe's presidential security team in 1961 and was then exiled with Tshombe in Spain.[43] He received guerrilla training in Portugal and participated in the Schramme and Denard operations in 1967. As commander of the Cazombo camp in the early 1970s, Muland had clashed with Nathanaël Mbumba.[44] Following Shaba II, he refused to be integrated into FAPAC. From

1982 to 1990, he was coordinator of a group of Congolese refugees at Pelengue. In nearby Saorimo in 1985, this former Tshombist established a cooperative named the Associacão Agro-Prenaria Patrice E. Lumumba do Pelengue.[45] Muland's decision reflects the fact that nonmilitary options were available to some ex-Tigres during this period.

Muland nevertheless claimed to be the "true" leader of the FLNC and during this period made numerous attempts to turn this claim into reality. His attempts to link up with Nguz Karl I Bond ended in failure.[46] Alongside André Kaloba, a representative of one wing of the FLNC, and the Lumumbist MNC/L of Albert Onawelho and Daniel Mayele, they formed an anti-Nguz faction.[47] The Muland group proved incapable, amid its perpetual quarrels, of establishing an effective organization.

In 1990, Muland allied with the military wing of a new FLNC re-created by Henri Mukachung Mwambu.[48] This faction regrouped intellectual elites who had joined the ex-Tigres in 1977. Mukachung had served as a state geologist and a *préfet des études* at Musumba secondary school in Zaire's Lunda heartland. He was abducted by the Tigres in 1977 and became coordinator of a refugee camp in 1977–1978. He gained the confidence of President Neto and became attached to the military affairs secretariat of the Angolan presidency. In 1990 Mukachung (re)established a "new FLNC" (hereafter FLNC II), which, befitting his political patronage, he gave a leftist orientation.[49] Mukachung became its general secretary, with Jean-Delphin Muland its military commander. This FLNC II was, along with the MCS, supported by the Angolan authorities as well as by left-wing Zairian intellectuals previously allied to the MNC/L.[50] Muland and Mukachung's leadership skills were not, however, matched by fighting capacity. According to several sources, the FLNC's leaders could count on a mere 157 soldiers.[51] Nevertheless, by the mid-1990s, Jean-Delphin Muland was playing an essential role in the activities of the ex-Tigres, as seen below.

Nathanaël Mbumba's FLNC in Exile

After his expulsion from Angola, Mbumba found himself in Guinea-Bissau with only a small group of loyal supporters and family members. Building on the credibility gained through his leadership during the Shaba wars, he sought to rebuild the FLNC with aid from Algeria, Libya, and/or Tanzania. In the first half of the 1980s, Mbumba stayed for prolonged periods in Tripoli, which had become an important backer of radical African politico-military movements. Opposition groups were also enticed by President Muammar Gaddafi's funding of scholarships to study in Europe. Many beneficiaries did not return to central Africa until the late 1980s, by which time their armed movements had almost disappeared.[52]

In March 1986, Congolese opposition movements were invited to the so-called Mathaba conference, at which they competed for Gaddafi's favors (among them was Kabila's PRP). As in Angola a decade earlier, the prospect of Libyan support probably encouraged declarations of unity and alliances between Congolese parties that otherwise had little in common. An important role in these alliance-building processes was played by Andre Kaloba. Elected in 1965 as a substitute member of parliament for Tshombe's Conaco movement in Kipushi, Kaloba had since before Shaba I been considered an official representative of the FLNC in Europe. In the 1980s, alongside secretary-general of the MNC/L Daniel Mayele, he was the most active external representative of the FLNC, supported by Mbumba. An FLNC-MNC/L alliance was accordingly established in November 1985, designated the Cartel d'Union Nationale Congolais.

After Mbumba traveled to Tanzania the following month, the FLNC-MNC/L cartel discussed various projects to attack Zaire, involving ex-Tigres, former Simba rebels under Louis Bidalira, and a group run by former general Nicolas Olenga in Brazzaville. According to several witnesses, Mbumba was not very serious about this new endeavor and spent significant sums of money on women and beer.[53] This considerably irritated President Nyerere, who, according to one source, put him in prison.[54] This suggests the reduced standing by the mid-1980s of the man who had led the FLNC in its finest hour.

Political Change in Angola and Zaire, 1990–1993

After hopes were raised for political change in Zaire in the late 1970s, stimulated in particular by the reforms put in place after Shaba I, the 1980s proved a decade of unfulfilled hopes amid chronic political and economic decline. One important legacy of the reforms that followed Shaba I was, however, the creation of a (temporarily) more independent parliament. On November 1, 1980, thirteen parliamentarians issued a manifesto condemning the government's human rights record and the endemic nature of corruption.[55] This group went on to found the Union pour la Démocratie et le Progrès Social (UDPS), led by Étienne Tshisekedi. The UDPS provided an important voice of opposition within Zaire for the remainder of the decade and beyond. During this time, the economy continued to decline; in a context of stagnant mineral prices, a series of IMF reform programs did nothing to arrest the situation and indeed contributed to lower employment and living standards. Meanwhile, Mobutu continued to salt away vast sums in external bank accounts.

In the wake of the sudden overthrow of communism in Eastern Europe in 1989, a similarly unexpected democratic wave swept across sub-Saharan Africa in the early 1990s. This brought down many dictatorships and military regimes that had hitherto seemed an immovable element of the African political landscape.⁵⁶ The end of the Cold War likewise enabled the resolution of long-standing conflicts on the continent, with the superpowers now cooperating to bring their clients to the negotiating table and enabling the withdrawal of Western support for dictators like Mobutu. Among these outcomes was the conclusion of the lengthy and linked Angolan and Namibian peace process, resulting in the May 1991 Bicesse Accords between the MPLA and UNITA. Bicesse initially created the potential circumstances for the peaceful return of the ex-Tigres to Zaire, but its failure in fact made these forces more, not less, important to the Angolan state.

Zaire was by no means immune to these phenomena. Mobutu's speech of April 24, 1990, announcing the liberalization of the regime, had a catalyzing effect on those ex-Tigres: the different factions now sought out allies among the burgeoning number of legal political parties inside Zaire. For his part, a beleaguered President Mobutu tried to control the ex-Tigres who returned to Zaire in 1989–1990 by integrating them into the paramilitary Civil Guard and later made an attempt to control those still in Angola by dispatching the pro-Mobutu Mwaant Yav to Luanda in 1994 to persuade them to return.

More generally, however, Mobutu demonstrated his aim to repeat his strategy of 1977, that is, to permit a limited democratic opening that he would control and dominate. The violent suppression of protests at the University of Lubumbashi in May 1991, in which about a hundred students were thought to have been killed, was followed by attacks on opposition leaders by state forces.⁵⁷ Mobutu did, however, convene the promised Sovereign National Conference, which opened in August 1991. This was a watershed event in Congolese history, enabling a critical examination of events since independence and an evaluation of the negative consequences of personalized and patrimonial rule. The CNS was a genuinely participatory initiative held in an atmosphere of free speech, with representatives of 200 political parties and civil society as well as church leaders among about 2,500 delegates from all layers of society. The opposition alliance, the Union Sacrée de l'Opposition—which included the UDPS and Nguz's Katanga-based party, UFERI—had the support of nearly half of all delegates.⁵⁸ The CNS was, however, undermined by rioting by unpaid FAZ troops and civilians in September 1991 and again in January 1993; the conference was temporarily halted, ostensibly over delegate accreditation. Following maneuvering by both Mobutu and the opposition, the Catholic Church suspended its participation; FAZ troops then engaged in a destructive wave of looting in urban centers.⁵⁹ Although unable to institute a fully fledged democratic transition, the CNS did set up a transitional government, led by Tshisekedi, in August 1992, and established the Haut Conseil de la République (HCR) as a legislative body to take the democratization process forward.

By 1992, it appeared possible that Zaire would reestablish a multiparty democracy led by civilian politicians. This led many exiled opposition figures to return to Zaire, including many linked to the ex-Tigres/FLNC. In reality, however, the ex-Tigres had very limited political capacity. With the flaring up of a violent confrontation between the Angolan state and UNITA in the wake of the failed peace process, the ex-Tigres were fully mobilized by the MPLA government, with some of their number now fully integrated into the Angolan army as the 24th Regiment (see below). They fought against the Zairian-backed UNITA and in so doing became once again a genuine threat to Mobutu's hold on power. During this transitional period, Zaire's desire to see the ex-Tigres return was matched by a fear that they might be deployed militarily, by either Angola or some combination of the Mobutu regime's internal and external enemies. In 1990, as part of bipartite meetings of the intelligence services of the two countries, a Zairian representative claimed that "Angola had the intention of attacking Zaire in collaboration with the ex-Katangese Gendarmes in Nambwangongo camp ... to punish Zaire for its support of UNITA."[60]

Meanwhile, the opening up of Zairian political life led not to a democratic transition but rather to a chaotic situation in which, as Mobutu's authority declined, political discontents meshed with myriad regional disputes. The fires of these local conflicts were stoked by the central authorities in a desperate and uncontrollable form of divide and rule. In this context, the various factions of the ex-Tigres were themselves involved in a variety of conflicts that arose anew or were revived in the newly competitive political dispensation.

FAPAC, UFERI, and Integration into the Civil Guard, 1990–1993

In the early 1990s, the FAPAC group led by Simon Kasongo became entangled in such a conflict, one that revolved around the historical antagonism between "authentic" Katangese and Kasaian "migrants" in urban Katanga, which had been central to the Katangese secession. In November 1991, Nguz Karl I Bond, whose UFERI party was a leading part of the Union Sacrée opposition alliance, was appointed prime minister by Mobutu. In Shaba Province, UFERI's provincial president Kyungu wa Kumwanza was made provincial governor the preceding month; both leaders were accused of betraying the opposition. UFERI, like Conakat forty years earlier, campaigned for greater autonomy and self-rule by autochthons and against a perceived domination by Kasaian "migrants" (many of whom were now third-generation residents of Shaba/Katanga) of urban and political space. This movement was cynically and effectively manipulated by Mobutu to divide the opposition, but it had genuine roots in the province.

When Tshisekedi was elected prime minister by the Sovereign National Conference on August 15, 1992, in a direct challenge to Mobutu's authority, Nguz and Kyungu launched an intensified campaign to evict Kasaians—considered to be supporters of Tshisekedi—from Shaba Province. Kyungu unleashed a wave of ethnic violence in which several hundred thousand Kasaians were expelled from the province.⁶¹ FAPAC officers, still based in Viana, sided during this period with UFERI's assertion of Katangese identity. FAPAC commander Kasongo, himself a Songye from Kasai, publicly declared his loyalty to Nguz.⁶² Despite this, Kasongo, suspected (for ethnic reasons) of supporting UDPS, was deposed in August 1992 under the pretext of misappropriation of funds.⁶³ He was replaced by André Tshingambo, once a battalion commander of the Tigres and therefore representing a link with the Katangese secession.⁶⁴ Indeed, during this period, long-dormant secessionist symbolism was widely revived. Kyungu actively deployed symbols of the secession, for example, driving around Lubumbashi in a car that had belonged to Moïse Tshombe. Godefroid Munongo played an important role in reviving Katangese political identity in the period before his death in 1992, for example in the creation of UFERI and in the restoration of the Yeke chieftaincy. Such initiatives were closely followed in the FAPAC camp in Viana, where UFERI membership cards were held by many FAPAC troops.⁶⁵ As always in the history of the ex-gendarmes, this more explicit Katangese exclusionary identity was symbolized in the adoption of a new organizational nomenclature, in which the inclusionary FAPAC was replaced with the name Forces Patriotiques Katangaises (FAPAK).

In this context, the around 8,000 refugees deported from Angola in 1989 (see above) were to play a significant role. The manner of their return had prevented them from making any political claims on the Zairian government. Nevertheless, their mere presence in Shaba created the potential for their political mobilization, something of which the Zairian immigration and security services were fully aware. The myth of the "Katangese gendarmes" was consciously inflated by both UFERI and the security forces: the former to put pressure on the central government, the latter to denounce UFERI as violent secessionists. The local press reported glimpses of the "ex-Katangese gendarmes" everywhere. Rumors abounded about training by "ex-Katangese gendarmes" of the violent UFERI youth movement, the *jeunesses*. It was suspected that Kyungu wanted to integrate the ex-Tigres into the *jeunesses* as a private militia at the service of his political objectives. Conversely, members of the *jeunesses* tried to infiltrate themselves among the returned ex-Tigres so as to benefit from the pay the latter received from the government (see below). On the other hand, Zairian newspapers suggested that the Special Presidential Division (DSP) distributed "Tigres" uniforms so as to suggest that UFERI had secessionist aspirations and thereby to justify the military occupation of Shaba.⁶⁶ The local security services made similar claims in order to undermine Kyungu. After the first wave of anti-Kasaian violence, the CNS sent a commission of enquiry to Shaba under General Singa Boyenge. In its report, presented to the CNS in October 1992, information provided by the provincial security services suggested that the UFERI *jeunesses* were being trained by "ex-Katangese gendarmes" led by a certain "General" Monga. Despite such manipulations, there was some truth in these rumors. Two former ex-Tigres confirmed that *jeunesse* training sessions were carried out by their colleagues on land owned by a prominent youth leader.[67]

In this context, the Mobutu regime took measures to control the various returnees, initially dispersed all over Katanga. A first section had already been integrated into the Civil Guard, a paramilitary corps created in the mid-1980s as a parallel structure to the "gendarmerie." To this end, a first census of ex-Tigres was organized in December 1990, which identified a total of 474 soldiers. These were to become part of the Civil Guard's so-called Special Battalion Shaba II as a concession to the ex-Tigres who had specifically requested this name during negotiations.[68]

In 1992, meanwhile, FAPAC/FAPAK had dispatched Brigadier General Mwepu Mukanda to contact the authorities regarding the potential return of its forces to Zaire under the auspices of Nguz Karl I Bond. Mwepu was arrested on his arrival at the border but went on to meet the provincial authorities and also Mobutu himself.[69] Mwepu was then appointed by Mobutu as president of a commission, not only to organize the census and regrouping of the 1989–1990 returnees, but also to convince those still in Angola to return to Zaire. This second census was carried out from September 1993 and included former Katangese gendarmes demobilized both after the secession and after the abolition of provincial autonomy in 1966; the regime thus showed its awareness of the risk of renewed political or even military engagement by this older generation in the wake of UFERI's activity.[70] This census identified 8,033 men, including some former gendarmes who had never been in Angola: the majority were, however, located in the subregion of Lualaba, on the frontier with Angola. Once integrated into the Civil Guard, this group formed the Division Speciale Commandos–Tigres. This division was then subdivided into the Battalion Shaba II (formed from elements who returned during the 1980s) and Battalion Shaba III (composed of elements who had returned later).

Following this integration, the ex-Tigres received the same salary as other members of the Civil Guard. The tricky problem of the equivalence of military ranks was resolved in 1994 by a harmonization commission, which awarded ranks on the basis of each soldier's seniority and reported bravery and performance.[71] Quite remarkably, this commission included members of four opposed factions of ex-Tigres.[72] This suggests that the political and ideological differences between the leaderships of the various groups were less relevant to the returned ex-Tigres themselves; for them what mattered was ensuring that their military grades were recognized and that they were paid accordingly.[73]

As has been indicated, the sheer presence of a significant number of ex-Tigres in Shaba fueled the fears and rumors circulated by FAZ officers or members of the security services opposed to their presence. Some FAZ officers remembered the Shaba wars and nourished a certain envy over the treatment accorded to the ex-Tigres, but above all they feared the extinguishing of the menace they represented. This menace was artificially inflated by the Zairian military command in Shaba to justify the payment of supplementary funds, which were looted by senior officers in the 1980s and 1990s. Thus, the FAZ officers tried to sabotage the Mwepu census mission and presented the presence of the ex-Tigres as a threat to national security.[74]

The MCS and Political Liberalization

The MCS leaders Mashiku and Mukalayi also participated in the CNS, forgoing in doing so their previously close relationship with the Angolan authorities. Emile Ilunga, a long-term opposition figure based in Belgium (see above), sought to ally with the MCS. However, the MCS practiced what amounted to a dual political/military strategy: its leaders Mashiku and Mukalayi also initiated a military operation with the help of Ilunga, the objective of which remains unclear. Ilunga channeled funds provided by a Belgian businessman, Johan Cools, to the MCS leaders for this purpose; however, as already noted, they had few troops at their disposal.[75] They nevertheless armed a group of officers, able to circulate freely in the wake of the 1991 Angolan peace agreement, who (it was envisaged) would take up armed resistance within Zaire. The MPLA, fearing that history was about to repeat itself as a form of Shaba III, initially detained them. They were, however, released, and in the first week of April 1992 a group of twenty-six armed troops entered Zaire at Dilolo and made contact with the Dilolo Zone commissioner, a Lunda allied to Shaba governor Kyungu (see above). Kyungu ordered them to conceal their arms and directed them toward Kolwezi. Here, they were arrested and interrogated before they were subsequently integrated into the Civil Guard.[76] This tiny operation, of virtually no military significance, nevertheless had the effect of contributing to the myth of the continuing potency of the "Katangese gendarmes" inside Zaire.

Mashiku and Mukalayi were meanwhile engaged in a commercial operation with Deogratias Symba, Johan Cools, and an official of the Angolan embassy in Windhoek. This appears to have irritated the Angolan government. In 1994 Ambroise Mashiku was removed from his hotel in Luanda by MPLA security and executed.[77] This brought the end of the MCS as a meaningful movement. After the failure of the military operation described above, Ilunga established contacts with the ex-Tigres through Mufu, Symba, and Symphorien Kyungu, all of whom shared his Hemba ancestry. He convinced General André Tshingambo, commander of the FAPAC in Viana, to establish a Conseil National de la Revolution (CNR), which was officially created in March 1996.[78] Ilunga sought by such means to demonstrate to potential political funders that he had the authority to mobilize the ex-Tigres, but in practice only the Angolan authorities had this capacity. Ilunga would go on to play a significant role in the AFDL operations of 1996–1997, subsequently becoming president of the Rassemblement Congolais pour la Démocratie during the second Congo war (1999–2001).

Nathanaël Mbumba and the FLNZ

Mbumba, having unsuccessfully sought to claim the contested assets of the FLNC in Angola, returned to Zaire in August 1990.[79] He renamed his version of the FLNC the Front Nationale de Libération du Zaïre (FLNZ). The return of Mbumba, among the regime's most enduring opponents in exile, was a major victory for Mobutu.[80] The Zairian authorities anticipated that this would soon be followed by the return of the ex-Tigres still in Angola. The December 1990 intelligence document referred to earlier clearly demonstrates the tension between the two countries, identifying the activities of ex-Tigres along the border with Bas-Zaire.[81] Zaire sought by various means to have them transferred to Zairian territory, where they could be more easily controlled.

Mbumba sought to convert his prestige as the leader of the FLNC during its 1970s heyday into political influence. As FLNZ leader he participated in the CNS, together with opposition figures he had worked with during his stay in Tanzania, Delphin Kapaya and Songolo Nura.[82] They sought to create a coalition between Mbumba and the various ex-Tigres, Antoine Gizenga, and even Laurent Kabila: the latter was to be presented as their candidate for prime minister at the CNS but canceled his journey to Zaire at the last moment, fearing for his personal security.[83] The FLNZ subsequently degenerated into a series of arguments over leadership positions: Mbumba was unable to translate his prestigious legacy into effective political action and was an unsuccessful parliamentary candidate in 2006.[84]

The Ex-Tigres in Angola, 1991–1996

As noted above, the renewed conflict between the MPLA and UNITA in the early 1990s forced the Angolan government to remobilize the ex-Tigres. According to the Bicesse Accords, the belligerents were, like the Portuguese colonial army in 1975, obliged to dismantle their foreign troops.[85] However, following the rejection by Jonas Savimbi of the Angolan election results in October 1992 and the rapid return to all-out warfare that followed, the ex-Tigres once again became a valuable military resource.[86] By the end of November 1992, UNITA had seized Ndalatando, Mbanza Congo, Uíge, and Negage, thereby threatening Luanda.[87] In December 1992 the governor of Cuanza Norte Province met FAPAC leader Tshingambo in Viana camp to assist in retaking Bengo, Cuanza Norte, and Lunda

Norte provinces from UNITA.[88] Until the signing of the Lusaka agreement in November 1994, the war between MPLA and UNITA was fought on all fronts, this time without either Cuban or South African assistance.

In May 1993, General João de Matos, head of the Angolan army (renamed the Forças Armadas Angolanas or FAA in 1991), placed all *tropas especiais* under the central command of the General Staff.[89] The following month it was decided to improve the salaries of the so-called Special Troops Tigres.[90] In August, de Matos created the 24th Regiment as an organizational home for these special troops and thus accomplished the full integration of the ex-Tigres into the FAA. In an almost exact parallel with the Portuguese colonial forces, the 24th Regiment was to be linked to the Ministry of Defense through the military security services, but with a degree of autonomy in its internal structures.[91] One "brigade" apiece of the regiment was to be stationed in each province in northern Angola (except Zaire and Uíge): Lunda Norte, Lunda Sul, Cuanza Norte, Cuanza Sul, and Malanje, as well as Moxico.[92] Three companies were given special commando training in Cabo Ledo camp near Luanda, placed under the command of General Kalala, and designated the 8th Brigade.

In early 1993 the FAA launched an offensive in which 3,000 ex-Tigres were deployed against UNITA positions at Ambriz and Ndalatando, the UNITA-held capital of Cuanza Norte.[93] The following March, they participated in a successful FAA offensive to retake Ndalatando. The same month, a separate offensive was launched in Lunda Norte to loosen UNITA's grip on the diamond areas. The Cambambe dam in Kwanza Norte, and the Mabubas dam—vital to Luanda's electricity supply—were protected by ex-Tigres. The 8th Brigade commandos helped capture Cafunfo, also in the diamond mining area, from UNITA. FLNC forces under Mukachung assisted in the retaking of Bengo Province in 1993–1994, while Mashiku's forces were deployed in Uíge.

Conclusion

Military unification and deployment also encouraged a degree of political unity among the ex-Tigres that had been lacking since the mid-1970s. A series of meetings was accordingly organized with the three factions of the ex-Tigres in Angola to establish a unified structure: the FAPAK (led by André Tshingambo), the MCS (led by Martin Mukalayi), and the FLNC II (led by Henri Mukachung). An account of one of these meetings held on September 3, 1993, demonstrates the strong animosity between FAPAC and MCS, on the one hand, and FLNC II, on the other.[94] Ultimately however, the command of the 24th Regiment was imposed by the Angolans on the respective military commanders of the three groups as follows:

- Supreme commander: André Tshingambo (FAPAK)
- Deputy supreme commander: Pascal Kapend (MCS)

- Chief of staff: Jean-Delphin Muland (FLNC II)
- Political commissioner: Symphorien Kyungu (FAPAK).[95]

Politically, however, the ex-Tigres remained as divided as ever, with FAPAK concluding short-lived alliances with former and current Congolese politicians during the mid-1990s.

The Lusaka agreement of November 1994 followed government gains achieved in part by the deployment of these forces. Although the agreement did not deliver peace, it did enable mutually beneficial private arrangements to extract and sell diamonds between FAA and UNITA commanders, laying the basis for the engagement of some ex-Tigres in securing diamond areas "owned" by FAA generals.[96] UNITA's failure to respect the agreement further reduced its already weakened international legitimacy, as it rearmed itself from a number of sources, including Zaire. As it became clear that support for the Mobutu regime was at a historical low, Angola saw its chance to topple the regime that had supported its archenemy for decades. Mobutu, however, made one last attempt to control these Angola-based forces in January 1994, when the Mwaant Yav Kawel (a.k.a. Thomas Tshombe) was sent to Angola to contact the ex-Tigres. Officially, the Mwaant Yav sought to bring the factions of the ex-Tigres into a new political structure called Conaco (the name Moïse Tshombe had given his Congo-wide party in 1965) and a new military structure called the Armée Nationale Congolaise (ANC) (again referring to the name of the national army before Mobutu's 1965 coup). Despite this apparent presentational return to the past by Moïse Tshombe's younger brother, most witnesses agree that, given this Mwaant Yav's loyalty to Mobutu, the initiative was designed to bring the ex-Tigres under the control of the Zairian president.[97] The founding document of this structure does not give any specific political or military objective and merely lists a group of military and political officers.[98] The ANC did not survive, because of the ever-present divisions and conflicts between the various factions, particularly the MCS.[99]

By the mid-1990s, the former Tigres remained fairly divided despite many efforts to establish a new political direction and orientation. Some were still part of the Angolan armed forces, albeit in the concealed form of the 24th Regiment. Others had returned to Zaire and become part of the Civil Guard, while yet others allied with UFERI in its conflict with the UDPS. Each faction debated its future, either in Angola (which still sought to utilize the ex-Tigres' military strength but curtailed their political self-expression) or Zaire (where, in the death throes of Mobutu's rule, space opened up for an internal, albeit violent, debate about Katangese autonomy and identity). Some sought a reformed Zaire, but for others, hopes for a revived autochthonous Katanga had been given concrete expression by Kyungu, enabled, with typically Congolese irony, by President Mobutu himself.

By this time, however, hopes had faded that Zaire's internal opposition might find a way to remove Mobutu through a combination of popular mobilization and coalition building. Many factors contributed to this, but uppermost was the unwillingness of opposition leaders to sacrifice their own position in favor of a nation to which most declared their allegiance but for which few were prepared to act. In this context and amid growing regional instability, political change in Zaire was to be enacted from without. In this process, both the myth and the reality of the ex-Katangese gendarmes, now significantly divorced from each other, would play an important role.

8 The Overthrow of Mobutu and After, 1996–2015

THE LATE 1990s saw the successful achievement of the self-proclaimed military objectives of the Katangese ex-Tigres and the survival, even the revitalization, of their historical and political agenda. The violent overthrow of Zairian president Mobutu Sese Seko in May 1997—an initiative in which the ex-Tigres played a significant role—created the prospect for political change that might address some of their long-standing grievances and aspirations. Just as important for many ordinary ex-Tigres, it finally allowed them to return home after decades in exile. However, because of their lack of a coherent political leadership, they were armed, mobilized, and equipped by the Angolans. They were then placed under the control of the Alliance des Forces Démocratiques pour la Libération du Congo-Zaïre (AFDL) president, Laurent Kabila, who ultimately ensured that his direction of the ex-Tigres' military capacity could not be used to pursue the political goals long associated with these forces—the granting of autonomy and recognition of the special political status of Katanga.

The ex-Tigres' participation in the AFDL's anti-Mobutu alliance was therefore not effectively questioned in the way seen during Nathanaël Mbumba's leadership of the FLNC. Mbumba had arguably prevented their meaningful participation in earlier anti-Mobutu opposition alliances, and the enduring dilemma of how to avoid being used militarily without achieving political influence was evident in 1997 in the inability of FLNC leaders to place any effective demands on the new Congolese authorities they helped bring to power. After Kabila's takeover, the ex-Tigres' forces were dispersed across the country. Kabila and his successor as Congolese president, his son Joseph, by the selective cooptation of the ex-Tigres' senior officers, prevented what Mobutu had long feared, the internal reconstitution of their military and political power and capital. Indeed, while the post-1997 Democratic Republic of Congo has been in many respects a different place from that ruled by Mobutu for thirty-two years, it was and is nevertheless characterized by enduring tensions that arose consistently throughout the long and complex history depicted in this book: the problematic nature of political sovereignty in postcolonial African states; the strengths and weaknesses of deploying military force to achieve political self-determination; the relationship between military and civilian political authority; and the enduring memory of the Katangese secession and its surprising relevance nearly half a century later, in the context of the renewed profitability and significance of Katanga's mining industry and the influence of Katangese governor Moïse Katumbi (see below). The failure of both Kabila governments to satisfactorily address these issues has meant that the resultant discontent finds expression, in Katanga at least, in the form of a renewed impulse toward autonomy or outright secession. This has demonstrated once again the inability of successive governments, notwithstanding their ostensible commitment to decentralization, to effectively incorporate Katanga into their centralized vision of the Congolese nation-state.

In this context, and despite their own marginality and even destitution, the historical legacy of the ex-Tigres has proved surprisingly persistent. In the minds of the security apparatus officials of both Kabila regimes, they remained a potential threat and an instrument by which Angola might destabilize the government in Kinshasa—more potent because they were now inside the DRC itself. More importantly, the ex-Tigres remained a central symbol of historical memory for anyone advocating Katangese self-rule. Until today, the claims of many Katangese movements for autonomy or independence are justified and politically imagined through the Tigres, even if the number of historical "gendarmes" or members of the FLNC involved in these movements is negligible. The political legacy of the ex-Tigres, largely independent of their control, has proved resilient and now arguably has greater appeal than at any previous period of postindependence history.

We will first summarize the ex-Tigres' role during the AFDL's 1997 overthrow of the Mobutu regime and, more briefly, during the 1998–2002 war. The analysis then turns to the ex-Tigres who remained in Angola, including an attempt by one of their members to re-create the FLNC as a politico-military movement. Finally, we will assess the emergence since 2006 of a new generation of "secessionists" in Katanga who make claims regarding the historical legacy of the Tigres and seek to offer an explanation for this recent turn of events.

Background: The Rwandan Genocide and the Formation of the AFDL, 1994–1996

It is necessary to briefly rehearse the well-known events leading up to the overthrow of President Mobutu in May 1997, which have been comprehensively detailed elsewhere.[1] With the end of the Cold War, Mobutu had ceased to offer to the United States a strategic ally in central Africa and, partly as a result, faced increasingly confident internal political opposition. This created an opportunity for Zaire's neighboring enemies to settle accounts with the aging dictator: led by Uganda and (from 1994) its new ally, Rwanda Patriotic Front (RPF)–ruled Rwanda, this initiative was supported by Tanzania, Burundi, and Angola. Politically acceptable leverage for the AFDL's operation was found in the alleged persecution of the Tutsi population of Zaire and in the presence, close to the Rwandan border, of the former Rwandan Hutu–dominated army, the Forces Armées Rwandaises (FAR), and the Interahamwe militia, which had implemented the 1994 genocide and which along with at least 700,000 Rwandan Hutu civilians, had flooded into Zaire in the wake of the RPF's military victory. As well as a massive and chaotic refugee presence, this created enormous political tension between Rwanda and President Mobutu.

Zaire's threat to close the refugee camps in late 1995, alongside the spread of anti-Tutsi political discourse and efforts by the ex-FAR/Interahamwe forces to carve out their own territory in North Kivu, led to widespread clashes between refugees and Zairians and the flight of Zairian Tutsi to Rwanda. The RPF accused Zaire and the FAZ of siding with the Hutu in such actions and ultimately of utilizing former Interahamwe in its military operations against Zairian Tutsis, increasingly perceived as a disloyal fifth column opposed to Zairian national interests and representing a "foreign" Rwandan presence.[2] Mobutu's use of Rwandan Hutu forces reflected his increasingly close relationship with France during this period and Western (primarily US) backing for the RPF. More generally, Mobutu's increasingly weak grip on Zairian territory or its armed forces led to the tacit or overt acceptance by the state of the activities of diverse rebel forces inside the country, including a resurgent UNITA in the southwest. The destabilizing effects of these rebel forces created increased unity among Zaire's regional enemies and a determination to remove Mobutu from power.

The extent to which the AFDL was dominated by these external powers was masked, as in previous such anti-Mobutu initiatives, by the promotion by foreign powers of internal rebel forces, sometimes invented by the former. The so-called Banyamulenge rebellion in South Kivu, among Zairian Tutsi who feared repression by Zairian and Rwandan Hutu forces and other "autochthon" groupings, provided the excuse for intervention in the last quarter of 1996 by Rwanda's new army and (to a lesser extent) that of Uganda.[3] In addition, Uganda and Rwanda consciously promoted a Congolese "leadership" of the AFDL, which was composed of a number of Zairian opposition groups. Laurent Kabila (PRP leader from 1967 to 1997) introduced to Rwanda and Uganda by former Tanzanian president Julius Nyerere, emerged as the main AFDL figurehead, with founding member Kisase Ngandu dying in mysterious circumstances during the early phase of AFDL operations.

The initial aim of these operations seems to have been to occupy the eastern half of Zaire and to force Mobutu to negotiate his resignation.[4] By the end of 1996, in a brutal operation to destroy Hutu refugee camps along the border, the RPA-led operation had established a buffer zone from Goma to Uvira; this was effectively justified as a self-defense operation against further genocidal violence by the FAR/Interahamwe and tacitly endorsed by most Western governments. Whatever its merits, it was an essentially limited operation; even in early 1997, only 5 percent of Zairian territory was under the control of the Rwandans and the AFDL.

The Ex-Tigres in the AFDL

Because Kabila lacked any meaningful military capacity, the AFDL was therefore particularly dependent on support from its external African patrons, primarily Rwanda. The decisive expansion in the war's aims took place in early 1997 with the entry of Angola on the side of the AFDL, opening a new front on Zaire's western border and making the prospect of a nationwide military victory plausible. Angola's involvement and deployment of the ex-Tigres increased the proportion of Congolese troops within the AFDL forces and reduced Kabila's dependence on the Rwandan and Ugandan military that dominated the AFDL's troops. Zaire's continuing concern about the ongoing threat posed by the ex-Tigres in Angola was demonstrated in December 1996 when, in a meeting in Brazzaville between Angolan president Eduardo dos Santos and Zairian prime minister Kengo wa Dondo, the former specifically pledged that Angola would prevent the ex-Tigres from crossing into Zaire in exchange for Zairian promises to suppress UNITA activity on its territory.[5] Angola was understandably doubtful about Zaire's ability or willingness to keep these promises, and at the end of December the senior Angolan general, Viera Dias "Kopelipa," visited Kigali to discuss Angolan participation in the invasion of Zaire that was already under way.[6] Angola, like Rwanda, sought to identify and mobilize "internal" Zairian forces to justify its actions. Kopelipa was thus accompanied by General Jean-Delphin Muland (formerly military commander of the FLNC II) and Gilbert Kafund.[7]

The surprisingly significant role of Muland is explained simply by the respective hospitalization and absence of the commander and deputy commander of the 24th Regiment, Andre Tshingambo and Pascal Kapend, at that moment. This left Muland, as chief of staff, in effective command. As always, the military role of the ex-Tigres was complicated by their own political aspirations and by the position taken by those who sought to represent them. As we have seen, notwithstanding their integration into the Angolan armed forces, the ex-Tigres retained their own representatives, who were directly involved in discussions regarding their deployment in the war. However, Muland proved either unable or unwilling to make meaningful political demands of the AFDL leadership in exchange for the proposed deployment of his forces, for example, about the future representation of Katanga within a reconstituted Congo or the integration of ex-Tigres into a post-Mobutu Congolese army (see below). Many other ex-Tigres blame him to this day for his failure in this regard.[8]

For his part, Kabila readily accepted military collaboration with the ex-Tigres, but he refused to share political leadership with anyone. Emile Ilunga and Deogratias Symba sought to represent the ex-Tigres via their recently created Conseil National de la Révolution (CNR) alliance within the AFDL. Kabila, however, refused to see them, and they were expelled from Angola.[9] Ilunga, notwithstanding his dubious credentials as a leader of the ex-Tigres, subsequently sought to deploy his CNR position to (misleadingly) suggest to European audiences that he was number two in the AFDL.

At the start of February 1997, the ex-Tigres' Angola-based forces, officially constituted as the 24th Regiment of the Angolan armed forces, were transferred to Bukavu by plane. Reyntjens summarizes these events: "During two weeks in mid-February 1997, several battalions (2000–3000 'Tigres') were airlifted to Kigali, and taken from there by road to Goma and Bukavu. This operation was logistically supported by the Angolan army, obviously in close cooperation with Rwanda."[10] Prunier similarly states that two battalions of "Tigres" were flown to Kigali from Luanda between February 12 and 25.[11]

The 24th Regiment was thereby in place when the AFDL commenced its all-out military offensive into Zaire. Laurent Kabila's long-held ambition for supremacy, the ease with which AFDL forces progressed (aided by the characteristic impotence of the FAZ), and the enthusiastic welcome they received from the population encouraged the rapid extension of their operation across most of Zaire and a new aim of physically ousting Mobutu. Central to the achievement of this aim were the ex-Tigres, who provided, as they had always threatened to, a key part of the military means to defeat the Mobutist regime. There is a general consensus that the ex-Tigres played an important role in some of the first Congo war's most important events. Reyntjens states, for example: "The Gendarmes played a major role in the capture of Kisangani, which they approached via two axes: Bunia-Bafwasende and Shabunda-Tingi-Tingi. Kisangani fell on 15 March. Another group progressed southwards, from Bukavu to Kalemie and further on to Kamina."[12]

As the AFDL advanced westward, the suspicion of many Zairians regarding the evidently foreign nature of many of its constituent elements was, Turner suggests, tempered by the presence of Katangese elements.[13] This was ironic, considering their secessionist origins, their long period in exile, and their tendency to display what might be termed "foreign" characteristics, for example speaking a number of non-Zairian languages, including Portuguese.[14] Temporarily at least, all such concerns were subsumed in the opportunity to destroy Mobutu's regime and his Hutu allies.

The ex-Tigres were also central to the battle for control of Katanga's strategic mining assets and for the city of Lubumbashi. Once it was clear that Mobutu's FAZ forces were being routed, Angolan army forces became directly involved in the war. With the tacit support of Zambia, FAA troops, including some ex-Tigres, flew into Ndola airport—once again ex-Katangese forces traveled via Zambian territory between Zaire and Angola. They crossed into Zaire at Kipushi, took Lubumbashi on April 9, and captured Tshikapa on April 23 with support from the FAA. Although a wide range of forces were involved in the AFDL's overthrow of Mobutu, the entry of the ex-Tigres (and, as importantly, their Angolan patrons) seems to have been decisive for the accelerated pace of the war, for some of the AFDL's key victories, and its ultimate success: Prunier states that the ex-Tigres played a "decisive role in the war."[15] This was successfully concluded with the entry of AFDL forces into Kinshasa on May 15, 1997, Mobutu himself having left the capital the day before. Kabila was sworn in as president of what was now renamed the Democratic Republic of Congo on May 29.

In the week before the AFDL entered Kinshasa, the sudden realization that Zaire was about to fall under its total control rapidly accentuated the existing rivalries within the alliance. The Angolans, under the cover of the ex-Tigres, sought to reach Kinshasa ahead of Rwandan forces. This, sources suggest, was the reason for Muland's detention on May 9: his and other arrests gave Rwandan forces, working closely with Kabila, the advantage.[16] Angola was subsequently marginalized in the establishment of the Kabila government, a process dominated by Rwandan actors. This arguably further weakened the political authority of the ex-Tigres, who lacked any meaningful political representation in the country they had helped to liberate.

Congo and Katanga, 1997–1999

With the accession to power of the Kabila government, the relationship between the central state and its provinces in general, and Katanga in particular, was significantly altered. Although Shaba was renamed Katanga and provincial structures of governance were reestablished, Kabila in practice pursued policies toward the province that closely resembled those of his predecessor. Yet to most observers it seemed that Katanga, in the person of Kabila—a son of Katanga—and his coterie of supporters had taken control of the central state. This was exemplified by the appointment of Gaëtan Kakudji, supposedly Kabila's cousin, to the position of governor of Katanga, accountable solely to the president. This prevented any meaningful accountability of the authorities to the local population.

Katanga/Shaba had under Mobutu been essential for Zaire's economic survival (providing 70 percent of national income via foreign exchange earnings) and had for that reason been systematically prevented from developing an autonomous political identity and project. Mobutu had used the historical division between northern and southern Katanga to weaken the province; he had as army chief in the mid-1960s used the ex-Katangese gendarmes to crush the Lumumbist rebellions—ideologically close to the Balubakat movement—before crushing the ex-gendarmes themselves. When Laurent Kabila took power, he recruited many Katangese Luba (so-called Lubakat) into the new Forces Armées Congolaises (FAC) and into senior political structures. Militarily, Lubakat commanders rather than their Lunda counterparts were promoted to senior FAC ranks: for example, Célestin Kifwa of the national police (and briefly the chief of staff in 1998, succeeding James Kabarebe) and Martin Mukalayi of the MCS (but who was also temporarily detained in 1998). Politically, he placed Lumumbists with Balubakat origins who had played a role in the 1964–1966 rebellions in senior positions, reflecting as they did his own nationalist and centralist convictions.[17] However, he also recruited to the armed forces younger Lubakat from the UFERI party and its militia led by former governor Kyungu wa Kumwanza—including John Numbi, former chief of the *jeunesses* of UFERI, who had in the 1990s advocated Katangese autonomy. Kyungu was perceived to be linked to the Balubakat who, under Chief Kasongo Niembo and Evariste Kimba, had allied with Conakat in 1960.[18]

Kabila named in his new government some of the more left-leaning overseas political representatives of the FLNC, such as Célestin Luanghy (appointed minister of justice) and Jean-Baptiste Mulemba (director of the so-called Office of Fraudulently Acquired Possessions).[19] But these appointments were made independently of the ex-Tigres as a movement. Despite the fact that Kabila publicly emphasized that his own mother was ethnically Lunda—as a way of stressing his friendship toward the Lunda—few Lunda ex-Tigres were appointed to senior army posts.[20]

Indeed, the military leaders who had under Angolan leadership brought the ex-Tigres into the AFDL's operations, including Jean-Delphin Muland himself, were arrested and imprisoned for eight months. This seems to have reflected both Kabila's fear of any autonomous power outside his control, particularly one in which the Lunda were arguably dominant, and Rwanda's parallel policy of preventing any Congolese group challenging Kabila's grip on power.

The radical decline of Gécamines in the final years of Mobutu's rule under the chaotic oversight of Governor Kyungu wa Kumwanza, combined with the historically low copper price and the international consensus around economic liberalization, now led to the highly corrupt semiprivatization of Katanga's mining assets to foreign elites prepared to give political and financial support to Kabila, particularly following the outbreak of the second Congo war in 1998.[21] The initial plan for the state to retain a 51 percent majority share of mines was gradually abandoned under pressure from the war economy and efforts by pro-Kabila regional powers to recoup part of their military expenses from the mining sector. A key person in setting up structures designed to underwrite the DRC's war effort was the new governor of Katanga, Katumba Mwanke, appointed in January

1998. The appointment of Billy Rautenbach as managing director of Gécamines in November of that year reflected the close relationship between Rautenbach and Zimbabwean president Robert Mugabe, as well as Zimbabwe's politico-military-commercial network of influence and interests in the DRC.

The Ex-Tigres in the FAC and the Second Congo War

It should be noted that at the start of the Kabila regime, the reorganization of the Congolese national army constituted a huge challenge, both because of its historical ineffectiveness and because of the extreme heterogeneity of the military units that were inherited from the former Mobutu army: the infantry, the gendarmerie, the Civil Guard, the Division Spéciale Présidentielle (DSP), the military intelligence body Service d'Action et de Renseignement Militaire (SARM), and so on, all of which were considered unreliable by the new regime. These were now joined by new units from among the AFDL forces, such as the Kadogo (child soldiers), the ex-Tigres, the troops of Kisase Ngandu, and a small number of members of former rebel forces including the PRP. It was always going to be difficult to overcome the great differences in experience, tactical methods, and grades among these forces, never mind the internal conflicts likely to arise as a consequence. It was decided to merge the soldiers of these different organizations into new, intentionally mixed sections. In retrospect, however, many Congolese commanders suggest that the internally divided and conflictual FAC that resulted was deliberately "disorganized" by its first chief of staff, James Kabarebe, whose loyalty remained with Rwanda.

The dilution of ex-Tigres across these new experimental units meant that their military expertise, reflecting as it did their distinct training and extensive combat experience, could not be effectively utilized. Various sources suggest that this reflected the regime's perspective that the ex-Tigres would constitute a threatening autonomous force within the new Congolese army, as they had in its predecessor in the mid-1960s. In this, Kabila replicated one of the most tragic characteristics of the Mobutu regime: every unit or person capable of effective military performance was regarded, because of that effectiveness, as a threat to the supremacy of the head of state. The historic fear of the "Katangese autonomists" continued under both Kabila regimes. It was a pretext that prevented agreement on suitable salaries and minimum living conditions, with only a few exceptions. It also made the ex-Tigres, and the wider FAC, a far less effective force than might otherwise have been the case when the second Congo war began.

In August 1998, growing tensions between President Laurent Kabila and the Rwandan and Ugandan governments that had helped place him in power led to the outbreak of a second, longer, and far more devastating war, which formally lasted until the Pretoria agreement of December 2002 but which partially continued until 2003. The war was once again characterized by the deliberate conflation and confusion of regional conflict between states and internal Congolese conflict: supposedly national Congolese forces, such as the newly constituted Rassemblement Congolais pour la Démocratie (RCD), were highly dependent, as the AFDL had been before them, on external support, and the Kabila government was likewise dependent on external backing from Angola, Zimbabwe, and Namibia. In this sense, the apparently extraordinary historical experience of the ex-Katangese gendarmes, with its ambiguous and evolving local, national, and international identity, can be understood as a precursor of the now more generalized ambiguity of military and political forces in Congo and the wider region that appeared simultaneously (and/or to different audiences) as regional, national, and transnational bodies. This is not to suggest that by the time they had been integrated into the FAC the ex-Tigres were anything other than loyal to the national cause of the reconstituted DRC and its Katangese president: indeed, compared to many of the other "pro-government" military forces active in the second Congo war, they were among the most loyal. Kabila's maternal Lunda ancestry and the August 1977 agreement between the PRP and the FLNC were cited as reasons for this loyalty, proving once again that historical justification for military affiliation was an active and decidedly imaginative process. Emile Ilunga, whose attempts to present himself as a senior AFDL figure had been rebuffed by Kabila in 1997, now showed his willingness to act as a new "internal" ally to Rwanda and Uganda. From May 19, 1999, to October 29, 2001, Ilunga presided over the RCD (later RCD-Goma) before being dismissed amid accusations of financial corruption. Despite the widespread discontent among ex-Tigres with both Kabila's leadership and their position in the FAC, Ilunga was unable to mobilize a single Tigre in either political or military support of the RCD, suggesting his lack of genuine influence over them.

During the second Congo war, many ex-Tigre officers held operational responsibility within the FAC. For example, Vindicien Kiyana "Mufu," veteran commander of Shaba II, was commander of the third military region (Maniema and Eastern Kasai) in 1999 and was second in command of the eighth region (Kivu) in 2003. Individual ex-Tigre commanders and troops played a significant role in the fighting, for example Mufu in Kindu in 1998.[22] In general, however, they remained unable to convert their military role into any meaningful political representation, during or after the war. A couple of ex-Tigres became involved in national politics: from 2000 to 2003, Henri Mukachung was a member of Laurent Kabila's appointed parliament, while Irung a Wan served first as deputy minister for foreign affairs (2000–2001) and then as minister of defense (2001–2003), but neither represented the concerns of the ex-Tigres in any way. While foreign-backed warlords became vice presidents in the 1 + 4 formula adopted to end the war, the ex-Tigres, loyal and effective troops within the FAC, were not represented at the negotiating table or in the political settlement. This situation is attributed by ex-Tigres to, variously, the Rwandan influence in 1997–1998, the Balubakat domination of the Congolese army from 1997 to the present, and, in particular, the influence of General John Numbi (see above), who was an important leader of the former FAZ soldiers incorporated into the national army, renamed the Forces Armées de la République Démocratique du Congo (FARDC) in 2004. In interviews with ex-Tigres who are now FARDC officers, hostility to Balubakat was constantly articulated; Numbi is perceived to have blocked their advancement.[23]

Those Who Stayed Behind: A New FLNC, 1998–2001

While the 24th Regiment was engaged in the overthrow of Mobutu, another, less important faction of former ex-Tigres, that of the so-called Armée Nationale Congolaise (ANC), was not mobilized by Angola. Its artificial existence was prolonged by the activities of its political president, Martin Mukalayi, and its chief of staff, Daniel Kamboyi. The ANC's vice president, Élie Kapend Kanyimbu, worked in civilian life as a driver and mechanic for the Endiama diamond mining corporation. Because of his supposed knowledge of the diamond concessions in both Lunda provinces, Élie Kapend was imposed by FAA officers, themselves active in diamond trading, onto ex-Tigres' structures in the Lunda provinces to provide military protection to diamond sites; as foreigners, their loyalty was easier to secure than that of local FAA troops.[24] To circumvent preexisting ex-Tigres' hierarchy, these officers boosted Kapend's status by giving him control of food distribution to ex-Tigres' camps in this area. When the central authorities discovered these goings-on, Kapend was removed to Luanda and presented there as the leader of a group of ex-Tigres. Kapend then established a "new FLNC," of which he was president, with Pascal Kapend as its military commander from 1998 to 1999.[25] This was, however, strongly contested by Henri Mukachung, the creator in 1990 of the FLNC II, who was by this time a member of the Congolese parliament.

Élie Kapend's control over diamond revenue gave him significant influence over groups of impoverished ex-Tigres in Angola, which he used to further his political ambitions in the DRC. The involvement of the ex-Tigres in the diamond trade, as has been previously documented, dates back to Portuguese rule. Lucrative alliances concluded between FAA and UNITA officers during the post-1992 civil war undermined Luanda's control over elements of the Angolan army. In this context, the ex-Tigres sometimes seemed a more reliable agent of state control than the lower ranks of the FAA. From 1996, a key strategic objective of Angolan army offensives was to wrest control of the Lunda diamond fields from UNITA. On their return from participation in the AFDL's overthrow of Mobutu in May 1997, the FAA troops involved launched an offensive in Lunda Sul and Norte, officially to protect Angola's northeastern border against Mobutu troops fleeing the AFDL.[26]

With the start of the second Congo war in August 1998, the Laurent Kabila regime, whose very survival was at risk, badly needed the support of FLNC troops under the control of Kabila's ally, Angola. In these circumstances, it was theoretically possible to negotiate with Kinshasa political conditions favorable to the ex-Tigres in exchange for their military support. This was, however, undermined by the lack of unified leadership among the ex-Tigres in Angola, and (probably) by the Angolan leadership's fear of losing access to valuable auxiliary troops in its war against UNITA. Angola's continued dependence on the ex-Tigres was exacerbated by its difficulties in recruiting sufficient numbers of "home" soldiers: as the conflict with UNITA reached a new intensity in January 1999, the reintroduction of compulsory conscription for all men between the ages of eighteen and twenty met with very limited success.[27]

One group of former FAZ troops, which had been detained in Kitona camp by the Kabila regime for "reeducation," had at the start of the second Congo war in August 1998 joined with James Kabarebe's Rwanda-instigated attack on Kabila's government. They subsequently fled to Angola, where they joined UNITA, but after Savimbi's death in 2002, some managed to return to Congo under the cover of Kapend's repatriation (see below), under the tortuously constructed designation "Foreign Congolese Troops."[28]

The embattled DRC government sent several missions to Angola between 1998 and 2000 to seek the return of the remaining ex-Tigres. During these negotiations with the Angolan authorities and with ex-Tigres themselves, the repertoire of history was constantly mobilized to support particular positions.[29] The ANC identified primarily with the Conaco party that the Mwaant Yav had sought to establish in 1994 and rejected the overtures of the Kinshasa government.[30] More significantly, they referred back to the Conakat-Balubakat struggle of the secession period in their criticism of Kabila, rejecting his claim to have united Luba and Lunda societies:

> We are ashamed in front of the whole world, by the neglect of our leadership by L. D. Kabila. What does he think of us? That we go back to the polemics of the 1960s? Does he have rancour, hatred, vengeance, as some of our fighters say? They say Kabila told hateful words about us to the Rwandese after the capture of Kisangani in 1997.... The man massacred our troops with sulphuric acid in the food. If he didn't have a Lunda mother, all would have been killed (by him) with poison, at the moment we looked for to unblock the impasse to democracy![31]

This resentment was undoubtedly directed against a perceived preference from Kabila for "the Rwandans" and his refusal to recognize the FLNC as an allied movement with legitimate claims rather than as a collection of individuals.[32] The unrealistic demands of Élie Kapend in these negotiations, in which he sought the post of vice president of the DRC, made it easy for the Kinshasa authorities to reject them. Internal divisions in the new FLNC were once again manifest in June 1999, when Kapend was removed by a group of senior officers and replaced by Kajama Kasaji Rodrigues.[33] Kapend wrote to the Angolan authorities to announce his "withdrawal" from the FLNC and the establishment of a new political movement, the Union des Neutralistes Indépéndants.[34] He would, however, stage a return as the FLNC leader in 2003 (see below).

On August 18, 2000, an accord was finally reached between presidents Laurent Kabila and Eduardo dos Santos for the repatriation of the approximately 800 ex-Tigres still in Angola.[35] Five months later, however, the repatriation process was brought to a halt by the assassination of Kabila on January 16, 2001.[36]

Katanga during and since the Congo Wars

At the height of the second Congo war, many of the largest mining investors pulled out of their operations in Katanga.[37] Those companies which remained tended to be drawn into the conflict on the government side. Even after the formal end to the war in October 2004, the planes and ground vehicles of Anvil Mining were used in an attack by the FARDC on army rebels in which one hundred civilians were killed.[38] The accelerated privatization of the mining sector after the death of Laurent Kabila shattered the integrated mining complex of southern Katanga into much smaller private units over which the state had little control and which were (and are) forced by national and provincial authorities to contribute informally to the expenses of the state and—more often—individual state actors.

As soon as the fighting stopped, amid the highest copper and cobalt prices for thirty years, a scramble for control of the province's privatized mineral resources, which had begun in the mid-1990s but which was halted by the outbreak of war, recommenced among the new generation of international mining companies, including giants such as BHP Billiton (itself a merger incorporating some older companies) and smaller, more adventurous operators such as First Quantum Minerals since 2000.[39] From 2007, Chinese state-owned or -sponsored firms moved into Katanga, and in April 2008 an enormous deal was reached in which US$6 billion (reduced from the original US$9 billion after IMF pressure) of nationwide infrastructural and social investment was traded for future production of 10 million metric tons of copper and 400,000 metric tons of cobalt.[40] A central role in cleaning up the mining industry was played by the governor of Katanga, Möise Katumbi, following his election in 2007. Billy Rautenbach was deported, partly as a result of a conflict between Katumba Mwanke and Jaynet Kabila (sister of Joseph Kabila), and Katumbi generally brought some respectability to what had in the past decade amounted to a semicriminal mining nexus in Katanga.[41] However, the renewed profitability of the mining industry accentuated, as it did in late-colonial/postcolonial Congo and as it has done elsewhere in postcolonial Africa, tension between the mineral-producing region and the centralized nation-state administering and perceived as benefiting from it.

Congo since 2003: The Ghosts of the Katangese Gendarmes

The long drawn-out end to the second Congo war, starting with the Pretoria Global and Inclusive Agreement of December 2002 and culminating in the elections of 2006, brought the curtain down on Africa's worst-ever war. It did not, however, bring about an effective peace. As is well known, periodic outbreaks of conflict continue to occur in eastern Congo among government-allied forces, local militias, and foreign forces of various types, while the conditions of insecurity, state-initiated violence and criminality, remain pervasive.

The end of the Laurent Kabila regime brought to a conclusion a remarkable historical cycle. President Kabila had sought to advance the Lumumbist military and political elites who had in general been marginalized from political and military power since Mobutu's accession in 1965; even those who had been co-opted by Mobutu never achieved senior positions during his presidency.[42] Members of this previously marginalized group, including those who went into exile after the defeat of the rebellion, were reintegrated into the Kabila power structure. This reflected the fact that the generation of Mobutu and Kabila, albeit politically opposed, shared the historical experiences of the independence period. However, when Joseph Kabila came to power in 2001, a younger generation, with different historical memories and frames of reference, progressively took over. This might have been expected to move the DRC beyond its traumatic experience of decolonization and early independence. Quite remarkably, however, the memory of the Katangese secession has remained very vivid in this recent period, for reasons we will now seek to explain.

While Laurent Kabila had effectively guaranteed an influential role for the Lubakat in central state power, this changed when Joseph Kabila became president. Under his rule, Katumba Mwanke gradually became the second most powerful personality in the DRC until his death in February 2012. As Katumba was from southern Katanga, competition was heightened at the central level between southern and northern Katangese. For the former, the historically potent threat of secession (though not the ex-Tigres themselves) could now be remobilized as their ultimate political weapon in this competition.

Within this configuration of power, the ex-Tigres themselves perceived that they were always on the losing side. Under Laurent Kabila, as noted above, they had the perception of being marginalized, despite or precisely because of their military expertise. Although Kabila turned back toward the ex-Tigres during the height of the second Congo war (that is, 1998–2001), and his son Joseph subsequently promoted a higher number of non-Lubakat commanders within the FARDC, the ex-Tigres' poor salaries and living circumstances, compared to their time in Angola, convinced many that the DRC government wished to neutralize them.[43] As a result, many returned to Angola, where they were still able to take up a better-paid military role.

Most significantly, the revival of the mining sector in Katanga, described above, enabled by the dramatic rise in international mineral prices in the early twenty-first century, has fueled a Katangese political revival around governor of Katanga Moïse Katumbi.[44] Katumbi's carefully cultivated media image as a promoter of the province's development meant that he was constantly in conflict with Kinshasa over control of mineral resources, earning himself a reputation as a defender of Katanga's wealth. Katumbi's positioning of himself as a successor to Moïse Tshombe's leadership of an assertive Katanga would have significant consequences. Just as the Laurent Kabila presidency restored the respectability of the Balubakat struggle, Katumbi restored the memory of the secession by, for example, installing a large statue of Tshombe in the center of Lubumbashi. Katumbi went to great lengths to refurbish infrastructure in Lubumbashi and southern parts of the province. His actions earned him enormous popularity, to the dismay of Joseph Kabila, who tried to mobilize Balubakat feeling against Katumbi but faced declining support among this group following Mwanke's death.

This evolution in the contemporary popular political imagination was linked not only to the revival of secessionist symbolism but also to the specific heritage of the Tigres in metaphorical form—certainly not directly linked to the actually existing historical ex-Tigres. While the organized existence and activity of the ex-Tigres has apparently come to an end, shadows of these forces, and the political ideas they partly embodied, continue to resurface as the political "half-life" of the Katangese secession (see below). Certainly, the apparently nonexistent Katangese ex-Tigres continue to be feared by the Congolese state and to be mobilized and manipulated by local actors in complex ways that raise the specter of secession and the Katangese enemy within. Two events illustrate this fear most clearly: the Élie Kapend affair and the more recent "Kata Katanga" events of 2012–2013.

Élie Kapend: Diamonds, Repatriation, and the Ex-Tigres in Congolese Politics, 2003–2013

As we have seen, the repatriation of the remaining ex-Tigres from Angola was agreed in 2000 without any of their political demands being fulfilled. After the death of Kajama Kasaji Rodrigues, who had replaced Kapend as the leader of the

FLNC in Angola, Kapend reestablished his authority among sections of the ex-Tigres in Luanda and Viana from around 2003. In December of that year, Kapend sent a delegation to Europe to make contacts and to increase his internal legitimacy with the ex-Tigres. However, one group under General Makaz a Nawej Ndjuma (approximately 250 soldiers) remained in another section of the Viana commune after their leadership was reportedly physically assaulted by the Kapend group. A further group remained in Dundo under General Wislos Nawej Mutchail, while the former collaborators with UNITA (see above) were still in Negage. Diplomatic observers considered that Kapend's personal ambitions endangered the entire community in Angola.[45] The subsequent events demonstrate that this was even more the case in the DRC.

Following the sudden end of the second Angolan civil war with the death of Jonas Savimbi in February 2002, negotiations led to the signing on April 4, 2002, of a memorandum between the Chiefs of Defense Staff of the FAA and UNITA concerning the repatriation of non-Angolan troops, including the ex-Tigres and the small UNITA-linked Congolese faction described earlier. One group of troops, Wislos's Troupes Spéciales Tigres and based in Txamba in the diamond area around Dundo, were reportedly also contacted by a DRC government mission in October 2002 to discuss their possible return.[46]

In January 2004, the FAA chief of staff sent a joint FAA/Tigres mission to Bié and Lunda Norte to conduct a census of those ex-Tigres still in Angola, alongside a DRC government delegation. Although the presence of ex-Tigres was identified in eight of Angola's eighteen provinces, the mission concluded that a full census was not possible because the FAA was involved in its own operation of relocation and restructuring.[47] It is nevertheless likely that the Angolans—or at least part of the FAA—wished the Katangese to return to the DRC: the Angolan press reported several instances of violent conflict between the Katangese and the FAA, as well as with the local population, around issues related to illegal diamond exploitation.[48] In 2004, "Katangese" forces in diamond-rich Cafunfo had reportedly attacked the local population and taken fifteen persons hostage in protest against the Angolan government's plan to repatriate Congolese who were illegally residing in the area.[49] Eighteen months later, in August 2005, violence erupted in Bié when a group of Katangese in search of diamonds caused destruction in the town.[50] That year, the Angolan authorities executed Operação Brilhante, in which thousands of Congolese diamond diggers were expelled from the country, creating tension between the two governments. Angolan media reports treated the return of the "Katangese" as part of this repatriation operation.[51]

Élie Kapend then tried to take the lead in organizing the repatriation of the ex-Tigres specifically to Kinshasa, with the intention of deploying his small army in the 2006 election campaign—a symptom of the continuing centrality of military force to national Congolese "civilian" politics.[52] In these efforts, Kapend was supported by Samba Kaputo, the powerful special security adviser to President Kabila. After Kapend's return to the DRC in September 2005, he was lodged in a state-owned mansion; with food provisions he received, he bought the loyalty from other historic commanders of the ex-Tigres.[53] Kapend succeeded in having his FLNC party recognized in October 2004[54] and obtained a "transfer of power" of the FLNC presidency from Nathanaël Mbumba to himself.[55] However, a court case he brought to register his presidential candidacy for the 2006 elections failed.

Élie Kapend also tried to establish his legitimacy via a procedure that will by now be familiar: the effective projection of an overseas profile, designed to demonstrate that he enjoyed the confidence of his patrons in the DRC. Contacts were established in Belgium, and some interviews were published in the Belgian press, effectively raising the profile and apparent credibility of Kapend as a Katangese leader with a force of Angola-based ex-Tigres at his disposal. Moreover, Kapend established an alliance with the political party Conaco, revived under the leadership of Andre Tshombe, son of its founder, Moïse Tshombe.

Some observers are convinced that Kapend's machinations had the support of General Fernando Garcia Miala, the head of Angola's external intelligence services.[56] According to this interpretation, Miala sought to strengthen his influence in Angola on an ethnic basis via the Bakongo, historically hostile toward the MPLA leadership. A return of the ex-Tigres to the DRC would give Miala, via Kapend, influence within the Congolese military forces. As a former employee of Diamang, Kapend was exploiting the artisanal diamonds in Dundo region on behalf of MPLA patrons, probably including Miala himself.[57] He used the resultant revenue to establish his leadership of the FLNC. It is further suggested that Miala cooperated with Samba Kaputo with the aim of using the Katangese returnees for their own political projects.[58] Evidence for the existence of a plan by Kapend to link his political and military initiatives can be found in a group of approximately 800 Congolese trained in Cabinda with ex-Tigres instructors. On July 17, 2006, a group of 318 persons, recruited by Kapend, were expelled from Cabinda. Be that as it may, Miala was dismissed on February 24, 2006, even as Kapend was executing his plan to have the ex-Tigres repatriated so as to support his participation in the 2006 elections.[59]

A repatriation operation of about 7,000 ex-Tigres was accordingly prepared by the UNHCR at the request of the DRC government. In April 2006, a delegation led by the deputy minister of defense prepared to travel to Luanda for the operation.[60] However, it was never implemented. To general surprise, in July 2006, in the midst of the presidential election campaign, a group of 4,673 "Katangese" (1,199 soldiers and 3,474 civilians) were suddenly and without publicity repatriated from Angola to the DRC.[61] It may be hypothesized that this sudden return was designed specifically to prevent their possible deployment as a politico-military threat by Kapend; this is suggested by the fact that the DRC's chief of defense staff ordered that no contact whatsoever should take place between this group and Kapend. The number of transferred ex-Tigres was lower than initially planned, probably because most chose to remain in Angola, most notably those in Lunda Norte's diamond regions (numbering 1,588 soldiers and 6,548 civilians). The returnees were transferred, variously, to Lubumbashi, Kitona, and Kibomango.

Élie Kapend, seeing that the base of his political campaign had collapsed, turned directly against President Joseph Kabila. On July 21, 2006, Kapend declared at a press conference that all the transitional institutions created in the 2002 Pretoria agreement (which had in any case ceased to exist on June 30, 2006) were thereby dissolved, and that "the organisation and the control of the DRC during a moratorium period were entrusted to the General of the Armed Forces, Élie Kapend Kanyimbu."[62] This amounted to a declaration of a coup, perhaps to be carried out with the returnees, and led to Kapend's detention by the military intelligence body Détection Militaire des Activités Anti-Patrie (DEMIAP) three days later.[63]

However, in March 2007 Kapend was accidentally freed by the militia of the opposition Mouvement de Libération du Congo (MLC) as it searched for weapons during its armed conflict with government forces. Kapend sought refuge in the Ndolo camp run by the United Nations Mission (MONUC), remaining there until he was freed in August 2008. He then moved in 2009 with about 600 newly demobilized soldiers to Joli Site, a former villa of Mobutu, on the outskirts of Kinshasa.[64] These were, it should be noted, not ex-Tigres but the ex-FAZ so-called Foreign Congolese Troops (see above), who had taken advantage of the July 2006 repatriation operation to hide among the Katangese and return thereby to the DRC—it is not known to what extent an alliance with ex-FAZ forces was a conscious part of Kapend's strategy.[65]

Kapend now combined his self-declared FLNC leadership with his presidency of the Union des Neutralistes Indépéndants, a group with a semimystical ideology: Kapend proclaimed himself a "divine king" and developed a sect-like following.[66] He started preparing for the 2011 electoral campaign: in November 2009 his FLNC party was officially recognized by the interior minister, and he began to train his forces in preparation.[67] This appears to have alarmed the Congolese authorities: when Kapend attempted to travel to Angola in June 2011, ostensibly to participate in his son's marriage, he was detained by the Congolese immigration authorities. An FLNC press release of June 23, 2011, apparently based on Kapend's interrogation, suggested that the Congolese authorities feared that Angola planned to use Kapend against the DRC's president. This certainly reflects the poor relations between the two countries during this period. No judicial procedure was launched against him, and he was released from prison in March 2015.[68]

Another interpretation suggests that Kapend had established contacts with the Paris-based Alliance des Patriotes pour la Refondation du Congo (APARECO) movement of Honoré N'Gbanda, Mobutu's former security adviser and a staunch opponent of President Kabila.[69] Witnesses indeed refer to a meeting among Kapend, N'Gbanda, and a military officer leading former FAZ troops in Brazzaville during Kapend's visit to Belgium in November 2005.[70] Any link between Kapend's FLNC and APARECO is, however, strongly denied by both organizations.[71]

During this period, Kapend demonstrated his understanding of the potential benefit to be reaped from redeploying the ex-Tigres in Congolese political life. He succeeded in re-creating the FLNC, then cut off from its historical roots, by co-opting the historic FLNC leadership and both Katangese and non-Katangese soldiers. On the one hand, his lack of political realism led him into adventurous initiatives that severely damaged what was left of the ex-Tigres' political project, confirming, in the eyes of their opponents, their status as a military unit dangerous to the state. On the other hand, by opportunistically keeping the heritage of the FLNC alive, he pioneered what has now become an established pattern of the deployment of the ex-Tigres by diffuse autonomist movements as an instrument in their vision for a new Katangese secession. The threat of a Tigres-led military action against the DRC, possibly with foreign support, was apparently very much alive in the DRC's action against Kapend. In June 2013, elements of the FARDC (including the military police) and the civilian Congolese National Police (PNC), encircled the Joli Site camp, searched the entire premises, and carried out significant destruction: the camp's school was closed, and several FLNC members were temporarily detained.[72]

Neosecessionist Movements and the Rebirth of the Tigres Myth

On October 14, 2004, seven persons entered and occupied the small town of Kilwa, in the Lake Mweru area of southern Katanga.[73] They were said to belong to the hitherto unknown Revolutionary Movement for the Liberation of Katanga (MRLK). Locally based soldiers and police offered no resistance to this action, and the occupying group was apparently joined by some of Kilwa's inhabitants. After the MRLK members had collected armaments, another group of about forty persons arrived the same day to join the "mobilization." Their leader, Kazadi Mukalayi, originally from Pweto and with no personal link to the ex-Tigres, proclaimed the liberation of Katanga and declared that the period of rule by President Joseph Kabila and then Katangese governor Katumba Mwanke was at an end. A number of youths from Kilwa and the local police now also joined with the movement.

However, national and international media, relying on information obtained from a humanitarian source, reported that the town of Kilwa had been taken by the "Mayi Mayi and ex-Katangese Gendarmes nicknamed Tigres."[74] The following day, the FARDC's 62nd Brigade, based at Pweto under Colonel Adhemar Ilunga, who was himself an ex-Tigre, attacked Kilwa to neutralize the movement. During its reoccupation of the town, the FARDC organized summary executions and committed numerous human rights violations. Human rights associations protested against the FARDC's abuses, which led to the imprisonment of Ilunga.

The causes of the Kilwa event remained unclear. One diplomatic source suggests that the MRLK was acting under the direction of John Numbi, then commander of the air force, who also controlled an important Lubakat network in the army and security forces (see above). The operation was, it seems likely, designed to suggest a persistent southern Katangese menace that could be effectively combated only by Lubakat, who historically positioned themselves as vital supporters of national unity in Katanga under Laurent Kabila and now sought to maintain this position under Joseph Kabila. The most significant aspect of this episode for the purposes of this history is the manipulation of the myth of the secession, symbolized by the "Katangese gendarmes," designed solely as part of a campaign to repress the MRLK in which no ex-gendarmes were actually involved, except ironically in the shape of the FARDC commander who led its brutal repression.

Events such as this might suggest that the threat of Katangese secession exists today only in the machinations of those whose position rests, as that of generations of Congolese politicians and officials has done, on the deployment of the very limited threat of a supposed enemy within, used to justify not only repressive state actions but also the deployment of resources and the allocation of political power to those officials. The reality is, however, that alongside such alarmist claims, the dream of a return to the mythic paradise of an independent Katanga has never disappeared. Long in abeyance during the ex-Tigres' exile in Angola, it was given a voice in the early 1990s by Kyungu wa Kumwanza's UFERI party. With the coming to power of Laurent Kabila, the movement took various forms, which are described in this section: the Notables Katangais bringing together part of the Katangese intellectual and political elite; the Congress of Peoples of Katanga (CPK), led by a witness to Tshombe's secession; and the group Coordination de l'Organisation de Référendum de l'Autodétermination pour le Katanga (CORAK), with its militant armed wing. Most significantly, the neo-secessionist movement is no longer the preserve of intellectual elites or of exiled political and military leaders but has taken on a popular form. Its autonomist dream rests, as did the secession of the early 1960s, on a relatively strong mining economy which is no longer formally state-controlled. This broad movement has sought to integrate the Tigres as a powerful symbol of secession, but in a form that has little or no relationship with the historical ex-Tigres.

While Katangese leaders were under Laurent Kabila (and indeed still are today) considered to hold the keys of power, it should be recalled that actual autonomist tendencies were suppressed. As Joseph Kabila tried to open up the power structure he had inherited from his father, Katangese elites resisted their reduced influence within the 2003–2006 transitional government. In 2003 a group of self-declared Notables Katangais (some of whom are long-term secessionists) sought to initiate a referendum regarding the autonomy of Katanga. This relatively marginal movement pitted a group of "southerners" against the "northerners" considered the protectors of the central state. The first public action of the Notables was to present their request for a referendum to the Lubumbashi office of the United Nations (that is, the MONUC office) on the anniversary of Katangese independence on July 11, 2008. Many Katangese see the United Nations as an important potential actor because it was decisive in ending the secession in 1963. A petition for such a referendum was, according to the organizers, signed by 3,290 persons and submitted on May 2009. This became something of a landmark for other, more radical organizations, among them CORAK, the leaders of which split from the Notables after 2008 to form this new organization. Because the United Nations was, through the 1962 U Thant Plan, considered the architect of Katanga's reunification with Congo, CORAK requested the United Nations to "pronounce the divorce" of Katanga and the DRC. CORAK produced a series of statements (written on an old typewriter) claiming that Katanga had an independent status before 1933 and even until Congolese independence in 1960; this remains a widely shared notion among ordinary Katangese people. However, CORAK also traced the origins of Katanga back to a Lunda cosmogony, probably as a historical base for the legitimacy of Moïse Tshombe's leadership.[75] In 2010 CORAK unilaterally proclaimed the Federal Multiracial Republic of Katanga and proposed a decentralized state structure resembling that proposed in the U Thant Plan. However, CORAK's leaders disagreed about the use of military means to further their aims; one of their leaders, Ngonga Tshinyama, broke away and began recruiting militia members. Drawing on the autochthonous discourse of Mayi Mayi groups in eastern DRC, CORAK leaflets emphasize the need for "legitimate" Katangese ethnicities to defend a "pure" Katanga against a foreign-dominated Kinshasa which controls an "illegitimate" Congolese state.[76] In addition, Tshinyama refers to a Katangese supreme being, Sakatanga, in reference to the Lunda cosmogony wherein Sakatang is the name of the supreme being.

However, a third autonomist group, the CPK, is responsible for the most spectacular activities. On February 4, 2011, CPK forces raised the Katangese flag at Lubumbashi airport, and on June 28–29 of the same year it attacked the FARDC's provincial logistics headquarters in the city. On July 11, 2011, a firefight took place between Republican Guard troops and alleged members of the CPK. The group is led by Ferdinand Kazadi Ntandaimena, born in Mitwaba in 1943 and of Muzela origin, who probably had direct experience of the Katangese secession. After several stays in European countries, Kazadi went into exile in Zambia and established a Katangese secessionist movement there in the late 1990s. From about 2010, the CPK initiated a series of pro-independence activities, while Kazadi himself remained in the background. The CPK first acquired notoriety in May 2010 when a Katangese flag was raised in the center of Lubumbashi, leading to the arrest of several CPK members. A cousin of Kazadi called Jean-Claude Ntandaimena organized armed combatants in the Pweto area, sometimes using the CPK label.

The remnant Mayi Mayi groups in northern Katanga were another source of recruits for this diffuse Katangan secession movement. Although northern Katanga has long been a fertile breeding ground for localized village-based militia, the current groups have their origins in the instigation of so-called popular self-defense forces (Forces Armées Populaires, or FAP) by Laurent Kabila during the second Congo war in 1999–2000; direct responsibility for these would-be guerrilla forces lay with John Numbi and Interior Minister Mwenze Kongolo, both from northern Katanga. A brief period of relative enthusiasm and military effectiveness was followed, in a context of poor organization, discipline, and structure, by a descent into banditry. One of the Mayi Mayi leaders, Gédéon Kyungu Mutanga, who surrendered in 2006, was condemned to death in 2008. However, when some detained CORAK members escaped from prison in September 2011, Gédéon Kyungu fled with them. He restarted his movement and placed himself under the command of Jean-Claude Ntandaimena, acting in the name of the CPK.

In 2013 the three movements of Gédéon (Manono area), Jean-Claude Ntandaimena (Pweto), and Ngonga Tshinyama (southern Katanga) allegedly coordinated a joint attack on three fronts to take over Lubumbashi, now operating under the umbrella name Kata Katanga (meaning "to cut Katanga" from the DRC). Facing a surprising lack of action from the security forces, the assailants took control of some villages before one group entered Lubumbashi on March 23, 2013, raising the flag of independent Katanga in the city center. Under fire from the Republican Guard, they fled to the local MONUSCO office, where they remained for two days. Finally, the 230 fighters, together with their family members, were transferred to Kinshasa, apparently to be forcibly integrated into the FARDC.[77] The episode is, at the time of writing, still largely unexplained; it appears, however, that Ntandaimena had promised his followers from villages in the Manono-Pweto-Mitwaba axis that he would wait for them in Lubumbashi to ask the United Nations to grant independence. However, some sources suggest that he may have been paid off by senior Katangese leaders and fled abroad, abandoning his followers to their fate. CORAK now considers Ntandaimena to be a traitor, and the movement seems temporarily demobilized. While the central authorities have taken measures to control the situation, the state's grip on events in the countryside is extremely limited, not only for logistical reasons—they lack effective troops—but also because of a widespread conviction in Katanga that the aims of the secessionist movements are noble, even if such methods are not acceptable. Gédéon Kyungu subsequently created his own political party in 2015, in the run-up to elections scheduled to take place the following year, and Kata Katanga activities declined significantly at this time.

The role of the ex-Tigres in these movements is not clear. Some individual ex-Tigres from Angola, specifically among those who had returned during the 1980s and who joined the FAZ, went on to train members of youth movements such as the UFERI *jeunesses*. More recently, some later returnees from Angola gathered in an area around Fungurume to support a secessionist movement. More generally, however, it appears that the ex-Tigres who participated in the overthrow of Mobutu are not involved in these activities. Currently, those ex-Tigres who were integrated into the FARDC in the late 1990s have been demobilized. Many received a paltry pension, some in the form of a bicycle, and are living in poverty in Lubumbashi and elsewhere. Most are old men, and although they are regularly accused by the intelligence and security services of being secessionists, they have no ambition to organize a new secession, merely wanting to survive. Yet the existence of the separate autonomist movement revived suspicions among state officials about the ex-Tigres and may have contributed to Élie Kapend's arrest in 2011 (see above). While the actual ex-Tigres present little or no threat to the Congolese state, they still present a symbolic threat from a now largely imaginary exile: rumors continue to circulate that about 4,200 of their number remain in Angola, ready to take power in Kinshasa when Joseph Kabila's second and final term in office ends in 2016. Their failure to act hitherto supposedly results from the restraint placed on them by the Angolan government and by their own lack of effective political leadership—constraints that have been used to explain the failure of the real ex-Tigres to bring much-desired political change to Congo since at least the 1970s.

Conclusion

It therefore appears that the Tigres' movement has been recreated in a symbolic way: the label, which arose from the regular army of the Katangese secession, and which remained a regularized armed force throughout its long Angolan exile, is now applied to anyone willing to take up arms to declare an independent Katanga, providing a powerful mobilizing agent across the province. This myth has been strengthened by the relegitimation of Katangese identity by Governor Moïse Katumbi and by the revival of the Katangese mining economy, now privatized and managed by a Katangese elite, tied to the state but not formally part of it. The Kinshasa government can control this valuable resource only through this network rather than via direct state control, creating the potential for increased Katangese autonomy.

However, the social basis for these movements is to be found among those who are socially excluded from the booming mining economy, including the artisanal miners driven out of their areas of activity. Northern Katanga, historically loyal to the central Congolese state since the independence period, has in general been neglected by both the central and the provincial government. The total absence of the state and its social or security services has created a fertile recruiting ground for the implementation of the myth of a reborn Katangese paradise, drawing on nostalgia for the Gécamines state mining company, which provided its employees with good living conditions and career prospects (as well as effectively funding the secession of the 1960s), and the SNCC railway company, which both provided province-wide transport services and unified Katangese territory. The continual frustration of such hopes, not addressed by any state or private actor, will almost inevitably lead to more violence.

In addition, periodic tensions between Angola and the DRC, focusing on the still somewhat uncontrolled and diamond-rich border region, which was the site of many of the struggles and movements related herein, mean that the potential deployment of some version of the ex-Tigres is, notwithstanding the obvious impracticalities, a historical shadow hanging over relations between these two nation-states. Several thousand ex-Tigres do remain in Angola, giving some potential weight, organizational and historical, to the threats articulated by the ragtag militias of the current secessionist forces operating in Katanga.

Despite the culmination of their long-standing exile-based struggle and their ostensible victory against Mobutu in the first Congo war, the ex-Tigres still failed to achieve their historic aims, about which their leaders were by the late 1990s less concerned than about negotiating a position in the new political dispensation. Their focus on the failures of some leaders (for example, Muland) and the betrayal of others (for example, Laurent Kabila) masks the underlying tension between military effectiveness and political autonomy that has been a constant thread in this story from its beginning. It was precisely the military strengths that made the ex-Tigres an attractive, even essential, participant in the AFDL's war against Mobutu, which also made them a dangerous element within a post-Mobutu state. The neutering of the ex-Tigres by their dispersal within the FAC followed in the late 1990s, despite the negative effect this had on their military capacity. The failure to convert the returning ex-Tigres, an experienced and well-trained army, into the backbone of the new national army reflected the competition of several factions that dominate the structures of the Congolese state which, in defending their particular interests, continually undermine the efforts of others, even when they would have the overall effect of enabling more effective state administration or defense. The control by leaders of Katangese origin of the central Congolese state has, paradoxically, prevented the possibility of a meaningful project for the self-conscious development of Katanga and the improvement of the lives of its people, which may perhaps emerge only when the Katangese elite have themselves lost control of the national state.

Meanwhile, the rebirth of the myth of the Tigres and the reemergence of secessionist thinking and action show that they remain a potent symbolic force within the DRC's political configuration, threatening precisely because of Katanga's problematic integration into the central state. Thus, post-Mobutu Congo resembles in some instructive ways the earlier phases of the country's history. The continuities and breaks in this narrative will be explored in a more sustained way in the conclusion.

Conclusion

The Military Significance of the Ex-Gendarmes

This study has sought to demonstrate that, over half a century, the Katangese ex-gendarmes played a significant and largely unheralded role in several of the most important politico-military conflicts that have taken place in southern-central Africa. The significance of their deployment in the secessionist conflict with the United Nations and the central Congolese state, in the 1964–1965 war in the east, and in the subsequent mutiny against Mobutu in 1966–1967 has been obscured both by the international illegitimacy of the secession itself and by the popular fascination with the role of white mercenaries in these conflicts, the importance of whom has been overstated both by their critics and by themselves.[1] The gendarmerie played a significant role in defending the secessionist state from UN forces and the Congolese National Army (ANC), successfully resisted attacks from Lumumbist forces, and was able to repress the activities of northern Katangese forces that Conakat regarded as "rebels" against its state. Following their recall from Angola and reorganization under Congolese prime minister Tshombe in 1964, they contributed to the crushing of the Mulelist or "Simba" rebellion in eastern Congo later that year. Their rebellion of 1966–1967 was the first military challenge to the rule of President Mobutu, following which they began their long-term exile in Angola.

It was this military effectiveness that led to their utilization by the Portuguese armed forces and intelligence services against Angolan nationalists; they played a significant role in restricting the gains made by the MPLA in particular, contributing to its lack of success relative to nationalist movements elsewhere in Portugal's African colonies at the moment of the April 1974 coup.[2] This effectiveness made the FLNC both a dangerous threat and a significant potential partner in the run-up to and during the war for control of the Angolan state that unfolded among the three liberation movements and their foreign backers in 1974–1975. The role of the ex-gendarmes in Portugal's war against Angolan nationalists, as well as in the MPLA's subsequent battle to take power in Angola, was consciously downplayed by their hosts but in the latter case was thought to be sufficiently important to warrant the signing of the Cossa Accords. While the evidence is not conclusive, it appears clear that FLNC forces played a significant role in helping the MPLA come to power in November 1975 and contributed to its retention thereafter.

All contemporary observers of the Shaba wars agreed on the effectiveness of the FLNC's military operations, the threat of which was implicitly acknowledged in the scale of the multinational counteroperation mounted by France, Belgium, and (indirectly) the United States. Despite Angola's subsequent demobilization of the Tigres, their military value was such that they were periodically redeployed in new forms, particularly against the continuing threat of UNITA in both the 1980s and following the failure of the Bicesse Accords in the 1990s. In 1996–1997 their successors proved militarily effective in the war initiated by the AFDL and its foreign backers to overthrow Mobutu.

The "military" significance of the ex-gendarmes, however, lies beyond the actual role they played in this succession of conflicts. As we have shown, the limited contemporaneous intelligence held by relevant nation-states about the ex-gendarmes led, from the late 1970s onward, to a growing disjuncture between their actual military capacity and their fearsome reputation. Their perceived military threat has, from the 1980s until today, been consistently deployed politically in the struggle for power within Zaire/DRC. Mobutu himself pioneered the exaggeration of the threat posed to his rule by the ex-gendarmes, among other opposition forces; he and the high command of the FAZ deliberately heightened the perception of the potential threat posed by the Tigres, both to seek Western military and economic support and to justify the periodic repression of political expression within Katanga, especially among the Lunda. The growing disconnect between the gendarmes' limited military threat potential and their fearsome reputation was further inflated in the 1980s by the FAZ and the security services as a way to justify their bloated resources and political influence. In the 1990s, it was anti-Mobutu opposition forces that maneuvered to deploy the ex-Tigres as a way of generating political support. As subsequent events have shown, the brief integration of some ex-Tigres into the renamed FAC during the presidency of Laurent Kabila did not prevent the continued deployment of the so-called Tigres as both promise and threat, in ways largely unrelated to their material reality, but which revealed the continuing potency of Katangese political expression within the DRC. We have sought to separate the reality and the myth, but it is equally important to recognize that both have had a bearing on the military and political relationship between the DRC and its neighbors and between the Kinshasa authorities and the province of Katanga.

The Political Significance of the Katangese Exile Movement

The importance of the ex-gendarmes goes considerably beyond the military role they have played over the past fifty years. We have been at pains to emphasize the significant political influence of these soldiers, both directly and indirectly. The recruitment of indigenous Katangese soldiers to, and their deployment as, the armed force of the secessionist state was important not only for military purposes. It also enabled the leaders of that state to project the image of a nation able to defend its asserted sovereignty. The rank and file of the Katangese army fought in significant battles that extended the life of the secession for a number of years, but Katanga's capacity for self-defense was equally performative, a conscious projection of meaningful statehood acted out in "national" and international media, in which visual and verbal representations of the Katangese army in action played a significant part.

Following the defeat of the secession, the integration of the Katangese gendarmes and police into the ANC was driven primarily by the political message of national reintegration advanced by the Congolese government, the United Nations, and the so-called international community. This was, however, undermined by both the continued aspirations of Katangese military and political leaders to reestablish the secessionist state and the continued suspicion of their Congolese counterparts about their motivations and loyalties. This was initially reflected in the violent action taken by the ANC against the ex-Katangese forces in 1963–1964 and in the uneasy inclusion of Katangese soldiers in the supposedly "national" Congolese army. These divisions were briefly papered over during Tshombe's premiership in 1964–1965 and in the action against the Mulelist rebels during that period, but they came to the fore again in 1966–1967 during the mutiny against Mobutu that coincided with Tshombe's final failed attempt to retake power.

Once in exile in Angola, the ex-gendarmes and the wider Congolese refugee community were the subject of new political challenges to Mobutu's increasingly total control of the country, in the organizational form of Fénaco and articulated through the FLNC publication *Reveil Congolais*. While these initiatives were evidently under the control of the Portuguese authorities, they had the support of Lunda royal authority, including the Mwaant Yav himself, who continued to advance Tshombe's articulation of Katangese national identity. The assertion in the late 1960s by Nathanaël Mbumba of an alternative, apparently more progressive form of exiled political organization rooted in military—rather than civilian—power led to the marginalization of the Tshombe family and to claims by the FLNC, as its name suggested, to speak for Congo as a whole. While the Portuguese authorities were not in complete control of these processes, they were able to restrict Mbumba's political ambitions and channel them in their own military interests in the early 1970s.

All this changed in 1974–1975, when the competing Angolan nationalist movements came into direct conflict following the Portuguese coup. While the MPLA's accord with the FLNC was, as already noted, based on the latter's undeniable military capacity, the FLNC's ability to negotiate (under Portuguese military auspices) the Cossa agreement reflected its capacity to project a coherent organizational position, contrasting sharply with all other Portuguese-affiliated African military groupings which lacked its politico-military capacity and coherence. Mbumba's tenacious defense of the FLNC's independence, in the face of considerable efforts by the MPLA to impose upon it leftist leaders and/or allies, certainly restricted its wider political influence but equally demonstrated that it was never simply a set of "guns-for-hire." This political independence was further demonstrated in the two Shaba invasions of Zaire in 1977–1978; although Shaba I was clearly supported by the MPLA, Shaba II was, the evidence suggests, initiated against the wishes of both superpowers and by their respective client states in the region. In asserting their right to oppose Mobutu's dictatorial control of Zaire, the FLNC paid a heavy price for destabilizing the fragile balance of power in Cold War–era central Africa.

For much of the following two decades, the direct political impact of the ex-gendarmes was negligible: while former leaders such as Mbumba engaged in a largely fruitless quest to secure alternative bases of support, some of the remaining rank-and-file forces in Angola were integrated in a new foreign army, albeit that of a country in which many had been resident for most of their lives. Although they split along ethnic and personal lines, at the heart of their divisions during this period was their central desire to return "home" to their fondly imagined "Katanga." In this regard, the ex-Tigres had much in common with exiled southern African liberation movements such as the African National Congress, whose internal conflicts and repression of dissent resulted in significant part from a similar failure to return home.[3] Notwithstanding their lack of direct political representation, the continued presence of this foreign armed force in a region racked by continual conflict made the ex-Tigres simultaneously a military asset and a political threat for the Angolan and Zairian states alike. During this difficult period, this threat helped solidify the fissure between Zaire and Katanga, demonstrating the impossibility of effectively integrating the province's history of autonomy and separate identity into the hegemonic discourse of the Zairian regime. Mobutu's opportunistic manipulation of the autonomist provincial government of Kyungu wa Kumwanza of the early 1990s, as well as his tacit approval of anti-Kasian violence as a way of undermining the UDPS, was possible only because of its indigenous basis. The governments of both Angola and Zaire, together with the UNHCR, sought but generally failed to return the ex-gendarmes to Zaire in a way that would not further destabilize that country or its regional relationships: this failure reflected above all the perception that the ex-Tigres represented a continued military and political threat to the centralized authoritarian state that Mobutu had constructed. Although, as has already been noted, a significant gap had opened up between the perception and the reality of the threat posed by the ex-Tigres, their involvement in the AFDL's operations of 1996–1997 that ultimately ousted the ailing dictator demonstrated that this perception was not entirely fanciful.

In the early twenty-first century, the political influence of the returned ex-Tigres in the post-Mobutu DRC has often mirrored earlier phases of their activities, albeit in greatly altered circumstances. As the hopes of most Congolese people for a transition to a more representative political system were destroyed during nearly a decade of devastating conflict, the military capacity of some ex-gendarmes was once again deployed in the latest manifestation of the poorly integrated and dysfunctional Congolese army, the FAC. As on previous occasions, the potential political threat posed by this historically secessionist force proved a more significant factor than its military strength. The dilution of the ex-Tigres within the FAC had the effect of weakening the military capacity of the new DRC army, leaving the Laurent Kabila regime particularly vulnerable when its regional friends became enemies with the advent of the second Congo war in 1998.

Under Laurent Kabila, Katanga was represented as never before at the center of Congolese political life, but this did not translate into material improvements in the lives of ordinary Katangese people in general or of the ex-Tigres in particular. Meanwhile, the continued presence of many ex-Tigres in Angola continued, and continues, to cast a shadow over Angolan-Congolese relations. As Katangese disillusionment has grown with the failure of the postwar minerals boom to translate into development and higher living standards, the ghosts of the secession have increasingly come to haunt the fragile Congolese state, barely presided over by President Joseph Kabila. As was starkly demonstrated in the Bakata Katanga militia incursion of Lubumbashi in March 2013, military effectiveness is arguably less important than the political impact achieved by summoning up the spirit of the ex-Tigres across the whole of the province; the legacy of these actions cannot as yet be meaningfully assessed.

Questions of Identity: Mercenaries or Nationalists-in-Exile

A common but highly problematic starting point for exploring the motivations of combatants is the "greed" or "grievance" bifurcation:[4] Is the force involved motivated primarily by financial reward—either by payment or other forms of material gain (for example, preferential access to minerals such as diamonds)—or by a "political" or ideological cause?[5] In most cases, other than those involving strictly professional mercenaries, the answer is almost always both, combined in complex ways which in practice do not distinguish so easily between material and moral causes.[6]

For their part, the ex-Tigres certainly fought for various political masters in exchange for tangible rewards: as the professional army of the Katangese state, they expected and demanded salaries, shelter, and some kind of security, and continued to do so in their relations with a series of political masters. This, for them, was not inherently contradictory to their long-term aim of restoring Katangese statehood—an aim, to be sure, that was abandoned after the seizure of power by the AFDL in 1997—or at least ensuring a significant degree of Katangese political autonomy within a more benevolent, decentralized Congolese state. Rather than viewing this as a simplistic bifurcation, it is more helpful to focus on the undoubted tensions and contradictions inherent in pursuing a form of national liberation via service to a foreign state: the initiatives taken by the ex-Tigres to return to the homeland they so desperately sought often took them further away from it. These tensions were mirrored in the difficulties faced by those who sought to deploy them: the Tshombe-led government of Congo in 1964–1965, and more obviously the Portuguese colonial army and the MPLA-controlled Angolan state. Each sought to exploit the military capacity of this well-trained force in "mercenary" forms, but each reckoned without the ex-Tigres' powerful capacity for independent agency and their continued pursuit of their own goals, a pursuit that severely troubled their political masters.

Despite their undoubted military strength, the leaders of the ex-Katangese gendarmes and their successor organizations perennially struggled to assert their political aims. By the late 1960s, the ex-army of secessionist Katanga had lost its original political leadership; the exile and then detention of Moïse Tshombe, along with the incorporation and/or complicity of most of the former Katangese leadership with the Mobutu-dominated political system, left the ex-gendarmes to the tender mercies of Portuguese colonialism. After an initial period in which the *fiéis* were mobilized primarily to restrict Congolese backing for Angolan nationalism, the expression of a degree of Katangese national identity was permitted by their Portuguese intelligence overseers (PIDE). It was, however, only after the FLNC was established in 1969 that the ex-gendarmes began to find some autonomous political direction. This was nevertheless constantly undermined by the dependent role of the *fiéis*, first on the Portuguese and then on the independent Angolan government, whose relationship with the Tigres was not dissimilar to that of their colonial predecessors. The FLNC leadership, dominated by the singular figure of Nathanaël Mbumba, carved out for the Tigres a significant degree of autonomy; but a high price was paid by the soldiers of the FLNC themselves, serving as they did under an authoritarian leadership whose campaign for Katangese self-determination was not matched in any respect by self-expression among its exiled armed forces regarding the trajectory of that campaign or the future of their movement. In this respect, at least, the FLNC resembled the reality, if not the rhetoric, of ostensibly radical southern African liberation movements such as the Zimbabwe African National Union (ZANU), the South West Africa People's Organization (SWAPO), and the South African ANC.[7]

In the mid-1970s, Mbumba, while painting the FLNC in radical colors that partly distanced the ex-gendarmes from their Tshombist roots and positioned them closer to the Marxist MPLA, continually resisted any challenge to his leadership from the FLNC's ostensible allies among leftist Congolese exile groups. Mbumba, apparently focused on his own dreams of power, equally rejected cooperation with powerful internal Katangese forces, for example, the Tshombe family and the Lunda king, the Mwaant Yav. While this single-mindedness may have prevented the hijacking of the military capacity of the Tigres for initiatives that might not have addressed their underlying aspirations for Katangese statehood, it also left the FLNC largely isolated, unable to achieve its immediate aim to remove Mobutu and exposed to the political winds of change within its host nation, Angola. Nearly two decades later, the ex-Tigres, lacking such effective leadership, were readily mobilized by Angola into the AFDL's successful overthrow of Mobutu; their leaders, such as they were by this time, were unable to impose any conditions on their role and consequently failed to assert meaningful influence over the Congolese political settlement under Laurent Kabila from 1997 onward.

Congo and Katanga: Rethinking the African Nation-State

The powerful legacy of the Katangese secession clearly demonstrates that the confidence of African rulers and political scientists in the sanctity of colonial borders, replicated in postcolonial form, has not been fulfilled in practice. Rather, the shadows of the often traumatic process of decolonization and nation-building have continued to be cast across some African states. During the 1960s and 1970s, the central(ized) nation-state was the flag-bearer in Africa of globalized notions of modernization and development, the agent charged with the—in retrospect impossibly ambitious—task of both overcoming and reconstructing colonial ideologies of power. Its antitheses were forms of "tribalism" or "regionalism," sometimes manipulated by foreign interests, of which the Katangese secession provided the paradigmatic example of what was now established as an illegitimate basis for political self-determination. The ban on redrawing African state borders after the OAU's 1963 declaration (reinforced by the bloodshed in both Katanga and Biafra) meant that little attention was paid to the generally marginal and subaltern articulation of secessionist imaginings. The Cold War, and the need to guard against the supposed threat of superpower destabilization supposedly disguised as irredentist threats, made the open expression of secessionist demands almost universally illegitimate. In their place, demands were made for political reform within nation-state borders, as the ex-gendarmes demonstrated with their nominative reinvention as Congolese nationalists in the form of the FLNC.

By the 1980s it was increasingly recognized that the effective capacity of independent African states was always overstated and now in decline.[8] The fall in state revenues (particularly marked in mineral-dependent economies such as Congo/Zaire), the growth of indebtedness, and the imposition of debt-related conditionalities by donor countries, combined with the redirection of aid to nonstate organizations to weaken the central state and to encourage attempts by local political actors to (re-)establish themselves on the regional or national political stage, sometimes through violent means. In this context, new forms of political mobilization around local or regional demands—many of which had bubbled below the surface for some decades—became newly viable, in Africa in general and in Congo in particular.[9]

Katanga thus found itself in a paradoxical position: on the one hand, the legacy of the secession made it the object of nearly universal condemnation; on the other one hand, it was for the reasons explained herein one of the few real candidates with a viable basis for autonomous statehood. Katanga as a colonial structure reproduced in essence the opposition between a "modern" but imposed state and a "traditional" but authentic rural community. But the partial reconstruction of the precolonial Luba and Lunda polities provided at least a basis for the reformulation of a Katangese identity. Katanga found itself once again at the center of competing claims for political and economic power, from both within and without the province, which had the cumulative effect of renewing the general claim to a legitimate Katangese identity. The secession and the subsequent iterations of autonomist thinking and association that followed represent an incomplete and decidedly imperfect attempt to develop a new form of legitimacy based on regional identification.

Such tendencies were only reinforced by the democratic revolutions of the early 1990s and their broader effects. It is certainly striking that, notwithstanding the warnings of some incumbent leaders, multiethnic African states did not, like many of their former communist counterparts, fragment into smaller, overtly ethnic nations during the continent's partial and problematic transition to multiparty democracy.[10] Electoral competition led instead to the more overt deployment (compared to the one-party state era) of ethnoregionalism as the basis of interparty divisions.[11] More recently, however, the precedent set by the internationally endorsed self-determination of newly independent South Sudan appears to have encouraged the more overt expression of new autonomist and/or secessionist demands in, for example, Zambia and Kenya.[12] In the DRC today, the official decentralization process and its endorsement by the so-called international community provide a partial legitimation of such demands, while the government's delay in implementing its declared commitment to decentralization has the potential to fuel antistate claims to more fully fledged autonomy.[13] In February 2015 it was announced that the long-delayed *découpage* (literally, to "cut up") process was to be completed by July of the same year, with the DRC's existing eleven provinces being divided into twenty-six new ones. Katanga itself was divided into four new provinces—Haut Katanga, Lualaba, Tanganyika, and Haut Lomani—closely resembling the division of the province following the secession. This sudden and ill-prepared step undoubtedly reflects President Kabila's attempt to clip the wings of his provincial opponents, and in particular Katumbi's Katanga power base; Katumbi has criticized Kabila's evident aim of standing for an unconstitutional third term in office, which prompted popular unrest in Kinshasa and other cities in early 2015. In September 2015, Katumbi resigned from the ruling party and is widely expected to mount a serious challenge for the Congolese presidency in elections constitutionally due in 2016.[14] Meanwhile, a powerful autonomist tendency exists elsewhere in the country, particularly in Ituri, fueled by a widespread perception that the authorities in Kinshasa are illegitimately extracting local resources but providing few if any state services. This is not to suggest that such movements are any more likely to succeed in the future than in the past, but rather to insist on their increasing importance as a mode of articulating political discontents with the central state.

As in Katanga, many neosecessionist movements across sub-Saharan Africa draw on a particular interpretation of history as the basis for their contemporary political demands. In making such claims, contested histories both of colonization and particular aspects of the precolonial past are universally deployed as a political resource. This renewed legitimacy of secessionist imaginaries is thus linked to a historical change in the perception of the role and efficiency of the state in Africa. But it also points to a deeper historical problem regarding the legitimacy of the state in many African localities. Since their forceful integration into new colonial authoritarian states, many local societies have been prohibited from finding their own path to modernity and to the development of linked local-national political structures that they perceive as their own. The colonial dichotomy between the "modern state" and the "traditional village" still hampers the conceptualization of these new forms of modernity. Efforts to reconceptualize political structures on the basis of existing ethnic groups inevitably fail because of the reproduction of this opposition, and the new or renewed ethnoregional movements that have emerged since the 1990s commonly have as their aim capturing the existing modern state and its most tangible manifestation as the capital city, or recreating it locally but in its existing form.

Such historically rooted contemporary demands are commonly articulated in relation to the drawing of borders at two decisive and interrelated historical moments: that of colonization in the late nineteenth century and of decolonization in the mid-twentieth century. During the "effective occupation" of sub-Saharan Africa that followed the Berlin Conference of 1884–1885, colonial territories were hastily constructed out of historically contestable claims by some African leaders, encouraged in such claims by agents of colonialism with no interest in establishing historical truth.[15] Powerful polities that found themselves divided or disempowered as a result of this process were often initially quiescent, consoled in part by the fact that some precolonial manifestations (for example, the continued expression of fealty by Lunda chiefs in Angola and Northern Rhodesia to the Mwaant Yav) could continue across relatively weak colonial borders. But this was thrown into doubt in the 1950s by the prospect of self-government under what threatened to be more interventionist nation-states. In Belgian Congo, historically rooted claims and counterclaims regarding the legitimacy of particular borders and identities were articulated in the late-colonial period, as the sudden and largely unheralded approach of independence generated not a singular nationalist movement, nor simply a series of opposed ethnoregional movements within Congo's borders, but rather an explosion of claims and counterclaims to demand and construct overlapping nation-state projects, seeking to utilize some of the same human and natural resources for what were ultimately incompatible visions of the future. In the case of Katanga, the secessionist project kept alive in exile by the ex-gendarmes imagined returning to an earlier set of (pre-1933) colonial boundaries, within which a multiethnic nation-state could be constructed. Although the Lunda majority among the ex-Tigres led occasionally to manifestations of a narrower ethnic but transborder Lunda polity, for example by Mbumba, this was never the primary basis of their political demands, which remained focused on a multiethnic Katangese nationhood.

All this was meant to be irrelevant after independence: the ultimate victory of the Leopoldville-based Congolese nation-state over its many internal enemies and competitors, ironically achieved only with the assistance of former colonial and neocolonial Western forces, appeared to have enabled President Mobutu to integrate, forcibly at times, the disparate regions of Congo into a highly centralized nation-state.[16] Yet Katanga proved ultimately impossible to integrate effectively: as this book has shown, the 1960s saw attempts by Tshombe and his chiefly and military allies to reestablish the secession or to bring about an alternative Congolese political order that would allow significantly increased provincial autonomy. In the 1970s fear of internal rebellion, backed by the ex-gendarmes across the Angolan border, led the militarized Zairian state to treat southern Katanga as a region under occupation and its peoples as an enemy within. Although such rebellious voices were mostly silenced in the following decade, the first shoots of democratic recovery in the early 1990s brought with them a rearticulation of autochthonous Katangese identification, led by UFERI and directed against the new generation of Kasaian politicians in UDPS—and this rearticulation was now fueled by the ever-opportunistic Mobutu to divide his potential enemies.

Such voices were again quieted during the presidency of Laurent Kabila and shortly thereafter: under Kabila père, Katangese figures were at the heart of

Congolese government for the first time since Tshombe's brief premiership in 1964–1965, and the province's concerns were apparently expressed at the highest level. But in the 2010s the government of Joseph Kabila reverted to a practice of central administration, treating Katanga simply as a space from which to extract revenue from mining and border customs. Today, in what is historically a relatively open political environment, there is a growing realization that, once again, the wealth produced in Katanga is, notwithstanding the new decentralized constitution, not ensuring meaningful development in the mineral-rich province. Most recently, the historic south-north Katangese division has been partly overcome, as Katanga's many political actors increasingly articulate a common ideal of increased autonomy, a goal that is widely shared among the general population. While Katanga's governor, Moïse Katumbi, created a framework for the expression of such feelings by his skillful deployment of Katangese imagery, it may prove to be the case that, in the long run, such articulations have fueled rather than legitimized the fires of Katangese political identification, well beyond the control of the politicians who unleashed them.

The resurgent myth of the Tigres has now been articulated by operational armed groups, and with this comes a range of claims to, variously, a historically rooted neosecessionism (the Congrès des Peuples du Katanga [CPK]), a "multiracial" Katanga (CORAK Matuka), and a pure "autochthonous" Katanga opposed to an externally dominated Congolese state (CORAK Ngonga). Each group makes political claims against the central state, alongside appeals to the military force of the Tigres, still in theory deployable from exile in Angola. In these forms, the Tigres act as an ideological reservoir of memories from which all Katangese movements can draw in order to advance their claims.

None of this should suggest the limited relevance of the nation or the state to either the ex-Katangese gendarmes or the wider Katangese population. Nostalgia for the secession is, in part at least, fueled by the remembered and decidedly relative functionality of the Katangese state: underwritten by mining capital and staffed in its initial period of existence by (ex-)colonial Belgian officials, but certainly able to generate a more meaningful presence in the lives and consciousness of many of its inhabitants than either its colonial predecessor or its Congolese/Zairian successor(s). As direct memory of the secession has faded with time, the idea of secession has become more mythic and politically potent.

The Katangese national imaginary was strengthened, not weakened, by the long gaze from exile of the ex-Katangese gendarmes. They, despite numerous reinventions of their own organization and role, retained above all a desire to return home to their fondly recalled "Katanga," which grew increasingly distant not only from its own historical reality but also from the Congolese/Zairian state that presided over the actually existing Katanga in an increasingly dysfunctional and brutal way. This was undoubtedly reinforced by the severe losses suffered by the ex-gendarmes in their military struggles over the long years in exile. As with other "liberation movements" (as they are constituted in the southern African political imagination), such sacrifices served to legitimate their cause and to strengthen their identity as the guardians of the flame of Katangese nationhood, both before and after their partial and problematic return in the late 1990s.

An idealized memory of Katanga was thus kept alive by the FLNC leadership, not only in Angola but also in Zaire itself. This memory could be built upon, in limited form by Nguz Karl I Bond in the 1980s and then more overtly by UFERI with the relative political opening of the early 1990s. This idealization of memory may be usefully compared to that of immigrant or settler communities that acted out their national identity of origin in their new society (for example, British settlers in Australasia or southern Africa, or immigrant communities in New York), retaining their national identity in a reified form while it evolved in new ways at home. In the case of the ex-gendarmes, this national identity was underwritten by the value of their military expertise and capacity, but it proved difficult to convert this valuable resource into effective political capital. Throughout their history, they retained the features and structure of a government army, with a surprising coherence of and longevity in their political objectives. This distinguishes them from the proliferation of armed groups in central Africa, particularly since the late 1990s. This is also why it has proved so difficult for civilian politicians from outside to displace from the FLNC leadership the officers of the Katangese military and police forces—Kalenga, Mbumba, Kasongo, and Tshingambo, for example—who physically embody the Tigres and their cause. This is why younger leaders such as Mashiku and Mukachung were forced to establish alternative factions in their ultimately unsuccessful efforts to do so.

Katanga is in many ways, as this analysis suggests, a particular and extreme example of contested national identity, yet not a qualitatively distinct one. As well as the more obvious comparisons with the RPF's long exile in Rwanda or the SPLA's war for an independent South Sudan, its enduring relevance, throughout the entire period of national independence, may be instructively compared to the otherwise very different Tuareg rebellion against the central Malian state, which has continued in one form or another for more than five decades.[17] For long periods this movement appeared largely irrelevant to the material concerns of nation-building and development in Mali, yet in particular periods, and owing to unpredictable historical developments—most recently, the ousting of pro-regime Tuareg fighters following the overthrow of Libyan president Muammar Gaddafi in 2011—it has directly threatened the central state's control of more than half of its territory, control that was (as in Katanga in the early 1960s and the late 1970s) maintained only by the intervention of non-African military forces. It is suggested that while few such rebellions have had such a dramatic impact, historians might fruitfully explore the African nation-state from the perspective of marginal movements and regions that have the potential to challenge central state control through a combination of military and ideational means.

Studying War in Central Africa—Historiographical and Methodological Challenges

As we have argued, research into conflict in Africa needs to go beyond the study of conflicts between nation-states on the one hand and nonstate guerrilla or rebel forces on the other. This has significant consequences for the methodological approach of researchers. At its most basic, state archives in much of Africa are inaccessible, poorly funded, and/or unable to maintain and make available documents detailing the decision-making processes that have led to conflicts on the continent.[18] In this context, it is often necessary to depend on Western state archives, and those have been of partial use in this study. However, it is equally necessary to recognize the inadequacy of those archives in reflecting the views and aspirations of movements such as the Katangese gendarmes and their successors. Western governments and intelligence agencies not only depicted the gendarmes' ideas and actions inaccurately but often deceived themselves regarding these ideas and actions because their own worldview, shaped by decolonization and the Cold War, failed to grasp the particular motivations of these actors, which could not easily be understood through the conventional geopolitical or modernist-developmental frameworks that dominated the considerations of policy makers (including those in the Eastern bloc, such as Cuba) and which continue to dominate the analytical approach of most diplomatic and political historians of this period.

To take one example: it is necessary to see beyond the visible aspects of affiliation of a particular group of soldiers at any one time, for example their uniforms or overtly declared allegiances. While these may reveal important aspects of their current loyalties, they should not be assumed to be a direct reflection of their underlying aims or affiliations. Rather, they should be understood in part as a form of militaristic performance or discourse, necessitating deconstruction. This does not mean, however, that the officers and soldiers of the ex-gendarmes did not have underlying and identifiable motivations for their actions, but that these motivations evolved over time and were the subject of contestation and conflict among the political and military leaders of the various successor movements and organizations. To identify them has, however, necessitated the collection of a wide range of additional sources, each in its own way as problematic as state archives: private papers painstakingly collected and preserved by some of the actors; interviews with ex-gendarmes and other actors; and other official materials (for example, the documents of the UNHCR) that enable researchers to bridge some of the gaps in comprehension and information that conventional archives reveal. The challenge of such research is, in analyzing the political messages embedded in archival and interview sources, to go beyond the external judgments normally imposed on Congolese political movements and by such means access the internal motives and aspirations of those movements as they range across national borders and through time.

More generally, and in line with our broader argument, it should be understood that historical materials, historical research, and even historians themselves are viewed by the protagonists in these political and military movements as an important resource in their struggles for power, liberation, and change. "Tin trunk memoirs" are not relics of the past; they have usually been carefully preserved in the expectation that historical evidence will play an important part in a range of contemporary and future political and cultural debates and conflicts. For some of the individuals whose papers have been vital to this project, the aim is to document their personal role in a political movement and to record the "misdeeds" of their political rivals. Indeed, this study has been made possible by the provision by respondents of carefully negotiated agreements, heated correspondence between protagonists, and (not least) competing "histories" of the FLNC and its predecessor movements, painstakingly reconstructed so as to make decidedly interested claims and counterclaims appear as uncontested, incontrovertible historical truth. Interviewees likewise deploy historical reference and apparently arcane detail with an eye determinedly fixed on the present and the future. While we have certainly sought to distance ourselves from such immediate claims in constructing a "professional" and "academic" history, we are aware that our construction has been made possible by political activists who see historical research and writing as a vital resource in their own search for a better future.

While the importance of competing historical claims based on the deployment and articulation of memory is well established, its centrality in centralsouthern Africa's contemporary political and military struggles is only now being fully understood. Far from focusing squarely on material or practical concerns, state actors and political activists alike can be seen (when one looks closely enough) to be constantly deploying historical references with which they themselves have only an indirect relationship. For example, Angolan youth groups, occupying their renamed Tahrir Square in Luanda, reference the violent suppression of the 1977 Nito Alves revolt against MPLA rule, in part because it remains the ruling party's greatest historical secret.[19] Youth activists of the South African Communist Party (SACP) invoke the party's icons, such as Chris Hani, in their pursuit of more effective "service delivery" in a postliberation environment that Hani and his comrades could not have envisaged.[20] In this respect, the Kata Katanga group's invocation of the flag of the secession in 2013 is just one example of the wider referencing of historical symbolism, language, and meaning that should be a primary focus of historians seeking to explain the nature of postcolonial political, social, and cultural change.

Notes

Introduction

1. Throughout the book, the various names adopted by the ex-gendarmes will be used to apply to their appropriate historically specific manifestation. For the purposes of clarity, this introduction will use the term "ex-gendarmes" throughout, but it should be borne in mind that it is necessarily applied to many soldiers who did not in fact serve as "gendarmes" in the Katangese secession of the early 1960s.

2. See, among many others, B. Davidson, *The Black Man's Burden: Africa and the Curse of the Nation-State* (London: James Currey, 1992); T. Ranger and O. Vaughan (eds.), *Legitimacy and the State in Twentieth Century Africa* (Basingstoke: Palgrave, 1993); A. D. Smith, *State and Nation in the Third World: The Western State and African Nationalism* (Brighton: Wheatsheaf, 1983); J.-F. Bayart, *L'état en Afrique: La politique du ventre* (Paris: Fayard, 1989); J. Herbst, *States and Power in Africa: Comparative Lessons in Authority and Control* (Princeton, NJ: Princeton University Press, 2000); G. Hydén, "The Problematic State," in *African Politics in Comparative Perspective* (Cambridge: Cambridge University Press, 2006), 50–71; C. Young, *The African Colonial State in Comparative Perspective* (New Haven, CT: Yale University Press, 1997); B. Berman, "Ethnicity, Patronage and the African State: The Politics of Uncivil Nationalism," *African Affairs* 97, no. 388 (1998): 305–341.

3. A. A. Mazrui and M. Tidy, *Nationalism and the New States in Africa from about 1935 to the Present* (London: Heinemann, 1984).

4. A. Temu and B. Swai, *Historians and Africanist History: A Critique; Post-Colonial Historiography Examined* (London: Zed Books, 1981).

5. Young, *The African Colonial State*.

6. R. Lemarchand, *Political Awakening in the Belgian Congo* (Berkeley: University of California Press, 1964), pp. 147–197.

7. Regarding citizenship, see S. Dorman, D. Hammett, and P. Nugent, "Introduction: Citizenship and Its Casualties in Africa," in S. Dorman, D. Hammett, and P. Nugent (eds.), *Making Nations, Creating Strangers: States and Citizenship in Africa* (Leiden: Brill, 2007), pp. 3–26; and B. Manby, *Struggles for Citizenship in Africa* (London: Zed Books, 2009). For a discussion of these issues in relation to the Democratic Repblic of Congo, see S. Jackson, "Of 'Doubtful Nationality': Political Manipulation of Citizenship in the D.R. Congo," *Citizenship Studies* 11 (2007): 481–500.

8. For examples, see J. Allman, *The Quills of the Porcupine: Asante Nationalism in an Emergent Ghana* (Madison: University of Wisconsin Press, 1993); G. Macola, *Liberal Nationalism in Central Africa* (New York: Palgrave Macmillan, 2010); M. Larmer, *Rethinking African Politics: A History of Opposition in Zambia* (Farnham: Ashgate, 2011); B. Lecocq, *Disputed Desert: Decolonisation, Competing Nationalisms and Tuareg Rebellions in Northern Mali* (Leiden: Brill, 2010).

9. For the external influence on the secession, see L. De Witte, *The Assassination of Lumumba* (London: Zed Books, 2001). For a more sophisticated analysis of the interaction of external and internal factors, see J. Gérard-Libois, *Katanga Secession* (Madison: University of Wisconsin Press, 1966).

10. A seminal contribution in this area is J. C. Scott, "Compulsory Villagization in Tanzania: Aesthetics and Miniaturization," in *Seeing Like a State: How Certain Schemes to Improve the Human Condition Have Failed* (New Haven, CT: Yale University Press, 1998), pp. 223–261.

11. M. Doornbos, "The African State in Academic Debate: Retrospect and Prospect," *Journal of Modern African Studies* 28, no. 2 (1990): 179–198.

12. See "Let's Talk about Bantustans," special issue, *South African Historical Journal* 64, no. 1 (2012), for the first important collection of writing in this area.

13. For Jean-François Bayart's explanation of the reappropriation of the colonial state, see his *L'état en Afrique*, p. 258.

14. A. Mpase, *Au service d'un Congo aux mille visages* (Kinshasa: Academic Express Press, 2008), pp. 141–192.

15. See, for example, C. Alden, "Making Old Soldiers Fade Away: Lessons from the Reintegration of Demobilized Soldiers in Mozambique," *Security Dialogue* 33 (2002): 341–356; more generally, K. Kingma (ed.), *Demobilization in Subsaharan Africa: The Development and Security Impacts* (New York: Palgrave Macmillan, 2000).

16. Among the most important studies of Congolese political history are Lemarchand, *Political Awakening in the Belgian Congo*; C. Young, *Politics in the Congo: Decolonization and Independence* (Princeton, NJ: Princeton University Press, 1965); C. Young and T. Turner, *The Rise and Decline of the Zairian State* (Madison: University of Wisconsin Press, 1985).

17. Young and Turner, *Rise and Decline*; M. G. Schatzberg, *The Dialectics of Oppression in Zaire* (Bloomington: Indiana University Press, 1988).

18. Young and Turner, *Rise and Decline*, pp. 64–77.

19. J. Herbst and G. Mills, "There Is No Congo," *Foreign Policy*, March 18, 2009, http://www.foreignpolicy.com/articles/2009/03/17/there_is_no_congo?page=0,1 (accessed July 3, 2014).

20. For a powerful rejoinder to Herbst and Mills developing this argument, see T. Raeymaekers, "Who Calls the Congo?," August 10, 2009, http://rubeneberlein.wordpress.com/2009/08/10/who-calls-the-congo-a-response-to-herbst-and-mills/ (accessed July 3, 2014).

21. R. Lemarchand, "Reflections on the Crisis in Eastern Congo," in S. Marysse and F. Reyntjens (eds.), *L'Afrique des Grands Lacs: Annuaire 2008–2009* (Paris: L'Harmattan, 2009), pp. 105–121.

22. During the second Congo war (1998–2003), the Rwandan-backed Rassemblement Congolais pour la Démocratie or Congolese Rally for Democracy (RCD) reintroduced the 1964 Congolese federal constitution and its flag, symbols decried in Kinshasa as enabling the annexation of the Kivus into Rwandan territory.

23. For the latter, see W. Reno, *Warfare in Independent Africa* (Cambridge: Cambridge University Press, 2011); C. Clapham, *African Guerrillas* (Oxford: James Currey, 1998); M. Bøås and K. C. Dunn (eds.), *African Guerrillas: Raging against the Machine* (Boulder, CO: Lynne Rienner, 2007).

24. Cited in J. Stockwell, *In Search of Enemies: A CIA Story* (New York: W. W. Norton, 1978), p. 51.

25. O. A. Westad, *The Global Cold War: Third World Interventions and the Makings of Our Times* (Cambridge: Cambridge University Press, 2005), pp. 3–5. See also S. Onslow (ed.), *Cold War in Southern Africa: White Power, Black Liberation* (London: Routledge, 2009), and V. Shubin, *The Hot "Cold War": The USSR in Southern Africa* (London: Pluto Press, 2008).

26. P. Gleijeses, *Conflicting Missions: Havana, Washington, and Africa, 1959–1976* (Chapel Hill: University of North Carolina Press, 2002).

1. Becoming Katanga

1. The title of this chapter is inspired by a groundbreaking history of the Zimbabwean nation-state that grapples with the challenge of reconstructing a national history without it becoming what Ranger terms "patriotic history": B. Raftopoulos and A. Mlambo (eds.), *Becoming Zimbabwe: A History from the Pre-colonial Period to 2008* (Harare: Weaver Press, 2009). See also T. O. Ranger, "Nationalist Historiography, Patriotic History and the History of the Nation: The Struggle over the Past in Zimbabwe," *Journal of Southern African Studies* 30, no. 2 (2004): 215–234.

2. This is a well-established argument, but a most lucid early articulation of it can be found in C. Neale, "The Idea of Progress in the Revision of African History," in B. Jewsiewicki and D. Newbury (eds.), *African Historiographies: What History for Which Africa?* (Beverly Hills, CA: Sage, 1986), pp. 112–122.

3. See, for example, B. Anderson, *Imagined Communities: Reflections on the Origins and Spread of Nationalism* (London: Verso, 1991); E. Hobsbawm and T. O. Ranger, *The Invention of Tradition* (Cambridge: Cambridge University Press, 1983); E. Gellner, *Nations and Nationalism* (Oxford: Blackwell, 1983). For an important counterargument, see A. D. Smith, *Nationalism and Modernism* (London: Routledge, 1989).

4. J. Vansina, *Kingdoms of the Savanna* (Madison: University of Wisconsin Press, 1966), p. 97; I. Ndaywel è Nziem, *Histoire générale du Congo* (Brussels: Duculot, 1998), pp. 131–138.

5. Ibid., pp. 142–146.

6. E. Bustin, *Lunda under Belgian Rule: The Politics of Ethnicity* (Cambridge, MA: Harvard University Press, 1973), p. 3.

7. Vansina, *Kingdoms of the Savannah*, p. 83; Bustin, *Lunda under Belgian Rule*, pp. 4–5.

8. E. M'Bokolo, "Le séparatisme katangais," in J.-L. Amselle and E. M'Bokolo (eds.), *Au coeur de l'ethnie* (Paris: La Découverte, 1999), pp. 192–194.

9. Bustin, *Lunda under Belgian Rule*, p. 5.

10. Ibid., pp. 20–22.

11. J.-L. Vellut, "Rural Poverty in Western Shaba, c. 1890–1920," in R. H. Palmer and N. Parsons (eds.), *The Roots of Rural Poverty in Central and Southern Africa* (London: Heinemann, 1977), p. 295.

12. R. Lemarchand, *Political Awakening*, p. 13; G. Macola, *The Kingdom of Kazembe: History and Politics in North-East Zambia and Katanga to 1950* (Hamburg: LIT, 2002), p. 26.

13. In this sense, the Msiri was the nearest thing to a pan-Katangese ruler, something that made his death at the hands of colonial officials in 1891 an important symbol of Katangese unity in the mid-twentieth century. W. G. Clarence-Smith, "Capital Accumulation and Class Formation in Angola," in D. Birmingham and P. M. Martin (eds.), *History of Central Africa*, vol. 2 (Harlow: Longman, 1983), p. 173.

14. Lemarchand, *Political Awakening*, p. 14.

15. Ibid., p. 24.

16. Bustin, *Lunda under Belgian Rule*, p. 40.

17. For the myth of gold wealth in Katanga, see J. Stengers, "Le Katanga et le mirage de l'or," in *Études africaines offertes à Henri Brunschwig* (Paris: EHESS, 1982), pp. 149–175. See also J.-L. Vellut, "Mining in the Belgian Congo," in Birmingham and Martin, *History of Central Africa*, 2:127.

18. C. Perrings, *Black Mineworkers in Central Africa* (London: Heinemann, 1979), pp. 6–7.

19. G. Nzongola-Ntajala, *The Congo from Leopold to Kabila: A People's History* (London: Zed Books, 2002), p. 44.

20. Bustin, *Lunda under Belgian Rule*, p. 40. Belgian recognition of Muteb as the Mwaant Yav did not end considerable internal Lunda conflict over the rightful holder of this position, which continued throughout the period covered by this chapter. Bustin provides an excellent summary of these conflicts, the detail of which is beyond the scope of this study.

21. Bustin, *Lunda under Belgian Rule*, p. 50.

22. B. Jewsiewicki, "Rural Society and the Belgian Colonial Economy," in Birmingham and Martin, *History of Central Africa* 2:97.

23. The history of the Comité Spécial du Katanga is analyzed in J. Gérard-Libois, "Les dissolutions successives du Comité Spécial du Katanga," *Études Congolaises* 8, no. 3 (1965): 1–55. See also R. Brion and J.-L. Moreau, *De la mine à Mars: La génèse d'Umicore* (Tielt: Lanoo, 2006), pp. 63–76.

24. J. Gérard-Libois, *Katanga Secession* (Madison: University of Wisconsin Press, 1966), pp. 47–48.

25. R. Anstey, *King Leopold's Legacy: The Congo under Belgian Rule* (London: Oxford University Press, 1966), p. 38.

26. F. Vandewalle, "La gendarmerie katangaise et sa filiation," *Bulletin Trimestriel du CRA-OCA* 2 (1982): 85–99.

27. A. Ndjate, *Gendarmerie et reconstruction d'un état de droit au Congo-Kinshasa*, Collection Études Africaines (Paris: L'Harmattan, 2007), pp. 111–129.

28. An influential variant of this history is that the Belgian king Albert I supposedly received Katanga as a wedding present from the British crown when he married his wife, Elisabeth, who was from Bavaria but was commonly confused with the British Queen Elizabeth II or her mother (also Elizabeth), the wife of King George VI.

29. Vellut, "Mining in the Belgian Congo," pp. 128–129.

30. Anstey, *King Leopold's Legacy*, p. 43.

31. Declaration to Belgium Parliament, February 1, 1911, cited in Gérard-Libois, *Katanga Secession*, p. 10.

32. J.-L. Vellut, "Les bassins miniers de l'ancien Congo Belge: Essai d'histoire économique et sociale (1900–1960)," *Les Cahiers du CEDAF* 7 (1981): 1–70.

33. Perrings, *Black Mineworkers in Central Africa*, pp. 21–29.

34. Ibid., p. 33.

35. B. Fetter, "The Union Minière and Its Hinterland: A Demographic Reconstruction," *African Economic History* 12 (1983): 67–81.

36. Vellut, "Mining in the Belgian Congo," p. 128.

37. Perrings, *Black Mineworkers in Central Africa*.

38. Vellut, "Rural Poverty in Western Shaba," p. 303.

39. Vellut, "Mining in the Belgian Congo," pp. 128–129.

40. Although the paramountcy of the Kasongo Nyembo was contested by other chiefs, namely, Kabongo and Mutombo Mukulu, it is clear that the Kasongo Nyembo's claim to the paramountcy was recognized by the Belgian authorities. The latter's division of the Luba "empire" subsequently fed into the secessionist conflict; see chapter 3.

41. Anstey, *King Leopold's Legacy*, p. 86.

42. Perrings *Black Mineworkers in Central Africa*, pp. 79–86.

43. Anstey, *King Leopold's Legacy*, p. 119.

44. Ibid., p. 106.

45. Ibid., p. 145.

46. Jewsiewicki, "Rural Society and the Belgian Colonial Economy."

47. Vellut, "Mining in the Belgian Congo," p. 135. See also B. Fetter, "L'Union minière du Haut-Katanga, 1920–1940: La naissance d'une sous-culture totalitaire, " *Cahiers du CEDAF* no. 6 (Brussels, 1973): 1–40.

48. Perrings, *Black Mineworkers in Central Africa*; H. Heisler, "The Creation of a Stabilized Urban Society: A Turning Point in the Development of Northern Rhodesia/Zambia," *African Affairs* 70, no. 279 (1971): 125–145.

49. J. Higginson, *A Working Class in the Making: Belgian Colonial Labor Policy, Private Enterprise, and the African Mineworker, 1907–1951* (Madison: University of Wisconsin Press, 1990), pp. 173–177; Perrings, *Black Mineworkers in Central Africa*, pp. 225–227; Bustin, *Lunda under Belgian Rule*, p. 141.

50. For the British and French experience, see F. Cooper, *Decolonization and African Society: The Labor Question in French and British Africa* (Cambridge: Cambridge University Press, 1996).

51. Nzongola-Ntajala, *The Congo from Leopold to Kabila*, p. 76.

52. Ibid., p. 53.

53. Jewsiewicki, "Rural Society and the Belgian Colonial Economy," p. 122. Bustin instructively notes that some of the mutineers escaped through Lunda areas, where they were offered assistance, and then into Portuguese-ruled Angola, where they were detained by the colonial authorities: Bustin, *Lunda under Belgian Rule*, p. 142. B. S. Fetter, "The Luluabourg Revolt at Elisabethville," *African Historical Studies* 2, no. 2 (1969): 269–277.

54. Reprinted in A. Rubbens, *Dettes de Guerre* (Elisabethville: Essor du Congo, 1945), pp. 128–129, quoted in C. Young, "Zaire: The Shattered Illusion of the Integral State," in J. D. Le Sueur (ed.), *The Decolonization Reader* (New York: Routledge, 2003), pp. 414–427.

55. Anstey, *King Leopold's Legacy*, pp. 53–56.

56. Bustin, *Lunda under Belgian Rule*, p. 61.

57. Anstey, *King Leopold's Legacy*, p. 68.

58. Bustin, *Lunda under Belgian Rule*, pp. 61–62.

59. Ibid., pp. 149–150.

60. Ibid., pp. 109–110.

61. Anstey, *King Leopold's Legacy*, p. 144.

62. Ibid., p. 153.

63. Ibid., pp. 160–161. In contrast, British and French late-colonial development was for the first time subsidized by the metropolitan exchequer: see Cooper, *Decolonization and African Society*.

64. Gérard-Libois, *Katanga Secession*, p. 5.

65. Bustin, *Lunda under Belgian Rule*, p. 160.

66. This issue is analyzed at some length in Lemarchand, *Political Awakening*, particularly p. 99.

67. Notwithstanding his family's claims of association with the Mwaant Yav, Joseph Kapend, once enslaved by the Tshokwe, was essentially a social climber who used the new possibilities created by the money economy to enrich himself and thereby achieve a high social position not otherwise available to him.

68. Bustin, *Lunda under Belgian Rule*, p. 158.

69. Ibid., p. 166.

70. Ibid., p. 167.

71. Ibid., p. 170.

72. Ibid., pp. 188–189.

73. Ibid., pp. 176–177.

74. Lemarchand, *Political Awakening*, p. 108.

75. Ibid., p. 236.

76. For Barotseland, see G. Caplan, *The Elites of Barotseland* (Berkeley: University of California Press, 1970), and, more recently, J. Hogan, "'What Then Happened to Our Eden?' The

Long History of Lozi Secessionism, 1890–2013," *Journal of Southern African Studies* 40, no. 5 (2014): 907–924.

77. This phenomenon has been most successfully analyzed in West Africa. See, for example, J. Allman, *The Quills of the Porcupine: Asante Nationalism in an Emergent Ghana* (Madison: University of Wisconsin Press, 1993). A more recent example is B. Lecocq, *Disputed Desert: Decolonisation, Competing Nationalisms and Tuareg Rebellions in Northern Mali* (Leiden: Brill, 2010).

78. R. Lemarchand, "The Limits of Self-Determination: The Case of the Katanga Secession," *American Political Science Review* 56, no. 2 (1962): 404–416.

79. M. Larmer, "Historical Perspectives on Zambia's Mining Booms and Busts," in M. Larmer and A. Fraser (eds.), *Zambia, Mining and Neo-liberalism: Boom and Bust on the Globalized Copperbelt* (New York Palgrave Macmillan, 2010), pp. 31–58.

80. In this sense, Katanga's rejection of Congo resembled the refusal of Ivorian leaders to remain within a reconstructed postcolonial version of French West Africa.

81. Lemarchand, *Political Awakening*, p. 108.

82. Such nostalgic reconstructions of the Lunda Empire were also taken up by some Belgian advisers during this period, some of whom went on to support the secession. See, for example, Albert Melot, adviser to Tshombe during 1964–1965: interview, Namur, January 11, 2007.

83. Quoted in Gérard-Libois, *Katanga Secession*, pp. 13–14.

84. Quoted in Lemarchand, *Political Awakening*, p. 237.

85. The preferential policy of Paelinck was reversed following the appointment of his successor in a newspaper article published in January 1959: Lemarchand, *Political Awakening*, pp. 237–238.

86. Correspondence with Henry Rosy, 1999.

87. A. Kishiba, "Katangais, ou es tu?," *Katanga* (Elisabethville), February 1, 1958. The article became a centerpiece in Katangese historiography during the 1990s.

88. Gérard-Libois, *Katanga Secession*, p. 16.

89. Quoted in Bustin, *Lunda under Belgian Rule*, p. 181.

90. Ibid., p. 180.

91. Lemarchand, *Political Awakening*, p. 236.

92. Communication by the Mwaant Yav, January 31, 1959, cited in Bustin, *Lunda under Belgian Rule*, p. 189.

93. Bustin, *Lunda under Belgian Rule*, p. 193, where his name is given as Fernand Crine; B. Crine-Mavar, "Histoire traditionnelle du Shaba," *Cultures au Zaïre et en Afrique* 1 (1973): 17–26. See also D. Biebuyck, "Fondement de l'organisation politique des Lunda du Mwaantyaav en Territoire de Kapanga," *Zaïre* 9, no. 8 (1957): 787–817.

94. Bustin, *Lunda under Belgian Rule*, p. 189.

95. Ibid., p. 191.

96. Similar tensions may be observed in relations between ethnically oriented politicians and the kings of the "tribes" they sought to represent, for example Godefroid Munongo and his brother the Msiri; and in a more stark way, between the Baluba king, the Kasongo Nyembo, and Balubakat leader Jason Sendwe.

97. Bustin, *Lunda under Belgian Rule*, pp. 183–184. Yakemtchouk claims that ATCAR initially affiliated with Conakat: *Aux origines du séparatisme katangais* (Brussels: Académie Royale des Sciences d'Outre-Mer, 1988), p. 90.

98. Lemarchand, *Political Awakening*, p. 238.

99. *Congo 1960*, quoted in Gérard-Libois, *Katanga Secession*, p. 17.

100. G. Munongo, "Comment est né le nationalisme katangais," Elisabethville, June 16, 1962 (mimeo), cited in R. Lemarchand, "Katanga: Background to Secession" (unpublished manuscript in the possession of authors, 1963), p. 1.
101. Lemarchand, *Political Awakening*, pp. 241–242.
102. C. Young, *Politics in the Congo: Decolonization and Independence* (Princeton, NJ: Princeton University Press, 1965), p. 271.
103. Gérard-Libois, *Katanga Secession*, pp. 63–65.
104. Young, *Politics in the Congo*, pp. 279–280.
105. A. A. J. Van Bilsen, *Vers l'indépendance du Congo et du Ruanda-Urundi: réflexions sur les devoirs et l'avenir de la Belgique en Afrique centrale* (Kinshasa: Presse Universitaire du Zaire, 1977).
106. Lemarchand, *Political Awakening*, pp. 155–156.
107. Ibid., p. 157.
108. Young, *Politics in the Congo*, pp. 276–278.
109. Gérard-Libois, *Katanga Secession*, p. 33.
110. Quoted in ibid., p. 41.
111. Ibid., p. 43.
112. Ibid., pp. 3, 18.
113. Ibid., pp. 56–58.
114. Indications that mining capital was considering support for Katangese secession can be found as early as 1956, in a note written by the Belgian officer Marcel Rongveaux in which he recalls being asked by the CSK president, "What would be your attitude, Major, if Katanga proclaimed its independence?" M. Rongveaux, "Note for Professor Jean Stengers: Memories of Katanga, 1956–1960"; interview, Marcel Rongveaux, Brussels, April 2000. Rongveaux went on to be appointed military chief of staff in Elisabethville in January 1960.
115. Lemarchand, *Political Awakening*, p. 243; interview, Professor Arthur Doucy, Brussels, April 4, 2000.
116. Such discourses mirrored debates elsewhere in Africa, for example the refusal of Ivory Coast to support the postcolonial continuation of French West Africa because of the recognition by Ivorian president Félix Houphouët-Boigny that this would involve the subsidization of poorer territories by his country's considerable cocoa revenue. F. Cooper, *Africa since 1940: The Past of the Present* (Cambridge: Cambridge University Press, 2002), p. 80.
117. T. O. Ranger, "Towards a Usable African Past," in C. H. Fyfe (ed.), *African Studies since 1945: A Tribute to Basil Davidson* (London: Longman, 1976), pp. 28–39.
118. C. Young, *The Politics of Cultural Pluralism* (Madison: University of Wisconsin Press, 1976), p. 175.

2. The Katangese Secession, 1960–1963

1. An earlier version of parts of this chapter appeared as an article by the authors: "Rethinking the Katangese Secession," *Journal of Imperial and Commonwealth History* 42, no. 4 (2014): 741–761. The authors are grateful to the editors of the journal for giving permission for sections of that article to be reproduced here.
2. US State Department Archives (hereafter USSD), RG 59, E3111, Box 7, File 5.2, Conferences, "Conversation between the Secretary of State and the Prime Minister of the Republic of the Congo, 27 July 1960," July 28, 1960.

3. L. De Witte, *The Assassination of Lumumba* (London: Zed Books, 2001), p. xxi. A very similar approach can be seen in Jules Chome's *Moise Tshombe et l'escroquerie katangaise* (Brussels: Fondation J. Jacquemotte, 1966).

4. A. Kishiba, "Katangais ou es tu?," *Katanga* (Elisabethville), February 1, 1958.

5. For evidence of the demonization of Lumumba, see M. Kalb, *The Congo Cables: The Cold War in Africa from Eisenhower to Kennedy* (New York: Macmillan, 1982), pp. 78–103; J. Kent, *America, the UN and Decolonisation: Cold War Conflict in the Congo* (London: Routledge, 2010), pp. 23–30; De Witte, *Assassination of Lumumba*, pp. 15–19.

6. Charter of the Organization of African Unity, agreed in Addis Ababa, 1963, in A. A. Mazrui, *Towards a Pax Africana: A Study of Ideology and Ambition* (London: Weidenfeld and Nicolson, 1967), pp. 219–229.

7. R. Yakemtchouk, *Aux origines du séparatisme Katangais* (Brussels: Académie Royale des Sciences d'Outre-Mer, 1988), p. 33.

8. R. Lemarchand, "The Limits of Self-Determination: The Case of the Katanga Secession," *American Political Science Review* 56, no. 2 (1962): 415.

9. A. Ndjate Omanyondo N'Koy, *Gendarmerie et reconstruction d'un état de droit* (Paris: L'Harmattan, 2007), pp. 116–123.

10. Proclamation of the Independence of Katanga, July 11, 1960, in J. Gérard-Libois, *Katanga Secession* (Madison: University of Wisconsin Press, 1966), Appendix 2, p. 328.

11. Telegram from Kasavubu and Lumumba to UN, July 13, 1960, in Centre de Recherche et d'Information Socio-Politiques (hereafter CRISP), *Congo 1960* (Brussels: CRISP, 1961), p. 545. For an excellent recent analysis of the Congo crisis and the UN intervention, see L. Namikas, *Battleground Africa: Cold War in the Congo, 1960–1965* (Washington, DC: Woodrow Wilson Center Press, 2013), pp. 62–126.

12. USSD, RG 59, E3111 (Bureau of African Affairs), Box 8, File 14.4, Communism, 1960–1, Hugh S. Cumming Jr. to the Secretary, Intelligence Note: "Prospects for Communist Inroads in the Belgian Congo under Alternative Conditions of Unity or Fragmentation," n.d. but ca. June 16, 1960.

13. A useful, by no means disinterested account of these debates is provided in L. Devlin, *Chief of Station, Congo: Fighting the Cold War in a Hot Zone* (New York: PublicAffairs, 2008).

14. C. Hoskyns, *The Congo since Independence, January 1960–December 1961* (Oxford: Oxford University Press, 1965), pp. 158–159.

15. Resolution adopted at 886th Session of UN Security Council, August 9, 1960, reprinted in Gérard-Libois, *Katanga Secession*, Appendix 2, p. 330.

16. For details of Hammarskjöld's report to the United Nations, see UK National Archives (hereafter TNA) FO/371/146775, Congo, 1960, UK UN Mission to FO, August 6, 1960.

17. The best accounts of these complex events are provided in CRISP, *Congo 1960*; CRISP, *Congo 1961* (Brussels: CRISP, 1962); and Young, *Politics in the Congo*.

18. Hoskyns, *Congo since Independence*, p. 163.

19. A total of 177 Belgian officers served in Katanga during the secession: although small in number, they had considerable influence over military affairs until their expulsion in August–September 1961.

20. F. Vandewalle, "A propos de la gendarmerie katangaise," *Bulletin Trimestriel du CRAOCA* 4 (1988): 60; R. Pire, "'La sécession katangaise: Impressions à chaud," *Bulletin Trimestriel du CRAOCA* 4 (1988): 45–59.

21. E. Kennes, *Fin du cycle post-colonial au Katanga, RD Congo, Rébellions, sécession et leurs mémoires dans la dynamique des articulations entre l'État central et l'autonomie régionale 1960–2007* (Saarbrucken: Editions Universitaires Européennes, 2014), pp. 481–484.

22. BTM/Mistebel was established in mid-July and led by Harold d'Aspremont Lynden and Robert Rothschild.
23. Gérard-Libois, *Katanga Secession*, p. 114.
24. Kennes, *Fin du cycle post-colonial au Katanga*, pp. 481–482.
25. Gérard-Libois, *Katanga Secession*, p. 114; *Moniteur Katangais*, no. 2, August 15, 1960, pp. 21–23, cited in Kennes, *Fin du cycle post-colonial au Katanga*, p. 416.
26. Vandewalle, "A propos de la gendarmerie katangaise."
27. Pire, "La sécession katangaise."
28. Vandewalle, "A propos de la gendarmerie katangaise," p. 66.
29. Quoted in F. Vandewalle, "Rapport négociations ONUC-Katanga," in *Mille et quatre jours: Contes du Zaïre et du Shaba* (Brussels: Self-published by author, 1976), pp. 153–154.
30. Vandewalle, "A propos de la gendarmerie katangaise," p. 66.
31. E. Kennes, *Essai biographique sur Laurent Désiré Kabila* (Paris: L'Harmattan, 2003), pp. 41–128.
32. Pire, " La sécession katangaise," p. 51; interview, René Pire, Namur, December 12, 2007.
33. Vandewalle, "A propos de la gendarmerie katangaise," p. 73.
34. Young, *Politics in the Congo*, p. 335.
35. Vandewalle, "A propos de la gendarmerie katangaise," pp. 65–92.
36. Major Perrad, commandant of the Force Terrestre, "Directive concernant l'ouverture éventuelle de négociations avec des communautés en insoumission," December 26, 1960, reprinted in Vandewalle, "A propos de la gendarmerie katangaise," p. 84.
37. C. Roosens, "La Belgique et la sécession du Katanga," in O. Lanotte, C. Roosens, and C. Clement (eds.), *La Belgique et l'Afrique Centrale: De 1960 à nos jours* (Brussels: GRIP-Editions Complexe, 2000), pp. 123–124.
38. I. Colvin, *The Rise and Fall of Moïse Tshombe* (London: Leslie Frewin, 1968) , pp. 18–19.
39. Brion and Moreau, *De la mine à Mars*, pp. 310–311.
40. Belgian Foreign Affairs Archives (hereafter BFA), File NA 15946, Congo-ONU, January–February 1960, telegram no. 192, Belg Brazza to Brussels, February 6, 1961.
41. USSD, RG 59, E3111 (Bureau of African Affairs), Box 8, File 17.2, Internal Research Reports, January–June 1963, Hare to Elting, February 2, 1961, "Belgian Assistance to the Congo." See also the records of the Katanga embassy to Belgium, held at the Contemporary History Library, Royal Museum of Central Africa, Tervuren, Belgium.
42. Young, *Politics in the Congo*, p. 340.
43. Namikas, *Battleground Africa*, p. 143.
44. Katanga's banknotes were introduced on January 9, 1961. The lyrics of the national anthem, "La Katangaise," referring to the Katangese flag shown on the cover of this book, read in part: "Allons allons marchons Katangais valeureux / notre bannière au vent / symbole pour tous ceux / que ses riches croisettes / et sa verte jeunesse / sa rouge force aussi soulèvent d'allégresse." The authors are grateful to Kimberley Chadwick for bringing this to their attention.
45. T. Vleurinck, *46 Angry Men: The 46 Civilian Doctors of Elisabethville Denounce U.N. Violations in Katanga of Its Own Charter, the Universal Declaration of Human Rights, [and] the Geneva Conventions* (Brussels: E. Guyot, 1962). See J. Brownell, "Diplomatic Lepers: The Katangan and Rhodesian Foreign Missions in the United States and the Politics of Nonrecognition," *International Journal of African Historical Studies* 47, no. 2 (2014): 209–237.
46. See, for example, the correspondence related to the request in July–August 1962 by Kibwe for the payment of "exceptional surcharges" imposed on UMHK's SOGECHIM subsidiary, in UMHK Papers, File 1942, BNA, Surtaxe exceptionnelle sur les dividendes, 1960–1962.

See also "Tensions croissantes avec les autorités Katangaises (1961)," in Brion and Moreau, *De la mine à Mars*, pp. 316–318.

47. See *L'Essor du Katanga* (Elisabethville), March 23, 1961, in which Tshombe spelled out these economic policies.

48. For example, the signing of accords with the state of South Kasai: *L'Essor du Katanga* (Elisabethville), February 3, 1961.

49. "Présentation du nouveau recteur de l'université de l'état," *L'Essor du Katanga*, January 16, 1961.

50. "La gendarmerie katangaise en action," *L'Essor du Katanga*, January 25, 1961. Photos of gendarmes on the battlefield appear in *L'Essor du Katanga*, January 27 and February 17, 1961. For a detailed analysis of the iconography and imagery of the secession, see C. L. Porter, "Nationalism, Authority and Political Identity in the Secession of Katanga, 1908–1963" (DPhil thesis, University of Cambridge, 2014).

51. "Messe de requiem à Elisabethville à la mémoire des héros katangais," *L'Essor du Katanga*, January 19, 1961.

52. *L'Essor du Katanga*, August 14, 1961.

53. Ibid., August 26, 1961.

54. "4000 ans d'histoire," special issue, *Katanga* (monthly review of the Friends of Katanga, Brussels) (July 1961): 16.

55. Interview with Evariste Kimba, *L'Essor du Katanga*, April 22, 1961. The location of the Kasongo Nyembo's throne at Kinkunki village provided the basis for this claim to the loyalty of the Luba kingdom: by this definition, those who allied with the central Congolese state against their king could be considered rebels.

56. Radio Katanga program schedule, listed daily in *L'Essor du Katanga*, for example, April 27, 1961. Radio Katanga is the subject of a book-length account by its founder: M. Nicolai, *Ici Radio Katanga* (Brussels: J. M. Collet, 1987).

57. "Le Président Tshombé's adresse aux femmes Baluba du Katanga," *L'Essor du Katanga*, January 9, 1961.

58. Kent, *America, the UN and Decolonisation*, pp. 58–59.

59. De Witte, *Assassination of Lumumba*, p. xiii.

60. See, for example, USSD, RG 59, E3111 (Bureau of African Affairs), Box 6, File 1.D/1.1, The President (Tshombe), 1961 and 1963, J. Wayne Fredericks to Mr McGhee, "Tshombe's Political Orientation," July 12, 1962.

61. USSD, RG 59, E3111 (Bureau of African Affairs), Box 8, File 14.3, The Katanga Question, J. Wayne Fredericks to Robert C. Good, "Neutralizing Extremist Congo Political Elements as a Prelude to Katanga Reintegration and Political Consensus," May 7, 1962.

62. Gérard-Libois, *Katanga Secession*, p. 188.

63. Namikas, *Battleground Africa*, p. 150.

64. C. Cruise O'Brien, *To Katanga and Back* (New York: Simon and Schuster, 1962), pp. 249–254.

65. Namikas, *Battleground Africa*, p. 151; Cruise O'Brien, *To Katanga and Back*, p. 257.

66. Cruise O'Brien, *To Katanga and Back*, pp. 241–242.

67. Interview, Grégoire Kabobo, Kinshasa, June 3, 2011.

68. Vleurinck, *46 Angry Men*.

69. Notwithstanding numerous official enquiries which have concluded that the plane crash was not caused by foul play, considerable suspicion still surrounds Hammarskjöld's death: see most recently S. Williams, *Who Killed Hammarskjöld? The UN, the Cold War and White Supremacy in Africa* (London: Hurst, 2011).

70. Kent, *America, the UN and Decolonisation*, p. 80.

71. In *To Katanga and Back*, Muke is continually presented by Cruise O'Brien as the puppet of mercenary commanders: for example, pp. 243, 250, 290. Cruise O'Brien is unwilling to admit that any African on the Katangese side played an active role in the military defense of Katanga apart from Munongo.

72. USSD, RG 59, E3111 (Bureau of African Affairs), Box 7, unnumbered file, 1960 UN Military Troops and Support, Robert Eisenberg to Governor Williams, memorandum, "Military Situation in Katanga," September 15, 1961.

73. Cruise O'Brien, *To Katanga and Back*, p. 240, describes the Lunda as "ignorant and backward" and the Luba as a "more advanced section" of Congo's population.

74. It should be noted that Katanga was hardly unique in its use of European officers in its early stages of "independence." Many African states did so, for example Ghana: indeed, the commander of the Ghanaian contingent of the UN forces in Congo was British. The ANC itself was already utilizing Belgian military advisers by the end of 1960 and continued to do so for the duration of the secession period (and indeed for decades afterward).

75. See, for example, B. Denard, *Corsaire de la République* (Paris: R. Laffont, 1998); M. Hoare, *Congo Mercenary* (Boulder, CO: Sycamore Island Books, 2008); J. Schramme, *Le Bataillon Léopard: Souvenirs d'un africain blanc* (Paris: R. Laffont, 1969).

76. USSD, RG 59, E3111 (Bureau of African Affairs), Box 4, File 1.3, Adoula, 1962–1963, Adoula communication to Tshombe, March 3, 1962.

77. USSD, RG 59, E3111 (Bureau of African Affairs), Box 6, File 1.C./1.1, Correspondence with Consulate, American Consul to Elisabethville Lewis Hoffacker to Robert Eisenberg, Deputy Director Bureau of Central African Affairs, April 18, 1962.

78. Ibid.

79. USSD, RG 59, E3111 (Bureau of African Affairs), Box 6, File 1.C./1.1, Correspondence with Consulate, Charles S. Whitehouse to Lewis Hoffacker, May 8, 1962.

80. USSD RG 59, E3111 (Bureau of African Affairs), Box 6, unnumbered file, Katanga Reconciliation, 1/8–27/8/62, CIA report, Subject: "SNIE 65-62: The Katanga Integration Problem," May 15, 1962.

81. USSD, RG 59, E3111 (Bureau of African Affairs), Box 7, File 5.2, Conferences, William Brubeck to McGeorge Bundy, "Our Congo Policy after the London Talks," May 21, 1962.

82. Regarding the support of Roy Welensky and the Central Africa Federation, see M. Hughes, "Fighting for White Rule in Africa: The Central African Federation, Katanga, and the Congo Crisis, 1958–1965," *International History Review* 25, no. 3 (2003): 596–615.

83. Namikas, *Battleground Africa*, pp. 162–173.

84. USSD, RG 59, E3111 (Bureau of African Affairs), Box 8, File 14.3, The Katanga Question, J. Wayne Fredericks to Robert C. Good, "Neutralizing Extremist Congo Political Elements as a Prelude to Katanga Reintegration and Political Consensus," May 7, 1962. UN officials such as Cruise O'Brien certainly saw Munongo, rather than Tshombe, as central to the expression of force by the Katangese state and believed that his arrest would end or significantly reduce tribal violence; *To Katanga and Back*, pp. 243, 249.

85. USSD, RG 59, E3111 (Bureau of African Affairs), Box 4, File 1.3, Adoula, 1962–1963, Ambassador Gullion to George McGhee, "Adoula Talking Paper," November 21, 1962.

86. USSD, RG 59, E3111 (Bureau of African Affairs), Box 6, File 1.D/1, Katanga, 1961 [1963], "Main Trends in Katanga, July 1962–July 1963," June 17, 1963.

87. Gérard-Libois, *Katanga Secession*, p. 273.

88. Ibid., p. 275; Brion and Moreau, *De la mine à Mars*, pp. 325–326; J.-J. Saquet, *De l'Union minière du Haut-Katanga á la Gécamines* (Paris: L'Harmattan, 2001), pp. 45–94.

89. Gérard-Libois, *Katanga Secession*, p. 275.

3. Into Exile and Back, 1963–1967

1. Z. Marriage, "Flip-Flop Rebel, Dollar Soldier: Demobilisation in the Democratic Republic of Congo," *Conflict, Security and Development* 7, no. 2 (2007): 281–309.
2. F. Vandewalle, *L'Ommegang: Odyssée et reconquête de Stanleyville 1964* (Brussels: Le Livre Africain, 1970); P. Gleijeses, "Flee! The White Giants Are Coming! The United States, the Mercenaries and the Congo, 1964–65," *Diplomatic History* 18, no. 2 (1994): 207–237.
3. Namikas, *Battleground Africa*.
4. USSD, RG 84, E3363 (Foreign Service Posts), Box 1, File, Political Affairs and Rel., Pol 22, 1963, Elisabethville to Secstate, telegram, January 18, 1963.
5. "Assurances to Mr Tshombe," *The Times* (London), January 17, 1963.
6. "Union Miniere Tax Move," *The Times*, January 14, 1963.
7. Interview, Victor Nendaka, Brussels, May 15, 2001.
8. USSD, RG 84, E3363 (Foreign Service Posts), Box 1, File, Political Affairs and Rel., Pol 18, 1963, Elisabethville to Washington, telegram, April 27, 1963.
9. Vandewalle, *L'Ommegang*, pp. 23–26.
10. USSD, RG 84, E3363 (Foreign Service Posts), Box 1, File, Political Affairs and Rel., Pol 2 Gen. Reports and Stat, 1963, US Consul Dean summary report, February 8, 1963 (hereafter Dean summary report).
11. A. Mpase, *Au service d'un Congo*, p. 185.
12. CRISP, *Congo 1963* (Brussels: CRISP, 1964), pp. 386–395; "Drafting a Congo Constitution," *The Times*, March 14, 1964.
13. Dean summary report.
14. USSD, RG 84, E3363 (Foreign Service Posts), Box 2, File, Political Affairs and Rel., Pol 18, Provincial, Municipal and State Government, January–June 1963, Elisabethville to Gov. Williams, February 17, 1963.
15. USSD, RG 84, E3363 (Foreign Service Posts), Box 2, File, Political Affairs & Rel., Pol 18, Provincial, Municipal and State Government, January–June 1963, Elisabethville to Secstate, January 29, 1963.
16. Young, *Politics in the Congo*, p. 458; USSD, RG 59, E3111 (Bureau of African Affairs), Box 4, File 1.3, Adoula, 1962–1963, "Katanga Reintegration," April 22, 1963.
17. An important source for the integration process is the memoir of Albert Mpase, Ileo's head of cabinet during this period: Mpase, *Au service*, pp. 141–181.
18. Interview, Charles Babah, Brussels, April 21, 1999. Babah, stationed in Stanleyville, decided to leave Congo entirely and eventually joined the CNL in Brazzaville.
19. Dean summary report.
20. "Disintegration Threat Facing Congo," *The Times*, March 4, 1963.
21. USSD, RG 84, E3363 (Foreign Service Posts), Box 2, File, Political Affairs and Rel., Pol 18, Provincial, Municipal and State Government, January–June 1963, Jonathan Dean to Dept. of State, "Indication of Possible Troubles amongst Katangan African Population," February 12, 1963.
22. USSD, RG 84, E3363 (Foreign Service Posts), Box 2, File, Political Affairs and Rel., Pol 18, Provincial, Municipal and State Government, January–June 1963, Elisabethville to Secstate, February 8, 1963.
23. "City of Empty Shops and Flaking Villas," *The Times*, March 2, 1964.
24. Dean summary report.
25. Ibid.

26. USSD, RG 84, E3363 (Foreign Service Posts), Box 2, File, Political Affairs and Rel., Pol 27-11 Guerrilla Warfare, 1963, Secstate McNamara to Leopoldville, August 9, 1963.
27. TNA, FO/371/167300, Activities of Mercenaries and Ex-Gendarmes, 1963, Elisabethville to Foreign Office, September 9, 1963.
28. TNA, FO/371/167300, Activities of Mercenaries and Ex-Gendarmes, 1963, Elisabethville to FO, September 21, 1963.
29. USSD, RG 84, E3363 (Foreign Service Posts), Box 1, File, Political Affairs and Rel., Pol 7, Visits and Meetings, 1963, Elisabethville to Secstate, November 7, 1963.
30. TNA, FO/371/167300, Activities of Mercenaries and Ex-Gendarmes, 1963, William Wilson, British consulate Elisabethville to E. M. Rose, British embassy Leopoldville, August 13, 1963. See also in same file Elisabethville to Foreign Office, September 9, 1963.
31. TNA, FO/371/167300, Activities of Mercenaries and Ex-Gendarmes, 1963, telegram, Lusaka to Salisbury, September 5, 1963.
32. TNA, FO/371/167301, Activities of Mercenaries and Ex-Gendarmes, 1963, Wilson to F. W. Morton, embassy in Leopoldville, October 4, 1963.
33. For example, TNA, FO 371/167303, Congo: Activities of Mercenaries and Ex-Gendarmes, 1963, Elisabethville consulate to FO, "Katanga Gendarmes," November 29, 1963.
34. See, for instance, TNA, FO/371/167299, Activities of Mercenaries and Ex-Gendarmes, 1963, telegram, Lusaka to FO, August 9, 1963.
35. Ibid.
36. TNA, FO 371/167303, Congo: Activities of Mercenaries and Ex-Gendarmes, 1963, Evelyn Hone to S. P. Whitley, Central African Office, "Katanga," November 21, 1963.
37. TNA, FO/371/167301, Activities of Mercenaries and Ex-Gendarmes, 1963, Wilson to Morton, Leopoldville embassy, October 10, 1963.
38. TNA, FO/371/167302, Activities of Mercenaries and Ex-Gendarmes, 1963, telegram, Lusaka to Leopoldville, November 22, 1963.
39. Arquivo Nacional da Torre do Tombo (hereafter ANTT), PIDE/DGS, Delegação de Angola, NP2184, Pr. Unf. 17.03.D/2m, "Polícia do Katanga"; R. Bonita Velez, *Salazar Tchombé: O envolvimento de Portugal na Questão do Catanga (1961–1967)* (Linda-a-velha: DG Edições, 2012).
40. Interview, Pascal Kapend, Lubumbashi, August 1, 2005.
41. A Portuguese intelligence report dated January 31, 1963, mentions 253 Katangese troops along with smaller groups of other nationalities: ANTT, PIDE/DGS, Del. A, L No. 9, UI 8978, "Refugiados Catangueses no Luso," Posto do Teixeira de Sousa, "Mapa de Refugiados."
42. USSD, RG 59, E5235, Box 43, File, Political Affairs and Rel., Angola, Pol 26, Rebellion, Coups, Insurgency, 1964, USARMA Lisbon to ASCI DA, January 2, 1964.
43. USSD, RG 84, E3363 (Foreign Service Posts), Box 2, File, Political Affairs and Rel., Pol 15-4, Administration of Govt., Elisabethville to Secstate, October 16, 1963.
44. See, for example, ANTT, PIDE Del A, L, No. 14, UI 8979, "Instruções sobre refugiados catangueses, April 15 1963–July 25 1964."
45. Ibid. See also interviews with Pascal Kapend (Lubumbashi, August 14, 2005) and Stany Kalala (Kinshasa, April 28, 2012). See also D. Spikes, *Angola and the Politics of Intervention* (Jefferson, NC: McFarland, 1993), pp. 45–46.
46. "Moïse Tshombe en Espagne," in *Le Dossier du Mois*, nos. 4/5 (April–May 1964): 23–26.
47. Anonymous source.
48. USSD, RG 59, E5235, Box 43, File, Political Affairs and Rel., Angola, Pol 37, Mercenaries, Pierre Laureys, 1964, memorandum of meeting between Belgian and US officials on "Katangan gendarme," March 11, 1964.

49. The CNL was formed in September 1963 by the Lumumbist radical forces in control of eastern Congo, led by Christophe Gbenye and Gaston Soumialot.

50. Centre de Recherche et d'Information Socio-Politiques, *Congo 1965* (Brussels: CRISP, 1966), pp. 133–138. The full text of this agreement is provided in this volume, pp. 136–137. It should not be regarded as a credible agreement for practical action, and the CNL signatories to the accords were not mandated to reach any such agreement. It had the desired effect, however, of panicking the Leopoldville government regarding the alarming prospect of such an agreement.

51. *Bulletin du CEDOPO*, February 15, 1961.

52. P. Cedomi (a.k.a. J.-P. Sonck), "L'étrange destin de la Gendarmerie katangaise," part 1, *Fire!* (Brussels) 16 (September–October 1994): 6; Vandewalle, *L'Ommegang*, pp. 178–179.

53. J.-P. Sonck, "Commandos Katangais, 1964–65," http://albertville.stools.net/text_commandos_kantangais.htm (accessed June 18, 2012).

54. Ibid.

55. Interviews, Jérôme Nawej and Joseph Kabwit, Kinshasa, May 19, 2012.

56. Arquivo Historico Militar (hereafter AHM), MU_GM_GNP_S027, Gendarmes e refugiados, General Bobozo to ANC Commander, February 2, 1964.

57. USSD, RG 59, E5235, Box 43, File, Political Affairs and Rel., Angola, Pol 37, Mercenaries, Pierre Laureys, 1964, G. McMurtrie Godley to US Consul General to Angola Henry Clinton Reed, February 3, 1964. Similar conclusions were reached by the British Foreign Office: see TNA, FO/371/167302, Activities of Mercenaries and Ex-Gendarmes, 1963, E. M. Rose, British embassy Leopoldville to G. E. Millard, FO, November 29, 1963.

58. USSD, RG 59, E3111 (Bureau of African Affairs), Box 4, File 1.11, Central Africa status report, G. Mennen Williams to the Secretary, "Status Report: Actions Being Taken to Deal with the Situation in the Congo," October 30, 1963. See also Vandewalle, *L'Ommegang*.

59. Among the considerable literature on the Kwilu rebellion, see B. Verhaegen, *Rebellions au Congo*, vol. 1 (Brussels: CRISP, 1966). More recently, see B. Verhaegen, J. Omasombo, E. Simons, and F. Verhaegen, *Mulele et la révolution populaire au Kwilu (République Démocratique du Congo)* (Paris: L'Harmattan, 2006); and Kennes, *Essai biographique sur Laurent Désiré Kabila*. For a recent useful summary in English, see Namikas, *Battleground Africa*, pp. 194–204.

60. "Mr Tshombe Takes Over in Congo," *The Times*, July 11, 1964; "Congo Frozen Out of African Unity Conference," *The Times*, July 17, 1964.

61. Gleijeses, "Flee!," p. 219; Namikas, *Battleground Africa*, pp. 199–200.

62. Vandewalle, *L'Ommegang*, pp. 192–193.

63. Sonck, "Commandos katangais, 1964–65."

64. Vandewalle, *L'Ommegang*, p. 196.

65. Quoted in Gleijeses, "Flee!"

66. Ibid.

67. "No Congo Plea for Foreign Troops," *The Times*, August 10, 1964.

68. F. Villafaña, *Cold War in the Congo: The Confrontation of Cuban Military Forces, 1960–1967* (New Brunswick, NJ: Transaction, 2009). There is an extensive literature on the battle for Stanleyville: see, among other sources, Vandewalle, *L'Ommegang*; Centre de Recherche et d'Information Socio-Politiques, *Congo 1964* (Brussels: CRISP, 1965), pp. 349–411; P. Nothomb, *Dans Stanleyville* (Paris: Duculot, 1993).

69. See, for example, "1,400 Rescued Hostages Flown from Stanleyville," *The Times*, November 26, 1964.

70. Eyewitness report of Antoine Hirsh, reported in CRISP, *Congo 1964*, p. 353. Once again, the behavior of the ANC was no better than that of the ex-gendarmes.

71. AHM, Governo-General de Angola, S.C.C.I.A., MU_GM_GNP_S027, Gendarmes e refugiados, "Relatório sobre a 'operação regresso,' " September 18, 1964.
72. Ibid. This report lists all the names of the returned soldiers.
73. Sonck, "Commandos katangais, 1964-65," p. 9.
74. "Belgian Protest to Mr. Tshombe," *The Times*, December 8, 1964.
75. "Congo Elections Start Today," *The Times*, March 18, 1965; CRISP, *Congo 1965*, pp. 203-233.
76. CRISP, *Congo 1965*, pp. 340-387, 409-418; "Mr. Tshombe Is Forced to Resign in Congo," *The Times*, October 14, 1965.
77. "Four Former Congo Ministers Sentenced to Death," *The Times*, July 1, 1966.
78. "Congo Government Wins Vote," *The Times*, November 29, 1965.
79. "Warrant Is Expected for Mr. Tshombe's Arrest," *The Times*, September 20, 1966.
80. Centre de Recherche et d'Information Socio-Politiques, *Congo 1967* (Brussels: CRISP, 1968), p. 227 (authors' translation).
81. "Congo Bans Union Minière Ore Exports," *The Times*, December 24, 1966.
82. Saquet, *De l'Union Minière du Haut-Katanga*, pp. 155-208; "Union Minière Wins Case—in All but Name," *The Times*, February 18, 1967.
83. Centre de Recherche et d'Information Socio-Politiques, *Congo 1966* (Brussels: CRISP, 1967), pp. 365-367.
84. "Belgians Training Congo Troops," *The Times*, December 8, 1964; "Belgium Trains Congo's Future Officers," *The Times*, May 13, 1966.
85. For the ANC's structure and operations, see CRISP, *Congo 1966*, pp. 35-37. See also "Army Keeps Firm Grip on Congo Cities," *The Times*, July 13, 1966. For details of Congolese city name changes, see CRISP, *Congo 1966*, p. 112. Others were changed in the early 1970s.
86. Vandewalle, *L'Ommegang*.
87. "Congo City Seized When Troops Mutiny," *The Times*, July 25, 1966.
88. Tshipola's memorandum is reproduced in CRISP, *Congo 1966*, pp. 348-349.
89. "Congo Breaks with Portugal," *The Times*, October 6, 1966.
90. ANTT, PIDE/DGS NT 7495, Proc. 7477 CI (2), Pasta 6, "Operação Tshombe"; R. Giordano, *Belges et Italiens du Congo-Kinshasa* (Paris: L'Harmattan, 2008), pp. 142-145.
91. CRISP, *Congo 1966*, pp. 339-370. See also CRISP, *Congo 1967*, pp. 362-363.
92. Pascal Kapend interview, August 1, 2005.
93. CRISP, *Congo 1967*, p. 365.
94. "Tshombe Given Sentence of Death," *The Times*, March 14, 1967.
95. CRISP, *Congo 1967*, p. 318.
96. Ibid. Authors' translation.
97. Interview, Ambassador Moïse Nawej, Brussels, December 14, 2007; interview, Joseph Kabwit, Kinshasa, March 31, 2012.
98. Denard, *Corsaire de la République*, p. 250; a description of the operation is given in CRISP, *Congo 1967*, p. 368.
99. "Fighting for Two Congo Cities," *The Times*, July 6, 1967.
100. "Congo Appeals to Security Council," *The Times*, July 7, 1967.
101. "Accusations at UN by Congo," *The Times*, July 8, 1967.
102. "Lumumba Ritual Precedes Talks," *The Times*, September 13, 1967.
103. "Mercenaries Repulsed by Artillery at Bukavu," *The Times*, August 8, 1967. A detailed account of the mutiny is provided in CRISP, *Congo 1967*, pp. 365-375.
104. "Congo Mercenaries Agree to Leave," *The Times*, October 7, 1967.
105. "Zambia Calls Off Congo Airlift," *The Times*, November 8, 1967.

106. Denard (*Corsaire de la République*, pp. 222–224) discusses his meeting with Jacques Foccart in Paris in May 1967, when the latter expressed his support for an operation to overthrow Mobutu and replace him with Tshombe. He then discusses the change of French attitude in November 1967 (p. 247).
107. "New Katanga Attack," *The Times*, November 9, 1967.
108. Pascal Kapend interview, August 1, 2005.

4. With the Portuguese, 1967–1974

1. Pascal Kapend (interview, Lubumbashi, March 20, 2008) reports that he arrived in June 1967 but was followed by a series of successive waves of arrivals. Throughout the period covered by this chapter, additional recruits arrived in Angola.
2. AHM, Fundo 43, "Situação," April 1975, p. 36.
3. It is impossible to do justice here to the complex and lengthy war of Angolan independence. Although significant additional information has subsequently emerged, the best single study remains J. A. Marcum, *The Angolan Revolution*, vol. 2, *Exile Politics and Guerrilla Warfare (1962–1976)* (Cambridge, MA: MIT Press, 1978). For UNITA's nonagression pact with the Portuguese, see B. Almeida, *Angola: O conflito na frente leste* (Lisbon: Ancora, 2011), pp. 37–40; and Estado-Maior do Exército, *Resenha histórico-militar das campanhas de África 1961–1974*, vol. 6, *Aspectos da actividada operacional*, book 2 (Lisbon: Comissão para o Estudo das Campanhas de África, 2006), pp. 379–421.
4. Britain in the same period had 593,000 soldiers and a defense budget of US$4.5 billion: J. P. Cann, *Counterinsurgency in Africa: The Portuguese Way of War, 1961–1974* (Westport, CT: Greenwood, 1997), p. 4.
5. Ibid., p. 91.
6. P. Pezarat Correia, "A participão local no desenvolvimento das campanhas: O recrutamento africano," *Instituto de Altos Estudos Militares: Estudos sobre as Campanhas de Africa (1961–74)* (Sintra: Atena, 2000), p. 154.
7. Cann, *Counterinsurgency in Africa*, pp. 96–103; AHM, Relatório 22.06.1988, ref. 1438/88/C, 2nd Div., 2nd Secc, Caixa 169, no. 17, Comp. Chefe Angola; AHM, CCFAA, 2nd Div., 2nd secc, Caixa 139, no. 05, Quartel General, "Forças Auxiliares: Situação actual, sua evolução," 1974[?].
8. A. Pires Nunes, *Angola, 1966–74: Vitória militar no leste* (Lisbon: Prefácio, 2002), pp. 63–64.
9. The most useful study of the Flechas is J. P. Cann, *The Flechas: Insurgent Hunting in Eastern Angola 1965–1974* (Solihull: Helion, 2013).
10. T. Drehsen, "The Militarization of the San in Southern Angola" (paper presented to the African Studies Association of the UK, Oxford, September 2010).
11. For more detail on the Zambian refugees in Angola, see Larmer, *Rethinking African Politics*, pp. 137–144.
12. Pires Nunes, *Angola 1966–74*, p. 67.
13. Marcum, *Angolan Revolution*, p. 201.
14. Centro de Instrução de Operações Especiais, *Apontamentos sobre o Emprego Táctico das Pequenas Unidades na Contra-Guerrilha: O exército na guerra subversiva* (n.p., 1961).
15. Cann, *Counterinsurgency in Africa*, pp. 37–59.
16. W. Van der Waals, *Portugal's War in Angola, 1961–1974* (Rivonia: Ashanti, 1993), p. 184.
17. Interview, Pascal Kapend, August 1, 2005; CRISP, *Congo 1967*, pp. 393–403; the anonymous testimony of a participant in Denard's's operation in *Ops Lucifer: Katanga 1967* (Brus-

sels: Kalmes, n.d.); D. Monguya Mbenge, *De Léopold II à Mobutu: Une conspiration internationale* (Mons: Privately published, 1993), pp. 51–52.

18. This is attested to by M. Mwando Nsimba (interview, Brussels, December 15, 1997); Justin Mushitu (interview, Stockholm, August 12, 2001); Justin Mushitu, "Le monde des méchants" (manuscript, 2003), p. 6, Papers of Justin Mushitu; and Nathanaël Mbumba (interview, Kinshasa, March 17, 2006). Direct evidence for the killing of ex-gendarmes is not available, but it seems highly likely. See, for example, T. Odom, *Shaba II: The French and Belgian Intervention in Zaire in 1978* (Fort Leavenworth, KS: Combat Studies Institute, US Army Command and General Staff College, 1993), p. 3; Young and Turner, *Rise and Decline*, p. 255.

19. ANTT, PT-TT-PIDE-D-C-1-7477-1, PIDE, Relatório imediato, no. 2466/67-GAB, November 21, 1967. This was confirmed by Nathanaël Mbumba, interview, Kinshasa, March 17, 2006.

20. AHM, CCFA, 2nd Div., 2nd L, Caixa 139, no. 6, 167a, "Factos de maior realce no historial dos fiéis," 1973.

21. ANTT, PIDE/DGS Delegação de Angola, NP2184, Pr. Unf. 17.03.D/2m, "Polícia do Katanga."

22. Pascal Kapend, interview, August 1, 2005.

23. AHM, CCFA, 2nd Div., 2nd L, Caixa 139, no. 6, 167a, "Relatório imediato realce no historial dos fiéis," 1973.

24. AHM, CCFA directive on the camps, April 4, 1968.

25. Raphaël Lumuna, interview, Lubumbashi, September 26, 2005.

26. Marcum, *Angolan Revolution*, pp. 67–69.

27. Ibid., pp. 149–156.

28. Ibid., pp. 197–198.

29. Gleijeses, *Conflicting Missions*, p. 238.

30. AHM, CCFAA, Div. 2, Secc 2, Caixa 139, no. 7, Cabinete de Forças Auxiliares, "Memorando: Acção Fidelidade," Luanda, August 3, 1974.

31. ANTT, PT-TT-PIDE-D-C-1-7477-1, PIDE, Directiva no. 1/68—Organisação e funcionamento dos campos de refugiados catangueses, Anexo (instruções complementares) a directiva no. 1/68, QG/RMA Luanda—GDP-36/01.

32. ANTT, PT-TT-PIDE-D-C-1-7477-1, PIDE, Relatório 11/05/1968, no. 3/68—GAB (2), Operação Phoenix, Campo de Gafaria. *Réveil Congolais* was widely distributed in a 1971 operation funded by PIDE. See also interview, Raphaël Lumuna, Lubumbashi, September 26, 2005.

33. This should not be confused with Bob Denard's 1967 operation of the same name (see chapter 3).

34. ANTT, PT-TT-PIDE-D-C-1-7477-1, PIDE, Informação no. 318-SC/CI (2), Operação Phoenix, March 28, 1968.

35. ANTT, PT-TT-PIDE-D-C-1-7477-1, letter from Thomas Tshombe, December 12, 1968.

36. ANTT, PT-TT-PIDE-D-C-1-7477-1, copy of "Réveil Congolais" and related correspondence, Angola Director to Director General, August 12, 1971.

37. Interview, Jérôme Nawej, Lubumbashi, April 8, 2008; interviews, Joseph Kabwit, Kinshasa, April 14 and July 14, 2008.

38. Young and Turner, *Rise and Decline*, pp. 53–54.

39. A mission to liberate Munongo from Bula Bemba was planned by the mercenaries with the aid of PIDE, but this never went ahead: D. Cabrita Mateus, *A PIDE/DGS na guerra colonial 1961–1974* (Lisbon: Terramar, 2004), pp. 180–181; CRISP, *Congo 1967*, 401–403.

40. Young and Turner, *Rise and Decline*, pp. 117–118.

41. Ibid., 57.

42. A detailed account of the negotiations can be found in Saquet, *De l'Union Minière du Haut-Katanga*, pp. 133–153.

43. Young and Turner, *Rise and Decline*, p. 70.

44. Ibid., pp. 54–63.

45. Regarding attempts to negotiate with the FLNC, see ANTT, PT-TT-PIDE-D-C-1-7477-1: PIDE, Informação no. 16/78-D, Inf/2° Sec (2), Acção Fidelidade, February 11, 1970; ANTT, DGS, MSG 83/71-D inf.—2°-CI, Diligencias para a recuperação de catangueses, March 3, 1971, report, February 11, 1970; PIDE 178-180, report, March 3, 1971. Concerning the reinforcement of Congolese forces on the border, see ANTT, PT-TT-PIDE-D-C-1-7477-1, SCCIA, "Aumento das possibilidades do FNLA (UPA-PDA)/GRAE, Attitude da RDC e dos EUA," no. 371, Proc. 22-10-95, October 12, 1970. Regarding the possibility of an amnesty, see ANTT, PT-TT-PIDE-D-C-1-7477-1, DGS, MSG 182/70—D. Inf/2 (2), Acção Fidelidade, December 16, 1970. According to this latter report, a majority of "gendarmes" wished to accept the offer to return to Congo. PIDE, however, sought to convince them that this was a trap set by Mobutu.

46. ANTT, PIDE UI 7477, GAB-2, "Informação 11/69," June 12, 1969.

47. Ibid.

48. Mbumba claimed to have single-handedly created the FLNC, but most witnesses and copious material in the PIDE archives attribute the original name, Army of the Front for the National Liberation of the Congo (AFLNC), to the Mwaant Yav David Tshombe, shortly before his brother Moïse Tshombe's death in 1969.

49. ANTT, PT-TT-PIDE-D-C-1-7477-1, PIDE, Informação, 21/71-DINF/2° (2), "Vinda de Thomas Tshombe ao TN em fins de maio passado," Luanda, July 21, 1971. See also interview, Justin Mushitu, Stockholm, May 17, 1998.

50. A Portuguese army witness describes a visit to the FLNC headquarters in Chicapa (probably in 1976), where a drunken Mbumba claimed he wanted to re-create the old Lunda Empire under his direction: M. J. Da Silva, *Sortilégio da cobra* (Lisbon: Esquilo, 2005), pp. 198–202. Portuguese military documents from 1974 express fear of a project to re-create a political entity incorporating Lunda territories in both Angola and Zaire: CCFAA, Div. 2, Secc 2, Caixa 139, no. 7, Cabinete de Forças Auxiliares, "Memorando: Acção Fidelidade," Luanda, August 3, 1974, p. 2. Tensions between Mwaant Yav Thomas Tshombe and Mbumba appear to have arisen from the fact that the former began a relationship with Mbumba's wife and had a child with her: interview, Pascal Kapend, March 20, 2008. An alternative version of this story suggests that the woman became Mbumba's wife after, not before, she had Thomas Tshombe's child: Justin Mushitu, interview, Stockholm, February 3, 2002.

51. Interview, Nathanaël Mbumba, Kinshasa, March 17, 2006.

52. "Décision de commissionnement no. 24, 19 March 1964," *Bulletin Provincial du Lualaba*, September 15, 1964, p. 26.

53. Interview, Gassomel president of this period Muteb a Fwamb, Lubumbashi, November 4, 2008.

54. Mbumba interview, March 17, 2006. Joseph Kabwit, however, claims that Mbumba got into debt and fled to escape his creditors: interviews, Kinshasa, July 14, 2008, and March 31, 2012. The inconsistency of Mbumba's activities is matched by the fluctuations and ambiguities of his aspirations, seeking at once political high office and chiefly authority and pursuing both secessionist aims and control over the whole of Congo.

55. Mbumba interview, March 17 2006. It should be noted that such a combination of intertwined political and religious motivations is commonly expressed by Congolese military and political leaders.

56. ANTT PT-TT-PIDE-D-C-1-7477-1, PIDE Informação no. 11/69-GAB-2, Acção Fidelidade, June 12, 1969.

57. Pires Nunes, *Angola 1966-74*, p. 66.
58. The name Tigre(s) had already been used by a squad of commandos, trained in Quibala Norte near Nambwangongo, who operated in 1963-1965: Estado-Maior do Exército, *Resenha histórico-militar das campanhas de África 1961-1974*, vol. 14, *Comandos, T. 1 Grupos Iniciais* (Lisbon: Comissão para o Estudo das Campanhas de África, 2009), pp. 261-262.
59. AHM, Fundo 43, "Situação," April 1975.
60. Marcum mentions the Katangese gendarmerie in reference to their subsequent relationship with the MPLA but says little about their relationship with the Portuguese: *Angolan Revolution*, p. 259. Gleijeses mentions the gendarmes' threat potential against the FNLA but similarly discusses only their later allegiance to the MPLA: *Conflicting Missions*, pp. 238, 249.
61. 25 April Documentation Centre, University of Coimbra, Espolio Antonio Belo (hereafter A25A), Companhia de Diamantes de Angola, "Memorando: Situação na Lunda no final de Julho de 1975," July 30, 1975; interviews with Deogratias Symba, various.
62. Cann, *Counterinsurgency in Africa*, p. 212.
63. Estado-Maior do Exército, *Resenha histórico-militar*, vol. 6, book 2, 465-466.
64. See, for example, documents in ANTT, PIDE/DGS SC CI(2) UI 7494 Processo No. 7477, Pasta 1: "Commando das Operações Especiais (COE), Frente de Libertação Nacional Congaleza."
65. Re Kalenga, e-mail from Justin Mushitu, October 22, 2008; on Mwakasu: responses of Professor Mulangu (University of Luanda) to questionnaire sent by author, Luanda, June 22, 1999.
66. The imprisonment of Kabwit is mentioned in a letter from Mwaant Yav David Tshombe to Mbumba dated July 14, 1972 (ANTT, PT-TT-PIDE-D-C-1-7477-1-3), and in Mbumba's response on August 7, 1972 (ANTT, PT-TT-PIDE-D-C-1-7477-3).
67. ANTT, PT-TT-PIDE-D-C-1-7477-3, FLNC, "Allocution de François Kapend à l'occasion de l'arrivée du Général Mbumba," July 21, 1972.
68. Lumuna interview, September 26, 2005.
69. Kennes, *Essai biographique sur Laurent Désiré Kabila*, pp. 187-317.
70. G. J. Bender, *Angola under the Portuguese: The Myth and the Reality* (Trenton, NJ: Africa World Press, 2004), p. 160.
71. Quoted in Pires Nunes, *Angola 1966-74*, p. 102.

5. The Katangese Gendarmes in the Angolan Civil War, 1974-1976

1. Gleijeses, *Conflicting Missions*.
2. Marcum, *Angolan Revolution*, p. 242.
3. F. A. Guimarães, *The Origins of the Angolan Civil War: Foreign Intervention and Domestic Political Conflict* (Basingstoke: Macmillan, 2001), p. 92.
4. Gleijeses dates UNITA's cooperation with the Portuguese military to 1969: ibid., p. 240. Portugal's official military history confirms that contacts with UNITA started in 1969 but that formal cooperation began only after a meeting in March 1972: Estado-Maior do Exército, *Resenha histórico-militar das campanhas de África 1961-1974*, vol. 6, book 2, pp. 379-396.
5. H. G. Ferreira and M. W. Marshall, *Portugal's Revolution: Ten Years On* (Cambridge: Cambridge University Press, 2011), p. 74; P. Pezarat Correia, *Descolonização de Angola* (Lisbon: Inquérito, 1991), p. 28.
6. F.-W. Heimer, *Der Entkolonisierungskonflikt in Angola* (Munich: Weltforum, 1979), p. 135.

7. J. Freire Antunes, *A guerra de África, 1961–1974* (Lisbon: Círculo de Leitores, 1995), pp. 579–580. See also interview with António Alvo Rosa Coutinho, Lisbon, February 10, 2008.

8. Marcum, *Angolan Revolution*, p. 252; interview, Rosa Coutinho, February 10, 2008.

9. António Gonçalves Ribeiro, *A vertigem da descolonização: Da Agonia do Êxôdo à Cidadania Plena* (Lisbon: Inquérito Memes Martins, 2002), p. 111; Guimarães, *Origins of the Angolan Civil War*, p. 92.

10. Interview with Rosa Coutinho, *Afrique-Asie*, May 19, 1975.

11. By the end of 1974, facing the threat of FNLA incursions, Rosa Coutinho gave orders to Portuguese troops to halt the FNLA, using FLNC forces to do so if necessary: A. Marques, *Segredos da descolonização de Angola* (Alfragide: Dom Quixote, 2013), p. 160.

12. Pezarat Correia confirms that this group of Portuguese officers sought to prevent the exclusion of the MPLA from the negotiations, as the more conservative group around Spínola desired. This permitted the equal treatment of the three movements at the Alvor summit: e-mail to authors, November 17, 2009.

13. A systematic and detailed analysis of this period is provided by Heimer, *Der Entkolonisierungskonflikt in Angola*.

14. Gonçalves Ribeiro, *A vertigem da descolonização*, p. 157.

15. Guimarães, *Origins of the Angolan Civil War*, p. 88.

16. Gleijeses, *Conflicting Missions*, p. 239.

17. Pezarat Correia, *Descolonização de Angola*, pp. 93–94.

18. Marcum, *Angolan Revolution*, p. 246.

19. Guimarães, *Origins of the Angolan Civil War*, p. 93.

20. Marcum, *Angolan Revolution*, p. 254. The text of the Alvor agreement is available in the *Boletim Oficial de Angola*, February 13, 1975.

21. Interview with Colonel Argentino Seixas, head of Cabinet of Auxiliary Forces, by General Marques Pinto, report, September 2, 2014.

22. Ibid.

23. M. Amaro Bernardo, *Memórias da revolução: Portugal 1974–1975* (Lisbon: Prefácio, 2004), p. 269.

24. The three main ethnic groups in Angola are the Bakongo (15 percent of the total population), Mbundu (25 percent), and Ovimbundu (37 percent): E. George, *The Cuban Intervention in Angola: From Che Guevara to Cuito Cuanavale* (Abingdon: Routledge, 2005), p. 6.

25. Estado-Maior do Exército, *Resenha histórico-militar das campanhas de África 1961–1974*, vol. 6, book 2, pp. 379–427. See also Pezarat Correia, *Descolonização de Angola*, pp. 37–40; Gleijeses, *Conflicting Missions*, p. 239. UNITA was in general militarily ineffective between 1969 and 1974: J. Chito Rodrigues, "Angola, a Military Victory," in J. P. McCann (ed.), *Memories of Portugal's African Wars, 1961–1974* (Quantico, VA: Marine Corps Association, 1998), p. 48.

26. Shubin, *The Hot "Cold War,"* p. 32. Milhazes suggest that the Soviet Union was initially reluctant to intervene because of the MPLA's divisions: J. Milhazes, *Angola: O princípio do Fim da União Soviética* (Lisbon: Vega, 2009), pp. 44–45.

27. Marcum, *Angolan Revolution*, p. 248.

28. Ibid., pp. 177–178; Freire Antunes, *A guerra de África*, pp. 851–852.

29. Gleijeses, *Conflicting Missions*, p. 237.

30. S. Chiwale, *Cruzei-me com a história* (Lisbon: Sextante, 2008), pp. 189–190.

31. M. Junior, *Forças armadas populares de libertação de Angola. 1º Exército Nacional (1975–1992)* (Lisboa: Prefácio, 2007), p. 159.

32. Marcum, *Angolan Revolution*, p. 252.

33. Gleijeses, *Conflicting Missions*, p. 237; Marcum, *Angolan Revolution*, pp. 248–258. The lack of troops for MPLA was an important argument for Rosa Coutinho to assist MPLA to gain

an equilibrium with the other groups; see interview with Rosa Coutinho in Cabrita Mateus, *Memórias do colonialismo*, pp. 151–152.

34. The Zairian press presented Chipenda as the MPLA president, against the "Neto faction": "Le president élu au premier congrès du MPLA M. Daniel Chipenda a fait une importante déclaration sur l'accord signé à Kinshasa entre le FNLA et l'UNITA," *Elima* (Kinshasa), November 29, 1974; "Le bureau politique du MPLA rompt ses liens avec la fraction Neto," *Elima*, December 18, 1974.

35. Marcum, *Angolan Revolution*, p. 251.

36. Heimer, *Der Entkolonisierungskonflikt in Angola*, pp. 135–142.

37. Pezarat Correia, *Descolonização de Angola*, p. 108; interviews with Pezarat Correia, Lisbon, November 6, 2009, and Nathanaël Mbumba, Kinshasa, March 17, 2006. For further information, see the book by one of the plotters: P. da Cruz, *Angola: Os vivos e os mortos* (Lisbon: Intervenção, 1976), pp. 199–206.

38. ANTT, PIDE/DGS Angola, NP 2559, Pasta 29, Comando Chefe das Forças Armadas de Angola, Cabinete Especial de Informações, "Reunião de Flechas com elementos do MPLA," October 29, 1974.

39. A25A, Presidência da República, Comissão Nacional de Descolonização, "Conversações entre as delegações portuguesa e do MPLA," Argel, November 18–19, 1974, pp. 20, 23.

40. AHM, Div. 2, Secc 2, Caixa 139, no. 7, 1974, Cabinete de Forças Auxiliares, "Memorando: Acção Fidelidade," August 3, 1974.

41. McCann, *The Flechas*, p. 61.

42. Gonçalves Ribeiro, *A vertigem da descolonização*, pp. 159–173; António Silva Cardoso, *Angola: Anatomia de uma tragédia* (Lisbon: Oficina do Livro, 2000), pp. 469–477; A25A, Comando da 2 Região Aérea, "Gabinete, Protocolo da reunião entre as delegações dos movimentos de libertação em Luanda e as autoridades portuguesas," December 3–4, 1974.

43. Marques, *Segredos da descolonização de Angola*, p. 127.

44. Ibid.

45. A25A, telegram from Diplomatic Consul of President Mobutu, Bula Mandungu, to High Commissioner Rosa Coutinho, December 6, 1974. See also Silva Cardoso, *Angola*, p. 491.

46. Silva Cardoso, *Angola*, pp. 478–480.

47. Guimarães, *Origins of the Angolan Civil War*, p. 119.

48. Gleijeses, *Conflicting Missions*, p. 238.

49. Marcum, *Angolan Revolution*, p. 246.

50. Ibid.

51. *AZAP Bulletin*, September 16, 1974; Young and Turner, *Rise and Decline*, p. 253.

52. T. Moreira de Sá, *Os Estados Unidos e a descolonizaçao de Angola* (Alfragide: Dom Quixote, 2011), p. 110.

53. Silva Cardoso, *Angola*, p. 469; Guimarães, *Origins of the Angolan Civil War*, p. 93.

54. Minutes of extraordinary meeting held November 21, 1974, Chicapa, November 22, 1974: Mushitu Papers. Mbumba suggests it was General Spínola himself who proposed that the FLNC forces would be sent to South Africa: interview, April 19, 2007.

55. Interview, Justin Mushitu, Stockholm, August 5, 2000.

56. Interview, Justin Mushitu, Stockholm, February 3, 2002.

57. Interviews with Deogratias Symba: Brussels, February 25, 1998, and Lubumbashi, March 18, 2008; interview with Jean-Baptiste Kibwe, Brussels, December 18, 2008. Following Kibwe's withdrawal from this plan, Symba continued to act as a leader of the FLNC.

58. A25A, letter from Nathanaël Mbumba to Rosa Coutinho, November 22, 1974.

59. ANTT, PIDE/DGS Angola, NP 2559, Pasta 29, MPLA, Estado de Angola, Comando-Chefe das Forças Armadas de Angola, Quartel-General, Relatório Diário 45/74-CI, November 21, 1974;

Relatório Diário 36/74-CI, November 19, 1974. The MPLA was represented at this meeting by Political Commissar Joaquim Capanga ("Kapango"), José Carias, Commandant Bolingo, and Jila Sapalo.

60. "Quem são e como aparecem os 'ex-gendarmes' catangueses que no Zaire perturbam os planos de Mobutu," *Expresso* (Lisbon), March 25, 1977.

61. The date December 17, 1974, which is likely but not entirely certain, is provided in a semi-official history of the FLNC: Cartel d'Union Nationale Congolais FLNC-MNC/L (Nathanaël Mbumba), "Naissance du FLNC," "Ailleurs au Congo" (Guinea-Bissau), May 31, 1981, p. 6 (hereafter cited as FLNC-MNC/L, "Naissance du FLNC"). In this document, Mbumba confirms the presence of Justin Mushitu at the Cossa meeting. Mushitu reports that he was promoted to major so that he would be sufficiently senior to participate: interview, Justin Mushitu, Stockholm, February 28, 2008.

62. "Quem sao e como aparecem os 'ex-gendarmes' catangueses."

63. AHM, Fundo 43, "Situação," April 1975, p. 42.

64. A slightly different attendance list is provided in A. C. Botelho, *Holocausto em Angola: Memórias de entre o cárcere e o cemitério* (Lisbon: Vega, 2007). The disputed presence of Dos Santos, who became Angolan president in September 1979 following Neto's death, is significant for subsequent relations between the FLNC and the Tigres. Mbumba claims he was present, while Symba and Mushitu claim otherwise: interviews.

65. A25A, text of press conference by General Nathanaël Mbumba, *Ailleurs au Congo*, December 17, 1974.

66. A25A, telex from Rosa Coutinho to Portuguese Presidency, December 24, 1974. Neto returned to Angola only in early 1975, so he could not have carried out such a visit.

67. A25A, letter from Nathanaël Mbumba to Rosa Coutinho, December 26, 1974. Accounts of Symba's abduction by Symba himself and by Mushitu (in interviews) are confirmed in A25A, Conselho Coordenador do Programa en Angola (hereafter CCPA), "Relação cronólogica dos factos mais importantes ocorridos em Angola (ou com ela relacionados) a partir de 31 Jan 75," Luanda, November 10, 1975. The CCPA was the MFA's Coordinating Council in Angola. Antonio Belo, its secretary, gave his archives to the University of Coimbra.

68. Symba interviews, various; AHM, Fundo 43, Serie 1, Caixa 839, no. 28, Elísio de Carvalho Figueiredo, "Relatório da visita effectuada aos Refugiados Zairienses (ex-Fiéis) em 4, 5 e 6 de abril 1975," April 9, 1975, pp. 3–4. Other sources, however, dispute Symba's account of these events and suggest that Symba was involved in negotiations with and even providing information to Kinshasa.

69. A meeting on March 14, 1975, between the CCPA and the Zairian consul general, Kitenge Yezu, is mentioned in A25A, CCPA, "Relação cronólogica dos factos mais importantes ocorridos."

70. AHM, Fundo 43, Serie 1, Caixa 839, no. 28, Figueiredo report, April 9, 1975; interview, Kitenge Yezu, Kinshasa, May 2013.

71. FLNC-MNC/L, "Naissance du FLNC."

72. E. Kambaj, "Les ex-gendarmes katangais: Récit critique d'une lutte héroïque de libération" (unpublished manuscript, n.d.), pp. 102–103.

73. Botelho, *Holocausto em Angola*, p. 279; interview, Colonel Oliveira Marques, Oeiras, August 29, 2014.

74. Communication from Elísio de Carvalho Figueiredo, related to the authors in e-mail from Pezarat Correia, July 2, 2013.

75. AHM, Fundo 43, Serie 1, Caixa 839, no. 28, Carvalho Figueiredo, "Relatório da visita," pp. 3–4. The secrecy surrounding the accord is indicated by the fact that Figueiredo makes no mention of his or Rosa Coutinho's involvement in it.

76. Ibid.
77. AHM, Fundo 43, Serie 1, Caixa 839, no. 28, Figueiredo report, April 9, 1975.
78. For the potential alliance with UNITA, see Justin Mushitu interview, June 18, 2011, Stockholm; correspondence from Mbumba to Savimbi can be found in A25A: Letter from Nathanaël Mbumba to Jonas Savimbi, April 19, 1975.
79. AHM, Fundo 43, "Situação," April 1975.
80. Joseph Kabwit supports the argument that the FLNC was not willing to rebel against the wishes of the pro-MPLA Portuguese, who were after all in power in Luanda during this period: interview, Kinshasa, July 14, 2008.
81. "Quem são e como aparecem os 'ex-gendarmes' catangueses."
82. Amaro Bernardo, *Memórias da revolução*, p. 270.
83. AHM, Fundo 43, "Situação," April 1975, p. 3.
84. Marcum, *Angolan Revolution*, p. 435, fn129.
85. Ibid., p. 259. Guimarães mentions the reinforcement of the MPLA by the ex-gendarmes, estimating their number as between 3,500 and 7,000 men, but offers no analysis of the importance of their role: *Origins of the Angolan Civil War*, p. 103.
86. Marcum, *Angolan Revolution*, p. 253.
87. George, *Cuban Intervention in Angola*, p. 55.
88. Guimarães, *Origins of the Angolan Civil War*, p. 93.
89. Ibid.
90. Rosa Coutinho interview, February 10, 2008.
91. Mushitu interview, February 28, 2008.
92. AHM, Fundo 43, Serie 1, Caixa 839, no. 28, Carvalho Figueiredo, "Relatório da visita," pp. 3-4. However, according to an officer stationed in Saurimo in 1975, Figueiredo obtained authorization from the military commander of all Portuguese forces to transfer his battalion's heavy weaponry to the Katangese, effectively supporting the MPLA. This reflected the MFA in Luanda's support for the MPLA against the wishes of the local commander: M. Jesus da Silva, *Sortilégio da cobra. Descolonização obrigatória* (Lisbon: Ésquilo, 2005), pp. 199-200.
93. Mbumba stated: "It is especially regrettable that the Portuguese government continues to insist on [the acceptance of] the amnesty signed by General Mobutu, which has already been rejected by the Congolese political refugees on three occasions." A25A, Nathanaël Mbumba, speech at Chicapa, July 5, 1975.
94. Guimarães, *Origins of the Angolan Civil War*, pp. 96-97; George, *Cuban Intervention in Angola*, p. 59.
95. AHM, Fundo 43, Serie 1, Caixa 839, no. 28, Carvalho Figueiredo, "Relatório da visita," pp. 16-17.
96. AHM, Fundo 43, Serie 3, Caixa 840, no. 30, CCPA (Secret) Capt Martins e Silva and Major Gomes de Abreu, "Estudo de Situação," April 19, 1975, p. 51.
97. AHM, Fundo 43, Serie 4, Caixa 841, no. 33, CCPA, "Reuniões da, CCPA," October 14, 1975; see also Marques, *Segredos da descolonização de Angola*, p. 476.
98. A25A, Nakuru Accord, June 21, 1975, paragraph 4, p. 6.
99. A25A, Companhia de Diamantes de Angola, "Memorando: Situação na Lunda no final de Julho de 1975."
100. P. Gleijeses, *Visions of Freedom: Havana, Washington, Pretoria, and the Struggle for Southern Africa, 1976-1991* (Chapel Hill: University of North Carolina Press, 2013); Vilafaña, *Cold War in the Congo*.
101. Gleijeses, *Conflicting Missions*, p. 227.
102. Shubin, *The Hot "Cold War,"* p. 26.

103. O. A. Westad, "Moscow and the Angolan Crisis, 1974–1976: A New Pattern of Intervention," *Cold War International History Project (CWIHP) Bulletin* 8–9 (1996): 21–31, cited in Gleijeses, *Conflicting Missions*, p. 244.
104. Gleijeses, *Conflicting Missions*, p. 247.
105. Quoted in ibid., p. 249.
106. Marcum, *Angolan Revolution*, pp. 258–259.
107. Gleijeses, *Conflicting Missions*, p. 252.
108. George, *Cuban Intervention in Angola*, p. 60.
109. Gleijeses, *Conflicting Missions*, pp. 254–255.
110. Ibid., pp. 256–257; Guimarães, *Origins of the Angolan Civil War*, p. 146. George agrees that Cuba did not immediately respond to the MPLA's requests for armaments and military instructors: *Cuban Intervention in Angola*, pp. 57–58.
111. Gleijeses, *Conflicting Missions*, pp. 260–265.
112. Guimarães, *Origins of the Angolan Civil War*, p. 147.
113. Gleijeses, *Conflicting Missions*, p. 267.
114. Marcum, *Angolan Revolution*, p. 257.
115. Shubin, *The Hot "Cold War,"* p. 43.
116. The military weakness of the MPLA during this period is acknowledged even by its sympathizers; see, for example, ibid., p. 40.
117. Marcum, *Angolan Revolution*, p. 260.
118. Report, Colonel Vincent de Paul Nguz, "L'aide que les Tigres ont amené en 1975 au MPLA avant l'arrivée des Cubains et les endroits où les Tigres ont combattu pour le MPLA après l'accord de Cosa," 2013. Ndalu was a leading FAPLA commander; see "Batalha de Kifangondo na voz do general Ndalu," http://jornaldeangola.sapo.ao/entrevista/batalha_de_kifangondo_na_voz_do_general_ndalu (accessed May 10, 2015).
119. Nguz, Report, "L'aide que les Tigres ont amené en 1975 au MPLA." See also Mushitu interview, November 6, 2005, and Pascal Kapend interview, August 14, 2005.
120. Gleijeses, *Conflicting Missions*, p. 266.
121. Ibid., p. 252.
122. Young and Turner, *Rise and Decline*, p. 254. These operations involved the 4th and 7th Battalions of the FAZ, under the command of Colonel Mamina: S. du Preez, *Aventuur in Angola: Die verhaal van Suid-Afrika se soldate in Angola 1975-1976* (Pretoria: J. L. van Schaik, 1989), p. 110.
123. Stockwell, *In Search of Enemies*, pp. 80–86.
124. Young and Turner, *Rise and Decline*, p. 265.
125. Gleijeses, *Conflicting Missions*, pp. 287–288. One explanation suggests that the posting of a US ambassador who had, during his previous posting in Chile, been instrumental in the overthrow of Allende led Mobutu to fear a similar fate, prompting a purge of suspect senior army officers: R. Omba, *Coup monté et manqué: Une voie de sanctification* (Kinshasa: Shomo, 2005), pp. 28–30.
126. Gleijeses, *Conflicting Missions*, pp. 288–289.
127. Ibid., pp. 291–292.
128. Mushitu interview, Stockholm, February 28, 2008.
129. Anonymous, document detailing history of Katangese gendarmes drafted under the leadership of Élie Kapend, Luanda, September 22, 1998.
130. FLNC-MNC/L, "Naissance du FLNC." According to a later history of the FLNC, Katangese troops were ambushed by South African forces, resulting in the deaths of 402 men, including their captain, Pierre Tshinyama: FLNC, "Mini-historique des ex-gendarmes katangais

du Congo-Kinshasa," Luanda, 1998, p. 13. This was confirmed by Mbumba: interview, Kinshasa, April 19, 2007. One source suggests that Figueirdo himself led Katangese forces at Luena: Jesus da Silva, *Sortilégio da cobra*, pp. 200–201.

131. Interviews, Justin Mushitu, various; François Kapend, Kinshasa, April 25, 2007.
132. Chiwale, *Cruzei-me com a história*, pp. 202–203.
133. George, *Cuban Intervention in Angola*, p. 74.
134. South African operations in conjunction with UNITA are documented in F. J. Du Toit Spies, *Operasie Savannah: Angola 1975–1976* (Pretoria: S.A. Weermag, Direktoraat Openbare Betrekkinge, 1989). This does not, however, mention the FLNC or the Tigres.
135. Gleijeses, *Conflicting Missions*, p. 269; Guimarães, *Origins of the Angolan Civil War*, p. 111.
136. Stockwell, *In Search of Enemies*, p. 157.
137. Lieutenant Colonel Enrique Buznego Rodriguez and Lieutenant Colonel Lazaro Cardenas Sierra, "La Batalla de Quifangondo," in M. Rey Cabrera (ed.), *La guerra de Angola* (Havana: Politica, 1989), pp. 43–56.
138. Young and Turner, *Rise and Decline*, p. 254.
139. Gleijeses, *Conflicting Missions*, p. 311. Similar figures are provided in Buznego Rodriguez and Cardenas Sierra, "La Batalla de Quifangondo," p. 31. Shubin's Soviet sources claim that these numbers of FAPLA and Katangese forces are exaggerated: Shubin, *The Hot "Cold War,"* p. 54. However, Marcum cites at least one journalistic source crediting the Katangese gendarmes with a major role in the defense of Luanda: *Angolan Revolution*, p. 443, fn262. A Brazilian journalist who witnessed the battle for Quifangondo attributes the outcome to Cuban and Soviet assistance: F. L. da Câmara Cascudo, *Angola: A guerra dos traídos* (Rio de Janeiro: Bloch, 1979), pp. 123–130.
140. Letter, Jacques Michel Grafé, December 13, 2006.
141. Gleijeses, *Conflicting Missions*, p. 270.
142. This figure was provided in interviews with Mbumba and Mushitu and is given in the "official history" of the FLNC: FLNC-MNC/L, "Naissance du FLNC."
143. Stockwell, *In Search of Enemies*, pp. 214–215; Gleijeses, *Conflicting Missions*, p. 312.
144. *New York Times*, January 30, 1976, quoted in Gleijeses, *Conflicting Missions*, p. 339.
145. South African sources are in turn critical of Holden's refusal to accept Mobutu's plans of attack and his desire to conquer Luanda in a spectacular manner: du Preez, *Aventuur in Angola*; M. Malan, *My Life with the SA Defence Force* (Pretoria: Protea, 2006), pp. 124–126.
146. Gleijeses, *Conflicting Missions*, p. 339.
147. G. Prunier, *Africa's World War: Congo, the Rwandan Genocide, and the Making of a Continental Catastrophe* (Oxford: Oxford University Press, 2009), p. 404.
148. Kennes, *Essai biographique*, pp. 236–237, 241–242.
149. Deogratias Symba interview, February 28, 1998; Kennes, *Essai biographique*, pp. 241–243.
150. A25A, letter from Nathanaël Mbumba to "Raul" Kabila, May 10, 1975.

6. The Shaba Wars

1. This chapter draws on some material originally published in the following article: M. Larmer, "Local Conflicts in a Transnational War: The Katangese Gendames and the Shaba Wars of 1977–78," *Cold War History* 13, no. 1 (2013): pp. 89–108. The authors are grateful to the publishers for allowing the use of this material in this chapter.
2. The figure 36,000 is cited in George, *Cuban Intervention in Angola*, pp. 13–17.

3. Ibid., pp. 119–120.

4. For Cuban and Soviet links: interviews with Robert Yav, Lubumbashi, February 28, 2006, and Pascal Kapend, Lubumbashi, August 14, 2005; Shaba I documents, Belgian Army Archives (hereafter BAA), Centre de Documentation Historique (hereafter CDH), Service Général de Renseignements et de Sécurité (hereafter SGR, the Belgian military intelligence service). Mbumba confirms the supply of armaments by the MPLA in a subsequent letter to Angolan president Eduardo dos Santos, June 11, 1983, Papers of Justin Mushitu (hereafter Mushitu Papers).

5. P. Gleijeses, "Truth or Credibility: Castro, Carter, and the Invasions of Shaba," *International History Review* 18, no. 1 (1996): 70–103.

6. Ibid., p. 73.

7. Memo, Risquet to Neto, n.d. but received February 1978; cited in ibid., pp. 73–74.

8. Gleijeses, "Truth or Credibility," pp. 94–95.

9. S. B. Snyder, "Helsinki Final Act (1975)," in J. R. Arnold and R. Wiener (eds.), *Cold War: The Essential Reference Guide* (Santa Barbara, CA: ABC-CLIO, 2012), p. 75.

10. Gleijeses, *Visions of Freedom*, p. 39.

11. This is confirmed by all relevant interviewees, including Mbumba interview, April 19, 2007; Cartel d'Union Nationale Congolais FLNC-MNC/L (Nathanaël Mbumba), "Naissance du FLNC" (Guinea-Bissau), May 31, 1981.

12. Mushitu was to play an important role in the history of the ex-Tigres—see subsequent chapters.

13. Interview, Emile Ilunga, Kinshasa, September 18, 2009.

14. Cedomi, "L'étrange destin de la Gendarmerie katangaise." A joint "final communiqué" (copy in authors' possession) dated October 22, 1975, declaring the fusion of these movements into the FLNC was, however, signed only by Mbumba and Mokede. An ABAKO-FLNC-Democratic Forces for the Liberation of the Congo (Fodelico) alliance was thought by French analysts to be engaged in the distribution of clandestine literature in 1977: "Le Zaire," April 7, 1977, in Archives diplomatiques, La Courneuve, Ministère des Affaires Etrangéres, Direction des Affaires Africaines et Malgaches (hereafter MAE DAM), Box 25-2, Réunions internationales, p. 6.

15. Letter, Mbumba to Jean-Delphin Muland, July 13, 1987, Papers of Daniel Mayele (hereafter Mayele Papers).

16. Cartel d'Union Nationale Congolais, "Naissance du FLNC," p. 9.

17. Interviews, Cartier Mutombo: Montargis (France), July 2, 2011, and Kinshasa, January 4, 2008.

18. Telephone interview, Justin Mushitu, December 1998; *Bulletin du CEDOPO*, nos. 13/77 and 54/77 (1977); Monguya Mbenge, *De Léopold II à Mobutu*, p. 79. Mpoyo later financed PRP activities, before he came to power in 1997 as one of Laurent Kabila's economic advisers.

19. Monguya Mbenge, untitled document, February 1, 1976. Monguya alleges that Neto wished him to take control of the FLNC but that this was strongly resisted by Mbumba. Monguya was simultaneously impressed by Mbumba's organization of the FLNC's military capacity and concerned that this force would be mobilized by Mbumba in the unrealistic cause of taking power in Kinshasa and reorganizing the Zairian state.

20. Monguya subsequently assured Mobutu by telegram that he had never been involved in the operations of the Tigres: D. Monguya Mbenge, *Histoire secrète du Zaïre: L'autopsie de la barbarie au service du monde* (Brussels: L'Espérance, 1977), p. 14.

21. Interviews: Deogratias Symba, February 25, 1998; Jean-Baptiste Kibwe, Brussels, December 17, 2007.

22. Kennes, *Essai biographique sur Laurent Désiré Kabila*, pp. 187–260; Cedomi, "L'étrange destin de la Gendarmerie katangaise."
23. A. Gizenga, *Ma vie et mes luttes* (Paris: L'Harmattan, 2011), p. 397.
24. C. Kabuya, *Zaïre: Quel changement pour quelles structures?* (Brussels: Éditions Africa, 1980), p. 142; Comité Zaïre, *Zaïre: Le dossier de la recolonisation* (Paris: L'Harmattan, 1978), pp. 257–258 ; Kennes, *Essai biographique*, p. 234; Gizenga, *Ma Vie*, pp. 392–394.
25. Interview, Jean-Baptiste Kibwe, Brussels, August 23, 2001.
26. Henri Mukachung explained that such a plan existed during this period but was only implemented subsequently: discussions, September 2013.
27. A PRP delegation was due to visit Luanda in March 1977: letter from Omari Mulikwa, secretary of the PRP Central Committee delegation, to Daniel Mayele, Bujumbura, Mayele Papers. It is not known if the visit took place. Deogratias Symba states that Kabila arrived in Luanda on the day that Shaba I commenced: interview, Lubumbashi, March 18, 2008.
28. "Contre révolution au Zaïre," report of an interview with Deogratias Symba, May 10, 1977, Thiange Papers.
29. Gizenga was presented as a member of the PRP in 1977. The proposal of a PRP-FLNC alliance led by Gizenga goes back to 1975: *Bulletin du CEDOPO*, nos. 45/75 (April 8, 1975). The MPLA supported the placing of Gizenga, with his Lumumbist credentials, at the head of a unified Zairian opposition movement; Gizenga, however, chose instead to protect his political autonomy via his own movement, Fodelico.
30. MAE DAM, Box 21.2, Zaire 1975–1978, "Zaïre: Perspectives après le retrait des forces françaises et belges," Annexe: Le Front National de Libération du Congo (FNLC), Premier Ministére, Secrétariat Général de la Défense Nationale, Groupe Permanent d'Evaluation de Situations, June 5, 1978, p. 3.
31. Letter, Jean-Delphin Muland to André Kaloba, Saurimo, March 29, 1987, Mayele Papers; interview, Pascal Kapend, Lubumbashi, August 14, 2005.
32. The respective commanders of these columns were as follows: for Kapanga, Nathanaël Mbumba; for Kisenge, Jean-Delphin Muland; and for Dilolo, Vindicien "Mufu" Kiyana: letter, Mbumba to Muland, July 13, 1987, Mayele Papers.
33. These are held in the BAA CDH, which are not publicly accessible: copies in possession of authors.
34. A supposedly official FLNC document giving details of the operational plan (FLNC, "Directives pour l'opération de l'Ouest du Katanga suivant la ligne Kaniama-Kolwezi," April 4, 1977) is reproduced in what amounts to Zaire's official account of Shaba I: Département de la Défense Nationale, État-Major Général des Forces Armées Zaïroises (DDNEMG), *Mobutu et la guerre de quatre-vingts jours* (Tournai: Casterman, 1978), pp. 339–343. It is clear, however, that the document is a falsification in terms of the routes taken and suspect in terms of the dates given for the operation.
35. This is referred to in a confidential document named "15 amazon" held in the BAA CDH, n.d. but probably March 1977, and probably of US intelligence provenance.
36. Interview, Jean-Baptiste Kibwe, Brussels, August 23, 2001; interview, Pascal Kapend, Lubumbashi, August 14, 2005.
37. Interview, Pascal Kapend, Lubumbashi, September 24, 2005.
38. Since the early 1960s, the center of mining activity in Katanga had shifted westward away from Elisabethville/Lubumbashi and toward the Kolwezi area.
39. Interview, General Paul Mukobo Mundende, Brussels, September 19, 2007.
40. The FAZ had been integrated into the MPR in 1972, and its commander, Brigadier Bumba Moaso, was a part of the eight-member Political Bureau from 1975: Young and Turner, *Rise and Decline*, p. 265.

41. Interview, Mukobo Mundende, Brussels, September 19, 2007. The Kamanyola Division was formed by the North Koreans and had existed for only six months at the time of Shaba I: T. Odom, *Shaba II: The French and Belgian Intervention in Zaire in 1978* (Fort Leavenworth, KS: Combat Studies Institute, US Army Command and General Staff College, 1993), pp. 17–19.

42. US embassy Kinshasa to US Secretary of State, March 16, 1977, quoted in Gleijeses, "Truth or Credibility," p. 76.

43. BAA CDH, SGR, Shaba I documents, March 9, 1977–May 26, 1977, *Rapport circonstancié voyage Lubumbashi-Kolwezi et retour (1 au 4 avril 1977) de Trio (B.2)*, R. Zaire/33.705, April 21, 1977, p. 2.

44. The wildest rumors during this period suggested the presence of ca. 200 nuclear warheads in Angolan hands! BAA CDH, Shaba I: manuscript note for Chiefs of Staff of Defence and Foreign Affairs, March 17, 1977. See also Gleijeses, *Visions of Freedom*, p. 39.

45. MAE DAM, Box 25.2, "Réunions internationales," Mobutu to President of OAU Sir Seewoojgur Ramgoolam, April 2, 1977, reprinted in French embassy Kinshasa to DAM, April 7, 1977.

46. Gleijeses, "Truth or Credibility," p. 77. Young and Turner suggest that Bumba's failure to support his accusations with evidence led in part to his removal: *Rise and Decline*, p. 265.

47. Gleijeses, *Visions of Freedom*, p. 41.

48. Gleijeses, "Truth or Credibility," p. 95.

49. Department of State, *Bulletin*, April 18, 1977, p. 361, quoted in Gleijeses, "Truth or Credibility," p. 76.

50. "The FLNC Speaks," *Africa*, May 1977, p. 25; International Press Service, "Congolese FLNC Leader Explains Goals," April 8, 1977.

51. Interviews, Cartier Mutombo: Montargis (France), July 2, 2011, and Kinshasa, January 4, 2008.

52. MAE DAM, Box 25.1, Aide et médiation étrangère, mars–juin 1977, "Nigeria, Resume of a Meeting between Nigerian Foreign Minister Garba and Secretary Vance on March 21 [1977]."

53. MAE DAM, Box 25.2, Réunions internationales, "Zaire," London COREU to all COREU, April 17, 1977, p. 2.

54. MAE DAM, Box 25.4, Réactions des pays étrangèrs, sauf " l'Afrique," "Belgian analysis of the Zairian situation," response, French embassy Lusaka to DAM, March 24, 1977, pp. 1–2.

55. BAA CDH, Shaba I, Very Secret Message, no. 314/206, May 2, 1977. Gizenga was expelled from France in April 1977, undoubtedly because of Shaba I.

56. MAE DAM, Box 25.4, Réactions des pays étrangèrs, sauf " l'Afrique," "La France et Le Zaire," French embassy Brussels to DAM, March 25, 1977, p. 2.

57. This meeting is reported by the French consul in Lubumbashi, Marcel Thauvin: report, March 25, 1977, in MAE, Centres des Archives Diplomatiques de Nantes (hereafter MAE CAD), Box 45, Zaire 1975–1978, Ambassade Kinshasa-Shaba correspondence, 1973–1978, I-134.

58. "Entretien avec l'Empereur Lunda," Pierre Guth, Lubumbashi consulate, April 5, 1977, in MAE CAD, Box 45, Zaire 1975–1978, Ambassade Kinshasa-Shaba correspondence, 1973–1978, I-134.

59. TNA, FCO/31/2116, Shaba Invasion, 1977, meeting at Luanda airport, April 17, 1977, item 261.

60. TNA, FCO/31/2117, Shaba Invasion, 1977, P. R. A. Mansfield (FCO) to C. M. James, Paris embassy, "French Views on Africa," May 10, 1977, item 284.

61. TNA, FCO/31/2115, Shaba Invasion, 1977, "French Assistance to Zaire," C. M. James, British embassy Paris to P. H. R. Mansfield, FCO, April 24, 1977, item 234a.

62. TNA, FCO/31/2115, Shaba Invasion, 1977, Rabat embassy to FCO, April 20, 1977, item 211; Morocco Ministry of Foreign Affairs communiqué, Rabat, April 27, 1977.

63. Gleijeses, "Truth or Credibility," p. 78; TNA, FCO/31/2115, Shaba Invasion, 1977, Kinshasa embassy to FCO, April 25, 1977. A British official commented, "This interview smells strongly of a put-up job." Gizenga was himself in Europe at this time: Gizenga, *Ma vie*, p. 396.

64. *Salongo*, April 26, 1977, quoted in Gleijeses, "Truth or Credibility," p. 78. Mobutu's supposedly triumphant victory in the "war of eighty days" was commemorated in the aforementioned official publication: Département de la Défense Nationale, *Mobutu et la guerre de quatre-vingt jours*.

65. BAA CDH, Shaba I, "Zaïre: Situation militaire au Shaba," May 24, 1977, no. 373/77.

66. TNA, FCO/31/2116, Shaba Invasion, 1977, "Belgian Views on Zaire," R. Janvrin to P. E. Rosling, FCO, May 5, 1977, item 273.

67. The exact name and quantity of these camps is hard to identify definitively and in any case fluctuated during this period. Nine of the Moxico camps bore the following names: Muxilindjindji, Lumege Cameia, Luxia Ponte, Leua, Mucusuege, Camanongue, Chingula, Luangi, and Musumba II. In Lunda Norte, in addition to the established military camps at Chicapa, Camissombo, and Cazombo, civilian camps were now established at Chimege and Chisele. Four civilian camps in Lunda Sul were called Cassege, Mwapezo, Sakambundji, and Muconda. État-Major Général des FAPAC, "Histoire des ex-gendarmes katangais de 1960–1992: 32 ans de maquis," Luanda (Viana), January 1992, p. 12.

68. The figure 9,240 is given in FLNC, *Mini-historique des ex-gendarmes katangais*, p. 14. This is supported by Belgian intelligence reports, which refer to 1,900 new recruits at Chicapa and four battalions at Caianda (about 2,000 men), plus fewer battalions at Luia: BAA CDH, Shaba I, bulletins dated September 9 and September 19, 1977.

69. Zaire, Conference Nationale Souveraine, Commission des Assassinats et des Violations des Droits de l'Homme, *Rapport de la Commission* (Kinshasa, 1992), p. 89.

70. Mbumba justified this action as an attempt to impose discipline on drunken troops: interview. Justin Mushitu reports at least another three executions in the wake of Shaba I: interviews, various.

71. A number of such incidents are referred to in Belgian army intelligence bulletins, BAA CDH, Shaba I. For this particular example, see MAE CAD, Box 45, Zaire 1975–1978, Ambassade Kinshasa-Shaba correspondence, 1973–1978, I-134, "Situation militaire au Shaba," French embassy Kinshasa to DAM, August 25, 1977.

72. MAE DAM, Box 24, Zaire 1975–1978, "Bulletin de situation," 767 and 786/ZAI/FA/CAD, November 4–20, 1977, p. 2.

73. MAE DAM, Box 24, Zaire, 1975–1978, "Situation militaire, octobre-1977–novembre 1978," "Situation au Shaba: Les évènements de 1977 et la situation au début de 1978," French embassy Kinshasa to DAM, June 1, 1978.

74. MAE DAM, Box 27.2, Zaire 1975–1978, "Evolution de la situation militaire, fevrier–avril 1977," "Gendarmes katangais," French embassy in Kinshasa to DAM, November 14, 1977. As indicated above, this should not suggest that Gizenga's influence was real.

75. For example, interview with Robert Yav, Lubumbashi, February 28, 2006; Pascal Kapend interview, August 14, 2005.

76. Colonel Vincent de Paul Nguz, interview, Kinshasa, December 13, 2013. Nguz claims that Cubans were paid in diamonds and sent in return ammunition and weapons to the FLNC hidden beneath foodstuffs in truck deliveries.

77. The ECP arose from the General Union of Congolese Students, a students' movement founded at Lovanium in 1961 that became increasingly left-wing and Lumumbist. J. Omasombo and E. Kennes, *Biographies des acteurs de la transition (juin 2003–juin 2006)* (Tervuren: MRAC-CEP-CERDAC, 2006), pp. 174–175.

78. C. N'Dom (on behalf of the ECP Coordination Committee), "La crise au sein du Comité extérieur du FLNC: Opportunisme et gauchisme" (Brussels, 1981), p. 16. The role of the ECP at this time was important in relation to the eventual accession to power of Laurent Kabila with the support of the FLNC.

79. Ibid., p. 8. It should be noted that not all leftist activists were so critical: for example, Ambroise Kalabela, a student of Katangese origin, mobilized support for the FLNC in Belgium from 1977.

80. It is now widely recognized that the effectiveness of southern African national liberation movements' guerrilla tactics in the 1970s often involved terrorization of the civilian community: see, for example, N. Kriger, "The Zimbabwean War of Liberation: Struggles within the Struggle," *Journal of Southern African Studies* 14, no. 2 (1988): 304–322.

81. Mbumba interview, April 19, 2007; a Belgian army intelligence bulletin (BAA CDH, Shaba I) reports a visit to Algeria on November 14, 1977.

82. Interviews, Jérôme Nawej, Kinshasa, April 8, 2008; Mwaant Yav Mushid III, Benjamin Tshombe Kaumb, Kinshasa, June 1, 2014.

83. Jesus da Silva, *Sortilégio da cobra*, pp. 199–200.

84. Interviews: David Kayombo, Brussels, May 7, 1997; Gaston Yambo, Oslo, December 1998; Daniel Monguya Mbenge, Mons, September 2001; Justin Mushitu, Stockholm, December 1998.

85. Symba may have joined the PRP in June 1977: Kabuya, *Zaïre*, p. 143. Symba allegedly established contacts in Belgium, France, Germany, Italy, Kenya, Lebanon, Mozambique, Switzerland, Tanzania, Zambia, and probably Libya.

86. Mushitu was appointed to this position on September 19, 1975: FLNC, Decision no. 1, 01/CAB/PDT/75, Mushitu Papers.

87. *Protocole d'accord entre le FLNC et le PRP relatif à la création du Conseil Suprême de Libération*, August 26, 1977, Papers of Monguya Mbenge. A joint communiqué announced the establishment of the CSL: *Le Soir*, August 28–29, 1977.

88. For FAZ attacks on the PRP in mid-1977, see Kennes, *Essai*, pp. 229, 244.

89. Mayele Papers, letter to Agostinho Neto, June 2, 1977, signed by Justin Mushitu and Jean-Désiré Fataki (PRP).

90. As noted above, Mbumba had already rejected collaboration with MARC. Monguya Mbenge, *De Léopold II à Mobutu*, pp. 77–90.

91. Interviews, Justin Mushitu, Stockholm, August 5, 2000, and February 3, 2002; "Le monde des méchants" (unpublished manuscript, 2003), pp. 31–32, Mushitu Papers. Mushitu arrived as a refugee in Stockholm in December 1977.

92. Cartel d'Union Nationale Congolais, "Naissance du FLNC," p. 10.

93. Gleijeses, *Visions of Freedom*, p. 43.

94. T. Trefon, *French Policy toward Zaire during the Giscard d'Estaing Presidency* (Brussels: CEDAF, 1989); N. Kinsey-Powell, "France's African Wars, 1974–1981" (PhD dissertation, Graduate Institute of International and Development Studies, Geneva, 2013).

95. Trefon, *French Policy toward Zaire*, pp. 68–69.

96. MAE DAM, Box 16, Zaire 1975–1978, Note, "Le Zaïre," April 7, 1977, p. 3.

97. MAE DAM, Box 16, Zaire 1975–1978, "Situation au Zaïre," May 17, 1977, p. 1. Emphasis in original.

98. MAE DAM, Box 16, Zaire 1975–1978, "Le Zaïre," February 22, 1978, p. 1.

99. Jimmy Carter Library, Atlanta, Georgia (hereafter JCL), "Secretary's meeting with Foreign Minister van Elslande," Secretary of State to Brzezinski, September 9, 1977.

100. *Le Soir*, April 27, 1977; *New York Times*, April 28, 1977; see also Gleijeses, "Truth or Credibility," p. 79.

101. *Le Soir*, June 14, 1977.
102. JCL, White House Central File, CO 177, Executive, January 20, 1977–January 20, 1981, Mobutu to Carter, July 23, 1977.
103. Young and Turner, *Rise and Decline*, p. 205.
104. D. Van der Steen, *Élections et réformes politiques au Zaïre en 1977: Analyse de la composition des organes politiques* (Brussels: CEDAF, 1978).
105. MAE DAM, Box 16, Zaire 1975–1978, "Zaire," March 29, 1978, p. 2.
106. J.-C. Willame, *Chronique d'une opposition politique: L'UDPS (1978–1987)* (Brussels: CEDAF, 1987).
107. Young and Turner, *Rise and Decline*, p. 74.
108. Gleijeses, "Truth or Credibility," p. 81.
109. MAE DAM Box 16, Zaire 1975–1978, "Zaire," March 29, 1978, p. 2.
110. MAE CAD, Box 45, Zaire 1975–1978, Ambassade Kinshasa-Shaba correspondence, 1973–1978, I-134, "Refugies du Shaba en Angola," French embassy Lusaka to French embassy Kinshasa, July 22, 1977.
111. Interview, Mukobo Mundende, Brussels, September 19, 2007.
112. MAE DAM, Box 27.2, Zaire 1975–1978, "Evolution de la situation militaire, fevrier–avril 1977," "Arrestations au Shaba," French embassy in Kinshasa to DAM, June 3, 1977.
113. N. Karl-i-Bond, *Mobutu ou l'Incarnation du Mal Zaïrois* (London: Rex Collings, 1982), p. 47.
114. "Le regime en peril," *Le Monde*, March 31, 1977, cited in R. Yakemtchouk, "Les deux guerres du Shaba," *Studia Diplomatica* 41, nos. 4/5/6 (1988): 443.
115. Nguz was released in July 1978 and reappointed minister of foreign affairs in March 1979 before going into exile in April 1981.
116. He was subsequently accused of being involved in the Shaba II attack: Monguya Mbenge, *De Léopold II à Mobutu*, pp. 90–91.
117. MAE DAM, Box 16, Zaire 1975–1978, "Zaire," March 10, 1978, pp. 1–2.
118. BAA CDH, Shaba II, "Climat de désorganisation accentuée au département de la défense nationale et à l'Etat-major général, " note no. 325/78, April 4, 1978.
119. Mbumba, interview, April 19, 2007. Most interviewees contest this account, but President Neto's approval of the operation is evident: Jean-Pierre Musasa, written response to questions, December 12, 2012.
120. Colonel Vincent de Paul Nguz interview, December 13, 2013.
121. Gleijeses, *Visions of Freedom*, pp. 54–57. The original Cuban documents can be consulted at the Woodrow Wilson Center's Cold War International History Project (CWIHP): http://digitalarchive.wilsoncenter.org.
122. MAE DAM, Box 24, Zaire 1975–1978, "Situation militaire, octobre-1977–novembre 1978," "Echec d'une infiltration katangaise," French embassy in Kinshasa to DAM, March 30, 1978.
123. Odom, *Shaba II*, p. 20; Cartel d'Union Nationale Congolais, "Naissance du FLNC," pp. 13–14.
124. "Mufu" in Swahili means "revenant" or able to return from the dead. With a reputation as a genuine soldier who fought alongside his men, Mufu would go on to play an important role in the history of the Tigres.
125. Cartel d'Union Nationale Congolais, "Naissance du FLNC," p. 14
126. MAE DAM, Box 21.2, Zaire 1975–1978, French embassy, Kinshasa, June 28, 1978, communiqué à DAM, "Prolongements diplomatiques des événements du Shaba," p. 2. While some Zambian officials may have known about the rebel presence in this remote border area, it is plausible that senior Zambian politicians, including President Kaunda, were ignorant of the movements of foreign forces in North-Western Province during this period.

127. The effectiveness of the Zambia path of entry was widely noted by contemporaneous diplomatic sources, for example TNA, FCO/99/162, Cuba/Zaire Shaba Invasion, 1978, Paris embassy to FCO, May 17, 1978, item 3.

128. Odom, *Shaba II*, pp. 31–32; BAA CDH, Shaba II, "Zaïre-Angola-Katangese," note no. 315/78, February 23, 1978.

129. Reports of soldiers in civilian clothes, reminiscent of the gendarmes' movement into Angola in 1963, can be found in MAE DAM, Box 21.2, Zaire 1975–1978, French embassy, Kinshasa, August 9, 1978, Ambassador André Ross to MAE Louis de Guiringaud, p. 5.

130. Statement by Colonel Ngongo Selembe, in G. Ilunga Malukula, *Après le terrorisme, la sorcellerie serait-elle un procédé de combat?* (Lubumbashi: Privately printed, 2006), p. 81.

131. TNA, FCO/31/2287, Zaire—Shaba Invasion, 1978, A. G. Munro, "Shaba: Present Situation," May 15, 1978, item 22.

132. Central Intelligence Agency Freedom of Information Act Electronic Reading Room (hereafter CIA FOIA ERR), "Zaire: New Katangan Attacks," in "National Intelligence Daily Cable," May 15, 1978, ESDN: CIA-RDP79T00975A030700010006-4.

133. MAE DAM, Box 21.3, Zaire 1975–1978, United Nations Press Communication, Weekly review no. 20, May 19–25, 1978, p. 15.

134. TNA, FCO/99/162, Cuba/Zaire Shaba Invasion, 1978, FCO (Owen) to British embassy Kinshasa, May 18, 1978, item 12. Lengema, having claimed that Kaunda, opposed to Soviet expansion in central Africa, would prevent further passage inside Zambia, admitted, "The fact that the Lunda spanned Zaire, Zambia and Angola complicate[s] surveillance."

135. TNA, FCO/99/162, Cuba/Zaire Shaba Invasion, 1978, British embassy Luanda to FCO, May 17, 1978.

136. TNA, FCO/99/162, Cuba/Zaire Shaba Invasion, 1978, Luanda embassy to FCO, May 17, 1978, item 14.

137. CIA FOIA ERR, "Chronology of FNLC Planning," January 1, 1978 (but in fact written in May? 1978), ESDN: CIA-RDP81B00401R002100020009-1.

138. CIA FOIA ERR, "Zaire: Military Situation Report," in "National Intelligence Daily Cable," May 17, 1978, ESDN: CIA-RDP79T00975A030700010010-9.

139. Ibid.

140. TNA, FCO/99/162, Cuba/Zaire Shaba Invasion, 1978, UK embassy Washington to FCO, May 18, 1978, item 20.

141. In May 1977, Angolan interior minister Nito Alves, having been expelled from the MPLA, mounted a coup attempt in Luanda, which Alves claimed was supported by the Soviet Union. The coup was violently suppressed by Cuban forces, and the ensuing repression of allegedly disloyal MPLA members in Luanda's shantytowns led to the deaths of thousands. See L. Pawson, *In the Name of the People: Angola's Forgotten Massacre* (London: I. B. Tauris, 2014).

142. This detention was confirmed by an eyewitness, Prof. Justin Mulangu of the University of Luanda: interview, Brussels, June 22, 1999.

143. Gleijeses, *Visions of Freedom*, p. 57.

144. Gleijeses. "Truth or Credibility," p. 100; various interviews.

145. Interview, Mundindi Didi Kilengo (former DRC ambassador to Angola), Kinshasa, April 14, 2008.

146. Rosa Coutinho interview, February 10, 2008.

147. Although an accord of this type was indeed signed in 1979 (see below), this hypothesis ignores the fact that, despite limited diplomatic exchanges under Nigerian auspices, no direct contact took place between the two presidents until after Shaba II. J. P. Nimy Mayidika, *Je ne renie rien. Je raconte . . .* (Paris: L'Harmattan, 2003), pp. 223–229.

148. Vindicien Kiyana to Nathanaël Mbumba, Guinea-Bissau, October 24, 1980, Mushitu Papers.
149. TNA, FCO/99/162, Cuba/Zaire Shaba Invasion, 1978, Paris embassy to FCO, May 17, 1978, item 18.
150. TNA, FCO/31/2288, Zaire Shaba Invasion, 1978, EAD "Briefing Note for Cabinet," May 17, 1978, item 85.
151. MAE DAM, Box 29, Zaire 1975–1978, "Français morts et disparus," "Assassinat de Belges," French embassy Kinshasa to DAM, May 15, 1978.
152. MAE DAM, Box 29 Zaire 1975–1978, "Situation of the Foreigners in Kolwezi," French embassy in Kinshasa to DAM, May 16, 1978. Although these reports may be accurate, it is important to question the sources for the situation in Kolwezi being received by Western embassies in Kinshasa.
153. MAE DAM, Box 29, Zaire 1975–1978, "Français morts et disparus," "Cooperants militaires," French embassy, Kinshasa to DAM, May 16, 1978.
154. Zaire, Département de la Défense Nationale de la Sécurité du Territoire et des Anciens Combattants, *Le bataillon Héros: L'exploit du 311me bataillon para au cours de la deuxième guerre du Shaba* (Kinshasa: Cible, 1978).
155. CIA FOIA ERR, "Zaire: Military Situation Report."
156. "Paris Troops Find Bodies of 44 Europeans in Zaire," *International Herald Tribune*, May 20, 1978.
157. BAA CDH, Shaba II, "Attitude des rebelles à Kolwezi entre le 13 et le 19 mai 1978," note no. 335/78, May 22, 1978. This is also stated in H. J. G. Depoorter, *Rapport sur les événements à Kolwezi et au Shaba dans la période mai–juillet 1978* (Brussels: ANPCV, 2005), p. 41: the author led the Belgian military operation in Kolwezi, which had, however, not arrived there when the massacre took place.
158. Odom, *Shaba II*, pp. 118–119.
159. P. Yambuya, *Zaïre: L'abattoir; Un pilote de Mobutu parle* (Anvers: EPO, 1991), p. 46.
160. C. Lourtie, "Kolwezi mai 1978: La seconde guerre du Shaba," *Tam Tam Ommegang* 31 (2006): 28.
161. Ibid., p. 23.
162. Depoorter, *Rapport sur les événements*, p. 23.
163. JCL, National Security Affairs 6, Brzezinski Material, Box 87, Zaire, 1979–1981, The White House, memo, 4:35 a.m., May 18, 1978.
164. TNA, FCO/99/162, Cuba/Zaire Shaba Invasion, 1978, FCO to Lusaka embassy, May 19, 1978, item 21.
165. Gen. Y. Gras, "L'opération Kolwezi," *Mondes et Cultures* 45, no. 4 (November 1985): 691–702.
166. Confirmed in numerous testimonies and in a Belgian military intelligence report: BAA CDH, Shaba II, "Ops Red Bean," R. Zaïre/36.210, May 24, 1978, Appendix 4.
167. R. Rousseau, *Légion je t'accuse! La face cachée de Kolwezi* (La Harmoie: Rexy, 2006), pp. 135–141. For the wider issue of Franco-Belgian rivalry during Shaba II, see S. Brabant, "La coopération belgo-française durant les événements de Kolwezi 1978" (seminar presentation, École Royale Militaire, Brussels, May 1982); and S. Brabant, "Aspects politiques et diplomatiques de l'intervention de Kolwezi en 1978: Réalité—information" (École Royale Militaire, Brussels, 1983–1984).
168. TNA, FCO/31/2289, Zaire Shaba Invasion, 1978, Brussels embassy to FCO, "Shaba: French Military Action," May 19, 1978, item 163.
169. TNA, FCO/31/2289, Zaire Shaba Invasion, 1978, Paris embassy (Henderson) to FCO, "Shaba," May 19, 1978, item 172.

170. TNA, FCO/31/2289, Zaire Shaba Invasion, 1978, Kinshasa embassy to FCO, May 20, 1978, item 183.

171. TNA, FCO/99/162, Cuba/Zaire Shaba Invasion, 1978, Parliamentary Statement briefing, May 22, 1978, item 27.

172. TNA, FCO/99/162, Cuba/Zaire Shaba Invasion, 1978, FCO to Lusaka embassy, May 19, 1978, item 21.

173. *Le Monde*, June 18, 1978, quoted in Gleijeses, "Truth or Credibility," p. 86. See also Yakemtchouk, "Les deux guerres du Shaba," pp. 605–608.

174. "No Cubans in Zaire Raid," *International Herald Tribune*, May 20, 1978; Gleijeses, "Truth or Credibility," p. 86; Yakemtchouk, "Les deux guerres du Shaba."

175. *Granma*, June 19, 1978, quoted in Gleijeses, "Truth or Credibility," p. 91.

176. TNA, FCO/99/162, Cuba/Zaire Shaba Invasion, 1978, Luanda embassy to FCO, June 13, 1978, item 41.

177. "Countering the Communists," *Time* magazine, June 5, 1978.

178. Gleijeses, "Truth or Credibility," p. 91.

179. For example, a CIA report compiled in the wake of Shaba II asserted that "the Katangans were not a significant threat until 1975 when they were reequipped and reorganized by Cuban advisers" and that the Cubans "had established guerrilla training bases for the ex-Katangan gendarmes in the Angolan towns of Cozambo [sic], Luacano, Nova Chaves, Chicapa, Mariege, Chiluage": CIA FOIA ERR, "Evidence of Cuban Involvement in Training FNLC Forces," May 28, 1978, ESDN: CIA-RDP81B00401R002100020010-9.

180. JCL, "Cuban Involvement with the Shaba Problem," CIA Director Adm. Stansfield Turner to Jody Powell (Presidential Press Secretary), May 24, 1978.

181. JCL, Rick Inderfurth to Zbigniew Brzezinski, "Cuban Assistance to the Katangese," June 2, 1978.

182. For example, Irung a Wan, interview, Kinshasa, April 19, 2007.

183. JCL, Memorandum of Conversation, Department of Commerce, Industry and Trade Administration, May 30, 1978, p. 1.

184. Gleijeses, "Truth or Credibility," pp. 87–90.

185. TNA, FCO/31/2291, Zaire Shaba Invasion, 1978, British embassy Lusaka to FCO, "Rebel Retreat through North West Zambia," May 23, 1978, item 342.

186. MAE DAM, Box 29, Zaire 1975–1978, "Français morts et disparus," French embassy Lusaka to DAM, "Otages du Shaba," May 25, 1978. As the title of this document suggests, the French believed that some of their nationals were being held hostage by the FLNC. It became clear some weeks later, following the interrogation of returned FLNC fighters by Angolan and Cuban authorities, that no hostages were being held. It is possible that FLNC claims to be holding hostages may have been a bluff to prevent hot pursuit by their enemies.

187. TNA, FCO/31/2291, Zaire Shaba Invasion, 1978, British embassy Lusaka to FCO, "Rebel Retreat through North West Zambia," May 23, 1978, item 342.

188. MAE DAM, Box 24, Zaire 1975–1978, "Forces interafricaines, mai–decembre 1978," "Shaba," French embassy in Lusaka to DAM, May 22, 1978.

189. TNA, FCO/31/2291, Zaire Shaba Invasion, 1978, British embassy Lusaka to FCO, "North West Zambia," May 24, 1978, item 356.

190. MAE DAM, Box 29, Zaire 1975–1978, "Français morts et disparus," "Shaba," French embassy in Luanda to DAM, June 13, 1978; editorial, *Times of Zambia* (Lusaka), May 27, 1978.

191. TNA, FCO/31/2292, Zaire Shaba Invasion, 1978, British embassy Lusaka to FCO, "Shaba," May 26, 1978, item 415.

192. CIA FOIA ERR, "Chronology of FNLC Planning." This document makes the basic error of referring to the Lunda as the "Luanda" people throughout.
193. Belgian intelligence did, however, continue to identify the threat posed by "Mufu's troops" operating inside Zambia for some time: see, for example, BAA SGR, État-Major Général, note pour M. le Ministre de la Défense Nationale sur coopération technique militaire belge au Zaïre, May 3, 1979, pp. 3–4; telex no. 219, August 24, 1979.
194. JCL, untitled telex report, White House Situation Room, May 22, 1978.
195. MAE DAM, Box 24, Zaire 1975–1978, "Situation militaire, octobre-1977–novembre 1978," "Situation au Shaba," French embassy Kinshasa to DAM, June 1, 1978.
196. TNA, FCO/99/162, Cuba/Zaire Shaba Invasion, 1978, A. G. Munro (EAD), June 20, 1978, "Zaire: After the Shaba Invasion," item 40.
197. Mobutu's ability to make a political virtue of his vulnerability, "to transform the very weakness of Zaire into an asset for the survival of his regime," was identified by Young and Turner, *Rise and Decline*, pp. 389–395.
198. JCL, Zbigniew Brzezinski collection, Special Coordination Committee (SCC) meetings, Box 28, Zbigniew Brzezinski to the President, "Next Steps to Zaire," May 26, 1978, pp. 1–2.
199. CIA FOIA ERR, "Africa Review," September 15, 1978, ESDN: CIA-RDP79T00912 A002700010014-5, p. 23.
200. Information on the PAF can be found in MAE DAM, Box 24, Zaire 1975–1978, "Forces interafricaines, mai-decembre 1978."
201. MAE DAM, Box 16, Zaire 1975–1978, "Le Zaïre après Kolwezi," September 13, 1978, p. 1.
202. George, *Cuban Intervention in Angola*, p. 136. The Cassinga raid of May 4, 1978, in which the South African military launched a devastating air raid on a military base and refugee camp controlled by the South West Africa People's Organization (SWAPO), led to claims by the Angolan authorities that 600 unarmed refugees had been killed: G. Baines, "The Battle for Cassinga: Conflicting Narratives and Contested Meanings," unpublished paper, December 2007, http://eprints.ru.ac.za/946/1/baines_Cassinga.pdf (accessed December 1, 2013).
203. Agence Zaire Presse (AZAP), "Angola-Zaïre: Les retrouvailles," Kinshasa, August 19, 1978, p. 14.
204. Symba interview, June 1–5, 2008.
205. R. Schmidt, "Zaïre after the 1978 Shaba Crisis," *Aussenpolitik* 30, no. 1 (1979): 92.
206. MAE DAM, Box 24.3, Refugies Zairois en Angola, "Refugies zaïrois civils et militaires," French embassy Luanda, September 1, 1978, p. 2.
207. Amnesty International, *Les violations des droits de l'homme au Zaïre* (London, 1980), p. 69.
208. MAE DAM, Box 21.2, Zaire 1975–1978, "Menaces sur Le Shaba," Première Ministre, Secrétariat Général de la Défense Nationale, Groupe Permanent d'Évaluation de Situations, December 18 1978, p. 1.

7. Disarmament and Division, 1979–1996

1. UNHCR, 100 ANG ZRE, Fonds II, Series 2, Box 45, Cable, "Sur reinstallation refugies," January 2, 1980.
2. UNHCR, 100 ANG ZRE, Fonds Subfonds 11, Series 3, Onésimo Silveira to UNHCR Headquarters, "Mission of Representative to Geneva", January 21–23, 1988, pp. 3–4.
3. UNHCR documents for this period underline the difficult living circumstances for the refugees and their lack of means of subsistence. Evidence for this is provided in letters sent to UNHCR by representatives of the refugees: see, for example, UNHCR, 100 ANG ZRE, Fonds II,

Series 2, Box 45, letter and documentation from Jean-Beauvin Kalenga, "Pour les réfugiés zaïrois du F.L.N.C.," June 19, 1980 (hereafter Kalenga, "Pour les réfugiés zaïrois").

4. UNHCR, 100 ANG ZRE, Fonds II, Series 2, Box 44, "Transfert des réfugiés zaïrois vers les sites d'installation," January 18, 1978; letter, Nicolas Bwakira, UNHCR delegate, to Maria de Assunção Vahekeni, Angolan Secretary of State for Social Affairs, January 24, 1978; and "Transfert des réfugiés zaïrois," February 16, 1978.

5. UNHCR, 100 ANG ZRE, Fonds II, Series 2, Box 45, report, "'Programme zaïrois, mission à Nambwangongo," January 3, 1980.

6. UNHCR, 100 ANG ZRE Fonds Subfonds 11, Series 3, Memorandum, Carlos Rodriguez to UNHCR Headquarters, "Situation of Zairian Refugees in Angola," September 3, 1986. This memorandum suggests a likely opposition between the Ministry of Social Affairs, which favored return, and the Angolan army (FAA), which opposed it.

7. *Times of Zambia* (Lusaka), April 16, 1982; M. Larmer (ed.), *The Musakanya Papers: The Autobiographical Writings of Valentine Musakanya* (Lusaka: Lembani Trust, 2010), 61.

8. See G. Y. Mumba, *The 1980 Coup: Tribulations of the One-Party State in Zambia* (Lusaka: UNZA Press, 2012). Interviews, Deogratias Symba, Kitwe, August 4, 2005, and Lubumbashi, June 1–5, 2008.

9. Larmer, *Musakanya Papers*, p. 61, fn8.

10. *Times of Zambia* (Lusaka), January 21, 1983.

11. Interview, François Kapend, Kinshasa, April 25, 2007; letter, Nathanaël Mbumba to Henri Mukachung, April 4, 1991, Mushitu Papers.

12. Interview, Colonel Vincent de Paul Nguz, Kinshasa, April 26, 2007.

13. Mbumba "Naissance du FLNC," Ailleurs au Congo, May 13, 1981, p. 16: Mushitu Papers.

14. Interview, Colonel Yav Nasser, Brussels, April 4, 2007.

15. "Exil historique des ex-gendarmes katangais 1963–1992" (copy in authors' possession). The name FAPC mirrored that of the MPLA's armed wing during the liberation struggle, the Armed Forces for the Liberation of Angola (FAPLA).

16. Kalenga was a member of the so-called Bataillon Kasongo Niembo serving under the pro-Tshombe Luba paramount chief in Kamina in 1960–1963.

17. Kalenga, "Pour les réfugiés zaïrois."

18. Report of the meeting between Zairian military authorities and FLNC representatives, July 23, 1980, Mushitu Papers.

19. Kalenga, "Pour les réfugiés zaïrois."

20. FCL founding documents ("Stockholm act"); minutes of meeting of FCL political and military leaders, Brussels, February 7, 1982; Front Congolais de Libération, Statutes, 1982, Mushitu Papers.

21. Article 3 of the FCD Charter, copy in authors' possession, Mushitu Papers.

22. M. G. Schatzberg, "Beyond Mobutu: Kabila and the Congo," *Journal of Democracy* 8, no. 4 (1997): 70–84; Kennes, *Essai biographique sur Laurent Désiré Kabila*, pp. 275–278.

23. Minutes, Réunion du Bureau Politique du FCL, April 22, 1986, Mushitu Papers.

24. For Kalenga's death: letter, Denis Kisunka to Justin Mushitu, March 4, 1983 and letter, Stéphane Lubange to Nguz Karl I Bond, March 10, 1983, both Mushitu Papers. Interview, David Kayombo, Brussels, May 7, 1997.

25. Letter, Daniel Kamboyi to Justin Mushitu, Luanda, n.d., but received May 24, 1985, Mushitu Papers.

26. Letter from Nguza Karl I Bond and decision no. 004/83/Com Sup/FAPAC, April 29, 1983, Mushitu Papers.

27. A UNHCR document from this period suggests that Angola was angered that Kasongo had given information to Mushitu about a UNITA operation: UNHCR, ANG ZRE Subfonds 11 Series 3, Rapport de Mission, "Visite du camp de Mawa," July 24, 1985.
28. It is reported that, believing they would follow Nguz home to Zaire, FAPAC soldiers shouted, "Down with Socialism" or "Down with MPLA": ibid.
29. "Compte rendu de la réunion tenue entre le Citoyen Ambassadeur de la République du Zaïre en Angola et les responsables de la haute direction militaire des FAPAC," July 24, 1985; "Procès verbal de deux séances de travail," July 23–24, 1985, Mushitu papers.
30. Various interviews, including those with Justin Mushitu.
31. UNCHR, 100 ANG ZRE Fonds Subfonds 11, Series 3, UNHCR Kinshasa to UNHCR Geneva, telegram, November 21, 1986; UNHCR Geneva to UNHCR Luanda, telegram, November 24, 1986.
32. UNHCR, 610 ANG ZRE Subfonds 11, Series 3, Special Protection Problems Zairian Refugees, vol. B: UNHCR Luanda to UNHCR Geneva, December 22, 1987; Acting Regional Representative Heikki Keto, Note for the File, "Return to Angola of Zairian Repatriants on 21.12.1987," December 22, 1987.
33. UNHCR, 100 ANG ZRE, Fonds Subfonds 11, Series 3, letter, Kasongo to Secretary of State for Social Affairs, June 22, 1991.
34. UNHCR, 100 ANG ZRE, Fonds Subfonds 11, Series 3, Cable (ref.: 2013-07-05-15-15-01), February 20, 1990. An equivalent operation was organized for some of the Angolan refugees in Zaire.
35. Interview, former Zairian diplomat Nsola Koko, Kinshasa, January 25, 2013; written response to questions, Jean-Pierre Musasa, December 12, 2012.
36. Acte Constitutif du Conseil National de la Résistance, January 12, 1988, Mayele Papers.
37. Musasa, written response to questions, December 12, 2012.
38. S. L. Weigert, *Angola: A Modern Military History* (New York: Palgrave Macmillan, 2011), pp. 74–75.
39. UNHCR, 100 ANG ZRE, Fonds Subfonds 11, Series 3, cable, UNHCR Luanda, January 14, 1988; Colonel Vincent de Paul Nguz, research note, "Remise des armes," 2012. Martin Mukalayi, however, claims that the MCS group was never disarmed: interview, Kinshasa, September 15, 2004.
40. Colonel Vincent de Paul Nguz, research note, "Remise des armes," 2012.
41. Ibid.
42. República Popular de Angola, Ministério da Defensa, Seçção política do comando do sector no. 3—Kibaxe, June 7, 1989. In this document, the local FAA commander orders two companies of ex-Tigres to combat UNITA forces.
43. Curriculum vitae of Jean-Delphin Muland, dated October 3, 2002, given to authors by Muland.
44. PIDE interrogation document reports the demotion of Muland from lieutenant colonel to captain: ANTT PT-TT-PIDE-D-C-1-7477-1, "Operação Phoenix," January 21, 1970, pp. 196–198. See also ANTT PT-TT-PIDE-D-C-1-7477-1, Avelino Antonio Neves Rocha report, March 13, 1970, p. 170.
45. UNHCR, 100 ANG GEN, Salif Kagni, Rapport de Mission, Saurimo, Lunda-Sul, April 10–12, 1986.
46. Letter, Jean-Delphin Muland to Nguz Karl-I-Bond, April 12, 1983, Mayele Papers.
47. Kaloba and Mayele created an FLNC-MNC/L coalition that tried to link elements of the FLNC to remnants of the Lumumbist rebellion in East Africa.

48. Mukachung and Muland, letter from FLNC [II] leadership to European representatives of the FLNC, December 1, 1990, Mayele Papers.

49. FLNC [II], "Avant-garde révolutionnaire et bras armé du people congolais: Histoire, statuts et programme politique minimum du Front de Libération Nationale Congolais, n.d., but 1990, Mayele Papers.

50. This initiative to reestablish the FLNC triggered a furious reaction from Nathanaël Mbumba. See letter from Mbumba to Mukachung, April 4, 1991, and reply by Mukachung of April 27, 1991, in Mushitu Papers and Mayele Papers, respectively.

51. Note by Professor Justin Mulangu, June 22 1999; interview, Émile Ilunga, Brussels, May 1997.

52. Interview with one such trainee: "Risasse," Stockholm, May 16, 1998.

53. Interviews: Bayibsa Sosyo, Stockholm, August 12, 2001; Bienvenu Mwilambwe, Kinshasa, January 12, 2013.

54. Bienvenu Mwilambwe interview, Kinshasa, January 12, 2013.

55. "Lettre ouverte au Citoyen Président-Fondateur du Mouvement Populaire de la Révolution, President de la République par un Groupe de Parlementaires," Kinshasa, November 1, 1980, http://www.politique-africaine.com/numeros/pdf/003094.pdf (accessed December 13, 2013).

56. For general overviews of this period, see, for example, M. Bratton and N. van de Walle, *Democratic Experiments in Africa: Regime Transitions in Comparative Perspective* (Cambridge: Cambridge University Press, 1997); M. Cowen and L. Laakso (eds.), *Multi-party Elections in Africa* (Oxford: Oxford University Press, 2002).

57. It now appears that the number of students killed was lower than once thought.

58. A useful summary of this period is given in G. de Villers with J. Omasombo Tshonda, *Zaïre: La transition manquée (1990–1997)* (Tervuren: Institut Africain/Paris: L'Harmattan, 1997). See also C. D. Gondola, *The History of Congo* (Westport, CT: Greenwood Press, 2002), pp. 156–157.

59. De Villers, *Zaïre*, pp. 17–28.

60. Unnamed but probably the Service National d'Intelligence et de Protection (SNIP): "Aide-mémoire—Concerne: Bipartite de Sécurité Zaire-Angola," December 1990, pp. 2–3.

61. T. Bakajika Bankajikila, *Epuration ethnique en Afrique: Les "Kasaïens" (Katanga 1961–Shaba 1992)* (Paris: L'Harmattan, 1997), is one of several publications on this topic.

62. In a 1992 documentary, he explicitly named Nguz as his political chief and supreme commander. Documentary, "Ailleurs au Congo. Les orphelins du Katanga," RTBF, Brussels, 1992, by Jean-François Bastin and Jean-Michel Germys.

63. *Décision collective* no. 001/CR/FAPAC/67/08/92 and *Acte d'Investiture* no. 002/CR/FAPAC/67/08/92, both August 24, 1992, Mushitu Papers.

64. General Kamboyi discussed the accusations against Kasongo in a written intelligence report, entitled "Confidential information": "This man [Kasongo] has for a long time received money from an agent originating in the UDPS.... This is one reason that he ignores that, although we have reached out to work with them [UDPS] that this did not mean to say that we cease to be Katangese any more, we are foremost Katangese and then Zairian, then how does he wish us to rally to a party that does not share a history with us..." Bulletin, Kamboyi to Nguz, n.d. but 1992, Jean-François Bastin Papers.

65. Justin Mushitu, who had become UFERI representative in Stockholm, sent a large number of UFERI membership cards to the FAPAC camp in Viana: Mushitu interview, Stockholm, June 19, 2011.

66. This alleged event took place in 1990 but was reported in *Mukuba* (Lubumbashi), October 22, 1994.

67. Interviews: General Mwepu Mukanda, Kinshasa, July 13, 2008, and Major Robert Yav, Lubumbashi, January 15, 2012.

68. Republic of Zaire, Shaba Region, Division Spéciale Commandos-Tigres, General Staff "Tigres" Lubumbashi, "Effectif de recensement pour les combattants de la ville de Lubumbashi et ses environs," September 1993; Republic of Zaire, Shaba Region, Division Spéciale Commandos-Tigres, Colonel Muchail Ntambu Rindachi, Chief of Permanent Secretariat for the Shaba II and III Battalions, "Les Ex-Gendarmes Katangais et Tigres," April 12, 1996, both in Muchaila Papers. The irony of a section of the Mobutu-era Garde Civile named after the FLNC's most successful action should not go unnoticed.

69. "Le Général Mwepu Mukanda des Tigres a été arrêté, *Mukuba* (Lubumbashi), May 6, 1992; interview, General Mwepu Mukanda, July 13, 2008.

70. Indeed, some of these ex-gendarmes participated in the Moba I attacks of November 1984, led by Laurent Kabila's PRP and Alphonse Kalabe, a secessionist political leader: Kennes, *Essai biographique sur Laurent Désiré Kabila*, pp. 284–290.

71. Interviews: General Mwepu Mukanda, July 13, 2008, and General Joseph Muchaila, Kinshasa, April 26, 2007. See also Papers of General Joseph Muchaila (hereafter Muchaila Papers).

72. Republic of Zaire, Garde Civile, 2nd Detachment Regional General Staff Command, Minutes of meeting, "Sanctionnant l'harmonisation des effectifs et grades des ex-gd et tigres," Lubumbashi, August 4, 1994, Muchaila Papers.

73. Zaire, intelligence service report, "Rapport à 05/47," August 10, 1993, copy in authors' possession.

74. Division Spéciale Commando-Tigres, Commission Directrice pour le Recensement des Commandos-Tigres Lubumbashi, letter to Marshall Mobutu, October 9, 1993, Muchaila Papers. Interviews: General Mwepu Mukanda, July 13, 2008; General Joseph Muchaila, Kinshasa, April 26, 2007; Jean-Pierre Musasa, Kinshasa, January 19, 2013.

75. Interviews: Irung a Wan, Kinshasa, April 19, 2007; Émile Ilunga, Brussels, May 1997.

76. "26 ex-gendarmes katangais arrêtés à Dilolo," *Mukuba* (Lubumbashi), April 18, 1992. The reasons for this failure are not clear. One version says that the number of men controlled by Mashiku was so small that they were only able to send a group of twenty-six. Another version says that Émile Ilunga used most of the funds for other purposes: interview, Martin Mukalayi, September 15, 2004.

77. Papers of Johan Cools (hereafter Cools Papers); interview, Irung a Wan, Kinshasa, October 20, 2011.

78. Republique d'Angola, État-Major Général du Commando Spécial du 24me Régiment, "Mandat de représentation," March 25, 1996, in which the commanders of the 24th Regiment, acting as the CNR, mandate Émile Ilunga to represent the CNR: Cools Papers.

79. Letter, Mbumba to Angolan president Eduardo dos Santos, October 24, 1989, Mushitu Papers.

80. "Le lieutenant Mbumba rentre au Zaïre," *La Libre Belgique* (Brussels), August 8, 1990; "Mbumba Nathanaël doit être traduit en justice," *Elima* (Kinshasa), October 31–November 1, 1990.

81. Service National d'Intelligence et Protection (SNIP), "Aide-mémoire," p. 13.

82. The Commission for Defense, Security, and Civil Protection of the Sovereign National Conference discussed the various irregular armed forces in Zaire. The Commission on Assassinations and Human Rights Violations interrogated Mbumba for human rights violations allegedly committed during Shaba I. The FAZ troops were found responsible for serious human rights violations during Shaba II. Republic of Zaire, Conférence Nationale Souveraine, Commission Défense, Sécurité et Protection Civile, *Rapport de la Commission* (1992), pp. 43–48;

Commission des Assassinats et des Violations des Droits de l'Homme, *Rapport de la Commission*, part 2, pp. 93–98.

83. Interview, Delphin Kapaya, Kinshasa, May 9, 2013.

84. "Le général Mbumb Nathanael exclut le colonel Songolo du FLNC/Z," *La Conscience* (Kinshasa), no. 147 (January 25–26, 1993); "Mbumb Nathanael chassé du FLNC," *UMOJA* (Kinshasa), June 1, 1993; "Si le FLNC etait conté . . . ," *L'Observateur* (Kinshasa), no. 56 (July 9, 1993).

85. The Bicesse agreements included the creation of an integrated national Angolan army. According to paragraph VI, A 2c of the Estoril Protocol, the national army could include only Angolan citizens: reproduced in P. Pezarat Correia, *Angola: Do Alvor a Lusaka* (Lisbon: Hugin, 1996), pp. 285, 290.

86. For a useful summary of the military clashes that followed, see Weigert, *Angola*, pp. 111–119.

87. Ibid., p. 113.

88. Report, Colonel Vincent de Paul Nguz, "L'aide que les Tigres ont amené en 1975 au MPLA avant l'arrivée des Cubains et les endroits où les Tigres ont combattu pour le MPLA après l'accord de Cosa," 2013.

89. FAA, "Indicações do estado maior general sobre as tropas especiais," May 13, 1993, Papers of Symphorien Kyungu.

90. Directiva no. 0003/CEME/93 sobre as tropas especiais "Tigres," June 19, 1993, Papers of Nickel Rumb (hereafter Nickel Rumb Papers).

91. FAA, Cabinet of the Chief of the General Staff, "Sobre a entrada em vigor das normas para a formação do 24° regimento," Luanda, August 4, 1993, Nickel Rumb Papers.

92. As a brigade theoretically includes 3,125 soldiers, this would put the strength of the ex-Tigres at the highly unlikely figure of 15,625 soldiers. In Lunda Norte, the commander in Nzaji (Dundo) was Faustin Munene, the future chief of staff of the Forces Armées de la République Démocratique du Congo (FARDC). Munene, himself from Bandundu, was a latecomer among the ex-Tigres and does not seem to have been involved in political maneuvering. He, however, reportedly cooperated with Jean-Delphin Muland in diamond trading during this period.

93. Weigert, *Angola*, p. 115.

94. "Relatório da reunião com as forças Katangueses," September 3, 1993, Papers of Élie Kapend (hereafter Kapend Papers).

95. Internal document of the ex-Tigres, May 18, 1993, copy in authors' possession.

96. Weigert, *Angola*, p. 126.

97. Interviews: Jérôme Nawej, Kinshasa, June 23, 2012; Irung a Wan, Kinshasa, August 20, 2011. Others contend that the Mwaant Yav's visit was also meant to confirm his authority over the Lunda in Angola: interview, Symphorien Kyungu, Kinshasa, January 21, 2012. This finds some support in the fact that the Mwant Yav's visit was heavily publicized inside Angola.

98. "Décisions découlant de divers entretiens avec les Congolais vivant en exil," signed by Mwaant Yav Kawel, Luanda, January 29, 1994, Kapend Papers.

99. Interview, Pascal Kapend, Lubumbashi, August 17, 2008.

8. The Overthrow of Mobutu and After, 1996–2015

1. The best analyses of the Congo wars are R. Lemarchand, *The Dynamics of Violence in Central Africa* (Philadelphia: University of Pennsylvania Press, 2009); F. Reyntjens, *The Great African War: Congo and Regional Politics, 1996–2006* (Cambridge: Cambridge University Press, 2009); and Prunier, *Africa's World War*.

2. The basis of qualification for Zairian citizenship had been a major issue at the Sovereign National Conference (see chapter 7), an issue addressed by the subsequent Vangu Commission. The Vangu Commission report suggested in 1994 the removal from government positions of "Rwandan and Burundian refugees and immigrants." This was based on its interpretation that Tutsi were not Zairian citizens under the 1981 nationality law, which declared that Zairian nationality depended on one's mother or father being of one of the tribes living in Congolese territory in 1885. A useful summary is provided in Manby, *Struggles for Citizenship in Africa*, pp. 66–80.

3. Reyntjens, *Great African War*, pp. 54–55.

4. Information provided by Belgian military intelligence sources.

5. Reyntjens, *Great African War*, p. 62.

6. Ibid., p. 63.

7. Professor Mulangu, written response to authors, June 22, 1999. This general account of events is supported by the summary in Reyntjens, *Great African War*, p. 63. Another version claims the participation of Irung a Wan (of the FLNC) rather than Kafund (of FAPAC). According to one report, other participants included General Cirilo de Sa "Ita" and Brigadier Ngueti. FLNC, record of conversation with General Gilbert Kafund, Luanda, June 6, 1998, Élie Kapend Papers.

8. Interviews: Colonel Vincent de Paul Nguz, Kinshasa, April 11, 2009; Colonel Yav Nasser, Brussels, April 4, 2007; General Pascal Kapend, Lubumbashi, September 18, 2005.

9. Interview, Irung a Wan, Kinshasa, April 19, 2007.

10. Reyntjens, *Great African War*, p. 63.

11. Prunier, *Africa's World War*, p. 131.

12. Reyntjens, *Great African War*, pp. 63–65.

13. T. Turner, "Angola's Role in the Congo War," in J. F. Clark (ed.), *The African Stakes of the Congo War* (New York: Palgrave Macmillan, 2002), p. 82.

14. *Washington Post*, March 21, 1997, cited by Turner, "Angola's Role," p. 82.

15. Prunier, *Africa's World War*, p. 131.

16. Nickel Rumb, interview, Kinshasa, August 23, 2013. The rivalry between Rwandan and Katangese forces is attested to by interviewees, especially Jean-Delphin Muland, Kinshasa, September 12, 2006.

17. Relevant Balubakat leaders include Séverin Kabwe, Jeanson Umba, and Prosper Mwamba Ilunga; the latter group includes Yerodia, Tchamlesso, and Albert Kisonga.

18. Kyungu was perceived as such by the Tigres, who considered Nguz Karl I Bond as the new Tshombe and Kyungu as the new Kasongo Niembo: interview, Pascal Kapend, August 14, 2005.

19. This office, established to investigate the acquisition of wealth by members of the Mobutu regime by fraudulent means, actually enabled the transfer of some of those goods to members of the new regime.

20. It should be noted that this reluctance, at least during the 1997–1998 period, probably reflected tension between the Rwandans and the ex-Tigres: the repression and nonappointment of ex-Tigres were most probably due to the actions of the RPF military leadership; interview, Jean-Delphin Muland, Kinshasa, September 12, 2006.

21. E. Kennes, "The Mining Sector in Congo: The Victim or the Orphan of Globalisation?," in S. Marysse and F. Reyntjens (eds.), *The Political Economy of the Great Lakes Region of Africa: The Pitfalls of Enforced Democracy and Globalization* (Basingstoke: Palgrave Macmillan, 2005), pp. 152–189; J. Hönke, "Extractive Orders: Transnational Mining Companies in the Nineteenth and Twenty-First Centuries in the Central African Copperbelt," in. R. Southall

and H. Melber (eds.), *A New Scramble for Africa? Imperialism, Investment and Development* (Durban: University of KwaZulu-Natal Press, 2009), p. 281.

22. L. Nsanda Buleli, "La bataille de Kindu," *Cahiers Africains* 60 (2003): 77–116.

23. Anonymized interview sources.

24. Weigert (*Angola*, p. 126) refers to diamond trading between FAA and UNITA officers in the mid-1990s and to a 2001 report by the Angolan defense minister describing the involvement in the illegal diamond trade by high-ranking FAA officers (p. 163); see also R. Marques, *Diamantes de sangue* (Lisbon: Ediçoes Tinta-da-China, 2011). For Kapend, see "Monsieur Kapend Élie Kanyimbu Président du FLNC: Notes biographiques," 1998, Kapend Papers.

25. "Déclaration du FLNC sur la nécessité de sa réorganisation politique dans le cadre de la conjoncture nationale post-Mobutu," Luanda, September 22, 1997, Kapend Papers; interview, Henri Mukachung, Kinshasa, August 27, 2013.

26. Weigert, *Angola*, p. 130.

27. Ibid., pp. 140, 146. The Angolan regime's position seemed to be weakened by sending the best Katangese troops to the DRC, while the weaker ones left in Angola struggled to resist UNITA: interview, Nickel Rumb, Kinshasa, August 23, 2013.

28. Letter from Colonel Frédéric Ngongo on behalf of the "Foreign Congolese troops" in Negage, Uíge Province, October 6, 2004, copy in authors' possession.

29. Copies of the minutes of these negotiations are in the authors' possession. Reference is made therein to a delegation headed by the ex-Tigres Faustin Munene and Daniel Kamboyi, and another led by one Bilukidi Mvula.

30. FLNC, conversation with General Gilbert Kafund, Luanda, June 6, 1998, Kapend Papers.

31. FLNC, audience with Paulo Jorge, secretary of the Political Bureau and Foreign Affairs/MPLA, September 3, 1998, Kapend Papers. The mention of the "polemics of the 1960s" is a reference to the historic opposition between Lunda and Lubakat.

32. See FLNC, meeting of all Katangese factions in the mother movement FLNC under the leadership of Élie Kapend, Luanda, August 12, 1998, Kapend Papers.

33. FLNC, Election of FLNC President, June 5, 1999, Kapend Papers.

34. Letter, Élie Kapend to the Angolan authorities, February 8, 2000, Kapend Papers. According to this document, Kapend still considered himself the leader of the Congolese refugee community in Angola, whose return to the DRC he would direct.

35. The figure of 800 is provided by Pascal Kapend: interview, Lubumbashi, August 14, 2005.

36. Interview, Douglas Tefnin, Belgian military attaché to Luanda, Namur, August 31, 2007; note by Van Troyen, Belgian ambassador to Angola, "De tijgers in de Angolees-Congolese context," February 15, 2005.

37. Hönke, "Extractive Orders," p. 281.

38. Ibid., p. 287; E. Kennes, "Le secteur minier au Congo—'Déconnexion' et descente aux enfers," in F. Reyntjens and S. Marysse (eds.), *L'Afrique des Grands Lacs: Annuaire 1999–2000* (Paris: L'Harmattan, 2000), pp. 299–342.

39. Hönke, "Extractive Orders," p. 283.

40. "China to Seal $9bn DR Congo Deal," *BBC News*, April 14, 2008, http://news.bbc.co.uk/1/hi/programmes/newsnight/7343060.stm (accessed April 28, 2012). For recent assessments of the Sicomines deal, see J. Jansson, "The Sicomines Agreement Revisited: Prudent Chinese Banks and Risk-Taking Chinese Companies," *Review of African Political Economy* 40, no. 135 (2013): 152–162; and D. Curtis, "China and the Insecurity of Development in the Democratic Republic of the Congo (DRC)," *International Peacekeeping* 20, no. 5 (2013): 551–569.

41. "New Katanga Governor Deports Controversial Businessperson," *Mining Weekly* (South Africa), July 27, 2007, http://www.miningweekly.com/article/new-katanga-governor-deports-controversial-businessperson-2007-07-27 (accessed April 28, 2012).

42. These include Kazadi Nyembwe and Andre Kisase Ngandu.

43. The ex-Tigres were far from being the only former soldiers in such circumstances: even many former senior officials in Laurent Kabila's PRP live in poverty as of this writing. The current Congolese regime has in general shown little disposition to recompense the historical opponents of President Mobutu for their long period in exile or opposition.

44. Many key positions were controlled by natives from Katanga: the Central Bank governor, the governor of Katanga, the president of the Federation of Congolese Enterprises, a relative majority of ministries, the director of cabinet and several key advisers to the president, and less visible but very powerful advisers such as Katumba Mwanke or John Numbi.

45. Analysis from the military adviser to the Belgian embassy, internal report, March 10, 2006.

46. FAA, Agroupement des Forces Speciales Tigres EMG, Txamba—Lunda Nord, "Lettre á la Maison Militaire de la RDC á Kinshasa," May 6, 2004, copy in authors' possession. According to this source, a memorandum was signed between an FAA general and the DRC government envoy. See also Van Troyen, "De tijgers in de Angolees-Congolese context."

47. The provinces were Bié, Malanje, Moxico (Luena), Lunda Norte (Dundo, Txamba), Lunda Sul, Huambo, Zaire (Soyo), Huila (Jamba): FAA, Estado-Maior do Exército, Ordem de Missão no. 001/CEME/2004, January 2, 2004; FAA, Estado-Maior do Exército, "Proces verbal de fin de mission," February 6, 2004, copy in authors' possession.

48. For example: "Cafunfo: Confrontos entre populares e antigas tropas," *LAC* (Luanda), June 28, 2004, http://www.angonoticias.com/Artigos/item/1350 (accessed December 9, 2013); *Le Phare* (Kinshasa), September 8, 2004; "Polícia matou cinco ex-guerrilheiros congoleses, garimpeiros ilegais," *ANGOP* (Luanda), September 8, 2004.

49. "Cafunfo: Confrontos entre populares e antigas tropas catanguesas."

50. "Empossamento da CNE destacado pela VOA em revista de prensa," *Angonoticias*, August 19, 2005, http://www.angonoticias.com/Artigos/item/6149 (accessed December 9, 2013).

51. "Operação Brilhante detém mais de 300 mil estrangeiros ilegais," *Jornal de Angola* (Luanda), April 12, 2005, http://www.angonoticias.com/Artigos/item/4496 (accessed December 9, 2013).

52. Letter from Élie Kapend, February 20, 2006, Kapend Papers.

53. One of the authors visited Élie Kapend in this mansion on March 17, 2006, in the presence of Nathanaël Mbumba, Stany Kalala, and Sylvain Mbumba.

54. Letter from DRC interior minister Théophile Mbemba, October 4, 2004, Kapend Papers.

55. Minutes no. 02/PNF/MM/2006, on the appointment and reshuffle of the National FLNC Directorate, March 31, 2006, Kapend Papers.

56. Interviews: Douglas Tefnin, August 31, 2007; Nickel Rumb, Montreal, May 30, 2005, and Kinshasa, August 23, 2013.

57. In two interviews with Élie Kapend (Kinshasa, March 17, 2006, and March 29, 2008), he mixed apparently accurate historical elements with wildly imaginative statements.

58. Samba Kaputo may have used Kapend to ensure a return of the remaining ex-Tigres and to observe his movements and contacts.

59. Miala was initially accused of a coup d'état but was convicted in 2007 for insubordination.

60. UNHCR, Repatriation of former Congolese combatants, Kinshasa, letter from United Nations Development Programme (UNDP) DRC Country Director to UNDP Resident Representative in Luanda, April 12, 2006.

61. DRC intelligence services, report on the repatriation of the Tigres, July 2006, copy in authors' possession.

62. Declaration of Front pour la Défense du Congo, July 21, 2006, Kapend Papers.

63. Voice of the Voiceless organization, press release, July 24, 2006.

64. Kapend received his demobilization certificate on April 27, 2009, Kapend Papers.

65. At the time of our visit to the camp, the common language used by these soldiers was Lingala, the official language of the FAZ, not Swahili, used by the ex-Tigres. Visit to camp of Élie Kapend and interview, Kinshasa, September 20, 2009.

66. A painting of Élie Kapend at Joli Site bore the inscription "Delut Roi Divin" (Delut Divine King), and another was entitled *Kapend Elie Kanyimbu Sauveur du people congolais*: author's visit, August 11, 2011.

67. Letter from Interior Minister Mbuyu, November 6, 2009, Kapend Papers.

68. No official explanation has ever been offered regarding the reasons for Kapend's detention or his release. See http://latempete.info/lex-general-elie-kapend-libere-apres-plus-de-3-ans-de-detention/ (accessed May 10, 2015).

69. This is partly echoed in a letter from FLNC secretary-general Mukachung, dated June 15, 2011, in which he claimed that Kapend, while in Angola, maintained good relations with the Zairian embassy and the Zairian secret services.

70. Anonymous sources.

71. Conversations with the children of Élie Kapend, Kinshasa, August 2011; FLNC Belgium letter to APARECO, dated July 28, 2011; APARECO press release, July 30, 2011, copy in authors' possession.

72. FLNC press releases dated June 12, 19, and 21, 2011, Kapend Papers; Voice of the Voiceless, press release, June 27, 2011.

73. Estimates of the number of attackers varied from 7 to 30 ("Rapport sur les violations des droits de l'homme commises à Kilwa au mois d'octobre 2004: Supplément au périodique des Droits de l'Homme," *Azadho Katanga*, October 15, 2004) to between 50 and 100 (Anvil Mining news release, "Advice on Rebel Activity in Village of Kilwa," October 15, 2004).

74. "Rapport sur les violations des droits," *Azadho Katanga*, Ocober 15, 2004. The Mayi Mayi (a.k.a Mai-Mai) were one of the more important internal militia groups during the second Congo war and thereafter.

75. CORAK Statutes: "Préambule historique," Lubumbashi, August 4, 2008, p. 1, copy in authors' possession.

76. CORAK leaflets: "Lettre par la CORAK invitant à la libération par la force de la RFMK," July 2013; Coordination de Corak Kata Katanga, "Alerte à la communauté nationale katangaise et internationale," signed by La Coordination de Corak Kata Katanga, Tshinyama Ngonga Cingo Gedeon, Général des Armées, n.d. but received by authors in October 2013.

77. See http://radiookapi.net/actualite/2013/03/23/lubumbashi-le-calme-est-revenu-apres-la-reddition-des-miliciens-bakata-katanga-la-monusco/ (accessed March 24, 2013).

Conclusion

1. For example, Cruise O'Brien, *To Katanga and Back*; and Hoare, *Congo Mercenary*, respectively.

2. Marcum, *Angolan Revolution*, pp. 200–204.

3. H. Macmillan, "The African National Congress of South Africa in Zambia: The Culture of Exile and the Changing Relationship with Home, 1964–1990," *Journal of Southern African Studies* 35, no. 2 (2009): 303–329.

4. P. Collier and A. Hoeffler, "Greed and Grievance in Civil War," World Bank Policy Research Working Paper 2355, May 2000, http://papers.ssrn.com/sol3/papers.cfm?abstract_id=630727 (accessed January 28, 2012). See also M. R. Berdal and D. Malone (eds.), *Greed and Grievance: Economic Agendas in Civil Wars* (Boulder, CO: Lynne Rienner, 2000).

5. For an interesting discussion of this distinction and its applicability to a range of historical examples, see B. O. Collins and N. Arielli (eds.), *Transnational Soldiers* (New York: Palgrave Macmillan, 2012).

6. This is indeed one of the conclusions of P. Collier and N. Sambanis (eds.), *Understanding Civil Wars: Evidence and Analysis*, vol. 1, *Africa* (Washington, DC: World Bank, 2005). See also E. Kennes, "Democratic Republic of the Congo: The Structure of Greed, the Networks of Need," in C. J. Arnson and I. W. Zartman (eds.), *The Economics of War: The Intersection of Need, Creed, and Greed* (Baltimore: Woodrow Wilson Center Press/Johns Hopkins University Press, 2005), pp. 140–177.

7. C. Leys and J. S. Saul, *Namibia's Liberation Struggle: The Two-Edged Sword* (London: James Currey/Athens: Ohio University Press, 1995); P. Trewelha, *Inside Quatro: Uncovering the Exile History of the ANC and SWAPO* (Johannesburg: Jacana, 2009); J. Alexander, J. McGregor, and T. O. Ranger, *Violence and Memory: One Hundred Years in the "Dark Forests" of Matabeleland* (London: Heinemann, 2000).

8. For the former, see Herbst, *States and Power in Africa*.

9. See, for example, S. Lindberg, "It's Our Turn to Chop: Do Elections in Africa Feed Neo-patrimonialism Rather Than Counter-act It?," *Democratization* 10, no. 2 (2004): 121–140.

10. Warnings of this type were issued, for example, by President Kaunda in Zambia (*Times of Zambia*, May 14, 1990). Mobutu was fond of warning that the choice was between him and chaos, citing Louis XV's phrase "Après moi, le déluge": Young and Turner, *Rise and Decline*, p. 395.

11. See, for example, B. Berman, D. Eyoh, and W. Kymlicka (eds.), *Ethnicity and Democracy in Africa* (Oxford: James Currey, 2004), esp. pp. 1–22.

12. Some of this evidence can be seen in a new collection, W. Zeller and J. Tomas (eds.), *Secession in Africa* (New York: Palgrave, 2016). For a journalistic analysis of the current wave of secessionist initiatives, see "Secessionist Wave Sweeps through Africa," *Wall Street Journal*, September 17, 2013, http://online.wsj.com/news/articles/SB10001424127887323342404579079103174662692 (accessed November 17, 2013).

13. The need for rapid progress toward decentralization was endorsed by the Peace, Security and Cooperation Framework for the DRC and the Region agreed to in Addis Ababa in February 2013, http://www.peaceau.org/uploads/scanned-on-24022013-125543.pdf (accessed December 17, 2013).

14. I. Mpyana, "Is Katumbi's resignation a game changer in DRC?," October 21, 2015, http://democracyinafrica.org/is-katumbis-resignation-a-game-changer-in-drc (accessed November 18, 2015).

15. S. Katzenellenbogen, "It Didn't Happen at Berlin: Politics, Economics and Ignorance in the Setting of Africa's Colonial Boundaries," in P. Nugent and A. I. Asiwaju (eds.), *African Boundaries* (Edinburgh: Edinburgh University Press, 1996), pp. 21–34.

16. Young and Turner, *Rise and Decline*, pp. 54–73.

17. Lecocq, *Disputed Desert*.

18. See papers presented at the conference "Archives of Post-Independence Africa and Its Diaspora, Dakar," June 2–23, 2012; abstracts available at https://sites.google.com/site/archivesconferencedakar/alphabetized-links-to-papers (accessed December 13, 2013).

19. J. Pearce, "Contesting the Past in Angolan Politics" (paper presented at the Fifth European Conference on African Studies [ECAS], Lisbon, June 27–29, 2013). See also http://www.theguardian.com/commentisfree/2011/mar/08/angola-spirit-revolution (accessed September 20, 2013).

20. M. Moiloa, "A Youth Politics That Imagines Itself through the Past" (paper presented at the Fifth European Conference on African Studies [ECAS], Lisbon, June 27–29, 2013).

Bibliography

Primary Sources

State and International Official Archives

BELGIUM

Archives Institut Africain / Centre d'Études et de Documentation Africaines (CEDAF), Brussels

Acte Constitutif du Conseil National de la Résistance, January 12, 1988.

Belgian Army Archives (BAA), Centre de Documentation Historique (CDH), Evere

Service Général de Renseignements et de Sécurité (SGR), Shaba I documents
Bulletins dated September 9 and September 19, 1977.
Manuscript note for Chiefs of Staff of Defense and Foreign Affairs, March 17, 1977.
Rapport circonstancié voyage Lubumbashi-Kolwezi et retour (1 au 4 avril 1977) de Trio (B.2), R. Zaïre/33.705, April 21, 1977.
Very secret message, no. 314/206, May 2, 1977.
"Zaïre: Situation militaire au Shaba," May 24, 1977, no. 373/77.

Service Général de Renseignements et de Sécurité (SGR), Shaba II Documents
"Attitude des rebelles à Kolwezi entre le 13 et le 19 mai 1978," note no. 335/78, May 22, 1978.
"Climat de désorganisation accentuée au département de la défense nationale et à l'État-major général," note no. 325/78, April 4, 1978.
État-Major Général, note pour M. le Ministre de la Défense Nationale sur coopération technique militaire belge au Zaïre, May 3, 1979, pp. 3-4.
"Ops Red Bean," R. Zaïre/36.210, May 24, 1978, Appendix 4.
Telex no. 219, August 24, 1979.
"Zaïre-Angola-Katangese," note no. 315/78, February 23, 1978.

Belgian Foreign Affairs (BFA) Archives, Brussels

File NA 15946, Congo-ONU, January–February 1960, telegram no. 192, Belg Brazza to Brussels, February 6, 1961.

Belgian National Archives, UMHK Papers, Brussels

File 1942, Surtaxe exceptionnelle sur les dividendes, 1960–1962.

Royal Museum of Central Africa (RMCA), Tervuren
Records of Katanga embassy in Belgium.

FRANCE

Archives Diplomatiques, La Courneuve, Ministère des Affaires Etrangères, Direction des Affaires Africaines et Malgaches (MAE DAM)

Box 16, Zaire 1975–1978
Note, "Le Zaïre," April 7, 1977.
"Situation au Zaïre," May 17, 1977.
"Le Zaire," February 22, 1978.
"Zaire," March 10, 1978.
"Zaire," March 29, 1978.
"Le Zaïre âpres Kolwezi," September 13, 1978.

Box 21.2, Zaire, 1975–1978
French embassy, Kinshasa, Ambassador André Ross to MAE Louis de Guiringaud, August 9, 1978.
French embassy, Kinshasa, communique à DAM, "Prolongements diplomatiques des événements du Shaba," June 28, 1978.
"Menaces sur Le Shaba," Première Ministre, Secrétariat Général de la Défense Nationale, Groupe Permanent d'Evaluation de Situations, December 18, 1978.
"Zaïre: Perspectives après le retrait des forces françaises et belges," Annexe: Le Front National de Libération du Congo (FNLC), Premier Ministère, Secrétariat Général de la Défense Nationale, Groupe Permanent d'Evaluation de Situations, June 5, 1978.

Box 21.3, Zaire 1975–1978
United Nations press communication, Weekly review no. 20, May 19–25, 1978.

Box 24, Zaire 1975–1978
"Bulletin de situation," 767 and 786/ZAI/FA/CAD, November 4–20, 1977.
"Forces interafricaines, mai–decembre 1978," "Shaba," French embassy Lusaka to DAM, May 22, 1978.
"Situation militaire, octobre-1977–novembre 1978," "Echec d'une infiltration Katangaise," French embassy in Kinshasa to DAM, March 30, 1978.
"Situation militaire, octobre-1977–novembre 1978," "Situation au Shaba," French embassy Kinshasa to DAM, June 1, 1978.
"Situation militaire, octobre-1977–novembre 1978," "Situation au Shaba: Les évènements de 1977 et la situation au début de 1978," French embassy Kinshasa to DAM, June 1, 1978.

Box 24.3, Réfugiés Zaïrois en Angola
"Réfugiés zaïrois civils et militaires," French embassy Luanda, September 1, 1978.

Box 25.1, Aide et médiation étrangère, mars–juin 1977
"Nigeria, Résumé of a Meeting between Nigerian Foreign Minister Garba and Secretary Vance on March 21 [1977]."

Box 25.2, Réunions internationales
Mobutu to President of OAU Sir Seewoojgur Ramgoolam, April 2, 1977, reprinted in French embassy Kinshasa to DAM, April 7, 1977.
"Zaire," London COREU to all COREU, April 17, 1977, p. 2.

Box 25.4, Réactions des pays étrangers, sauf "l'Afrique"
"Belgian analysis of the Zairian situation," response, French embassy Lusaka to DAM, March 24, 1977, pp. 1–2.
"La France et Le Zaïre," French embassy Brussels to DAM, March 25, 1977, p. 2.

Box 27.2, Zaire 1975–1978, Évolution de la situation militaire, fevrier–avril 1977
"Arrestations au Shaba," French embassy in Kinshasa to DAM, June 3, 1977. "Gendarmes Katangais," French embassy in Kinshasa to DAM, November 14, 1977.

Box 29, Zaire 1975–1978, Français morts et disparus
"Assassinat de Belges," French embassy Kinshasa to DAM, May 15, 1978.
"Coopérants militaires," French embassy Kinshasa to DAM, May 16, 1978.
French embassy Lusaka to DAM, "Otages du Shaba," May 25, 1978.
"Shaba," French embassy in Luanda to DAM, June 13, 1978.
"Situation of the Foreigners in Kolwezi," French embassy Kinshasa to DAM, May 16, 1978.

Ministère des Affaires Etrangères, Centre des Archives Diplomatiques de Nantes (MAE CAD)

Box 45, Zaire 1975–1978
Ambassade Kinshasa-Shaba correspondence, 1973–1978, I-134, "Réfugiés du Shaba en Angola," French embassy Lusaka to French embassy Kinshasa, July 22, 1977.
Ambassade Kinshasa-Shaba correspondence, 1973–1978, I-134, report by French Consul in Lubumbashi, Marcel Thauvin, March 25, 1977.
Ambassade Kinshasa-Shaba correspondence, 1973–1978, I-134, "Situation militaire au Shaba," French embassy Kinshasa to DAM, August 25, 1977.

PORTUGAL

Arquivo Histórico Militar (AHM)

CCFA, 2nd Div., 2nd L, Caixa 139, no. 6, 167a, "Factos de maior realce no historial dos fiéis," 1973.
CCFA directive on the camps, April 4, 1968.
CCFAA, 2nd Div., 2nd secc, Caixa 139, no. 05, Quartel General, "Forças Auxiliares: Situação actual, sua evolução," 1974 (?).
CCFAA, Div. 2, Secc 2, Caixa 139, no. 7, Gabinete de Forças Auxiliares, "Memorando: Acção Fidelidade," Luanda, August 3, 1974.
Fundo 43, Serie 1, Caixa 839, no. 28, Elísio de Carvalho Figueiredo, "Relatório da visita efectuada aos Refugiados Zairienses (ex-Fiéis) em 4, 5 e 6 de abril 1975," April 9, 1975, pp. 3–4.
Fundo 43, Serie 3, Caixa 840, no. 30, CCPA (Secret) Capt Martins e Silva and Major Gomes de Abreu, "Estudo de Situação," April 19, 1975,

Fundo 43, Serie 4, Caixa 841, no. 33, CCPA, "Reunioes da CCPA", October 14, 1975
Governo-General de Angola, S.C.C.I.A., MU_GM_GNP_S027, Gendarmes e refugiados, "Relatório sobre a 'operação regresso,'" September 18, 1964.
MU_GM_GNP_S027, Gendarmes e refugiados, General Bobozo to ANC commander, February 2, 1964.
Relatório 22.06.1988, ref. 1438/88/C, 2nd Div., 2nd Secc, Caixa 169, no. 17, Comp. Chefe Angola.

Arquivo Nacional da Torre do Tombo (ANTT)

DGS, MSG 83/71-D inf.—2°-CI, Diligências para a recuperação de catangueses, March 3, 1971, report, February 11, 1970.
PIDE, Relatório imediato, no. 2466/67-GAB, November 21, 1967.
PIDE 178-180, report, March 3, 1971.
PIDE Del. A, L, no. 14, UI 8979, "Instruções sobre refugiados catangueses."
PIDE UI 7477, GAB-2, "Informação 11/69," June 12, 1969.
PIDE/DGS, Del. A, L no. 9, UI 8978, "Refugiados catangueses no Luso," Posto do Teixeira de Sousa, "Mapa de refugiados," January 31, 1963.
PIDE/DGS, Delegação de Angola, NP2184, Pr. Unf. 17.03.D/2m, "Polícia do Katanga."
PIDE/DGS Angola, NP 2559, Pasta 29, Comando Chefe das Forças Armadas de Angola, Gabinete Especial de Informações, "Réunião de Flechas com elementos do MPLA," October 29, 1974.
PIDE/DGS Angola, NP 2559, Pasta 29, MPLA, Estado de Angola, Comando-Chefe das Forças Armadas de Angola, Quartel-General, Relatório Diário 36/74-CI, November 19, 1974.
PIDE/DGS Angola, NP 2559, Pasta 29, MPLA, Estado de Angola, Comando-Chefe das Forças Armadas de Angola, Quartel-General, Relatório Diário 45/74-CI, November 21, 1974.
PIDE/DGS NT 7495, Proc. 7477 CI (2), Pasta 6, "Operação Tshombe."
PIDE/DGS SC CI(2) UI 7494, Processo no. 7477, Pasta 1, "Commando das Operações Especiais (COE), Frente de Libertação Nacional Congaleza."
PT-TT-PIDE-D-C-1-7477-1, Avelino Antonio Neves Rocha report, March 13, 1970.
PT-TT-PIDE-D-C-1-7477-1, DGS, MSG 182/70—D. Inf/2 (2), Acção Fidelidade, December 16, 1970.
PT-TT-PIDE-D-C-1-7477-1, letter from Thomas Tshombe, December 12, 1968.
PT-TT-PIDE-D-C-1-7477-1, "Operação Phoenix," January 21, 1970.
PT-TT-PIDE-D-C-1-7477-1, PIDE, copy of "Réveil Congolais" and related correspondence, Angola Director to Director General, August 12, 1971
PT-TT-PIDE-D-C-1-7477-1, PIDE, Directiva no. 1/68—Organisação e funcionamento dos campos de refugiados catangueses, Anexo (instruções complementares) a directiva no. 1/68, QG/RMA Luanda—GDP-36/01.
PT-TT-PIDE-D-C-1-7477-1, PIDE, Informação, 21/71-DINF/2° (2), "Vinda de Thomas Tshombe ao TN em fins de maio passado." July 21, 1971.
PT-TT-PIDE-D-C-1-7477-1, PIDE, Informação no. 11/69-GAB-2, Acção Fidelidade, June 12, 1969.
PT-TT-PIDE-D-C-1-7477-1, PIDE, Informação no. 16/78-D, Inf/2° Sec (2), Acção Fidelidade, February 11, 1970.

PT-TT-PIDE-D-C-1-7477-1, PIDE, Informação no. 318-SC/CI (2), Operação Phoenix, March 28, 1968.
PT-TT-PIDE-D-C-1-7477-1, PIDE, Relatório 11/05/1968, no. 3/68—GAB (2), Operação Phoenix, Campo de Gafaria.
PT-TT-PIDE-D-C-1-7477-1, SCCIA, "Aumento das possibilidades do FNLA (UPA-PDA)/ GRAE, Attitude da RDC e dos EUA," no. 371, Proc. 22-10-95, October 12, 1970.
PT-TT-PIDE-D-C-1-7477-3, Mwaant Yav David Tshombe to Nathanaël Mbumba, July 14, 1972.
PT-TT-PIDE-D-C-1-7477-3, Nathanaël Mbumba to Mwaant Yav David Tshombe, August 7, 1972.

25 April Documentation Centre, University of Coimbra, Espólio António Belo (A25A)

These documents are available online: http://www1.ci.uc.pt/cd25a/wikka.php?wakka=HomePage.
Comando da 2 Região Aérea, "Gabinete, Protocolo da reunião entre as delegações dos movimentos de libertação em Luanda e as autoridades portuguesas," December 3-4, 1974.
Companhia de Diamantes de Angola, "Memorando: Situação na Lunda no final de Julho de 1975."
Conselho Coordenador do Programa para Angola (CCPA), "Relação cronologica dos factos mais importantes ocorridos em Angola (ou com ela relacionados) a partir de 31 Jan 75," Luanda, November 10, 1975.
Letter from Mouvement des Réfugiés Politiques Congolais (Zaïrois) en Angola (FLNC), Camissombo, to High Commissioner in Angola, April 19, 1975.
Letter from Nathanaël Mbumba to "Raul" Kabila, May 10, 1975.
Letter from Nathanaël Mbumba to Rosa Coutinho, November 22, 1974.
Letter from Nathanaël Mbumba to Rosa Coutinho, December 26, 1974.
Letter from Nathanaël Mbumba to Jonas Savimbi, April 19, 1975.
Nakuru Accord, June 21, 1975.
Nathanaël Mbumba, speech at Chicapa, July 5, 1975.
Presidência da República, Comissão Nacional de Descolonização, "Conversações entre as delegações portuguesa e do MPLA," Argel, November 18-19, 1974.
Telegram from Diplomatic Consul of President Mobutu, Bula Mandungu to High Commissioner Rosa Coutinho, December 6, 1974.
Telex from Rosa Coutinho to Portuguese Presidency, December 24, 1974.
Text of press conference by Gen. Nathanaël Mbumba, *Ailleurs au Congo*, December 17, 1974.

UNITED KINGDOM

UK National Archives (TNA)

FCO/31/2115, Shaba Invasion, 1977
"French Assistance to Zaire," C. M. James, British embassy Paris, to P. H. R. Mansfield, FCO, April 24, 1977, item 234a.

Kinshasa embassy to FCO, April 25, 1977.
Rabat embassy to FCO, April 20, 1977, item 211; Morocco Ministry of Foreign Affairs communiqué, Rabat, April 27, 1977.

FCO/31/2116, Shaba Invasion, 1977
"Belgian Views on Zaire," R. Janvrin to P. E. Rosling, FCO, May 5, 1977, item 273.
Meeting at Luanda airport, April 17, 1977, item 261.

FCO/31/2117, Shaba Invasion, 1977
P. R. A. Mansfield (FCO) to C. M. James, Paris embassy, "French Views on Africa," May 10, 1977, item 284.

FCO/31/2287, Zaire—Shaba Invasion, 1978
A. G. Munro, "Shaba: Present Situation," May 15, 1978, item 22.

FCO/31/2288, Zaire Shaba Invasion, 1978
EAD "Briefing Note for Cabinet," May 17, 1978, item 85.

FCO/31/2289, Zaire Shaba Invasion, 1978
Brussels embassy to FCO, "Shaba: French Military Action," May 19, 1978, item 163.
Kinshasa embassy to FCO, May 20, 1978, item 183.
Paris embassy (Henderson) to FCO, "Shaba," May 19, 1978, item 172.

FCO/31/2291, Zaire Shaba Invasion, 1978
British embassy Lusaka to FCO, "North West Zambia," May 24, 1978, item 356.
British embassy Lusaka to FCO, "Rebel Retreat through North West Zambia," May 23, 1978, item 342.

FCO/31/2292, Zaire Shaba Invasion 1978
British embassy Lusaka to FCO, "Shaba," May 26, 1978, item 415.

FCO/99/162, Cuba/Zaire Shaba Invasion, 1978
British embassy Luanda to FCO, May 17, 1978.
FCO (Owen) to British embassy Kinshasa, May 18, 1978, item 12.
FCO to Lusaka embassy, May 19, 1978, item 21.
Luanda embassy to FCO, May 17, 1978, item 14.
Luanda embassy to FCO, June 13, 1978, item 41.
A. G. Munro (EAD), "Zaire: After the Shaba Invasion," June 20, 1978, item 40.
Paris embassy to FCO, May 17, 1978, item 3.
Paris embassy to FCO, May 17, 1978, item 18.
Parliamentary statement briefing, May 22, 1978, item 27.
UK embassy Washington to FCO, May 18, 1978, item 20.

FO/371/146775, Congo, 1960
UK UN Mission to FO, August 6, 1960.

FO/371/167299, Activities of Mercenaries and Ex-Gendarmes, 1963
Telegram, Lusaka to FO, August 9, 1963.

FO/371/167300, Activities of Mercenaries and Ex-Gendarmes, 1963
Elisabethville to Foreign Office, September 9, 1963.
Elisabethville to Foreign Office, September 21, 1963.

Telegram, Lusaka to Salisbury, September 5, 1963.
William Wilson, British Consulate Elisabethville to E. M. Rose, British embassy Leopoldville, August 13, 1963.

FO/371/167301, Activities of Mercenaries and Ex-Gendarmes, 1963
Telegram, Lusaka to FO, October 3, 1963.
Wilson to F. W. Morton, Leopoldville embassy, October 4, 1963.
Wilson to Morton, Leopoldville embassy, October 10, 1963.

FO/371/167302, Activities of Mercenaries and Ex-Gendarmes, 1963
"Activities of Mercenaries and Ex-Gendarmes, 1963," E. M. Rose, British embassy Leopoldville to G. E. Millard, FO, November 29, 1963.
Telegram, Lusaka to Leopoldville, November 22, 1963.

FO 371/167303, Congo: Activities of Mercenaries and Ex-Gendarmes, 1963
Elisabethville Consulate to FO, "Katanga Gendarmes," November 29, 1963.
Evelyn Hone to S. P. Whitley, Central African Office, "Katanga," November 21, 1963.

UNITED NATIONS

United Nations High Commission for Refugees (UNHCR), Geneva

100 ANG GEN
Salif Kagni, Rapport de Mission, Saurimo, Lunda-Sul, April 10–12, 1986.

100 ANG ZRE, Fonds II, Series 2, Box 44
Letter, Nicolas Bwakira, UNHCR delegate, to Maria de Assunção Vahekeni, Angolan Secretary of State for Social Affairs, January 24, 1978.
"Transfert des réfugiés zaïrois," February 16, 1978.
"Transfert des réfugiés zaïrois vers les sites d'installation," January 18, 1978.

100 ANG ZRE, Fonds II, Series 2, Box 45
Cable, "Sur réinstallation réfugiés," January 2, 1980.
Letter and documentation from Jean-Beauvin Kalenga, "Pour les réfugiés zaïrois du F.L.N.C.," June 19, 1980.
Report, "Programme zaïrois, mission à Nambwangongo," January 3, 1980.

100 ANG ZRE, Fonds Subfonds 11, Series 3
Acting Regional Representative Heikki Keto, Note for the File, "Return to Angola of Zairian Repatriants on 21.12.1987," December 22, 1987.
Cable (ref.: 2013-07-05-15-15-01), February 20, 1990.
Cable, UNHCR Luanda, January 14, 1988.
Letter, Kasongo to Coordination des Réfugiés zairois en Angola, July 6, 1991.
Letter, Kasongo to Secretary of State for Social Affairs, June 22, 1991.
Memorandum, Carlos Rodriguez to UNHCR Headquarters, "Situation of Zairian Refugees in Angola," September 3, 1986.
Rapport de Mission, "Visite du camp de Mawa," July 24, 1985.
Onésimo Silveira to UNHCR Headquarters, "Mission of Representative to Geneva," January 21–23, 1988.

Special Protection Problems Zairian Refugees, vol. B: UNHCR Luanda to UNHCR Geneva, December 22, 1987.
UNHCR Geneva to UNHCR Luanda, telegram, November 24, 1986.
UNHCR Kinshasa to UNHCR Geneva, telegram, November 21, 1986.

UNITED STATES

Central Intelligence Agency Freedom of Information Act Electronic Reading Room (FOIA ERR)

"Africa Review," September 15, 1978, Electronic Standard Document Number (hereafter ESDN) CIA-RDP79T00912A002700010014-5.
"Chronology of FNLC Planning," January 1, 1978 (but in fact written in May? 1978), ESDN CIA-RDP81B00401R002100020009-1.
"Evidence of Cuban Involvement in Training FNLC Forces," May 28, 1978, ESDN CIA-RDP81B00401R002100020010-9.
"Zaire: Military Situation Report," in "National Intelligence Daily Cable," May 17, 1978, ESDN CIA-RDP79T00975A030700010010-9.
"Zaire: New Katangan Attacks," in "National Intelligence Daily Cable," May 15, 1978, EDSN CIA-RDP79T00975A030700010006-4.

Jimmy Carter Library (JCL), Atlanta, Georgia

"Cuban Involvement with the Shaba Problem," CIA Director Adm. Stansfield Turner to Jody Powell (Presidential Press Secretary), May 24, 1978.
Memorandum of conversation, Department of Commerce, Industry and Trade Administration, May 30, 1978.
National Security Affairs 6, Brzezinski Material, Box 87, Zaire, 1979–1981, The White House, memo, 4.35 a.m., May 18, 1978.
Rick Inderfurth to Zbigniew Brzezinski, "Cuban Assistance to the Katangese," June 2, 1978.
"Secretary's Meeting with Foreign Minister Van Elslande," Secretary of State to Brzezinski, September 9, 1977.
Untitled telex report, White House Situation Room, May 22, 1978,White House Central File, CO 177, Executive, January 20, 1977–January 20, 1981, Mobutu to Carter, July 23, 1977.
Zbigniew Brzezinski collection, Special Coordination Committee (SCC) meetings, Box 28, Zbigniew Brzezinski to the President, "Next Steps to Zaire," May 26, 1978.

US State Department (USSD), College Park, Maryland

RG 59, E3111 (Bureau of African Affairs)
Box 4, File 1.11, Central Africa status report, G. Mennen Williams to the Secretary, "Status Report: Actions Being Taken to Deal with the Situation in the Congo," October 30, 1963.
Box 4, File 1.3, Adoula, 1962–1963, Adoula communication to Tshombe, March 3, 1962.

Box 4, File 1.3, Adoula, 1962–1963, Ambassador Gullion to George McGhee, "Adoula Talking Paper," November 21, 1962.
Box 4, File 1.3, Adoula, 1962–1963, "Katanga Reintegration," April 22, 1963.
Box 6, File 1.C./1.1, Correspondence with Consulate, American Consul to Elisabethville Lewis Hoffacker to Robert Eisenberg, Deputy Director Bureau of Central African Affairs, April 18, 1962.
Box 6, File 1.C./1.1, Correspondence with Consulate, Charles S. Whitehouse to Lewis Hoffacker, May 8, 1962.
Box 6, File 1.D/1, Katanga, 1961 [1963], "Main Trends in Katanga, July 1962–July 1963," June 17, 1963.
Box 6, File 1.D/1.1, The President (Tshombe), 1961 and 1963, J. Wayne Fredericks to Mr McGhee, "Tshombe's Political Orientation," July 12, 1962.
Box 6, unnumbered file, Katanga Reconciliation, 1/8–27/8/62, CIA report, Subject: "SNIE 65-62: The Katanga Integration Problem," May 15, 1962.
Box 7, File 5.2, Conferences, William Brubeck to McGeorge Bundy, "Our Congo Policy after the London Talks," May 21, 1962.
Box 7, File 5.2, Conferences, "Conversation between the Secretary of State and the Prime Minister of the Republic of the Congo, 27 July 1960," July 28, 1960.
Box 7, unnumbered file, 1960 UN Military Troops and Support, Robert Eisenberg to Governor Williams, memorandum, "Military Situation in Katanga," September 15, 1961.
Box 8, File 14.3, The Katanga Question, J. Wayne Fredericks to Robert C. Good, "Neutralizing Extremist Congo Political Elements as a Prelude to Katanga Reintegration and Political Consensus," May 7, 1962.
Box 8, File 14.4, Communism, 1960–1961, Hugh S. Cumming Jr. to the Secretary, Intelligence Note, "Prospects for Communist Inroads in the Belgian Congo under Alternative Conditions of Unity or Fragmentation," n.d. but ca. June 16, 1960.
Box 8, File 17.2, Internal Research Reports, January–June 1963, Hare to Elting, "Belgian Assistance to the Congo," February 2, 1961.

RG 59, E5235
Box 43, File, Political Affairs and Rel., Angola, Pol 26, Rebellion, Coups, Insurgency, 1964, USARMA Lisbon to ASCI DA, January 2, 1964.
Box 43, File, Political Affairs and Rel., Angola, Pol 37, Mercenaries, Pierre Laureys, 1964, G. McMurtrie Godley to US Consul General to Angola Henry Clinton Reed, February 3, 1964.
Box 43, File, Political Affairs and Rel., Angola, Pol 37, Mercenaries, Pierre Laureys, 1964, memorandum of meeting between Belgian and US officials on "Katangan gendarmes," March 11, 1964.

RG 84, E3363, Foreign Service Posts
Box 1, File, Political Affairs and Rel., Pol 2 Gen. Reports and Stat., 1963, US Consul Dean summary report, February 8, 1963.
Box 1, File, Political Affairs and Rel., Pol 7, Visits and Meetings, 1963, Elisabethville to Secstate, November 7, 1963.
Box 1, File, Political Affairs and Rel., Pol 18, 1963, Elisabethville to Washington, telegram, April 27, 1963.

Box 1, File, Political Affairs and Rel., Pol 22, 1963, Elisabethville to Secstate, telegram, January 18, 1963.
Box 2, File, Political Affairs and Rel., Pol 15-4, Administration of Govt., Elisabethville to Secstate, October 16, 1963.
Box 2, File, Political Affairs and Rel., Pol 18, Provincial, Municipal and State Government, January–June 1963, Jonathan Dean to Dept. of State, "Indication of Possible Troubles amongst Katangan African Population," February 12, 1963.
Box 2, File, Political Affairs and Rel., Pol 18, Provincial, Municipal and State Government, January–June 1963, Elisabethville to Gov. Williams, February 17, 1963.
Box 2, File, Political Affairs and Rel., Pol 18, Provincial, Municipal and State Government, January–June 1963, Elisabethville to Secstate, January 29, 1963.
Box 2, File, Political Affairs and Rel., Pol 18, Provincial, Municipal and State Government, January–June 1963, Elisabethville to Secstate, February 8, 1963.
Box 2, File, Political Affairs and Rel., Pol 27-11, Guerrilla Warfare, 1963, Secstate McNamara to Leopoldville, August 9, 1963.

Personal Papers and Other Nonarchival Primary Sources

PAPERS OF JEAN-FRANÇOIS BASTIN

Bulletin, Daniel Kamboyi to Nguz, n.d. but 1991–1992.
Bulletin, Kasongo to Nguz, n.d. but ca. 1991–1992.
État-Major Général des FAPAC, "Histoire des ex-gendarmes katangais de 1960–1992: 32 ans de maquis," Luanda (Viana), January 1992.
"Exil historique des ex-gendarmes katangais 1963–1992," n.d.

PAPERS OF JOHAN COOLS

Republic of Angola, État-Major Général du Commando Spécial du 24me Régiment, "Mandat de représentation," March 25, 1996.

PAPERS OF ÉLIE KAPEND

"Décisions découlant de divers entretiens avec les Congolais vivant en exil," signed by Mwaant Yav Kawel, Luanda, January 29, 1994.
Declaration of Front pour la Défense du Congo, July 21, 2006.
"Déclaration du FLNC sur la nécessité de sa réorganisation politique dans le cadre de la conjoncture nationale post-Mobutu," Luanda, September 22, 1997.
Document detailing history of Katangese gendarmes: "Resenha histórico de FLNC," drafted under the leadership of Élie Kapend, Luanda, September 22, 1998.
FLNC, audience with Paulo Jorge, Secretary of the Political Bureau and Foreign Affairs/MPLA, September 3, 1998.
FLNC, Election of FLNC President, June 5, 1999.
FLNC, "Mini-historique des ex-gendarmes katangais du Congo-Kinshasa," Luanda, 1998.
FLNC, record of conversation with Gen. Gilbert Kafund, Luanda, June 6, 1998.

Letter, Élie Kapend to the Angolan authorities, February 8, 2000.
Letter from Élie Kapend, February 20, 2006.
Letter from Interior Minister Mbuyu, November 6, 2009.
Minutes no. 02/PNF/MM/2006, on the appointment and reshuffle of the National FLNC Directorate, March 31, 2006.
"Monsieur Kapend Elie Kanyimbu Président du FLNC: Notes biographiques," 1998.
"Relatório da reunião com as forças Katangueses," September 3, 1993.

PAPERS OF SYMPHORIEN KYUNGU

FAA, "Indicações do Estado-Maior general sobre as tropas especiais," May 13, 1993.

PAPERS OF DANIEL MAYELE

FLNC [II], "Avant-garde révolutionnaire et bras armé du people congolais: Histoire, statuts et programme politique minimum du Front de Libération Nationale Congolais," n.d. but 1990.
Letter, Mbumba to Jean-Delphin Muland, July 13, 1987.
Letter, Nathanaël Mbumba to Jean-Delphin Muland, July 13, 1987.
Letter, Henri Mukachung to Nathanaël Mbumba, April 27, 1991.
Letter, Jean-Delphin Muland to André Kaloba, Saurimo, March 29, 1987.
Letter, Jean-Delphin Muland to Nguz Karl-I-Bond, April 12, 1983.
Letter, Omari Mulikwa, secretary of the PRP Central Committee delegation, to Daniel Mayele, Bujumbura, n.d.
Letter to Agostinho Neto, June 2, 1977, signed by Justin Mushitu and Jean-Désiré Fataki (PRP).
Mukachung and Muland, letter from FLNC [II] leadership to European representatives of the FLNC, December 1, 1990.

PAPERS OF DANIEL MONGUYA MBENGE

Monguya Mbenge, untitled document, February 1, 1976.
"Protocole d'accord entre le FLNC et le PRP relatif à la création du Conseil Suprême de Libération, " August 26, 1977.

PAPERS OF GENERAL JOSEPH MUCHAILA

Division Speciale Commando-Tigres, Commission Directrice pour le Recensement des Commandos-Tigres Lubumbashi, letter to Marshall Mobutu, October 9, 1993.
Gen. Joseph Muchaila, document, April 12, 1996.
Republic of Zaire, Civil Guard, 2nd Detachment Regional General Staff Command, Minutes of meeting, "Sanctionnant l'harmonisation des effectifs et grades des ex-gd et tigres," Lubumbashi, August 4, 1994.
Republic of Zaire, Shaba Region, Special Division Commandos-Tigres, General Staff "Tigres" Lubumbashi, "Effectif de recensement pour les combattants de la ville de Lubumbashi et ses environs," September 1993.

Republic of Zaire, Shaba Region, Special Division Commandos-Tigres, Colonel Muchail Ntambu Rindachi, Chief of Permanent Secretariat for the Shaba II and III Battalions, "Les Ex-Gendarmes Katangais et Tigres," April 12, 1996,

PAPERS OF JUSTIN MUSHITU

Acte d'Investiture no. 002/CR/FAPAC/67/08/92.
Cartel d'Union Nationale Congolais FLNC-MNC/L (Nathanaël Mbumba), "Naissance du FLNC," "Ailleurs au Congo (Guinea-Bissau)," May, 31 1981.
"Compte rendu de la réunion tenue entre le Citoyen Ambassadeur de la République du Zaïre en Angola et les responsables de la haute direction militaire des FAPAC," July 24, 1985.
Décision collective no. 001/CR/FAPAC/67/08/92.
FCL founding documents: minutes of meeting of FCL political and military leaders, Brussels, February 7, 1982; Front Congolais de Liberation, Statutes, 1982.
FLNC, Decision no. 1, 01/CAB/PDT/75), September 19, 1975.
Letter, Daniel Kamboyi to Justin Mushitu, Luanda, n.d. but received May 24, 1985.
Letter, Nathanaël Mbumba to Angolan president Eduardo dos Santos, June 11, 1983.
Letter, Nathanaël Mbumba to Angolan president Eduardo dos Santos, October 24, 1989.
Letter, Nathanaël Mbumba to Henri Mukachung, April 4, 1991.
Mbumba report on FLNC assets, 1982.
Minutes of extraordinary meeting held November 21, 1974, Chicapa, November 22, 1974.
J. Mushitu, "Le monde des méchants" (unpublished manuscript, 2003).
"Procès verbal de deux séances de travail," July 23–24, 1985.
Report of the meeting between Zairian and FAPC representatives, July 1980.
Vindicien Kiyana to Nathanaël Mbumba, Guinea-Bissau, October 24, 1980.

PAPERS OF NICKEL RUMB

Directiva no. 0003/CEME/93 sobre as tropas especiais "Tigres," June 19, 1993.
FAA, Cabinet of the Chief of the General Staff, "Sobre a entrada em vigor das normas para a formação do 24° regimento," Luanda, August 4, 1993.

PAPERS OF RÉGINE THIANGE

"Contre révolution au Zaïre," report of an interview with Deogratias Symba, May 1, 1977.

MISCELLANEOUS PRIMARY DOCUMENTS IN POSSESSION
OF OR ACCESSED BY AUTHORS

Analysis from the military adviser to the Belgian embassy, internal report, March 10, 2006.
Anvil Mining news release, "Advice on Rebel Activity in Village of Kilwa," October 15, 2004.

APARECO, press release, July 30, 2011.
Coordination de Corak Kata Katanga, "Alerte à la communauté nationale katangaise et internationale," n.d. but received by authors in October 2013.
CORAK leaflet, "Lettre par la CORAK invitant à la libération par la force de la RFMK," July 2013.
CORAK Statutes, "Préambule historique," Lubumbashi, August 4, 2008.
Curriculum vitae of Jean-Delphin Muland, October 3, 2002.
Documentary, "Ailleurs au Congo. Les orphelins du Katanga," RTBF, Brussels, 1992, by Jean-François Bastin and Jean-Michel Germys.
DRC intelligence services, report on the repatriation of the Tigres, July 2006.
FAA, Agroupement des Forces Speciales Tigres EMG, Txamba—Lunda Nord, "Lettre á la Maison Militaire de la RDC á Kinshasa," May 6, 2004.
FAA, Estado-Maior do Exército, Ordem de Missão no. 001/CEME/2004, January 2, 2004.
FAA, Estado-Maior do Exército, "Proces verbal de fin de mission," February 6, 2004.
FLNC Belgium, letter to APARECO, July 28, 2011.
FLNC II Statutes.
Letter, Jacques Michel Grafé, December 13, 2006.
Letter from Colonel Frédéric Ngongo on behalf of the "Foreign Congolese troops" in Negage, Uíge Province, October 6, 2004.
"Lettre ouverte au Citoyen Président-Fondateur du Mouvement Populaire de la Révolution, Président de la République par un Groupe de Parlementaires," Kinshasa, November 1, 1980, http://www.politique-africaine.com/numeros/pdf/003094.pdf.
C. N'Dom (on behalf of the ECP Coordination Committee), "La crise au sein du Comité extérieur du FLNC: Opportunisme et gauchisme" (Brussels, 1981).
Note by Van Troyen, Belgian Ambassador to Angola, "De tijgers in de Angolees-Congolese context," February 15, 2005.
Report, Colonel Vincent de Paul Nguz, "L'aide que les Tigres ont amené en 1975 au MPLA avant l'arrivée des Cubains et les endroits où les Tigres ont combattu pour le MPLA après l'accord de Cosa," 2013.
Service National d'Intelligence et de Protection (SNIP): "Aide-mémoire—Concerne: Bipartite de Securité Zaïre-Angola," December 1990.
UNHCR, Repatriation of former Congolese combatants, Kinshasa, letter from United Nations Development Programme (UNDP) DRC Country Director to UNDP Resident Representative in Luanda, April 12, 2006.
Voice of the Voiceless, press releases, July 24, 2006, and June 27, 2011.
Zaire, intelligence service report, "Rapport à 05/47," August 10, 1993.

Newspapers, News Agencies, and Periodicals

Afrique-Asie (Paris)
Agence Zaïre Presse (AZAP-Kinshasa)
Ailleurs du Congo (Kinshasa)
Angonoticias (Luanda)

ANGOP (Luanda)
Azadho Katanga (Lubumbashi)
La Conscience (Kinshasa)
Le Dossier du Mois (Paris)
Elima (Kinshasa)
L'Essor du Katanga (Elisabethville)
Expresso (Lisbon)
The Guardian (London)
International Herald Tribune (New York)
International Press Service
Jornal do Angola (Luanda)
Katanga (Elisabethville)
LAC (Luanda)
La Libre Belgique (Brussels)
Moniteur Katangais (Elisabethville)
Mukuba (Lubumbashi)
New York Times (New York)
L'Observateur (Kinshasa)
Le Phare (Kinshasa)
Radio Okapi (Kinshasa)
Le Soir (Kinshasa)
Time magazine (New York)
The Times (London)
Times of Zambia (Lusaka)
UMOJA (Kinshasa)

Interviews

Charles Babah, Brussels, April 21, 1999.
Professor Arthur Doucy, Brussels, April 4, 2000.
Muteb a Fwamb, Lubumbashi, November 4, 2008.
Émile Ilunga, Kinshasa, April 1997; Brussels, May 1997; Kinshasa, 1998; and Kinshasa, September 18, 2009.
Grégoire Kabobo, Kinshasa, June 3 2011.
Joseph Kabwit, Kinshasa, April 14, 2008, July 14, 2008, and March 31 2012.
Stany Kalala, Kinshasa, April 28, 2012.
Delphin Kapaya, Kinshasa, May 9, 2013.
Élie Kapend, Kinshasa, March 17, 2006, March 29, 2008, and September 20, 2009.
François Kapend, Kinshasa, April 25, 2007.
Pascal Kapend, Lubumbashi, August 1, 2005, August 14, 2005, September 18, 2005, September 24, 2005, March 20, 2008, and August 17, 2008.
David Kayombo, Brussels, May 7, 1997.
Jean-Baptiste Kibwe, Brussels, August 23, 2001, December 17, 2007, and December 18, 2008.

Mundindi Didi Kilengo, Kinshasa, April 14, 2008.
Nsola Koko, Kinshasa, November 2012 and January 25, 2013.
Symphorien Kyungu, Kinshasa, January 21, 2012.
Raphaël Lumuna, Kinshasa, September 26, 2005.
Colonel Oliveira Marques, Oeiras, August 29, 2014.
Daniel Monguya Mbenge, Mons, September 2001.
Nathanaël Mbumba, Kinshasa, March 17, 2006, and April 19, 2007.
Albert Melot, Namur, January 11, 2007.
General Joseph Muchaila, Kinshasa, April 26, 2007.
Henri Mukachung, Kinshasa, May 2003, March 27, 2011, and August 27, 2013; discussions, September 2013.
Martin Mukalayi, Kinshasa, September 15, 2004.
General Mwepu Mukanda, Kinshasa, July 13, 2008, and January 2012.
General Paul Mukobo Mundende, Brussels, September 19, 2007.
Jean-Delphin Muland, Kinshasa, September 12, 2006.
Jean-Pierre Musasa, Kinshasa, January 19, 2013.
Justin Mushitu, Stockholm, May 17, 1998, December 1998 (telephone), August 5, 2000, August 12, 2001, February 3, 2002, February 28, 2008, and June 19, 2011.
Cartier Mutombo, Kinshasa, January 4, 2008; Montargis (France), July 2, 2011.
Bienvenu Mwilambwe, Kinshasa, January 12, 2013.
Colonel Yav Nasser, Brussels, April 4, 2007.
Jérôme Nawej, Lubumbashi, April 8, 2008; Kinshasa, June 2, 2012.
Jérôme Nawej and Joseph Kabwit, Kinshasa, May 19, 2012.
Moïse Nawej, Brussels, December 14, 2007.
Victor Nendaka, Brussels, May 15, 2001.
Colonel Vincent de Paul Nguz, Kinshasa, April 26, 2007, April 11, 2009, and December 13, 2013.
M. Mwando Nsimba, Brussels, December 15, 1997.
Pedro de Pezarat Correia, Lisbon, November 6, 2009.
René Pire, Namur, December 12, 2007.
"Risasse," Stockholm, May 16, 1998.
Marcel Rongveaux, Brussels, April, 2000.
António Alvao Rosa Coutinho, Lisbon, February 10, 2008.
Nickel Rumb, Montreal, May 30, 2005; Kinshasa, August 23, 2013.
Colonel Argentino Seixas, head of Cabinet of Auxiliary Forces, by General Marques Pinto, report, September 2, 2014.
Bayibsa Sosyo, Stockholm, August 12, 2001.
Deogratias Symba, Brussels, February 25, 1998; Kitwe, August 4, 2005; Lubumbashi, March 18, 2008; Lubumbashi, June 1–5, 2008.
Douglas Tefnin, Namur, August 31, 2007.
Irung a Wan, Kinshasa, April 19, 2007, and October 20, 2011.
Gaston Yambo, Oslo, December 1998.
Major Robert Yav, Lubumbashi, February 28, 2006, and January 15, 2012.
Kitenge Yezu, Kinshasa, May 2013.

Correspondence and Written Responses to Authors

Pedro de Pezarat Correia, emails to authors, November 17, 2009, and July 2, 2013.
Professor Justin Mulangu (University of Luanda), Luanda, June 22, 1999.
Jean-Pierre Musasa, written response to questions, December 12, 2012.
Justin Mushitu, e-mail to authors, October 22, 2008.
Colonel Vincent de Paul Nguz, research note, "Remise des armes," 2012.
Correspondence with Henry Rosy, 1999.

Secondary Sources

Books

J. Alexander, J. McGregor, and T. O. Ranger, *Violence and Memory: One Hundred Years in the "Dark Forests" of Matabeleland* (London: Heinemann, 2000).
J. Allman, *The Quills of the Porcupine: Asante Nationalism in an Emergent Ghana* (Madison: University of Wisconsin Press, 1993).
B. Almeida, *Angola: O conflito na frente leste* (Lisbon: Âncora, 2011).
M. Amaro Bernardo, *Memórias da revolução: Portugal 1974–1975* (Lisbon: Prefácio, 2004).
B. Anderson, *Imagined Communities: Reflections on the Origins and Spread of Nationalism* (London: Verso, 1991).
R. Anstey, *King Leopold's Legacy: The Congo under Belgian Rule* (London: Oxford University Press, 1966).
T. Bakajika Banjikila, *Épuration ethnique en Afrique: Les "Kasaïens" (Katanga 1961–Shaba 1992)* (Paris: L'Harmattan, 1997).
K. Barber (ed.), *Africa's Hidden Histories: Everyday Literacy and Making the Self* (Bloomington: Indiana University Press, 2006).
J.-F. Bayart, *L'État en Afrique: La politique du ventre* (Paris: Fayard, 1989).
J.-F. Bayart, *The State in Africa: The Politics of the Belly* (London: Longman, 1992).
G. J. Bender, *Angola under the Portuguese: The Myth and the Reality* (Trenton, NJ: Africa World Press, 2004).
M. R. Berdal and D. Malone (eds.), *Greed and Grievance: Economic Agendas in Civil Wars* (Boulder, CO: Lynne Rienner, 2000).
B. Berman, D. Eyoh, and W. Kymlicka (eds.), *Ethnicity and Democracy in Africa* (Oxford: James Currey, 2004).
M. Boås and K. C. Dunn (eds.), *African Guerrillas: Raging against the Machine* (Boulder, CO: Lynne Rienner, 2007).
R. Bonita Velez, *Salazar Tchombé: O envolvimento de Portugal na Questão do Catanga (1961–1967)* (Linda-a-velha: DG Edições, 2012).
A. C. Botelho, *Holocausto em Angola: Memórias de entre o cárcere e o cemitério* (Lisbon: Nova Vega, 2007).
M. Bratton and N. van de Walle, *Democratic Experiments in Africa: Regime Transitions in Comparative Perspective* (Cambridge: Cambridge University Press, 1997).
R. Brion and J.-L. Moreau, *De la mine à Mars: La génèse d'Umicore* (Tielt: Lannoo, 2006).

E. Bustin, *Lunda under Belgian Rule: The Politics of Ethnicity* (Cambridge, MA: Harvard University Press, 1973).
D. Cabrita Mateus, *A PIDE/DGS na guerra colonial 1961–1974* (Lisbon: Terramar, 2004).
D. Cabrita Mateus, *Memórias do colonialismo e da guerra* (Lisbon: ASA, 2006).
F. L. da Câmara Cascudo, *Angola: A guerra dos Traídos* (Rio de Janeiro: Bloch, 1979).
J. P. Cann, *Counterinsurgency in Africa: The Portuguese Way of War, 1961–1974* (Westport, CT: Greenwood Press, 1997).
J. P. Cann, *The Flechas: Insurgent Hunting in Eastern Angola 1965–1974* (Solihull: Helion, 2013).
G. Caplan, *The Elites of Barotseland* (Berkeley: University of California Press, 1970).
I. Carreira, *Memórias* (Luanda: Nzila, 2005).
Centre de Recherche et d'Information Socio-Politiques, *Congo 1960* (Brussels: CRISP, 1961).
Centre de Recherche et d'Information Socio-Politiques, *Congo 1961* (Brussels: CRISP, 1962).
Centre de Recherche et d'Information Socio-Politiques, *Congo 1963* (Brussels: CRISP, 1964).
Centre de Recherche et d'Information Socio-Politiques, *Congo 1964* (Brussels: CRISP, 1965).
Centre de Recherche et d'Information Socio-Politiques, *Congo 1965* (Brussels: CRISP, 1966).
Centre de Recherche et d'Information Socio-Politiques, *Congo 1966* (Brussels: CRISP, 1967).
Centre de Recherche et d'Information Socio-Politiques, *Congo 1967* (Brussels: CRISP, 1969).
S. Chiwale, *Cruzei-me com a história* (Lisbon: Sextante, 2008).
J. Chome, *Moïse Tshombe et l'escroquerie katangaise* (Brussels: Fondation J. Jacquemotte, 1966).
C. Clapham, *African Guerrillas* (Oxford: James Currey, 1998).
P. Collier and N. Sambanis (eds.), *Understanding Civil Wars: Evidence and Analysis*, vol. 1, *Africa* (Washington, DC: World Bank, 2005).
B. O. Collins and N. Arielli (eds.), *Transnational Soldiers* (New York: Palgrave Macmillan, 2012).
I. Colvin, *The Rise and Fall of Moïse Tshombe* (London: Leslie Frewin, 1968).
Comité Zaïre, *Zaïre: Le dossier de la recolonisation* (Paris: L'Harmattan, 1978).
F. Cooper, *Africa since 1940: The Past of the Present* (Cambridge: Cambridge University Press, 2002).
F. Cooper, *Decolonization and African Society: The Labor Question in French and British Africa* (Cambridge: Cambridge University Press, 1996).
M. Cowen and L. Laakso (eds.), *Multi-party Elections in Africa* (Oxford: Oxford University Press, 2002).
C. Cruise O'Brien, *To Katanga and Back* (New York: Simon and Schuster, 1962).
P. da Cruz, *Angola: Os vivos e os mortos* (Lisbon: Intervenção, 1976).
M. J. Da Silva, *Sortilégio da Cobra. Descolonização obrigatória* (Lisbon: Esquilo, 2005).
B. Davidson, *The Black Man's Burden: Africa and the Curse of the Nation-State* (London: James Currey, 1992).

B. Denard, *Corsaire de la République* (Paris: R. Laffont, 1998).
H. J. G. Depoorter, *Rapport sur les événements à Kolwezi et au Shaba dans la période mai– juillet 1978* (Brussels: ANPCV, 2005).
L. Devlin, *Chief of Station, Congo: Fighting the Cold War in a Hot Zone* (New York: PublicAffairs, 2008).
L. De Witte, *The Assassination of Lumumba* (London: Zed Books, 2001).
F. J. Du Toit Spies, *Operasie Savannah: Angola 1975–1976* (Pretoria: S.A. Weermag, Direktoraat Openbare Betrekkinge, 1989).
Estado-Maior do Exército, *Resenha histórico-militar das campanhas de África 1961–1974*, vol. 6, *Aspectos da actividada operacional*, book 2 (Lisbon: Comissão para o Estudo das Campanhas de África, 2006).
Estado-Maior do Exército, *Resenha histórico-militar das campanhas de África 1961–1974*, vol. 14, *Comandos, T. 1 Grupos Iniciais* (Lisbon: Comissão para o Estudo das Campanhas de África, 2009).
H. G. Ferreira and M. W. Marshall, *Portugal's Revolution: Ten Years On* (Cambridge: Cambridge University Press, 2011).
J. Freire Antunes, *A Guerra de África, 1961–1974* (Lisbon: Circulo de Leitores, 1995).
E. George, *The Cuban Intervention in Angola: From Che Guevara to Cuito Cuanavale* (Abingdon: Routledge, 2005).
J. Gérard-Libois, *Katanga Secession* (Madison: University of Wisconsin Press, 1966).
E. Gellner, *Nations and Nationalism* (Oxford: Blackwell, 1983).
R. Giordano, *Belges et Italiens du Congo-Kinshasa* (Paris: L'Harmattan, 2008).
A. Gizenga, *Ma vie et mes luttes* (Paris: L'Harmattan, 2011).
P. Gleijeses, *Conflicting Missions: Havana, Washington, and Africa, 1959–1976* (Chapel Hill: University of North Carolina Press, 2002).
P. Gleijeses, *Visions of Freedom: Havana, Washington, Pretoria, and the Struggle for Southern Africa, 1976–1991* (Chapel Hill: University of North Carolina Press, 2013).
A. Gonçalves Ribeiro, *A Vertigem da Descolonização: Da Agonia do Exôdo à Cidadania Plena* (Lisbon: Inquérito Memes Martins, 2002).
F. A. Guimarães, *The Origins of the Angolan Civil War: Foreign Intervention and Domestic Political Conflict* (Basingstoke: Macmillan, 2001).
F.-W. Heimer, *Der Entkolonisierungskonflikt in Angola* (Munich: Weltforum, 1979).
J. Herbst, *States and Power in Africa: Comparative Lessons in Authority and Control* (Princeton, NJ: Princeton University Press, 2000).
J. Higginson, *A Working Class in the Making: Belgian Colonial Labor Policy, Private Enterprise, and the African Mineworker, 1907–1951* (Madison: University of Wisconsin Press, 1990).
M. Hoare, *Congo Mercenary* (Boulder, CO: Sycamore Island Books, 2008).
E. Hobsbawm and T. O. Ranger, *The Invention of Tradition* (Cambridge: Cambridge University Press, 1983).
C. Hoskyns, *The Congo since Independence, January 1960–December 1961* (Oxford: Oxford University Press, 1965).
G. Ilunga Malukula, *Après le terrorisme, la sorcellerie serait-elle un procédé de combat?* (Lubumbashi: Privately printed, 2006).
M. Junior, *Forças armadas populares de libertação de Angola. 1° Exército Nacional (1975–1992)* (Lisboa: Prefácio, 2007).

C. Kabuya, *Zaïre: Quel changement pour quelles structures?* (Brussels: Éditions Africa, 1980).
M. Kalb, *The Congo Cables: The Cold War in Africa from Eisenhower to Kennedy* (New York: Macmillan, 1982).
N. Karl-i-Bond, *Mobutu ou l'Incarnation du mal zaïrois* (London: Rex Collings, 1982).
E. Kennes, *Essai biographique sur Laurent Désiré Kabila* (Paris: L'Harmattan, 2003).
E. Kennes, *Fin du cycle post-colonial au Katanga, RD Congo, Rébellions, sécession et leurs mémoires dans la dynamique des articulations entre l'État central et l,autonomie régionale 1960–2007* (Saarbrucken: Editions Universitaires Européennes, 2014).
J. Kent, *America, the UN and Decolonisation: Cold War Conflict in the Congo* (London: Routledge, 2010).
K. Kingma (ed.), *Demobilization in Subsaharan Africa: The Development and Security Impacts* (New York: Palgrave Macmillan, 2000).
M. Larmer (ed.), *The Musakanya Papers: The Autobiographical Writings of Valentine Musakanya* (Lusaka: Lembani Trust, 2010).
M. Larmer, *Rethinking African Politics: A History of Opposition in Zambia* (Farnham: Ashgate, 2011).
B. Lecocq, *Disputed Desert: Decolonisation, Competing Nationalisms and Tuareg Rebellions in Northern Mali* (Leiden: Brill, 2010).
R. Lemarchand, *The Dynamics of Violence in Central Africa* (Philadelphia: University of Pennsylvania Press, 2009).
R. Lemarchand, *Political Awakening in the Belgian Congo* (Berkeley: University of California Press, 1964).
C. Leys and J. S. Saul, *Namibia's Liberation Struggle: The Two-Edged Sword* (London: James Currey / Athens: Ohio University Press, 1995).
G. Macola, *The Kingdom of Kazembe: History and Politics in North-East Zambia and Katanga to 1950* (Hamburg: LIT, 2002).
G. Macola, *Liberal Nationalism in Central Africa* (New York: Palgrave Macmillan, 2010).
M. Malan, *My Life with the SA Defence Force* (Pretoria: Protea, 2006).
B. Manby, *Struggles for Citizenship in Africa* (London: Zed Books, 2009).
J. A. Marcum, *The Angolan Revolution*, vol. 2, *Exile Politics and Guerrilla Warfare (1962–1976)* (Cambridge, MA: MIT Press, 1978).
R. Marques, *Diamantes de sangue* (Lisbon: Edições Tinta-da-China, 2011).
A. Marques, *Segredos da descolonização de Angola* (Alfragide: Dom Quixote, 2013).
A. A. Mazrui, *Towards a Pax Africana: A Study of Ideology and Ambition* (London: Weidenfeld and Nicolson, 1967).
A. A. Mazrui and M. Tidy, *Nationalism and the New States in Africa from about 1935 to the Present* (London: Heinemann, 1984).
J. Milhazes, *Angola: O princípio do Fim da União Soviética* (Lisbon: Vega, 2009).
D. Monguya Mbenge, *De Léopold II à Mobutu: Une conspiration internationale* (Mons: Privately published, 1993).
D. Monguya Mbenge, *Histoire secrète du Zaïre: L'autopsie de la barbarie au service du monde* (Brussels: L'Espérance, 1977).
T. Moreira de Sá, *Os Estados Unidos e a descolonização de Angola* (Alfragide: Dom Quixote, 2011).
A. Mpase, *Au service d'un Congo aux mille visages* (Kinshasa: Academic Express Press, 2008).

G. Y. Mumba, *The 1980 Coup: Tribulations of the One-Party State in Zambia* (Lusaka: UNZA Press, 2012).
L. Namikas, *Battleground Africa: Cold War in the Congo, 1960–1965* (Washington, DC: Woodrow Wilson Center Press, 2013).
I. Ndaywel è Nziem, *Histoire générale du Congo* (Brussels: Duculot, 1998).
A. Ndjate Omanyondo N'Koy, *Gendarmerie et reconstruction d'un état de droit* (Paris: L'Harmattan, 2007).
M. Nicolai, *Ici Radio Katanga* (Brussels: J. M. Collet, 1987).
J. P. Nimy Mayidika, *Je ne renie rien. Je raconte . . .* (Paris: L'Harmattan, 2003).
P. Nothomb, *Dans Stanleyville* (Paris: Duculot, 1993).
G. Nzongola-Ntajala, *The Congo from Leopold to Kabila: A People's History* (London: Zed Books, 2002).
T. Odom, *Shaba II: The French and Belgian Intervention in Zaire in 1978* (Fort Leavenworth, KS: Combat Studies Institute, US Army Command and General Staff College, 1993).
J. Omasombo and E. Kennes, *Biographies des acteurs de la transition (juin 2003–juin 2006)* (Tervuren-Kinshasa-Lubumbashi: MRAC-CEP-CERDAC, 2006).
R. Omba, *Coup monté et manqué: Une voie de sanctification* (Kinshasa: Shomo, 2005).
S. Onslow (ed.), *Cold War in Southern Africa: White Power, Black Liberation* (London: Routledge, 2009).
Ops Lucifer: Katanga 1967 (Brussels: Kalmes, n.d.).
L. Pawson, *In the Name of the People: Angola's Forgotten Massacre* (London: I. B. Tauris, 2014).
C. Perrings, *Black Mineworkers in Central Africa* (London: Heinemann, 1979).
P. Pezarat Correia, *Angola: Do Alvor a Lusaka* (Lisbon: Hugin, 1996).
P. Pezarat Correia, *Descolonização de Angola* (Lisbon: Inquerito, 1991).
A. Pires Nunes, *Angola, 1966–74: Vitória militar no leste* (Lisbon: Prefácio, 2002).
S. du Preez, *Aventuur in Angola: Die verhaal van Suid-Afrika se soldate in Angola 1975–1976* (Pretoria: J. L. van Schaik, 1989).
G. Prunier, *Africa's World War: Congo, the Rwandan Genocide, and the Making of a Continental Catastrophe* (Oxford: Oxford University Press, 2009).
B. Raftopoulos and A. Mlambo (eds.), *Becoming Zimbabwe: A History from the Pre-colonial Period to 2008* (Harare: Weaver Press, 2009).
T. Ranger and O. Vaughan (eds.), *Legitimacy and the State in Twentieth Century Africa* (Basingstoke: Palgrave, 1993).
W. Reno, *Warfare in Independent Africa* (Cambridge: Cambridge University Press, 2011).
F. Reyntjens, *The Great African War: Congo and Regional Politics, 1996–2006* (Cambridge: Cambridge University Press, 2009).
R. Rousseau, *Légion je t'accuse! La face cachée de Kolwezi* (La Harmoie: Rexy, 2006).
A. Rubbens, *Dettes de guerre* (Elisabethville: Essor du Congo, 1945).
J.-J. Saquet, *De l'Union minière du Haut-Katanga à la Gécamines* (Paris: L'Harmattan, 2001).
M. G. Schatzberg, *The Dialectics of Oppression in Zaire* (Bloomington: Indiana University Press, 1988).
J. Schramme, *Le Bataillon Léopard: Souvenirs d'un Africain blanc* (Paris: R. Laffont, 1969).
V. Shubin, *The Hot "Cold War": The USSR in Southern Africa* (London: Pluto Press, 2008).

A. Silva Cardoso, *Angola: Anatomia de uma tragédia* (Lisbon: Oficina do Livro, 2001).
A. D. Smith, *Nationalism and Modernism* (London: Routledge, 1989).
A. D. Smith, *State and Nation in the Third World: The Western State and African Nationalism* (Brighton: Wheatsheaf, 1983).
D. Spikes, *Angola and the Politics of Intervention* (Jefferson, NC: McFarland, 1993).
J. Stockwell, *In Search of Enemies: A CIA Story* (New York: W. W. Norton, 1978).
A. Temu and B. Swai, *Historians and Africanist History: A Critique: Post-Colonial Historiography Examined* (London: Zed Books, 1981).
T. Trefon, *French Policy toward Zaire during the Giscard d'Estaing Presidency* (Brussels: CEDAF, 1989).
P. Trewelha, *Inside Quatro: Uncovering the Exile History of the ANC and SWAPO* (Johannesburg: Jacana, 2009).
A. A. J. Van Bilsen, *Vers l'indépendance du Congo et du Ruanda-Urundi: Réflexions sur les devoirs et l'avenir de la Belgique en Afrique centrale* (Kinshasa: Presse Universitaire du Zaire, 1977).
D. Van der Steen, *Élections et réformes politiques au Zaïre en 1977: Analyse de la composition des organes politiques* (Brussels: CEDAF, 1978).
W. Van der Waals, *Portugal's War in Angola, 1961-1974* (Rivonia: Ashanti, 1993).
F. Vandewalle, *Mille et quatre jours: Contes du Zaïre et du Shaba*, vol. 1 (Brussels: self-published by author, 1976).
F. Vandewalle, *L'Ommegang: Odyssée et reconquête de Stanleyville 1964* (Brussels: Le Livre Africain, 1970).
J. Vansina, *Kingdoms of the Savannah* (Madison: University of Wisconsin Press, 1966).
B. Verhaegen, *Rébellions au Congo*, vols. 1 and 2 (Brussels: CRISP, 1966, 1970).
B. Verhaegen, J. Omasombo, E. Simons, and F. Verhaegen, *Mulele et la révolution populaire au Kwilu (République Démocratique du Congo)* (Paris: L'Harmattan, 2006).
F. Villafaña, *Cold War in the Congo: The Confrontation of Cuban Military Forces, 1960-1967* (New Brunswick, NJ: Transaction, 2009).
G. de Villers with J. Omasombo Tshonda, *Zaire: La transition manquée (1990-1997)* (Tervuren: Institut Africain / Paris: L'Harmattan, 1997).
T. Vleurinck, *46 Angry Men: The 46 Civilian Doctors of Elisabethville Denounce U.N. Violations in Katanga of Its Own Charter, the Universal Declaration of Human Rights, [and] the Geneva Conventions* (Brussels: E. Guyot, 1962).
S. L. Weigert, *Angola: A Modern Military History* (New York: Palgrave Macmillan, 2011).
O. A. Westad, *The Global Cold War: Third World Interventions and the Makings of Our Times* (Cambridge: Cambridge University Press, 2005).
L. White, S. F. Miescher, and D. W. Cohen (eds.), *African Words, African Voices: Critical Practices in Oral History* (Bloomington: Indiana University Press, 2001).
J.-C. Willame, *Chronique d'une opposition politique: L'UDPS (1978-1987)* (Brussels: CEDAF, 1987).
S. Williams, *Who Killed Hammarskjöld? The UN, the Cold War and White Supremacy in Africa* (London: Hurst, 2011).
R. Yakemtchouk, *Aux origines du séparatisme katangais* (Brussels: Académie Royale des Sciences d'Outre-Mer, 1988).
P. Yambuya, *Zaïre: L'abattoir: Un pilote de Mobutu parle* (Anvers: EPO, 1991).

C. Young, *The African Colonial State in Comparative Perspective* (New Haven, CT: Yale University Press, 1997).
C. Young, *Politics in the Congo: Decolonization and Independence* (Princeton, NJ: Princeton University Press, 1965).
C. Young, *The Politics of Cultural Pluralism* (Madison: University of Wisconsin Press, 1976).
C. Young and T. Turner, *The Rise and Decline of the Zairian State* (Madison: University of Wisconsin Press, 1985).
Zaire, Département de la Défense Nationale, État-Major Général des Forces Armées Zaïroises (DDNEMG), *Mobutu et la guerre de quatre-vingts jours* (Tournai: Casterman, 1978).
Zaire, Département de la Défense Nationale de la Sécurité du Territoire et des Anciens Combattants, *Le bataillon Héros: L'exploit du 311me bataillon para au cours de la deuxième guerre du Shaba* (Kinshasa: Cible, 1978).
W. Zeller and J. Tomas (eds.), *Secession in Africa* (New York: Palgrave, 2016).

Book Chapters

J. Chito Rodrigues, "Angola, a Military Victory," in J. P. McCann (ed.), *Memories of Portugal's African Wars, 1961–1974* (Quantico, VA: Marine Corps Association, 1998), pp. 45–91.
W. G. Clarence-Smith, "Capital Accumulation and Class Formation in Angola," in D. Birmingham and P. M. Martin (eds.), *History of Central Africa*, vol. 2 (Harlow: Longman, 1983), pp. 163–199.
S. Dorman, D. Hammett, and P. Nugent, "Introduction: Citizenship and Its Casualties in Africa" in S. Dorman, D. Hammett, and P. Nugent (eds.), *Making Nations, Creating Strangers: States and Citizenship in Africa* (Leiden: Brill, 2007), pp. 3–26.
J. Hönke, "Extractive Orders: Transnational Mining Companies in the Nineteenth and Twenty-First Centuries in the Central African Copperbelt," in. R. Southall and H. Melber (eds.), *A New Scramble for Africa? Imperialism, Investment and Development* (Durban: University of KwaZulu-Natal Press, 2009), pp. 274–298.
G. Hydén, "The Problematic State," in G. Hydén, *African Politics in Comparative Perspective* (Cambridge: Cambridge University Press, 2006), pp. 50–71.
B. Jewsiewicki, "Rural Society and the Belgian Colonial Economy," in D. Birmingham and P. M. Martin (eds.), *History of Central Africa*, vol. 2 (Harlow: Longman, 1983), pp. 95–125.
S. Katzenellenbogen, "It Didn't Happen at Berlin: Politics, Economics and Ignorance in the Setting of Africa's Colonial Boundaries," in P. Nugent and A. I. Asiwaju (eds.), *African Boundaries* (Edinburgh: Edinburgh University Press, 1996), pp. 21–34.
E. Kennes, "Democratic Republic of the Congo: The Structure of Greed, the Networks of Need," in C. J. Arnson and I. W. Zartman (eds.), *The Economics of War: The Intersection of Need, Creed, and Greed* (Baltimore: Woodrow Wilson Center Press/Johns Hopkins University Press, 2005), pp. 140–177.
E. Kennes, "The Mining Sector in Congo: The Victim or the Orphan of Globalisation?," in S. Marysse and F. Reyntjens (eds.), *The Political Economy of the Great Lakes*

Region of Africa: The Pitfalls of Enforced Democracy and Globalization (Basingstoke: Palgrave Macmillan, 2005), pp. 152–189.

E. Kennes, "Le secteur minier au Congo—'Déconnexion' et descente aux enfers," in F. Reyntjens and S. Marysse (eds.), L'Afrique des Grands Lacs: Annuaire 1999-2000 (Paris: L'Harmattan, 2000), pp. 299–342.

M. Larmer, "Historical Perspectives on Zambia's Mining Booms and Busts," in M. Larmer and A. Fraser (eds.), Zambia, Mining and Neo-liberalism: Boom and Bust on the Globalized Copperbelt (New York Palgrave Macmillan, 2010), pp. 31–58.

R. Lemarchand, "Reflections on the Crisis in Eastern Congo," in S. Marysse and F. Reyntjens (eds.), L'Afrique des Grands Lacs: Annuaire 2008-2009 (Paris: L'Harmattan, 2009), pp. 105–121.

Lieutenant Colonel Enrique Buznego Rodriguez and Lieutenant Colonel Lazaro Cardenas Sierra, "La Batalla de Quifangondo," in M. Rey Cabrera (ed.), La guerra de Angola (Havana: Politica, 1989), pp. 43–56.

E. M'Bokolo, "Le séparatisme katangais," in J.-L. Amselle and E. M'Bokolo (eds.), Au coeur de l'ethnie (Paris: La Découverte, 1999), pp. 185–226.

C. Neale, "The Idea of Progress in the Revision of African History," in B. Jewsiewicki and D. Newbury (eds.), African Historiographies: What History for Which Africa? (Beverly Hills, CA: Sage, 1986), pp. 112–122.

P. Pezarat Correia, "A participão local no desenvolvimento das campanhas: O recrutamento africano," in Instituto de Altos Estudos Militares: Estudos sobre as Campanhas de África (1961–74) (Sintra: Atena, 2000).

T. O. Ranger, "Towards a Usable African Past," in C. H. Fyfe (ed.), African Studies since 1945: A Tribute to Basil Davidson (London: Longman, 1976), pp. 28–39.

C. Roosens, "La Belgique et la sécession du Katanga," in O. Lanotte, C. Roosens, and C. Clément (eds.), La Belgique et l'Afrique Centrale: De 1960 à nos jours (Brussels: GRIP–Editions Complexe, 2000), pp. 107–132.

J. C. Scott, "Compulsory Villagization in Tanzania: Aesthetics and Miniaturization," in Seeing Like a State: How Certain Schemes to Improve the Human Condition Have Failed (New Haven, CT: Yale University Press, 1998), pp. 223–261.

S. B. Snyder, "Helsinki Final Act (1975)," in J. R. Arnold and R. Wiener (eds.), Cold War: The Essential Reference Guide (Santa Barbara, CA: ABC-CLIO, 2012), p. 75.

J. Stengers, "Le Katanga et le mirage de l'or," in Études africaines offertes à Henri Brunschwig (Paris: EHESS, 1982), pp. 149–175.

T. Turner, "Angola's Role in the Congo War," in J. F. Clark (ed.), The African Stakes of the Congo War (New York: Palgrave Macmillan, 2002), pp. 75–92.

J.-L. Vellut, "Mining in the Belgian Congo," in D. Birmingham and P. M. Martin (eds.), History of Central Africa, vol. 2 (Harlow: Longman, 1983), pp. 126–162.

J.-L. Vellut, "Rural Poverty in Western Shaba, c. 1890–1920," in R. H. Palmer and N. Parsons (eds.), The Roots of Rural Poverty in Central and Southern Africa (London: Heinemann, 1977), pp. 294–316.

C. Young, "The African Colonial State and Its Political Legacy," in D. Rothchild and N. Chazan (eds.), The Precarious Balance: State and Society in Africa (London: Westview, 1988), pp. 25–66.

C. Young, "Zaire: The Shattered Illusion of the Integral State," in J. D. Le Sueur (ed.), The Decolonization Reader (New York: Routledge, 2003), pp. 414–427.

Journal Articles

C. Alden, "Making Old Soldiers Fade Away: Lessons from the Reintegration of Demobilized Soldiers in Mozambique," *Security Dialogue* 33 (2002): 341–356.
B. Berman, "Ethnicity, Patronage and the African State: The Politics of Uncivil Nationalism," *African Affairs* 97, no. 388 (1998): 305–341.
D. Biebuyck, "Fondement de l'organisation politique des Lunda du Mwaantyaav en Territoire de Kapanga," *Zaïre* 9, no. 8 (1957): 787–817.
J. Brownell, "Diplomatic Lepers: The Katangan and Rhodesian Foreign Missions in the United States and the Politics of Nonrecognition," *International Journal of African Historical Studies* 47, no. 2 (2014): 209–237.
P. Cedomi (a.k.a. J.-P. Sonck), "L'étrange destin de la Gendarmerie katangaise," part 1, *Fire!* (Brussels) 16 (September–October 1994): 22–27.
B. Crine-Mavar, "Histoire traditionnelle du Shaba," *Cultures au Zaïre et en Afrique* 1 (1973): 17–26.
D. Curtis, "China and the Insecurity of Development in the Democratic Republic of the Congo (DRC)," *International Peacekeeping* 20, no. 5 (2013): 551–569.
M. Doornbos, "The African State in Academic Debate: Retrospect and Prospect," *Journal of Modern African Studies* 28, no. 2 (1990): 179–198.
B. Fetter, "The Union Minière and Its Hinterland: A Demographic Reconstruction," *African Economic History* 12 (1983): 67–81.
B. Fetter, "L'Union Minière du Haut-Katanga, 1920–1940: La naissance d'une sous-culture totalitaire," *Cahiers du CEDAF* 6 (Brussels, 1973): 1–40.
B. S. Fetter, "The Luluabourg Revolt at Elisabethville," *African Historical Studies* 2, no. 2 (1969): 269–277.
J. Gérard-Libois, "Les dissolutions successives du Comité Spécial du Katanga," *Études Congolaises* 8, no. 3 (1965): 1–55.
P. Gleijeses, "Flee! The White Giants Are Coming! The United States, the Mercenaries and the Congo, 1964–65," *Diplomatic History* 18, no. 2 (1994): 207–237.
P. Gleijeses, "Truth or Credibility: Castro, Carter, and the Invasions of Shaba," *International History Review* 18, no. 1 (1996): 70–103.
Gen. Y. Gras, "L'opération Kolwezi," *Mondes et Cultures* 45, no. 4 (November 1985): 691–702.
H. Heisler, "The Creation of a Stabilized Urban Society: A Turning Point in the Development of Northern Rhodesia/Zambia," *African Affairs* 70, no. 279 (1971): 125–145.
J. Hogan, "'What Then Happened to Our Eden?' The Long History of Lozi Secessionism, 1890–2013," *Journal of Southern African Studies* 40, no. 5 (2014): 907–924.
M. Hughes, "Fighting for White Rule in Africa: The Central African Federation, Katanga, and the Congo Crisis, 1958–1965," *International History Review* 25, no. 3 (2003): 596–615.
S. Jackson, "Of 'Doubtful Nationality': Political Manipulation of Citizenship in the D.R. Congo," *Citizenship Studies* 11 (2007): 481–500.
J. Jansson, "The Sicomines Agreement Revisited: Prudent Chinese Banks and Risk-Taking Chinese Companies," *Review of African Political Economy* 40, no. 135 (2013): 152–162.

N. Kriger, "The Zimbabwean War of Liberation: Struggles within the Struggle," *Journal of Southern African Studies* 14, no. 2 (1988): 304–322.
M. Larmer, "Local Conflicts in a Transnational War: The Katangese Gendames and the Shaba Wars of 1977–78," *Cold War History* 13, no. 1 (2013): 89–108.
R. Lemarchand, "The Limits of Self-Determination: The Case of the Katanga Secession," *American Political Science Review* 56, no. 2 (1962): 404–416.
S. Lindberg, "It's Our Turn to Chop: Do Elections in Africa Feed Neo-patrimonialism Rather Than Counter-act It?," *Democratization* 10, no. 2 (2004): 121–140.
C. Lourtie, "Kolwezi mai 1978: La seconde guerre du Shaba," *Tam Tam Ommegang* 31 (2006): 15–28.
H. Macmillan, "The African National Congress of South Africa in Zambia: The Culture of Exile and the Changing Relationship with Home, 1964–1990," *Journal of Southern African Studies* 35, no. 2 (2009): 303–329.
Z. Marriage, "Flip-Flop Rebel, Dollar Soldier: Demobilisation in the Democratic Republic of Congo," *Conflict, Security and Development* 7, no. 2 (2007): 281–309.
L. Nsanda da Buleli, "La bataille de Kindu," *Cahiers Africains* 60 (2003): 77–116.
R. Pire, "La sécession katangaise: Impressions à chaud," *Bulletin Trimestriel du CRAOCA* 4 (1988): 45–59.
T. O. Ranger, "Nationalist Historiography, Patriotic History and the History of the Nation: The Struggle over the Past in Zimbabwe," *Journal of Southern African Studies* 30, no. 2 (2004): 215–234.
M. G. Schatzberg, "Beyond Mobutu: Kabila and the Congo," *Journal of Democracy* 8, no. 4 (1997): 70–84.
R. Schmidt, "Zaïre after the 1978 Shaba Crisis," *Aussenpolitik* 30, no. 1 (1979): 88–99.
F. Vandewalle, "A propos de la gendarmerie katangaise," *Bulletin Trimestriel du CRAOCA* 4 (1988): 59–95.
F. Vandewalle, "La gendarmerie katangaise et sa filiation," *Bulletin Trimestriel du CRAOCA* 2 (1982): 85–99.
J.-L. Vellut, "Les bassins miniers de l'ancien Congo Belge: Essai d'histoire économique et sociale (1900–1960)," *Les Cahiers du CEDAF* 7 (1981): 1–70.
O. A. Westad, "Moscow and the Angolan Crisis, 1974–1976: A New Pattern of Intervention," *Cold War International History Project (CWIHP) Bulletin* 8–9 (1996): 21–31.
R. Yakemtchouk, "Les deux guerres du Shaba," *Studia Diplomatica*, 41, nos. 4/5/6 (1988).

Online Articles

G. Baines, "The Battle for Cassinga: Conflicting Narratives and Contested Meanings," unpublished paper (December 2007), http://eprints.ru.ac.za/946/1/baines_Cassinga.pdf (accessed December 1, 2013).
"Batalha de Kifangondo na voz do general Ndalu," http://jornaldeangola.sapo.ao/entrevista/batalha_de_kifangondo_na_voz_do_general_ndalu (accessed May 10, 2015).
P. Collier and A. Hoeffler, "Greed and Grievance in Civil War," World Bank Policy Research Working Paper 2355 (May 2000), http://papers.ssrn.com/sol3/papers.cfm?abstract_id=630727 (accessed January 28, 2012).

J. Herbst and G. Mills, "There Is No Congo," *Foreign Policy*, March 18, 2009, http://www
.foreignpolicy.com/articles/2009/03/17/there_is_no_congo?page=0,1 (accessed
November 15, 2015).
I. Mpyana, "Is Katumbi's Resignation a Game Changer in DRC?," October 21, 2015,
http://democracyinafrica.org/is-katumbis-resignation-a-game-changer-in-drc
(accessed November 18, 2015).
T. Raeymaekers, "Who Calls the Congo?," August 10, 2009, http://rubeneberlein
.wordpress.com/2009/08/10/who-calls-the-congo-a-response-to-herbst-and-mills/
(accessed July 3, 2014).
J.-P. Sonck, "Commandos Katangais, 1964–65," http://albertville.stools.net/text
_commandos_kantangais.htm (accessed June 18, 2012).

Other Publications

"4000 Ans d'Histoire," special issue, *Katanga* (monthly review of the Friends of
Katanga, Brussels) (July 1961).
Amnesty International, *Les violations des droits de l'homme au Zaïre* (London, 1980).
Boletim Oficial de Angola, February 13, 1975.
Bulletin du CEDOPO, February 15, 1961; April 8, 1975; and nos. 13/77 and 54/77 (1977).
Centro de Instrução de Operações Especiais, *Apontamentos sobre o emprego táctico
das pequenas unidades na contra-guerrilha: O exército na guerra subversiva*
(n.p., 1961).
"Décision de commissionnement no. 24, 19 March 1964," *Bulletin Provincial du Lualaba*,
September 15, 1964.
"The FLNC Speaks," *Africa*, May 1977.
A. Kishiba, "Katangais, ou es tu?," *Katanga* (Elisabethville), February 1, 1958.
"Let's Talk about Bantustans," special issue, *South African Historical Journal* 64, no. 1
(2012).
M. Rongveaux, "Note for Professor Jean Stengers: Memories of Katanga, 1956–1960."
Zaïre, Conférence Nationale Souveraine, Commission Défense, Sécurité et Protection
Civile, *Rapport de la Commission* (Kinshasa, 1992).
Zaïre, Conférence Nationale Souveraine, Commission des Assassinats et des Violations
des Droits de l'Homme, *Rapport de la Commission* (Kinshasa, 1992).

Unpublished Secondary Sources

S. Brabant, "Aspects politiques et diplomatiques de l'intervention de Kolwezi en 1978:
Réalité—information" (École Royale Militaire, Brussels, 1983–1984).
S. Brabant, "La coopération belgo-française durant les événements de Kolwezi 1978"
(seminar presentation, École Royale Militaire, Brussels, May 1982).
T. Drehsen, "The Militarization of the San in Southern Angola" (paper presented to the
African Studies Association of the UK, Oxford, September 2010).
E. Kambaj, "Les ex-gendarmes katangais: Récit critique d'une lutte héroïque de libéra-
tion" (unpublished manuscript, n.d.).

E. Kennes, "Fin du cycle post-colonial au Katanga, RD Congo: Rébellions, sécession et leurs mémoires dans la dynamique des articulations entre l'État central et l'autonomie régionale 1960–2007" (PhD thesis, University of Laval, Quebec, and University of Paris I, 2009).
N. Kinsey-Powell, "France's African Wars, 1974–1981" (PhD dissertation, Graduate Institute of International and Development Studies, Geneva, 2013).
R. Lemarchand, "Katanga: Background to Secession" (unpublished manuscript, 1963, in possession of authors).
M. Moiloa, "A Youth Politics That Imagines Itself through the Past" (paper presented at the Fifth European Conference on African Studies [ECAS], Lisbon, June 27–29, 2013).
J. Pearce, "Contesting the Past in Angolan Politics" (paper presented at the Fifth European Conference on African Studies [ECAS], Lisbon, June 27–29, 2013).
C. L. Porter, "Nationalism, Authority and Political Identity in the Secession of Katanga, 1908–1963" (DPhil thesis, University of Cambridge, 2014).

Index

Adoula, Cyrille, 11, 53–55, 57–58, 62–64, 69
African National Congress, 193
Albert I (king of Belgium), 208n28
Albertville (city), 54, 56, 69–70, 72
Algeria, 39, 79, 81, 84–85, 89, 98, 125, 128–29, 155
Alliance des Bakongo (ABAKO), 21, 38, 121, 230n14. *See also* Kongo
Alliance des Forces Démocratiques pour la Libération du Congo (AFDL), 4, 9, 12, 14–15, 97, 148, 162, 166–77, 188, 191, 193–96
Alliance des Patriotes pour la Refondation du Congo (APARECO), 183
Almeida, Silvino, 107
Ambriz, Angola, 163
ANC. *See* Armée Nationale Congolaise
Angola: aftermath of Portuguese revolution, 100–101; Cossa Accords, 108–10; forming a provisional government, 101–102; KG exile, 2–4, 61–62, 65–69, 80–81; Lusaka agreement, 162–63, 164; Marxist influence, 119, 150; nationalist movements, 102–104, 110–12; Portuguese withdrawal, 4; struggle for independence, 1, 3, 113–16
Angolan Armed Forces (FAA): integration of FLNC, 145–47; integration of Tigres, 104–108; KG organization and identity, 5; 24th Regiment (KG), 5, 158, 163–64, 169–70, 175
Angolan Civil War: early 1970s actions, 97–98; FLNC actions, 4; South Africa intervention, 115–16, 119–21, 163, 228n130, 239n202; Tigres' role in independence war, 1, 99–100, 104–108
Angolan Government in Exile (GRAE). *See* Governo Revolucionário de Angola no Exílio
Armée Nationale Congolaise (ANC): Belgian advisors, 50; fighting ability, 53; forcing an end to secession, 45–48, 62–63; FP mutiny, 44; integration of KG, 2, 8–9, 43–44, 54, 58, 70–71, 75, 79; KG mutiny, 75–79; mercenary forces, 77–78; military actions in Katanga, 57, 68–69, 76; remaining elements in Angola, 175–77; resisting integration, 61–66, 90–91; retaking of Stanleyville, 69–72

Armée Secrète de Libération Nationale (ASLN), 85, 94
d'Aspremont Lynden, Harold, 50
Associação Agro-Prenaria Patrice E. Lumumba do Pelengue, 155
Association des Anciens Combattants du Katanga, 52
Association des Tshokwe du Congo de l'Angola et de la Rhodésie du Nord (ATCAR), 35, 37, 40
"autochthon" relations: Banyamulenge rebellion, 168; formation of Gassomel, 34; formation of MNC-L, 36; formation of UFERI, 146; Katangan identity, 1–2, 13, 53, 158, 164, 199–200; politics and ethnic struggle, 36–37, 40, 185

Babah, Charles, 64
Balubakat movement, 27, 35–37, 39, 43, 48–49, 53–56, 60, 63, 73, 172, 175–76, 179, 245n17
Banyamulenge rebellion, 168
Battle of Quifangondo, 115–16
Baudouinville (town), 65
Belgian Congo: colonial rule in Congo and Katanga, 29–30; diversity and lack of identity, 6–7; Katangan autonomy, 24–25, 52, 199; late colonial policy, 30–32; planned transition to independence, 38–39; postcolonial nationalism, 18, 32–37; resistance to exploitation, 28–29; rule by Leopold II, 10, 23–24. *See also* Congo/Zaire
Belgian Technical Mission (BTM/Mistebel), 47, 49–50, 213n22
Bemba (people/ethnicity), 25–26, 152
Bengo, Angola (province), 128, 147, 162–63
Biafra, 7
Bicesse Accords, 191
Bidalira, Louis, 156
Boma (Congolese capital), 25
Bomboko, Justin, 49
Botelho, Américo, 108
Botswana, 130
Bourse du Travail du Katanga (BTK), 25

280 | Index

Britain: colonial policies, 28, 31–32, 81, 83–84, 126; immigrant communities, 201; mining interests, 24; policy toward Katangese secession, 51, 57, 59, 65–66; policy toward Shaba war, 127, 135–37, 141–42
British South Africa Company (BSAC), 22
Brzezinski, Zbigniew, 138, 140, 142–43
Bukavu (town), 77–78
Bula Bemba (island), 89, 221n39
Bumba Moaso, Antoine, 124, 231n40
Bunche, Ralph, 46
Bunkeya (town), 47
Burundi, 167, 245n2
Bustin, E., 21, 35–36, 209n53

Cabinda, Angola, 82–83, 114, 116, 181
Cacanda, Angola, 147, 153
Caetano, Marcelo, 98, 100
Cafunfo, Angola, 163
Caianda, Angola, 84, 233n68
Camissombo, Angola, 84–86, 95, 107, 114, 129, 147
Camp Massart mutiny, 44
Carnation Revolution, 100–102
Carreira, Henrique ("Iko"), 134
Cartel d'Union Nationale Congolais, 156
Carter, Jimmy, 125, 131, 140, 142
Cartier Mutombo, Jacques, ix, 122, 125
Cassinga raid (1978), 143, 239n202
Castro, Fidel, 139–40
Cathedral of St. Peter and Paul (Elisabethville), 52
Catholic missionaries/schools, 26, 28, 30, 49, 93, 157
Cazage, Angola, 67
Cazombo, Angola, 67, 84–85, 127, 147, 154, 233n67
Central African Federation (CAF), 39, 58–59, 65–66
Charte Coloniale, Article 22, 24
Chimbalile, Albert, 148
Chimbila, Angola, 85, 92, 95, 147, 153
China, 96, 106, 135, 177
Chipenda, Daniel, 86, 97–98, 103–104, 106, 109, 225n34
Chiwale, Samuel, 115
CIA. See U.S Central Intelligence Agency
Clemens, René, 50
colonialism: artificiality of nation-states, 5–8, 18; Belgian rule in Congo, 10; creation of postcolonial armies, 13–16; KG support of Portuguese, 1, 4; Portuguese withdrawal, 4, 100–102; sanctity of colonial borders, 196–99
Comité Spécial du Katanga (CSK), 24
Communism: Angola and, 100–101, 114, 117; Cold War politics and, 16–17, 51–52, 62, 69, 85; embrace by Lumumba in Congo, 11, 44–45, 49; Katangan anticommunism, 19, 52, 67; Mobutu anticommunist stance, 11, 17; threat throughout Africa, 127–28, 142, 156–57; Western interventionism, 131. *See also* Marxism/Marxist influence; Soviet Union
Compagnie du Chemin de Fer du Bas-Congo au Katanga (BCK), 24, 26–27, 32
Compagnie du Congo pour le Commerce et l'Industrie (CCCI), 23
Compagnie du Katanga, 23–24, 26
Conaco (Convention Nationale Congolaise), 72–73, 121, 156, 164, 176, 181
Conakat (Confédération des Associations Tribales du Katanga), 21, 32–39, 51–55, 60, 63, 91, 172, 176, 190
Congo wars (1997–2003): division of mineral resources, 10; first war, 170, 188; Pretoria agreement, 173–74, 178, 182; results and aftermath, 177–79; second war, 13, 162, 172–77, 186, 194, 206n22, 248n60
Congolese army. *See* Armée Nationale Congolaise
Congolese Force Publique (FP), 10, 14, 24, 44, 46–48
Congolese National Police (PNC), 183
Congo/Zaire: colonial rule, 29–30; declaration of independence, 41–44; European influence, 39–40; Katangan secession, 2–3, 8–9; nationalist politics, 38–39; postcolonial political changes, 10–13; redrawing provincial boundaries, 196–98; support from China, 106; support of FNLA, 105–106. *See also* Belgian Congo; Léopoldville/Congolese government; Mobutu Sese Seko
Congrès des Peuples du Katanga (CPK), 184–86, 200
Conscience Africaine, 38
Conseil National de la Révolution (CNR), 161, 170
Conseil Suprême de Libération (CSL), 130
Cools, Johan, 161
Coordination d'organisation du référendum d'autodétermination du Katanga (CORAK), 184–86, 200

Cossa Accords, 108–10
Costa Gomes, Francisco da, 97, 101
Côte d'Ivoire, 9
Crèvecoeur, Jean-Marie, 47
Crine-Mavar, Bruno, 35
Cruise O'Brien, Conor, 56
Cuanza Norte/Sul (provinces), 128, 162–63
Cuba, 16, 71, 96, 99, 112–16, 119–21, 124–28, 131, 134–36, 138–41, 143–44, 202

de Matos, João, 163
De Witte, Ludo, 41, 53
Dean, Jonathan, 65
Denard, Bob, 56, 76–79, 154
Détection Militaire des Activités anti-Patrie (DEMIAP), 182
Dilolo (region), 36, 67, 76, 85, 91, 123–24, 127–28, 161
Direcção Geral de Segurança (DGS), 92
Division Spéciale Présidentielle (DSP), 159, 173
Dos Santos, Jose Eduardo, 107, 153, 169, 177, 226n64
Dundo, Angola (town), 95, 107, 112, 115, 121, 163, 180–81

Egge Plan (1961), 61
Egypt, 71
Elisabeth (queen of Belgium), 208n28
Elisabethville (city): anti-US demonstrations, 59; Belgian military presence, 98; Camp Massart mutiny, 44; population, 31, 33; as seat of government, 24, 52, 54, 57, 73, 76; UN military presence, 55–57, 62. *See also* Lubumbashi
Engels, Walter, 47
Engulu, Leon, 74
Eritrea, 14
Ethiopia, 138
Étudiants Congolais Progressistes (ECP), 128–29, 233n77, 234n78
évolués, 29, 31, 32, 38
Eyskens, Gaston, 49

FAA. *See* Angolan Armed Forces
Federal Multiracial Republic of Katanga, 185
Fédération Kasaïenne (FEDEKA), 37
Fédération Nationale Congolaise (Fénaco), 85–86, 96, 192
fiéis (faithful ones), 4, 5, 87–88, 111. *See also* photo gallery

Figueiredo, Elsio de Carvalho, 95, 102, 107–11, 114, 226n75, 227n92
Flechas (*fleches noires*), 80, 83, 104–105
FLNC. *See* Front de Libération Nationale Congolais
FLNC II ("new FLNC"), 154–55, 163–64, 169, 175, 177
Forças Armadas Populares Libertação de Angola (FAPLA), 103, 113–16, 120, 147, 240n15
Force Publique (FP), 10, 14, 24, 44, 46–49
Forces Armées Congolaises (FAC), 172–75, 188, 191, 194
Forces Armées de la République Démocratique du Congo (FARDC), 175, 177, 179, 183–87, 244n92
Forces Armées Patriotiques du Congo (FAPAC), 150–55, 158–64
Forces Armées Populaires du Congo (FAPC), 150–51, 240n15
Forces Armées Rwandaises (FAR), 168–69
Forces Patriotiques Katangaises (FAPAK), 159–60, 163–64
Ford, Gerald, 114
Foreign Congolese Troops, 176, 182
46 Angry Men (Vleurinck), 55
"4000 Ans d'Histoire" (*Katanga*, 1961), 52–53
France, 76, 78, 81, 84, 127, 130–32, 135, 138–44, 168
Franck, M. Louis, 29–30
Frente de Libertação de Moçambique (Frelimo), 100, 119. *See also* Mozambique
Frente Nacional de Libertação de Angola (FNLA), 67; beginning of independence struggle, 67, 82; competition with rival groups, 100–103, 110–13; fighting Cuban forces, 120–23; MPLA alliance, 98, 104–105, 108, 110; offensive operations in Angola, 113–16; Shaba wars, 123–42; support from Chinese, 96; support from Mobutu, 85–86, 106; UNITA alliance, 109
Frente para a Libertação do Enclave de Cabinda (FLEC), 83. *See also* Cabinda, Angola
Front Commun, 38
Front Congolais de Libération (FCL), 151–52
Front Congolais pour la Restauration de la Démocratie (FCD), 151–52
Front de Libération Nationale Congolais (FLNC): leadership of Mbumba, 91–94; Marxist influence, 119–20, 196; military training and deployment, 94–97; organization and identity, 4–5; Shaba I,

Front de Libération Nationale
Congolais (FLNC) (cont.)
123–27; Shaba II, 133–42; Shaba wars,
objectives, 11, 116–18, 120–23; Shaba wars,
period between, 127–33; Shaba wars, results/
aftermath, 142–46. See also FLNC II ("new
FLNC")

Gabon, 143
Gaddafi, Muammar, 155–56
Garba, Joseph, 125
Garde Civil, 146, 157, 160–61, 164, 173
Garenganze (state), 22
Gassomel. See Groupement des Associations
Mutuelles de l'Empire Lunda
Gavage, Achille, 39
Gécamines (a.k.a. Gécomin), 26, 74, 88–89, 135,
137, 172–73, 188
Gérard-Libois, J., 34, 47, 54
Giscard d'Estaing, Valéry, 127, 131
Gizenga, Antoine, 46, 51, 53, 56, 69, 74, 122–23,
126–28, 162, 231n29, 232n55
Gleijeses, P., 16, 71, 86, 99, 112–13, 116, 120, 131,
134, 136, 140, 223n60
The Global Cold War (Westad), 16
Government of National Union, 73
Governo Revolucionário de Angola no Exílio
(GRAE), 67–68, 82, 86
Grandjean, André, 48
Group de Travail, 38
Groupement des Associations Mutuelles
de l'Empire Lunda (Gassomel), 34–35, 40, 93
Guinea-Bissau, 98, 100
Guiringaud, Louis de, 139
Gullion, Edmund, 58

Hammarskjöld, Dag, 46, 53, 55, 214n69
Hani, Chris, 203
Hassan II (king of Morocco), 127
Haut Conseil de la République (HCR), 157
Haut-Katanga (province), 198
Haut-Lomani (province), 198
Helsinki Accords of 1975, 120
Hemba, ki- (language), 53
Hemptinne, Jean Félix de, 30
Herbst, J., 13
Herter, Christian, 41
Hoare, Mike, 71
Hone, Evelyn, 66
Hoskyns, C., 46
Huambo (town), 148

Ileo, Joseph, 63–65, 67
Ilunga, Adhémar, 184
Ilunga, Émile, 148, 151, 161–62, 170, 174, 243n76
Interahamwe militia, 168–69
International Monetary Fund (IMF), 131, 156,
177
International Red Cross, 78, 147
Irung a Wan, ix, 174, 245n7. See also photo
gallery
Isiro (town), 76

Jadotville (city, renamed Likasi), 55, 56, 59
Janssens, Émile, 44, 46
jeunesses, 9, 56, 159–60, 172, 187
Jewsiewicki, Bogumil, ix, 28
Junta Governativa para o Estado de Angola, 101

Kabalo (town), 49, 70
Kabarebe, James, 172
Kabila, Jaynet, 177–78
Kabila, Joseph, 13, 178–79, 182–87, 194, 200
Kabila, Laurent: assassination, 177; command
of Balubakat forces, 56, 72; creation of FCD,
151; leadership of AFDL, 168; leadership
of PRP, 96–97, 117, 121–22, 129, 243n70;
leadership role in CNS, 162; overthrow of
Mobutu, 2, 4, 12, 166, 169–71; rise to power, 1,
171–73, 184–86, 191, 234n78; second Congo
War, 173–79, 193–94
Kabobo, Grégoire, ix
Kabongo (Baluba chief), 208n40
Kabongo (town), 70
Kabwit, Joseph, ix, 88, 96, 222n54, 227n80
Kabwita, Roger, 148
Kafund, Gilbert, 169
Kafunga, Simon, 148
Kajama Kasaji, Rodrigues, 177, 179
Kakoma, Northern Rhodesia, 66
Kakudji, Eustache, 70
Kalabe, Alphonse, 243n70
Kalabela, Ambroise, 234n79
Kalala, Stany, 163. See also photo gallery
Kalenga, Jean-Beauvin, 94, 96, 150–52, 201,
240n15
Kalenga, Paul, 106–107
Kaloba, André, 155, 156, 241n47
Kalonda Moanda, 77
Kalonji, Albert, 69
Kamboyi, Daniel, 175, 242n64
Kaniama (territory), 47, 154
Kanyimbu, Laurent, 148

Kanyoka (people/ethnicity), 20
Kapanga (town), 20, 64, 123–24, 127
Kapend, Élie Kanyimbu, ix, 175, 177, 179–83, 246n34, 247n58, 248n66, 248nn68–69
Kapend, François, ix, 149
Kapend, Joseph, 209n67
Kapend, Pascal, ix, 67, 76, 85, 134, 163, 169, 175
Kapend Tshombe, Joseph, 34
Kasai (people/ethnicity), 7, 9, 19–20, 26–29, 33–37, 40–41, 124, 132, 158–59
Kasai River, 20
Kasaji (town), 123, 134
Kasanje (kingdom), 21
Kasavubu, Joseph, 46, 50, 69, 73
Kasenga (town), 65
Kasongo, Simon, 84, 151–54, 158. *See also* photo gallery
Kata Katanga, 186–87, 203
Katanga (renamed Shaba Province): Belgian withdrawal, 8; colonial rule, 22–24, 29–30; creating a sense of identity, 1–2; declaration of independence, 41, 50; development, economic/political, 26–29; development, mining economy, 25–26; following the Congo wars, 177–78; legitimacy as a nation-state, 5–8, 18–19, 51–53, 196–98; nationalism and politics following independence, 32–39; origins of, 20–22; political centralization, 73–74; population, 31, 33, 38; post–World War II development, 30–32; provincial autonomy, 24–25; redrawing provincial boundaries, 198. *See also* Shaba wars
Katanga, secession: assertion as authentic nation-state, 41–44; beginnings of, 2, 44–45; creating an army, 46–48; international politics of, 49–51; intervention by UN, 45–46, 53–56; termination and demobilization, 8–9, 62–66
Katangese gendarmes/ex-gendarmes (KG): as an army without borders, 13–15; creation and organization, 46–48; dealing with Balubakat rebellion, 48–49, 56–57; exile in Angola, 2–4, 61–62, 65–69, 80–81; identity, 15–16, 194–96; importance to secessionist effort, 43–44; integration into ANC, 2, 8–9, 43–44, 54, 58, 70–71, 75–76, 79; military significance and effectiveness, 190–91; political significance, 191–94; recall from Angola, 69–70; withdrawal of Belgian officers, 56. *See also* military units; Tigres/ex-Tigres; *photo gallery*

Katumba Mwanke, 172, 177–78, 183, 247n44
Katumbi, Moïse, 16, 167, 177–79, 187, 198, 200
Kaunda, Kenneth, 103, 143, 148, 235n126
Kazadi, Pierre ("Cobra"), 94
Kazadi Mukalayi, 183
Kazadi Ntandaimena, Ferdinand, 185–86
Kemishanga, Mathias, 122
Kenya, 14, 84, 197
Kibomango, 182
Kibwe, Jean-Baptiste, 39, 52, 54–55, 58, 62–63, 74, 88–89, 107, 122, 133, 223n57
Kifwa, Célestin, 172
Kilala, David, 151–52
Kilo (Watsa territory), 72
Kilwa (town), 183–84
Kimba, Evariste, 36–37, 43, 53–54, 73, 88, 172
Kinshasa, 9, 13, 78, 84, 91, 97, 107–108, 124, 127–28, 171, 180, 186–87. *See also* Léopoldville/Congolese government
Kipushi (city), 59, 142, 156, 171
Kisangani (formerly Stanleyville), 89, 106, 170, 176. *See also* Stanleyville
Kisenge (town), 78, 91, 123
Kishiba, Alexis, 34
Kisunka, Denis, 151
Kitona, 176, 182
Kitona agreement, 55
Kivu, North/South, 13, 75, 168, 174, 206n22
Kiyana, Vindicien Kasuku ("Mufu"), 134, 151, 174
Kiyeke (people/ethnicity), 53
Kolwezi (city), 26, 56, 59, 62, 91, 93, 119, 124, 127, 134–35, 137–43, 161
Kongo (people/ethnicity), 21, 103, 181, 224n24. *See also* Alliance des Bakongo
Kongolo (town), 55–56, 71. *See also photo gallery*
Kongolo dynasty, 20
Kwango River, 21
Kwilu (town), 133
Kyundu Mutanga, Gédéon, 186–87
Kyungu, Symphorien, 161, 164
Kyungu wa Kumwanza, Gabriel, 16, 158–59, 172, 193

Lake Kisale, 20
Lamouline, Robert, 46
Le Réveil Congolais, 94
Leais (Loyals), 83
Lefèvre, Théo, 49
Lemarchand, Réne, 22, 36, 39, 43
Leopold II (king of Belgium), 10, 22–24

Léopoldville/Congolese government, 11, 25, 36, 50–51, 68–71, 79, 89. *See also* Congo/Zaire
L'Essor du Congo (newspaper), 39
Libya, 128–29, 149, 155–56, 201
Likasi. *See* Jadotville
Lingala (language), 90, 248n65
Llara, Lucio, 107
Lobito, Angola, 25
Lourtie, C., 138
Lualaba (province), 198
Lualaba River, 22
Luanda, Angola, 101, 106–108, 110–16, 121–23, 130, 135–36, 143–44, 150–53, 162–63, 170, 180, 203
Luanghy, Celestin, 125, 172
Luapula Province (Rhodesia), 25
Luapula Valley/River, 21–22, 65
Luba (kingdom), 16, 20–22, 26–29, 35, 43, 71, 176, 197, 208n40, 214n55, 215n73
Luba (people/ethnicity), 22–23, 36–37, 46, 49, 53, 55–56
Luba, ki- (language), 27, 53
Luba Kasai, 27–29, 33–35, 37, 40, 86, 132
Luba Katanga (a.k.a. Lubakat, Luba Shankadi), 2, 20, 27, 172, 178–79, 184, 246n31
Luba Lubilanji, 20, 27
Lubange, Stéphane, 94, 151–52
Lubumbashi, 25–26, 33, 91, 123, 126, 142–43, 153, 170–71, 179, 182, 185–87, 194. *See also* Elisabethville
Ludy, Lopes, 107
Luembe, Antoine, 76, 94, 107, 128, 134
Lukasa agreement (1964), 162–63, 164
Lulimba (town), 70
Luluabourg (city), 29, 36
Lumumba, Patrice: assassination, 10, 41, 49–50; embracing communism, 11; formation of MNC-L, 36; leadership of postcolonial government, 10, 41–42; memorialized as national hero, 78, 89, 155; response to Katangese secession, 44–46
Lumumbist ideology/groups, 12, 14, 51–52, 62, 69, 74, 112, 121–23, 125, 129, 146, 150, 153, 171–72, 190
Lumuna, Raphaël, 85, 96
Lunda (people/ethnicity): colonial conquest, 22–23, 26; development as political force, 20–22, 29–30; identity under colonial rule, 28; Katangese secession, 43, 46; loss of political authority, 32–37; origins and traditions of, 1, 19–20. *See also* Mwaant Yav

Lunda Kazembe, 21, 23
Lundula, Victor, 44
Lunguebungo, Angola, 67
Lutuai, Angola, 67

Maïkissa, Robert, 121
Makaz a Nawej Djuma, 180
Malanje, Angola (province), 128, 147, 163, 247n47
Malonga (town), 123
Manono (territory), 53, 56, 71, 186
Manzikala, Jean-Foster, 74, 89, 91, 93
Maoism/Maoist ideology, 16, 129
Marandura, Antoine, 154
Marcum, J. A., 105, 110, 223n60, 229n139
Martinez, Sergio, 141
Marxism/Marxist influence, 1, 4, 17, 96–97, 119–20, 125–26, 146, 150, 196. *See also* Communism
Masela, Gustave, 150, 153
Mashiku, Ambroise, 153–54, 161, 163, 201, 243n76
Massiala (General), 76, 86
Mawa, Angola, 147, 152, 153–54
Mayele, Daniel, ix, 155–56, 241n47
Mayi Mayi (a.k.a. Mai Mai), 14, 184–86, 248n74
Mbandaka (city), 84
Mbanza Congo, Angola, 162
Mbuji Mayi, 123
Mbumba, Nathanaël: arrest and exile, 136–37, 148–49, 155–56; arrival in Angola, 81; assistance with book, ix; becoming leader of KG, 91–97, 150; break with Lunda authority, 93, 199; leadership at FLNC, 100–110, 121–23, 141, 143–44, 166, 193, 195; leadership during Shaba wars, 125–26, 128–30, 133–35; leadership of FLNZ, 162; military actions in Angolan war, 115–16, 231n32; political ambitions, 129, 153, 192, 196; political relationships, 116–18; removal from leadership, 145–46, 181; support from Cuba, 120. *See also* photo gallery
Mbumba, Sylvain ("Kadhafi"), ix, 247n53
Mbundu (people/ethnicity), 103, 224n24
McNamara, Robert, 65
mercenaries/mercenary forces, 2, 4, 8, 16, 17, 47–51
Methodist missionaries/schools, 26, 30–31, 64, 93
Miala, Fernando Garcia, 181, 247n59
migrant labor, 7, 27, 30, 33, 36, 40, 43, 158

military actions: Battle of Quifangondo, 115–16; Operation Carlota, 113; Operation Lucifer, 78, 87; Operation Morthor, 55; Operation Red Bean, 138–39; Operation Rumpunch, 51, 54; Operation Savannah, 115; Operation Tshombe, 76

military units, ANC: 2nd Katangese Company, 70; 3rd Battalion, 70; 5th Battalion (South African mercenaries), 71; 5th Brigade, 72, 75; 7th Battalion of Hemba, 71, 72; 9th Battalion, 72; 10th Battalion of Batabwa, 71; 12th Battalion, 70; 14th Brigade, Kamanyola Division, 134; 14th Commando of Mboyo, 72; Baka Regiment, 72, 75

military units, FAA: 8th Brigade, 163; 24th Regiment, 5, 158, 163–64, 169–70, 175

military units, FARDC, 62nd Brigade, 184

military units, FAZ: 4th Battalion, 228n122; 7th Battalion, 228n122; 311st Battalion, 137

military units, FLNC: 1st Battalion, 123; 2nd Battalion, 123; 3rd Battalion, 123; 4th Battalion, 123

military units, FP, Liberation Battalion from Kamina, 46

military units, Garde Civil: Special Battalion Shaba II, 160; Special Battalion Shaba III, 160

military units, MPLA, 9th Brigade, 116

Mills, G., 13

mining/mining industry, 4–5, 8, 88, 91, 119, 135, 142–43, 167, 170, 184, 200, 211n114, 231n38; copper, 19–20, 22–28, 38–41, 43–45, 49–50, 64, 124, 172, 177–79; diamonds/diamond trade, 95, 97, 112, 116, 121, 128–29, 147–49, 154, 163–64, 175, 180, 187–88, 246n24. *See also* Union Minière du Haut Katanga

missionaries/mission schools, 26, 28, 30–31, 34, 36, 64

MNC-L. *See* National Congolese Movement—Lumumba

Mobutu Sese Seko: dealing with Katangese secession, 45, 49, 51; fight against communism, 17; interference in Angola, 102–16; opposition, 116–23 (*see also* Shaba wars); overthrow/removal, 1, 4, 12, 78–79, 85–86, 99–100, 109, 146, 166–67, 170–71; post-Shaba reaction/concessions, 148–62; relationship with Mwaant Yav, 87–88, 164; relationship with Tshombe and KG, 54, 64–65, 69–76, 84–87, 145–46; rise of, and consolidation of power, 2, 4, 9–12, 15, 41, 62, 73–75, 88–90; rule in Congo (1967–1974), 88–90; rule in Katanga (1969–1973), 91–94; support from China, 96; support from United States, 62, 88, 146. *See also* Congo/Zaire

Mokede, Roger, 121

Monga, Leonard, 78

Monguya Mbenge, Daniel, 122, 133

Morocco, 127, 135, 143

Moto (Faradje territory), 72

Mouvement d'Action pour la Résurrection du Congo (MARC), 122, 130, 133

Mouvement de Libération du Congo (MLC), 182

Mouvement des Combattants Socialistes (MCS), 152–55, 161–64, 172, 241n39

Mouvement Populaire de la Révolution (MPR), 12, 74, 89–90, 96, 124, 132, 231n40

Mouvement Révolutionnaire pour la Libération du Katanga (MRLK), 183–84

Movimento das Forças Armadas (MFA), 98, 100–103, 106, 111–12, 227n92

Movimento Popular de Libertação de Angola (MPLA): Bicesse Accords, 157–58; Cossa Accords, 118; Cuban and Soviet aid, 112–13, 119–20, 144; *fiéis* alliance, 95–96; FLNC alliance, 4, 99–100, 106–10, 116–18, 121–23, 145, 190, 192–93; infiltration into Angola, 84–85; leadership of Neto, 103–104; MCS affiliation, 153–54, 161–62; military effectiveness, 91–92, 97–98; military victory in Angola, 113–16, 119; Nito Alves affair, 136, 203; relations with other groups, 82, 86, 100–106, 110–12; removal of Mobutu, 121; rise to power, 1, 4; role of KG, 17; role of Tigres, 149–50; UNITA conflict, 158, 162–63

Moxico, Angola (province), 97, 103–104, 115, 128, 147, 149, 163, 233n67

Mozambique, 9, 98, 100–101, 119, 130

Mpoyo, Pierre-Victor, 122, 230n18

"Mufu." *See* Kiyana, Vindicien Kasuku

Mugabe, Robert, 173

Muhona, Paul, 73–74

Mukachung Mwambu, Henri, ix, 155, 163, 174–75, 201

Mukalayi, Martin, 153, 161, 163, 172, 175

Muke Masuke, Norbert, 56, 59, 63–64, 67, 215n71. *See also photo gallery*

Mukulu, Mutombo, 208n40

Mukulubundu, Felix, 122

Muland, Jean-Delphin, 94, 107, 152, 154–55, 164, 169–72, 188, 241n44, 244n92

Mulele, Pierre, 49, 69, 122
Mulelist rebellion (a.k.a. Simba rebellion), 2, 14, 62, 69–72, 190, 192
Mulemba, Jean-Baptiste, 172
Mulombo, Grégoire, 114, 123
Munongo, Antoine, 65, 210n96
Munongo, Godefroid, 34, 36, 39, 54–55, 58, 69, 73, 76, 88–89, 159, 210n96
Munongo, Msiri, 210n96
Munongo Mutampuka (people/ethnicity), 30
Musakanya, Valentine, 148
Mushid, Gaston, 32, 68
Mushitu, Justin, ix, 107, 121, 130, 151–52, 226n61, 226n64, 241n27, 242n65. *See also photo gallery*
Musonda Mukandasa Kingandya, 148
Musuumb (town), 20
Mutshatsha (town), 78, 123–24, 127, 134–35, 141
Mwaant Yav (Lunda king): assassination attempt, 84; KG relationship with, 81, 87–88, 92–93, 98, 157; Mbumba challenges, 93, 129, 196, 222n50; monopolization by Tshombe family, 68; 1907–1920, Muteb a Kasang, 23, 208n20; 1920–1951, Kaumb, 30–31; 1951–1963, Mbako Ditend, 31–32, 34–36, 45–46; 1963–1965, Gaston Mushid, 68; 1965–1973, Daniel Tshombe (Muteb II Mushid), 68, 126, 133; 1994–present, Thomas Tshombe (a.k.a. Kawel), 77, 164, 176, 222n50; role of, and political power, 20–22, 192, 199. *See also* Lunda; *photo gallery*
Mwakasu, David, 96
Mwamba Ilunga, Prosper, 26, 245n17
Mwambu, Antoine, 67–68
Mwenze Kongolo, 186
Mwepu Mukanda, 160–61
Mwinilunga District (Northern Rhodesia), 66

Nakuru Accord of 1975, 112
Nambwangongo, Angola, 147, 154, 158
Namibia, 102, 105, 157, 174
Nascimento, Lopo de, 107
National Congolese Movement—Lumumba (MNC-L), 36, 38, 121
National Reconciliation Plan (a.k.a. U Thant Plan), 58–59, 62, 63, 91, 185
National Security Study Memorandum (NSSM) 39, 16
Nawej, Jérôme, 66, 68, 88
Nawezi, Georges, 94
Ndalatando, Angola, 162–63

Ndalu, Antonio França, 114, 228n118
Ndjoku, Eugene, 54
Ndola, Northern Rhodesia, 55
Negage, Angola, 162, 180
Neto, Agostinho, 98, 103–10, 112–13, 117, 120, 122–23, 126, 128–30, 134, 136–37, 140–41, 143, 155, 226n64, 230n19
N'Gbanda, Honoré, 183
Nguz, Vincent de Paul, ix, 228n118, 233n76
Nguz Karl I Bond, Jean, 125, 133, 141, 146, 150–51, 155, 158, 160, 201, 245n18. *See also photo gallery*
Niembo (captain), 70
Nkrumah, Kwame, 6
Northern Rhodesia, 22–23, 25–26, 28, 33, 35, 39, 44, 55–57, 61, 65–68, 79, 199. *See also* Southern Rhodesia; Zambia
Nsanga a Lubangu, 20
Ntandaimena, Jean-Claude, 186
Numbi, John, 172, 175, 184, 186, 247n44
Nyembo (Niembo), Kasongo, 23, 27, 37, 43, 46, 48, 52–53, 71, 172, 208n40, 210n96, 214n55, 240n16
Nyerere, Julius, 117, 156, 168
Nzongola-Ntajala, G., 29

Odom, T., 138
Olenga, Nicolas, 156
Onawelho, Albert, 121, 155. *See also photo gallery*
Operação Brilhante, 180
Operation Carlota, 113
Operation Lucifer, 78, 87
Operation Morthor, 55
Operation Red Bean, 138–39
Operation Rumpunch, 51, 54
Operation Savannah, 115
Operation Tshombe, 76
Organization of African Unity (OAU): confirmation of colonial borders, 6; intervention in Katanga, 127, 131; recognition of colonial borders, 42; recognition of GRAE, 86; redrawing African borders, 196; relationship with Mobutu, 124–25; Tshome banned from meetings, 69
Ovimbundu (people/ethnicity), 103, 224n24
Owen, David, 126

Paelinck, Jean, 34–35
Paluku, Denis, 74
Pan-African Force (PAF), 143

Parti de Libération Congolais (PLC), 154
Parti Lumumbiste Unité (PaLu), 123
Parti Solidaire Africain (PSA), 122
Partido Africano da Independência da Guiné e Cabo Verde (PAIGC), 100, 112
Pelengue, Angola, 155
pendus de la pentecôte, 73
People's Republic of China (PRC). See China
Perrad, Paul, 49
Pezarat Correia, Pedro, x, 101, 104, 224n12
Pire, René, ix, 47
Polícia Internacionale de Defesa do Estado (PIDE), 67, 83–85, 87, 92–95, 97, 101, 108, 195
Port Francqui (city), 27
Portugal: anticolonial uprisings, 80–84; decolonization, 100–102, 105; 1891 Lunda border agreement, 23; fighting Angolan independence, 1, 4, 97–100, 190; relationship with Congo, 76–79; relationship with Katanga, 66–69; revolution of 1974, 4, 100–101, 105, 112, 118; use of KG and *"fiéis"* forces, 4–5, 83–87, 91–97, 111; withdrawal, 100, 114
Portugal and the Future (Spínola), 100
Pretoria Global and Inclusive Agreement of 2002, 173–74, 178, 182
Protin, André, 71
Prunier, G., 170, 171
Puren, Jerry, 77, 78
Pweto (town), 47, 65

Quifangondo (town), 115
Quitota, Angola, 147

Radio Katanga, 53, 122, 214n56
Rassemblement Congolais pour la Démocratie (RCD), 162, 174, 206n22
Rautenbach, Billy, 173, 177
Reagan, Ronald, 154
refugees: Congolese diaspora, 15; Katanga secession, 55, 77; KG camps, 62, 66–67, 82, 92, 192; management by FLNC, 155; management by Portugal, 84–85; political refugees, 83, 102, 148; Portuguese and Belgian, 101; as potential recruits, 132, 141; repatriation to Zaire, 143, 147, 153; Rwandan Genocide, 168; Shaba war, 123, 127–28; troops posing as, 135, 140. See also UN High Commission for Refugees
Réveil Congolais, 88, 94, 192
Revolta Activa, 103
Reyntjens, Filip, ix, 170

Rhodesia. See Northern Rhodesia; Southern Rhodesia
Risquet, Jorge, 120, 125, 136
Roberto, Holden, 67, 69, 82, 86, 89, 103, 106, 116, 229n145
Rodrigues, Bettencourt, 97
Rosa Coutinho, António Alva, 101–107, 109–10, 136, 224n11, 224n33, 226n75
Rosy, Henry, 34
Rukonkish Kamin (queen mother), 129
Rwanda, 13, 15, 26, 78, 206n22
Rwandan Genocide, 167–76, 201
Rwandan Patriotic Front/Army (RPF/RPA), 15, 167–68, 201, 245n20

Salazar, António de Oliveira, 98
Samba Kaputo, Guillaume, 181, 247n58
Sandoa (region), 36, 86, 123
Sanga, ki- (language), 53
Sangondo, Angola, 147, 149
Santa Eulalia, Angola, 147
Santos, Almeida, 95
Savimbi, Jonas, 82, 106, 109, 115, 162, 176, 189. See also União Nacional para a Independência Total de Angola
Schöller, André, 34–35
Schramme, Jean, 56, 67–68, 70–71, 76–78, 84, 87–88, 154
Sendwe, Jason, 35, 37, 43, 210n96
Senegal, 143
Service d'Action et de Renseignement Militaire (SARM), 173
Shaba wars: Angolan involvement, 119–20; beginnings, 4, 11, 16–17; conduct of Shaba I, 123–27; conduct of Shaba II, 133–42; fear of a Shaba III, 144, 161; FLNC objectives, 116–18, 120–23; period between, 127–33; postwar refugees, 146–48; results and aftermath, 142–44, 177–78
Shubin, V., 103, 112, 114, 115–16, 229n139
Silva, José Emildio da, 101
Silva Cardoso, António, 106, 109–11
Simba rebellion. See Mulelist rebellion
Société Générale de Belgique (SGB), 24–25, 39
Somalia, 138
Sonck, Jean Pierre, 68, 70
Songye (people/ethnicity), 20, 159
Soumialot, Gaston, 69, 72, 218n49
South Africa: apartheid, 7–8; Cassinga raid (1978), 143, 239n202; fighting in Angola, 115–16, 119–21, 163, 228n130, 239n202; FLNC

South Africa (*cont.*)
    forces in, 105, 109, 225n54; intervention in Congo politics, 76; liberation movement, 87, 102–103; mercenary soldiers, 56, 71, 77–78; migrant labor model, 27
South African Communist Party (SACP), 203
South Sudan, 7
South West Africa People's Organization (SWAPO), 195, 239n202
Southern Rhodesia, 39, 56–57, 68, 102, 104. *See also* Northern Rhodesia
Sovereign National Conference (CNS), 12, 146, 157, 159, 161–62
Soviet Union: FLNC alignment, 119–20, 125–26; influence in Africa, 11, 17, 127; involvement in Shaba wars, 135–36, 138–40; military aid and arms shipments, 110, 112–13; MPLA alignment, 103, 106, 114; training and advisers, 116, 120, 128. *See also* Communism
Spínola, António de, 100–101, 106, 224n12, 225n54
Stanleyville, 2, 46, 51, 56, 60, 62, 69–72, 75–78. *See also* Kisangani
Sudan, North/South, 7, 14–15, 197, 201
Sudan People's Liberation Army/Movement (SPLA/SPLM), 15
Swahili (language), 22, 90, 248n65
Symba, Déogratias, ix, 107, 117, 121–22, 130, 148, 161, 170, 225n57, 226n64, 226n68, 234n85. *See also photo gallery*

Tabwa (people/ethnicity), 43, 70, 71
Tanganyika (province), 198
Tanganyika Concessions, 24
Tanzania, 14, 87, 97, 102, 117, 130, 149, 154–56, 162, 167–68
Teixeira de Souza, Angola, 67
Thyssens, George, 39, 50
Tigres/ex-Tigres: adoption of the name, 95; contributions to this book, x; evolution of identity, 4–5; goal of Katangan autonomy, 9, 16, 145–46; integration into Angolan army, 102, 108; leadership of Mbumba, 155–56; leadership of Muland, 154–55; leadership of Tshombe, 89; legacy of Cossa Accords, 108–10; MPLA alliance, 102–104, 117–18; overthrow of Mobutu, 166–67; relationship with ANC, 84, 175–77; relationship with FLNC, 116–18, 121–23; relationship with Kabila government, 172, 178–79; remobilization of, 162–65; repatriation to DRC, 179–89; repatriation to Zaire, 146, 153, 157–62; role in AFDL, 169–71; role in Angolan wars, 99–100, 110–16; role in FAPC, 150–52; second Congo War, 173–75; Shaba wars, 119–37; Shaba wars, P2 massacre, 137–38; Shaba wars, postwar, 139–50; support from Cubans, 112–13, 120–21; Zambia coup attempt, 148. *See also* Katangese gendarmes/ex-gendarmes; *photo gallery*
Togo, 143
Troupes Speciales Tigres, 180
Tshatshi, Joseph-Damien, 70, 75, 77–78
Tshibinda Ilunga, 20
Tshingambo, André, 159, 161, 162, 163, 169, 201
Tshiniama, Pierre-Damien, 107, 121
Tshinyama, Ngonga, 186
Tshinyama, Pierre, 228n130
Tshipola, Ferdinand, 67–68, 70, 72, 75–77
Tshisekedi, Étienne, 156–59
Tshokwe (people/ethnicity), 22–23, 32, 35–37, 43, 53, 68, 73, 86–88, 129
Tshombe, Daniel, 68, 126, 133
Tshombe, Moïse: detention and death in Algeria, 81, 85, 89, 92; exile in Paris, 63, 68; exile in Spain, 73, 75, 154; named prime minister, 69; as prime minister, 2, 11, 72–75; return to power, 76–79. *See also photo gallery*
Turner, T., 89–90, 116, 170

U Thant Plan, 58–59, 62–63, 91, 185
Ucol. *See* Union Katangaise
Uganda, 14–15, 71, 167–69, 173–74
Uíge, Angola, 82, 162–63
Umba Di Lutete, 135, 138
União Nacional para a Independência Total de Angola (UNITA), 82–83, 95–98, 101–103, 109–11, 114–16, 119–23, 134, 137, 144–48, 152, 154, 157–58, 162–64, 168–69, 175–76, 191, 223n4. *See also* Savimbi, Jonas
Union des Fédéralistes et Républicains Indépendants (UFERI), 146, 158–60, 164, 172, 184, 187, 199, 202, 242n65
Union des Neutralistes Indépéndants, 177, 182
Union Katangaise, 36–37, 39
Union Minière du Haut Katanga (UMHK), 24–28, 30–33, 37–39, 50–53, 60, 62, 74–75, 213n46. *See also* mining/mining industry
Union of Peoples of Angola (UPA), 82, 86
Union pour la Démocratie et le Progrès Social (UDPS), 132, 156–59, 164, 193, 199, 242n64

Union Sacrée de l'Opposition, 157–58
United National Independence Party (UNIP), 39
United Nations (UN): beginning intervention in Katanga, 45–46; dealing with Balubakat rebellion, 48–49; military pressure and negotiations, 53–56; negotiating a settlement, 49–51; Operation Morthor, 55; Operation Rumpunch, 51, 54; overseeing KG demobilization, 62–66; terminating the secession, 8–9, 55, 57–62
UN High Commission for Refugees (UNHCR), 145–47, 150, 153–54, 181, 193, 202. *See also* refugees
UN Security Council Resolution 161 (1961), 50–51, 54
UN Security Council Resolution 169 (1961), 55
United States: anti-US demonstrations, 59; Carter administration, 125, 131, 140, 142; Congolese policy/support, 69, 70–71; Ford administration, 114; Katanga secession policy, 45, 53; negotiating a settlement, 57–60; Reagan administration, 154; Shaba war policy, 138–39, 142–43; "smoking Cuban" evidence, 140; support of FNLA, 114; support of Mobutu, 62, 88, 146; support of UNITA, 103, 114; training KG forces, 57; Vance "Africanist" policy, 125, 131, 138
Université d'État d'Elisabethville, 52
U.S Central Intelligence Agency (CIA): relationship with Mobutu, 11, 114; relationship with Tshombe, 112; report on Cuban activities, 136, 238n179

Van Bilsen, A. A. J., 38
Vance, Cyrus, 125, 131, 138
Vandewalle, Frédéric, 47–49, 70
Vansina, J., 21
Verhaegen, Benoit, 73
Verissimo Sarmento, Angola, 84
Viana, Angola, 147, 152, 153, 159, 161, 162, 180. *See also photo gallery*
Viera Dias, Manuel Hélder, Jr. ("Kopelipa"), 169
Vila Luso, Angola, 67

Watsa (town), 76
Weber, Guy, 46, 48. *See also photo gallery*
Welensky, Roy, 39, 59
Westad, O. A., 16
Whitehouse, Charles S., 57
Wislos (General), 180
World War II, 30–31

Yeke (people/ethnicity), 22–23, 30, 43, 47, 65, 89
Yolhamu, Vénance, 94
Young, Andrew, 231
Young, C., 37–38, 48, 64, 89–90, 116

Zambia: FLNC presence, 129–30, 133–34, 141–44; KG exile, 3–4, 78–80, 87; MPLA presence, 82, 84, 97, 102–103; 1980 coup attempt, 148; secessionist demands, 197; Shaba rebels' presence in, 235n126. *See also* Northern Rhodesia
Zimbabwe, 52, 87, 173–74, 207n1
Zimbabwe African National Union (ZANU), 195

ERIK KENNES is Research Associate at the Africa Museum, Department for Contemporary History, in Tervuren, Belgium, and at the Institute of Development Policy and Management of the University of Antwerp, Belgium. He has published widely on the history and politics of the Democratic Republic of Congo.

MILES LARMER is Associate Professor of African History at the University of Oxford and Research Fellow at the Department of Historical and Heritage Studies, University of Pretoria. He has written extensively on the political and social history of central Africa in the twentieth century.

www.ingramcontent.com/pod-product-compliance
Lightning Source LLC
Chambersburg PA
CBHW070300240426
43661CB00057B/2602